ENCYCLOPEDIA OF
ENGLISH

ENCYCLOPEDIA OF
ENGLISH

DICTIONARIES OF:

GRAMMAR • USAGE

SPELLING • PUNCTUATION

PRONUNCIATION

ROOTS • PREFIXES & SUFFIXES

RHETORIC • RIMES

WORLD LITERATURE

EDITED BY **ARTHUR ZEIGER**

ARCO PUBLISHING COMPANY, INC.
New York, New York

Published by ARCO PUBLISHING COMPANY, INC.
219 Park Avenue South, New York, N. Y. 10003

Revised Edition, 1959
Fourth Printing, 1973

Library of Congress Catalog Card Number 59–8821
ISBN 0–668–00655–X

Printed in the United States of America

Preface

To SERVE BOTH as a manual of instruction and as a work of reference—such is the two-fold purpose of this Encyclopedia. The plan subserves the purpose. Wherever feasible, two books have been devoted to a subject: the first systematically presenting fundamentals, the other exploring ramifications. Thus, the needs of the beginning and the advanced reader are fairly met. The content and intent of the individual books are outlined below:

I and II: "Grammar for Use" describes the "persistent pattern of related words," and its aim is to be illuminating rather than exhaustive on such various matters as case, inflection, and concord. The "Dictionary of Grammar" is comprehensive and complex, and ought to be studied intensively only by those estimable people who peruse dictionaries with enjoyment.

III and IV: The first of the two books on English spelling is a guide through its mazes, setting forth the few rules and the many exceptions. The second book is a dictionary listing the mavericks of the spelling range, with suggestions for their corralling.

V and VI: The book on "Punctuation" answers such questions as: Why punctuate? What is essential punctuation? How does "open punctuation" differ from "close punctuation"? The "Dictionary of Punctuation" is concerned with practice rather than principles. It is based on the Government Printing Office *Style Manual*, a work chosen because its source makes it authoritative; because it is relatively complete; and because it embodies a logical and practicable code.

VII and VIII: The book on "Pronunciation" recognizes the "sanctions of section," but specifies and analyzes those elements of pronunciation that are the same for North, South, East and West. The "Dictionary" indicates as simply and accurately as may be the correct pronunciations of a large number of words often mispronounced.

IX and X: Both of the books on usage are decidedly *un*puristic. However, though emphatically liberal, each declares for certain values and recognizes certain standards. The first of the two books dealing with usage considers the constructions most frequently abused; examines reference, agreement, idiom; and tries to suggest reasonable norms for writing and for speaking. The "Dictionary" supplies a selective list of words and expressions often misused, emphasizing the different franchises granted by usage to oral and to written language.

XI, XII, XIII: The three books on vocabulary have a single objective: to show the reader how he can improve his active vocabulary. The techniques are amply described in the first of the three books. Perhaps, though, it would be well to emphasize that the "Dictionary of Affixes" and the "Dictionary of Roots and Stems" are specialized dictionaries. Consequently, in the columns headed *Examples,* definitions are distorted—twisted so that the meaning and function of the prefix, suffix, or root becomes clear. The dictionaries are stringently edited versions of James Stormonth's and John Kennedy's excellent compilations.

XIV and XV: The book entitled "Rhetoric and Composition" is a synthesis of observations on the writer's craft—usually the observations of expert writers—that have proved helpful to beginning writers. The "Dictionary of Rhetoric" records the figures of speech. These traditional "embellishing" devices vary in modern esteem from desirable to reprehensible, and the "Dictionary" is a brief anthology of good and of horrible examples.

XVI and XVII: The book on "Prosody" discusses both the traditional techniques, forms, and types of verse and the recent departures from tradition. The "Dictionary of Rimes" is a modified and modernized version of Thomas Hood's famous compendium.

XVIII: The "History of the English Language" records the successive changes in grammar and vocabulary from Anglo-Saxon to Anglo-American. Representative word-lists—culled, for most part, from Skeat, Nesfield, and Earle—point up the foreign debt of English.

XIX: The forms and types of world literature are briefly analyzed in "The Dictionary of World Literature" and the chief names connected with them are cited. The entries are especially relevant to the "History of English and American Literature."

XX: Any short survey of twelve centuries of English and four of American prose and poetry must obviously adopt a highly selective approach. The "History of English and American Literature—from Beowulf to Thomas Wolfe" stresses those writings which are part of our living literature, scanting those which are important mainly from a historical viewpoint. Consequently this book is as much a recommended-reading list as it is a history.

Abbreviations in this volume for which reference is at all necessary will be found on pages 158 to 161 and on page 180.

Some acknowledgment of sources is made in the bibliography and in the body of the text itself. The number of authorities consulted, however, makes it practicable to issue only a general "Thanks!"

ARTHUR ZEIGER

Contents

BOOK ONE

Grammar for Use

Usage

Grammar comes not from the gods but from grammarians. Man communicates his thoughts, feelings, desires by means of words. Grammarians note that many of these words are concerned with naming, and these they term *nouns*. Similarly, chemists note that many compounds have certain characteristics in common and call them *acids*. Both *words* and *acids,* the things-in-themselves, may have been created by whatever gods may be; but the peculiar systems of classification are undeniably man-made.

From Formalism to Functionalism

We emphasize the human as against the divine origin of grammar because not until grammarians learned that basic fact of language-life did they discard a false and dead formalism. Supposing that grammar was inherent in a language, not a series of generalized statements *about* a language, grammarians supposed that they could discover the norm by logic, and so authoritatively correct errant constructions. Consequently they combated attempts to establish usage as the touchstone of acceptable speech.

Further, since most of them had much Latin but little or no German, they discovered parallels between English and

Latin where none in fact existed—and disregarded the plentiful Germanic parallels.[1] Thus, though English nouns have only two case forms,[2] the false analogy with the Latin that the early grammarians forced has brought into English such essentially foreign case terms as *Genitive, Dative, Accusative, Vocative,* and *Locative.*

The chief functions of the grammarians who in the eighteenth century (the period of greatest grammatical activity) attempted to "ascertain our language," were, they conceived, prescription and proscription—telling what was and what was not "correct" speech. They assumed the role of the lawgiver, rejected that of the reporter. They succeeded in establishing as "incorrect" such native English locutions as the double negative, the split infinitive, *this here* and *that there;* and as "correct," *different from* instead of *different than* or *to, I would rather* instead of *I had rather, you were* instead of *you was.*

There were, however, a few anticipations of the modern concept of the primacy of usage in determining grammar. Joseph Priestly, the most clear-headed of the eighteenth-century grammarians, declared that "the custom of speaking is the original and only just standard of any language." Grammar could not be established, he held, by "the arbitrary rules of any man, or body of men whatever." George Campbell set up a triple criterion for usage (which, he affirmed, was the ultimate authority and which it was the grammarians' business to note, collect, and methodize): usage to be authoritative must be *present, national,* and *reputable.* There is no better modern statement of the functional attitude toward grammar.

Usage—Theory and Practice

Grammar is based on function or usage. But there are levels of usage. What would be a right and fitting expression

---

[1]In early English usage, *grammar* meant only Latin grammar. Not until the seventeenth century was the word used generically, so that there was no need to refer explicitly to English grammar.

[2]The common form, which does not vary whether it is used as subject or object, and the possessive form.

in an army barracks might not be acceptable at a meeting of the Modern Language Association. The soberest functionalist would (in practice) rather split a quart than an infinitive—though he would (in theory) enthusiastically agree that there was nothing wrong in splitting an infinitive. For example, Philip Krapp, a complete modern in his attitude toward grammar, regards the old rule, to the effect that *one* must always be referred to by itself or a form of itself, as making for an unnecessary awkwardness. (A possible sentence—grammatically immaculate—might read: "One thinks oneself one of a select group if one invariably minds one's ones.") Yet Professor Krapp consistently practices the rule he does not preach.

Levels of Usage

The levels of usage—vulgar, colloquial, formal—establish separate forms. *It's me* is unexceptionable, normally; and *it is I,* normally, is affected. St. Peter standing at the Pearly Gates is alleged to have asked an applicant for entrance, "Who's there?" and to have been answered, "It is I." The Saint is supposed to have groaned and said, "Damn! Another English teacher!" Nevertheless, if you *are* an English teacher (or if you are making a formal presentation) it would be advisable to say, "It is I." Communication is the *"without-which-nothing"* of grammar; but communication appropriate to the time, the place, and the group is the *all* of grammar.

Rules and Usage

There is only one "law" of grammar: if any construction is used often enough and widely enough, it is right and proper. There are no invariable "rules of grammar." However, there are descriptive generalizations concerning grammar. They are valuable, when they conform to reality, in the same way that a periodic chart of chemical elements is valuable: both abridge the total learning process. But remember: if a generalization and a usage do not agree, the generalization is not necessarily wrong, and the usage certainly is not. It is merely that the generalization is not comprehensive enough to cover the usage.

The Vocabulary of Grammar

Grammatical terms and their definitions are a short-cut to the learning of usage. They are imperfect, but they will do. Why compound confusion by creating a new set of terms and a new set of definitions? Let us anticipate for the sake of illustration. A sentence has long been defined as a complete communication, containing both subject and verb. So be it. But it is pointed out that a number of complete communications have neither subject nor verb. "Huh?" for example, though less elegant, may be as complete a communication, as, "I am amazed!" Let us, then, call communications which present a complete (or relatively complete) communication by some other term, one which indicates how it is like and how unlike the sentence. Two such terms have been suggested: *presentative sentence* and *nonsentence*. Either will do, but the former is becoming the standard term. If we redefine *sentence* itself to include the variation which does not include the verb-subject combination, we shall have to redefine clause, phrase, and an indeterminate number of other fairly standard terms. The paraphernalia of grammar is already too cumbersome to weight it with alternative terms and definitions. A common-sense approach will solve many of the so-called perennial problems of grammar.

What Is Grammar?

Grammar was once a synonym for learning in general.[1] Its scope has narrowed a good deal. Today grammar signifies: "That department of the study of a language which deals with its inflectional forms or other means of indicating the relations of words in the sentence, and with the rules for employing them in accordance with established usage."[2]

[1] The *NED* says, "As this was popularly supposed to include magic and astrology, the Old French *gramaire* was sometimes used as a name for these occult sciences. In these applications it still survives in certain corrupt forms, French *grimoire*, English *glamour, gramary*."

[2] The *NED* criticizes the definitions of such formal grammarians as Lindley Murray ("English grammar is the art of speaking and writing the English

Psychology of Grammar

Grammar has logic, a definite form and structure. There is, though, a psychology and a sociology of grammar too, and these have been habitually neglected. Grammar is the product of the social group and of the individuals who comprise it. Even the simplest example of communication, Pillsbury has remarked, "such as 'Please pass the butter!' . . . or even the single word 'Butter!' are life processes, intelligible only as part and parcel of the particular situation within which they came into being and of which they are an essential and formative factor, both determined by the situation and, in turn, affecting it, growing out of the needs of the individual in his surroundings, employing those surroundings for his self-realization, and, in turn modifying those surroundings by his action." Unless we remember the psychological base of English, we shall be at a loss to analyze a tremendous number of locutions. Examine this sentence: *Conn was given a stiff right uppercut.* The construction is a familiar one, and it is apparent that not *Conn* but the *uppercut* was given. Yet the logic of English word order is violated. To derive the intended meaning it is necessary to bridge a psychological gap. Frequently in the sections which follow we shall have to appeal from the logic to the psychology of English grammar.

Words: The Parts of Speech

Words have certain functions in communicating thought, and grammarians have classified words, according to function, into eight groups—the "parts of speech." They are: *nouns* and *pronouns,* together often termed *substantives,* words which name; *verbs,* which assert; *adjectives* and *adverbs,* which modify; *prepositions* and *conjunctions,* which connect; and *interjections,* which exclaim. The functions are not exclusive one of the other. Frequently a noun—or any other part of speech—may assert. Compare *The rains came*

language with propriety") as being at once too narrow and too wide; too narrow because "it applies only to a portion of this branch of study"; and too wide because "many questions of 'correctness' in language are outside its province" —*e.g.,* spelling and pronunciation.

with *It rains*. The word *rains* asserts in both communications, but the *action of raining* is subordinated in the first and central in the second. Hence, in the second, *rains* is said to be a *verb*.

Again, there is nothing necessary and eternal in this eight-fold division of words. Aristotle counted only four: the substantive, the adjective, the verb, and the particle.[1] And if you choose, you can say that there are two—or four —or six dozen parts of speech and defend your stand. Adjectives, for example, are sometimes subdivided into the qualitative, the descriptive, the numbering, and the demonstrative. You can give each of these a separate name and declare each a separate part of speech. The functions differ somewhat, and you could justify your procedure on the basis of function. We hope you will not embark on the procedure though, because the eight parts of speech are a fair working compromise. They are general enough to summarize the totality of English words and specific enough to distinguish, roughly, any one function from any other.

One other thing to remember about the parts of speech: *once an adjective,* it does *not* follow, *always an adjective.* The parts are not given for all time; if a word functions differently in different sentences—plays a different "part"— it will be called something else. Look at the sentences quoted a little while ago: *The rains came* and *It rains.* The same word is used in both sentences; yet *rains* has a noun, or naming, function in the first and a verb, or asserting, function in the second. Remember this very important principle of grammar, and you will find the going relatively easy on the succeeding pages: The *function of* a word *determines its classification;* or, differently put, *how it is used determines what it is called.* Not even such an eminently assertive word as *run* can be called a verb out of context. A young lady's stocking may *run* (verb), or she may have a *run* (noun) in her stocking. The same consideration of context applies to the other parts of speech.

[1]The particle is defined as "a minor part of speech, especially a short, indeclinable one." The "minor" is debatable. Adverbs, conjunctions, prepositions, numerals, and some pronouns are considered particles.

Words in Meaningful Combination: The Sentence

Any combination of words in which something meaningful is said about something or someone else is called a **sentence**. (Latin *sententia,* a judgment, opinion.) It may consist of two words,[1] *Jesus wept* (the shortest verse in the *Bible*), or of a thousand (the longest recorded English sentence, in Edward Phillips's "Preface" to *Theatrum Poetarum,* consists of 1012 words).

Sentences may be **declarative, interrogative, imperative,** or **exclamatory,** depending on the kind of communication made. Thus, any sentence which makes an affirmation (or denial) is classified as declarative: *Men must die.* Any sentence which asks a question is classified as interrogative: *Must men die?* Any sentence which expresses a command (or demand, desire, entreaty, or wish) is classified as imperative: *Let the men die.* Any sentence which declares, asks, or commands in an energetic enough manner is classified as exclamatory: *The men must die!*

Note that these are not logic-tight categories. Conversion is largely a matter of substituting one of the end-stops (period, question mark, or exclamation point) for another. The intent and the emotional charge establish the category. Again, the combination of kinds of sentences is frequent: *The men asked, "Must we die?" He ordered, "The men must die!"* Both of these sentences are usually considered declarative, because they are essentially statements. Yet there is room for argument, if you have a taste for grammar-mongering. However, only where doubt concerning the proper mark of punctuation to employ is involved does the argument become at all important; and that doubt can be resolved by considering the intention of the sentence.

The **nonsentence** or the **presentative sentence** expresses a complete thought, but without one of the necessary sentence elements, subject and verb. This is not to be confused with the omission of the subject in imperative sentences. When the gun commander of a battery issues the order to "Fire!"

[1] Certain types of sentences may consist of only one word, usually with subject understood, as, [You] Go!

the subject *you* is understood by his men. (*You* [understood]
is said to be the subject of the sentence.)

We have been employing the terms **subject** and **predicate**
throughout as if they, too, were understood. The subject
(Latin *subjectus,* placed under) was supposed to be under
the domination of the predicate (Latin *predicatus,* proclaim). In a sense it is, no doubt, since it is the person or
thing spoken about, and the predicate is what is said. In
the following sentences the subject is underlined once, and
the predicate twice:

Man proposes.

The best-laid schemes o' mice and men gang aft agley.

The winds of heaven mix for ever with a sweet emotion.

To determine which is subject and which predicate, simply
remember their meanings: *what is spoken of,* and *what is
said.*[1]

One other sentence element should receive brief attention here. The **object** (Latin *objectus,* placed against) receives whatever action the verb generates. To determine
whether a verb has an object, ask *Who?* or *What?* after it.
Thus, in *The mountains kiss high heaven,* heaven is the answer to *What?*—it receives the kiss which the mountains bestow. Often no answer to *Who?* or *What?* will be forth-
coming: there will, then, be no object.

Inflection: The Change in Form

Inflection (Latin *inflexis,* bending[2]) describes the variation in a word to express some variation in function or meaning—a variation, though, which is not so basic as to create a
new word. *Men* is an inflection of *man* and signifies "more
than one man." *Him* is the inflection of *he* which indicates
the objective case. *Was* is an inflection of *am,* the one being
a form of the past tense, the other of the present.

[1]Thus, even where their normal positions are inverted (as *Gone are they*),
by keeping their meanings in mind, no difficulty in determining subject and
predicate should be encountered.

[2]An inflection may be considered "a bending away from the ordinary form
of a word."

The dictionary defines inflection as "The change of form which words undergo to mark distinctions of case, gender, number, tense, person, mood, voice, etc." Noun and pronoun inflection is termed **declension,** and refers to changes in the forms of the substantives to indicate gender, number, and case. Verb inflection, or **conjugation,** denotes the changes in the form of the verb to indicate voice, mood, tense, number, and person. Actually, in English, there are only two "major or live" inflections—number and tense. The other inflections are dead or dying. The employment of particles and of a logical word order rather than of inflections characterize modern English.[1]

Declension: Gender of Nouns

Gender (Latin *genus,* a kind or sort) is that modification of a word by means of which objects are distinguished in regard to sex. In English, grammatical gender is almost completely logical. *Husband* and *wife, boy* and *girl, hart* and *roe, wizard* and *witch, monk* and *nun* are pairs,[2] but they have different referents. The difference between any pair is organic, not inflectional. Perhaps pairs like *actor* and *actress, count* and *countess, hero* and *heroine, sultan* and *sultana* may be legitimately regarded as embodying inflectional changes, particularly when their histories are taken into account. However, it is better and simpler to say only that male names (*boy, hart, actor, hero, sultan*) are of **masculine gender;** that female names (*girl, roe, actress, heroine, sultana*) are of **feminine gender;** and that the names of objects (*thing, hand, book*) are of **neuter gender.** If the sex is indeterminate (*sheep, bird, parent, writer, servant*), the animals or persons are said to be of **common gender.** The whole subject of noun gender may be dismissed with three words: *gender follows sex.*[3]

[1]Consequently modern English is referred to as an **analytic** language, whereas Latin and Old English are termed **synthetic** languages.

[2]See "Dictionary of Grammar" for a complete listing.

[3]Natural gender does not prevail in most European languages, nor did it in Old English. In Old English nouns ending in *dom* (as *freedom*) were masculine; nouns ending in *ness* (*goodness*), feminine; and nouns ending in *en* (*maiden*), neuter.

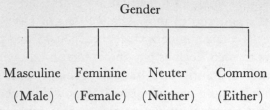

Personifications—that is, things or abstractions factitiously endowed with personality—may be either masculine or feminine. The *Sun, Time, Ocean, Anger, War* are generally made masculine when personified; *Moon,* a *ship, Earth, Virtue, Religion, Pity, Peace, Philosophy, Charity* are generally made feminine. The explanation for these assigned genders is partly psychological, partly mythological, partly etymological.

The psychological phase of the explanation is explored by Cobbett in his remarks concerning the reasons for saying *she* when speaking of a ship: "The mower calls his scythe a *she;* the plowman calls his plow a *she,* but a prong, or a shovel, or a harrow, which passes promiscuously from hand to hand, and which is appropriated to no particular laborer, is called a *he.* It was, doubtless, from this sort of habitual attachment that our famous maritime solecism arose."

The mythological phase of personification is illuminated by considering *the Sun.* The Germans still say "the sun in her glory, the moon in his wane."[1] We have reversed the gender because of the pervasive influence of classical mythology, in which Phoebus is the sun-god and Diana the moon-goddess.

The classical (etymological) influence also operates on such abstractions as *philosophy, charity, liberty.* They are personified as feminine because they were of feminine gender in Latin, and our poets learned their rhetoric from Latin literature.

Noun Declension: Case

By the **case** of a noun grammarians mean "the changes of form it undergoes to show its relationship to another

---

[1]Compare this extract from an Icelandic Edda: "Mundifori had two children, a son, Mani (Moon), and a daughter, Sol (Sun)."

word." In the English noun, then, there is really only one variation from the standard form: the possessive case when *apostrophe s* (*'s*) is added (*John's*). The **possessive case**— also called the **genitive**—denotes ownership, of course, but also origin or source (*Pope's poetry, John's son*), extent or duration (*a stone's throw, a month's leave*), and quality or characteristic (*a poet's poet, an artist's eye*). Except in the possessive, all English nouns are constant in form whether used objectively or subjectively (*Louis hit Conn, Conn hit Louis*). And the use of the possessive case with *apostrophe s* is shrinking. Formerly, it was considered proper to speak of a *thing's peculiarities;* now, except where the possessive is embedded in a traditional idiom (*a stone's throw*), the possessive termination is usually restricted to people.[1] Furthermore, the current tendency seems to favor an *of + noun* construction in place of the possessive with *apostrophe s,* even where the latter is admissible. Again, the *apostrophe s* is occasionally omitted on purpose where, by the "laws" of grammar, it should appear (*Veterans Administration, Teachers College*).[2]

The word *case* derives from the Latin *casus,* which means "falling." The nominative was regarded as the *upright* case, and the other cases as *slanting* or *oblique.*

Consider these sentences which are illustrative of the various cases (italicized) once supposed to exist in English:

Nominative:	*Caesar* heard.
Genitive:	*Caesar's* hearing.
Dative:	Give *Caesar* the tidings.
Objective:	They heard *Caesar.*
Vocative:	Hear, *Caesar.*

Note that only in the genitive is there any change in the form of *Caesar.* The other cases are all alike, and rather

---

[1] The inflection for the genitive case in Old English was *es,* and the *apostrophe s* substitutes for the omitted *e;* thus, Old English *moones* becomes Modern English *moon's.* Not until the eighteenth century did the apostrophe come into general use to indicate the possessive. Previously, but after the disappearance of the *es,* the word was written solid, and whether it was possessive or plural had to be decided from context [for illustration, see *Twelfth Night,* Act I, scene 4, lines 31–34].

[2] This is particularly true of words which end in *s,* including plurals.

than *Nominative, Dative, Accusative,* and *Vocative,* they ought all to be viewed as belonging to the common case of English nouns. In grammar, as elsewhere, that explanation should be accepted which covers the most facts most simply.[1]

Noun Declension: Number

Number is the distinction in the form of a word which shows whether it refers to one or more than one; whether, in the more technical phrase, it is **singular** or **plural**. There is a certain inconsistency in our use of number, as Aiken and Bryant point out, largely reducible to the fact that "our language has only two numbers instead of an infinite number as in mathematics. . . . The singular number covers one, zero, and infinity (or the whole), while the plural number is used for fractions of one."[2]

Again, English has a class of nouns, called **collective nouns,** which may be construed as either singular or plural, according to their intention. Thus *jury, committee, class, team, army, crowd* may be conceived of as entities, or as composed of separate individuals. Thus: *The jury was quick to bring its verdict;* but: *The jury were confused by the lawyer, and instead of hanging the criminal, they were hung.*

Collective nouns are singular, but by psychological processing are sometimes converted to plural. The fused subject effects a reversal of the process. When Kipling writes "The shouting and the tumult dies" he is considering the two types of racket to be so closely allied as actually to be one; thus the singular verb. Similarly, in the sentence "The one hundred dollars is cheerfully given," the sum, rather than the individual dollars, is chiefly being thought of, and that fact determines the choice of the singular verb.

Number, we have said, remains a live inflection, though hardly as healthy as in its Old English prime. Of the many ways of forming plurals in Old English, one has prevailed: the adding of *s* or *es* to the singular form.[3] So we have

---

[1] In conformity with this stricture, we prefer to view *of* + *noun* construction as being akin to the other *preposition* + *noun* constructions rather than as being genitive.

[2] In *The Psychology of English.*

[3] The *es* is the Modern English equivalent of the Old English *as* termination: *stanas—stones.*

devils, drugs, and *doctors;* as well as *witches, wolves,* and *wives.*[1]

There are a variety of survivals from the Old English terminations for the plural. Thus, some nouns take *en* or *ne,* with or without a vowel change, to form their plurals: *children, brethren, kine.*[2] Other nouns change the root vowel: *men, feet, geese.* A small group of nouns, for the most part naming animals of one kind or another, have an identical form for both singular and plural: *deer, sheep, partridge, quail, pike, mackerel.*[3] A few nouns, from their very nature, can only be plural: *bellows, pincers, shears, pliers, trousers.* Several real singulars appear to be plurals, and in fact are frequently so construed: *alms,*[4] *riches, eaves.*[5]

Foreign nouns incompletely assimilated into the body of English form their plurals in conformity with the rules of the language of their origin. Thus, the plural of *phenomenon,* derived from the Greek, is *phenomena;* the plural of *datum,* from the Latin, is *data;* the plural of *Monsieur,* French, is *Messieurs;* the plural of *bandit,* Italian, is *banditti.*[6]

The Pronoun

The familiar definition of pronoun (Latin *pro nomen,* instead of a noun) is "a word used in place of a noun."[7]

---

[1] For the change from singular *f* to plural *ves* see Book Two.

[2] Where there are two plural forms for a word, there is normally some distinction in their employment. Thus:

brothers (by blood)	brethren (of a community)
cloths (kinds of cloth)	clothes (garments)
dies (stamps for coining)	dice (cubes for gaming)
geniuses (men of rare talent)	genii (powerful spirits)
indexes (to books)	indices (to quantities in Algebra)

[3] Most were neuter gender in Old English.

[4] *Acts,* iii, 3, speaks of "an alms."

[5] *News* is a plural construed as a singular. Horace Greeley always insisted that it be employed as a plural: He once wired a reporter, "Are there any news?" The reporter, conforming to the Greeley style, wired back, "Not a new!" The old derivation (false, but perhaps determinative of its present construction) was from the initial letters of the four points of the compass. In the shape of a cross they were placed at the top of some early newspapers to indicate that their contents were gathered from North, East, West, and South.

[6] As the word becomes naturalized, it usually develops a normal English plural, as *bandits,* while retaining its native plural. Eventually, however, the latter becomes obsolete.

[7] This may be deceptive nomenclature because many philologists believe that

Nouns and pronouns are often given the same grammatical accounting and termed substantives. The noun, or noun equivalent, in place of which the pronoun is used, is called an antecedent. But suppose there is no referent stated or implied? In *It rains*—to what, precisely, does *it* refer? The word is without real meaning, and consequently grammarians have relegated it to a class of its (and perhaps their) own—the **expletive**. That *it*, in such constructions, is a noun, however, might reasonably be maintained. Again, in "that not impossible *she*," or in "the bravest *he*, the fairest *she*," the italicized words, though pronouns in form, are in function nouns. Similarly, *none* has, by definition, no antecedent, and the case for calling *none* a noun rather than a pronoun is logically the stronger. Sometimes, too, it is arguable whether ostensible pronouns are not really adjectives. In the sentences, *This book is my book* and *This is my book*, the former *this* is held to be an adjective, the latter a pronoun. The distinction is tenuous, since *book* is clearly understood in the second sentence. Once again, it is patent that a rigid system of classification is essentially artificial. Language eludes formal grammar.

Pronouns are grouped according to function. Their designations are descriptive: **Personal, Demonstrative, Interrogative,** and **Relative.** These are the main categories; however, there are further distinctions. Grammarians, not without reason, have discerned Indefinite, Possessive, Reflexive, Reciprocal, Intensive, and Identifying Pronouns.[1] The synoptic diagram on page 15 will demonstrate their functions with sufficient clarity.

The durability of inflection is most apparent in the pronouns, probably because they are simple and strongly ac-

---

the pronoun developed prior to the noun: primitive man, it would seem likely, would employ words as pointers for "him," "her," and "it," rather than say "John," "Joan," or "gin." The matter of priority is confused. A reasonable case has been made out for the adjective, since, in some languages, words for specific trees have been proved to exist before the concept of tree, a rather complex abstraction, is endowed with a name; for the verb, since action words are obviously of prime importance in communicating even the most primitive thoughts; and for the interjection, since verbal ejaculations of pain, anger, joy, fright, hate are nearly as natural as breathing. For none of these theories can scientific proofs be adduced. The time for demonstration is long past.

[1] A complete list will be found in the "Dictionary."

PRONOUNS

Personal	Demonstrative	Relative	Interrogative	Indefinite	Possessive	Reflexive and Intensive	Reciprocal	Identifying
I, you, we, us, he, him, his, she, her, it, its, they, their, them	this, these, that, those,	who (m. and f.), whom, which (n.), what (n.), that (m., f., and n.), whose	who? which? what? whom? whose?	any, some, every, each, few,	mine, his, hers, whose,	myself, yourself, himself, herself, itself, ourselves, yourselves, themselves	each other one another	same (the only identifying pronoun)
I smile and say,	*This* is no flattery, *these* are counsellors,	*That* feelingly persuade me *what* I am.	*Who* is Sylvia?	*Each* to the other.	*Whose* broad stripes and bright stars.	We must free *ourselves* from cant. Ha! here is Hephzibah *herself.*	Therefore, love, let us be true to *one another.*	Another, yet the *same.*

cented words. The declension of pronouns, as the declension of nouns, includes gender, number, case, and one other— person. Person signifies one of the three relations involved in discourse: a pronoun of the first person denotes the speaker (*I, we*); of the second person, the one who is spoken to (*you*); of the third person, the one who or that which is spoken of (*he, she, it, they*).

In spite of the diversity of properties which the pronoun embraces, there are surprisingly few changes in its structure. For example, only six pronouns have distinguishing forms for the nominative and objective cases: *I—me; we—us; he—him; she—her; they—them; who—whom.*[1] A real question exists as to whether we can properly list many of the changes as being in fact inflectional. Entirely different words are sometimes employed to indicate different relationships. Is *we* the plural of *I?* Obviously *I+I+I* does not equal *we,* since there is only one *I.* Even in its last stronghold, the pronoun, inflection holds none too strongly.

Verb Inflection: Conjugation

Traditionally the verb (Latin *verbum,* word) has been examined with respect to five or six supposedly standard properties: *person, number, tense, mood, voice,* and occasionally *aspect.* This does not constitute a necessary, an unavoidable division, and certainly the properties are not of equal value; but it does have the advantages of expediency and custom. Where the old paths of approach will do, it is quixotic and quirky to attempt forging others.

Perhaps the meaning of the divisions will become apparent if we parse[2] a simple verb specimen in context. Let us choose a line from a popular song which makes an uninhibited declaration in three words: *I love life.*

The verb *love* is:

first person
singular number
present tense
indicative mood
active voice

[1] If archaic forms are not exempt, *thou—thee* swells the total to seven.

[2] To parse (Latin *pars,* a part; *pars orationis,* a part of speech) a word is, among other things, to account for its inflections.

Let us now examine the items in order.

First person: Since *I* shows that the speaker refers to himself, the verb *love* is said to be in the first person. If *love* appeared out of its context, no such analysis could be made. Only in the third person singular of the present tense has the verb a distinctive personal form (*loves*).[1]

Singular number. Since *I* is singular, and since the verb must "agree" in number as well as person with its subject, *love* is said to be in the singular number. Again, this is an analysis wholly dependent on syntax, for only the third person singular has a form from which number can be determined by simple inspection.[2]

Present tense: Tense derives from the Latin word (*tempus*[3]) meaning time. Tense is "that form or modification of the verb by which time is expressed." That, at any rate, is the definition you will discover in most dictionaries. It is, we think, an incomplete one. Time is uniform, continuous, and infinite in the real world of physics (though perhaps not in Einstein's universe). The present divides time from eternity to eternity. Any action falls into one of three categories, the *past*, the *present*, and the *future*. Yet there are six inflectional tenses listed in all grammars: Present, past, and future; present perfect, past perfect, and future perfect. The forms are given below.

Present	— I love
Past	— I loved
Future	— I shall love
Present Perfect	— I have loved
Past Perfect	— I had loved
Future Perfect	— I shall have loved

The difference between the simple and the perfect tenses is not a temporal one but rather a difference in the *degree of completeness* ascribed to an action. Thus, *I loved life* implies that my affection has diminished or disappeared. *I have*

[1] That is, if we exclude the first person singular of the copulative verb *to be*, and certain archaic or poetic forms such as (*thou*) *lovest*.

[2] The same exceptions as those noted in the previous footnote apply. As Kennedy points out, "The six auxiliaries *can, may, shall, will, must,* and *ought* do not even have the ending of the third person singular."

[3] The mediate source was the Old French *tens*.

loved life implies that my affection which began at some time in the past, continues *to* (but not necessarily *into*) the present.

The latter tense is called *perfect* because the action it comprehends, rather than the time of action, is perfect or complete. The so-called *imperfect* tenses derive their designation from the incompleteness or imperfection of the actions they comprehend. For obvious reasons they are also termed the *continuous* or *progressive* tenses. There is a corresponding imperfect or progressive form for any of the tenses: *I am loving, was loving, shall be loving; I have been loving, had been loving, shall have been loving.*

Some grammarians prefer, with reason, to treat all verb constructions which are formed with the auxiliary or helping verbs separately; as verb phrases rather than as distinct tenses. Logical organization would be enhanced, however, if they could be considered together, as customarily they have been. They can be. Only, to justify the organization, a rather wider definition of *tense,* one which subsumes the relevant facts, must be formulated. *Tense,* then, is the form which a verb assumes, either by inflection or by the addition of auxiliary verbs, to locate the time at which an action took place, or to describe the degree of completeness of that action.[1]

The table below may clarify much of the foregoing.

FORM	PRESENT TENSE	PAST TENSE	FUTURE TENSE
Indefinite[2]	I love	I loved	I shall love
Progressive (or *Imperfect*)	I am loving	I was loving	I shall be loving
Perfect	I have loved	I had loved	I shall have loved

The principal parts of a verb are those basic forms from which all others of whatever tense, mood, or person, may be deduced. Three are particularly important: the first person singular of the present or the simple infinitive with *to;* the

---

[1] This definition is modeled after Nesfield's in *English Grammar, Past and Present.*

[2] *Indefinite* denotes simple past, present, or future. The term has been applied by grammarians because nothing in the verb form indicates the degree of completeness attaching to the action.

first person singular of the past; and the past participle.[1] Thus the principal parts of *love* are (to) *love, loved, loved.* Note that the past and the past participle forms are identical, and that the root vowel remains constant. This is not always so. **Regular** or **weak verbs** add *d, ed,* or *t* to the present tense in forming the past tense; but **irregular** or **strong verbs** undergo internal vowel changes in forming the past tense.[2] Formerly, all verbs of the strong conjugation formed their past participles by adding *en, n,* or *ne;* now, either the old suffix is an alternate (*proved* or *proven*) or else discarded (*abode, sat, wrung*).

	PRESENT	PAST	PAST PARTICIPLE
Weak Verb	live	lived	lived
	select	selected	selected
	dwell	dwelt	dwelt
Strong Verb	arise	arose	arisen
	sing	sang	sung
	tread	trod	trodden or trod

Active voice: The verb in *I love life* is, then, in the first person, of singular number, in the present tense, and active in voice. Voice shows whether the subject is acting or acted upon. If acting, it is active; if acted upon, it is passive. In Latin and other languages the change in voice is made manifest by a change in form; in English the change in voice is accomplished by prefixing some form of the verb *to be* to the past participle. Thus, *Life is loved by me,* though not so "suitable for saying," is an equivalent passive version of the line we have quoted. Note that the object of the verb becomes its subject when the voice shifts from active to passive, and the subject of the active verb becomes an adverbial phrase (*by me*) modifying the passive verb.

---

[1]Sometimes the present participle form (*loving*) is included; but since it is invariable, there is not much point in listing it each time.

[2]Strong verbs are of Old English stock, and most are monosyllabic. The weak verb (perhaps so called because "it has no inherent strength for forming its past tense, but requires the help of a suffix") is the living conjugation, and all borrowed and coined words are formed by analogy with it. The strong formation persists in about a hundred or less words. See "Dictionary of Grammar" for full list.

Any transitive verb may be similarly changed from the active to the passive voice. A verb is used transitively if its action is not self-contained, but is directed toward some person or thing (an *object*). All other verbs are intransitive. The categories are not absolute. A verb transitive in one context may be intransitive in another. In *I love life* the verb takes an object (*life*), and consequently is transitive; but in *I love deeply* there is no object and consequently transitivity is absent. It is true, however, that certain words (*die, listen, rise*), because of their meaning, are essentially intransitive. Other words, the **copulative verbs,** which express not action, but *state of being,* are necessarily intransitive. The forms of *to be* (*am, is, was, were, shall be, will be*), *remain, seem, become,* can never pass an action to an object for the reason that they contain no action. They may, though, take a complement,[1] a word or words which "complete" the thought. The complement equates with or defines the subject. *I am* is an incomplete predication as it stands; *I am the state* completes it. Some verbs of *choosing, making, naming,* and *thinking* (along with a few others), which in the active voice take a direct object, are followed by a complement of the kind described when passive. Compare *We elected FDR President four times* with *FDR was elected President four times.* In the second example, *President* achieves a new function as complement.

Indicative mood. The verb *love* in the sentence under desultory consideration is in the indicative mood.[2] Mood signifies the way in which a verb makes an assertion. Occasionally a difference of form accompanies a distinction of mood, but normally mood is a syntactical element.[3] As a consequence, the problem of mood is minor. Further, because of the current tendency to use the indicative mood where formerly the subjunctive was obligatory, the problem becomes progressively more negligible.

[1] The complement described is classified as a subject complement or attribute or predicate nominative.

[2] Sometimes spelled *mode* and pronounced accordingly.

[3] There is no form which is exclusively subjunctive. The verb in *If I be* might be indicative or imperative as well as subjunctive.

Three moods are ordinarily distinguished: The **indicative,** which is the mood of assertion or fact; the **subjunctive,** which is the mood of condition or contingency; and the **imperative,** which is the mood of command or entreaty.

The indicative is the dominant mood in current English. There is very little that can be said subjunctively which cannot be said indicatively. This was not always so. In the Old and Middle English periods, the subjunctive was the specific mood for a large number of constructions, and it had its own peculiar forms. Examine the paradigms[1] which follow; you will discover no form which might not be indicative or imperative:

PRESENT TENSE

	SINGULAR	PLURAL
1st Person	If[2] I love	If we love
2nd Person	If you love	If you love
3rd Person	If he love	If they love

PAST TENSE[3]

	SINGULAR	PLURAL
1st Person	If I loved	If we loved
2nd Person	If you loved	If you loved
3rd Person	If he loved	If they loved

PERFECT TENSE

	SINGULAR	PLURAL
1st Person	If I have loved	If we have loved
2nd Person	If you have loved	If you have loved
3rd Person	If he has loved	If they have loved

PAST PERFECT TENSE

	SINGULAR	PLURAL
1st Person	If I had loved	If we had loved
2nd Person	If you had loved	If you had loved
3rd Person	If he had loved	If they had loved

[1]A paradigm is a model of inflectional forms.

[2]*If* is prefixed not as part of the inflection, but because most subjunctives are found in *if* clauses.

[3]The past tense of the subjunctive, as it will become evident, actually has reference to present or future conditions.

The subjunctive forms of the verb *to be* differ from the corresponding indicatives in the present tense only:

PRESENT TENSE

	SINGULAR	PLURAL
1st Person	If I be	If we be
2nd Person	If you be	If you be
3rd Person	If he be	If they be

Until the end of the nineteenth century, and even later, it was standard to list the following uses of the subjunctive:[1]

Wishes or Exhortations	Thy Kingdom *come,* Thy will *be* done.
Doubt or Suppositions	When I ask her If she *love* me
Purpose or Expectation	Love not sleep, Lest thou *come* to poverty
Condition or Concession	If she *be* not so to me, What care I how fair she *be?*

Of the variety of subjunctives, only one remains alive— the subjunctive employed in a *condition contrary to fact:*

> If love *were* what the rose is
> And I *were* like the leaf,
> Our lives would grow together
> In sad or singing weather.

Since love is, in fact, not what the rose is, and Mr. Charles A. Swinburne (the author of the lines quoted) is totally unlike the leaf, the condition the *if* clause states is contrary to fact, and the subjunctive is employed. Yet even in this vestigial construction, there is a growing tendency to use the indicative. Matthew Arnold, hardly a revolutionary in grammar, writes: "It rained all night, as if the sky was coming down." And similar usages by Thackeray, Dickens, Auden, Eliot, and Maugham might also be cited.

[1]This is a minimum list.

Aspect. As applied to the verb, aspect has but lately entered English grammar. Old-fashioned grammarians regard it suspiciously, and modern ones employ it in several significations. Used as it is most useful, aspect refers to tense distinctions for which there are no set tense forms, or which escape the set forms. It is, in essence, a psychological concept: it entails examining the verb in its context and ascertaining intention. Illustrations are certainly required. Consider, then, a sentence like *I am going to leave*. The tense form is present progressive; but the action is to take place in the future. *I shall leave* is clearly intended. Again, the verbs in both *The Avon to the Severn runs* and *The machine runs smoothly* are present indicative, but there is plainly a large difference: The Avon has been running to the Severn for a long time, and there is no likelihood that its course will change in the predictable future; however, since the prospects for a perpetual motion machine are dim, we are probably safe in predicting that the machine will eventually run down. The one use of the verb constitutes a timeless present; the other, a definitely limited present.[1]

Aspect simplifies grammar. Instead of postulating tenses like *Future in the Past* to account for the verb in sentences like *I should love Caesar,* grammarians should analyze its aspect. They would then realize that *should,* in this instance, is not simply the past tense of *shall,* and that the action of *should* does not take place at "some past time viewed as future."[2] Rather, *should love* expresses a conditional unreality: it implies, "I ought to love Caesar, but I do not."

Aspect conforms to historical reality. Most students of language agree that there were originally no forms by which tense could be distinguished. There were, however, primary intentions made manifest in frequently repeated word patterns. From these aspects, tense distinctions were gradually evolved. Logic likes tenses: they are monuments to the organizing genius of grammarians. But there are literally hundreds of verb constructions which cannot be fitted into existing tense molds. To create others is scarcely possible. The

[1] This aspect of verbs is called the "durative."
[2] The standard definition of the tense called "Future in the Past."

structure of English grammar would topple. The only solution is to consider aspect—the intention which context reveals. And this is a psychological rather than a logical procedure.[1]

Words Which Modify: Adjectives

An adjective (Latin *adjectivum,* added) is defined as a word which qualifies a substantive (noun or pronoun); that is, the adjective restricts the application of a noun or pronoun to that which has "the quality, the quantity, or the relation which the adjective denotes."[2] The adjective has been classified according to the manner in which it restricts or qualifies. The names are of slight importance, but they are customarily given. We shall not in this instance depart from custom.

Descriptive Adjectives:[3] *dead* lion, *venial* sin, *blue* Monday.

Proper Adjectives: *American* dream, *Freudian* wish, *Byronic* attitude.

Quantative Adjectives: money *enough,*[4] *half* a loaf, *any* idiot.

Possessive Adjectives: *my* eye, *thy* faith, *our* troubles.

Distributive Adjectives: *each* and *every* one, *neither* pronunciation, *either* alternative.

Demonstrative Adjectives: *the* quick and *the* dead,[5] *these* mortals, the *other* woman.

Numeral Adjectives: *two* things, *second* chance, *double* dealer,[6] *all* mortals, *many* men, *divers* books.[7]

As do the other parts of speech, adjectives occasionally shift identity. Sometimes they function like nouns ("the home of the *brave* and the *free,*" "the *quick* and the *dead,*" "the *beautiful* and *true*"); and sometimes like adverbs (*red* hot, *wide* open, *pale* blue sky). There are few generalizations in grammar which are open to no exceptions.

[1] See "Dictionary of Grammar" for the kinds of aspect.

[2] The latter part of this definition is borrowed from Mason's *English Grammar.*

[3] Most adjectives belong to this group.

[4] Adjectives usually, but not invariably, precede the noun.

[5] *The* is also termed a definite article, in contrast to *a* and *an,* the indefinite articles.

[6] *Two* is called a Cardinal, *second* an Ordinal, and *double* a Multiplicative.

[7] Words (*all, many, divers*) that denote number, but not precisely, are classed as indefinite numerals, whereas the Cardinals, Ordinals, and Multiplicatives are classed as definite numerals.

In Modern English the adjective has lost all inflections of number, gender, and case. Comparison, the modification of form to show "how much," still persists. There are three degrees of comparison: positive, comparative, and superlative. Most monosyllables are compared regularly; that is, by adding *r* or *er* to the positive to form the comparative, and *st* or *est* to form the superlative. Thus: *long, longer, longest; large, larger, largest.* A few frequently used monosyllables are compared irregularly, by changing the root vowel—*old, elder, eldest.*[1] Most of the common monosyllables, however, are compared by using different words for the different degrees—*good, better, best; bad, worse, worst.* Many dissyllables and almost all polysyllables[2] are compared by the use of *more* and *most: beautiful, more beautiful, most beautiful; repulsive, more repulsive, most repulsive.*[3]

Some adjectives (*lovely, handsome, remote*) are compared either by adding the *er* and *est* suffixes or by prefixing *more* and *most*. There are, too, allowable variations from standard practice for the purpose of securing a particular rhetorical effect—euphony, balance, emphasis, or another. Shakspere speaks of "Ingratitude *more strong* than traitors' arms," and Spenser of a "lowly ass *more white* than snow." On the other hand, Bacon writes "honourablest and ancienter," Sidney, "repiningest," Coleridge, "safeliest."

Whether doubling of comparatives is admissible has been much mooted. It seems needlessly repetitive, yet it has been done from the earliest times:

> Most cleanest flesh of brides.—Langland, *Piers Plowman.*
> After the most straitest sect of our religion I lived a Pharisee.—*Acts.*
> Let not my worser spirit tempt me again [*i.e.,* more worse].
> —Shakspere, *King Lear.*

[1]Another comparison would be *old, older, oldest.* As is usual when there are variant forms, the uses of the comparative and superlative have become differentiated. Thus *elder* and *eldest* apply to persons only, and, as a rule, to persons who are related. (*He is the elder of the two sons, and the eldest of the children.*) *Older* and *oldest* apply to both persons and things. (*All thoughts and things look older; when the oldest colors have faded.*)

[2]A dissyllable has *two* syllables and a polysyllable *more than two* syllables.

[3]The suffix *most* is fused to the adjective in some of the older forms derived from adverbial roots of time and place; *e.g., utmost, hindermost, foremost, nethermost, northernmost.*

Liberals tend to condone the usage, conservatives to condemn it. The modern writer or speaker who employs it must justify it on grounds of achieving a grace beyond the reach of grammar.

Whether absolutes (*perfect, square, unique, empty, extreme*) can, with logic, be compared is a closely allied question. The answer, those qualified to supply it would generally agree, is: "Not with logic, but with several other sanctions." Reputable practice is certainly one. Shakspere employs *chiefest;* the Bible, *more perfect;* Milton, *extremest.* That the usage is widespread, a casual reading of your newspaper —particularly its advertising columns—ought to convince you. It is an unusual issue which does not include *more unique, more utter,* or *most complete.* There is no doubt that people compare words like these partly because they do not fully grasp the concept of the absolute; but also because they are addicted to taking short cuts in language as elsewhere. The framers of the *Declaration of Independence,* for example, did not mean that though they regarded other unions as perfect they nevertheless proposed to make "a more perfect union." Rather, they thought the others imperfect and proposed to make one *more nearly* perfect. It is a false economy to save one word and cloud a sentence.

Words Which Modify: Adverbs

The adverb, in spite of its derivation (Latin *ad+verbum,* added to the verb), modifies *any* part of speech except the noun or pronoun. The usual definition of adverb as modifying verbs, adjectives, or adverbs *only* is demonstrably incomplete. In *Partly through intelligence but mostly through luck, man has survived,* the adverb *partly* modifies the preposition *through.* In *Simply because we hate are we unhappy,* the adverb *simply* modifies the conjunction *because.* Prof. Nesfield, who first proposed this heretic definition of *adverb,* remarks: "It is immaterial whether we say that the verb qualifies the *preposition only,* or the *entire clause* introduced by the preposition. Similarly, we could say with truth that the ad-

verb qualifies the *conjunction only* or the *entire clause* that
follows it."

The usual definition, of course, applies in practically all
cases. But exceptions help enforce the principle we are attempting to emphasize—that grammatical categories are
fluid, not to say vague. The adverb is assigned all the words
and phrases which are difficult to deposit elsewhere. It has
been cleverly observed that all words tend to become adverbs. Here are a few words which may be classed "adverbs
by courtesy":

> *Accordingly,*[1] they attacked.
> *Well,* what next?
> They must *needs* be borne, because they cannot go.
> *There* was a man in the land of Uz.[2]
> *Yes. No.*
> We arrive *today.*

Adverbs, like adjectives, have three degrees of comparison.
Almost all adverbs are compared by means of *more* and *most*
(*bravely, more bravely, most bravely*), but a few are compared by means of the *er* and *est* endings (*near, nearer,
nearest.*)[3]

At least five classes of adverbs have been distinguished on
the basis of meaning:

> Adverbs of Time: *now, instantly, late, tomorrow.*
> Adverbs of Place: *here, above, in, far, near.*
> Adverbs of Quality: *slowly, badly, asleep, certainly, thus.*
> Adverbs of Number: *again, seldom, secondly, never, twice.*
> Adverbs of Quantity: *almost, little, rather, partly, wholly.*

The adverb is supposed to be a baffler, difficult to recognize
and identify. But simply ask yourself, when doubt assails
you, these questions: "When?" "Where?" "How?" and
"How much?" The words which answer the questions will
be, respectively, adverbs of time, place, quality and quantity,
or number.

---

[1] The *ly* termination is the "sign" of the adverb (from Old English *lic, like*).
But the adjective—as in *manly man*—has it occasionally also.

[2] *There* is an expletive, as *It* is in *It is a fact that* . . .

[3] A few, too, are compared irregularly: *little, less, least.*

Particles: The Preposition

The particle is sometimes defined as a "relatively unimportant part of speech." The preposition, a particle, discounts the definition. Its great reason for being is that it serves as a substitute for the lost inflections of case. In the (usually) short preposition frequently resides the sense of the sentence. Proof is simply furnished. Eliminate the preposition, or supply another, in the following sentence, and the meaning will have been rendered indefinite or else have been transformed:

The boy stood *on* the burning deck . . .

The preposition (Latin *praeponere*, to place before) is the relation of one thing or person to another. The relation may be of place (*at* home), cause (struck *by* lightning), instrumentality (*in* this sign we conquer), manner (*with* kind words and loving hearts), purpose (*for* God and Country), and a variety of others.

Prepositions are firmly imbedded in any number of idiomatic phrases, and attempts to alter them by logical analysis "gang aft agley." To say, for example, that *of* does not express agency or instrumentality, and that *by,* which does, should be substituted when the preposition is to serve such a function, is to disregard a fundamental fact of English speech—the versatility of function which inheres to prepositions. Thus Matthew (xxiii, 5) says: "all the works they do to be seen *of* men." *By men* is standard; but Matthew's phrase has a stylistic rightness which the logicians of language cannot undermine. Similarly the old rule to the effect that "*to* and *into* are not to be used after verbs of rest" has gone the way of all such rules. Hardly anyone would suspect that *Have you ever been to Hawaii?* is considered even faintly improper. The verb *have been* is the psychological equivalent of an "action" verb; certainly much of its "resting" quality has been altered. The preposition, more than most parts of speech, defies analysis and rules based on analysis. One authority has declared that "there is no English preposition which has a clear and consistent meaning and use."[1]

In classical Latin the verb ended the sentence. Since verbs are important, English grammarians inferred that important words should end a sentence. The preposition was alleged to be unimportant. Hence prepositions were not to end sentences.[2] Fallible as logic, the rule is nonsense as grammar. From Old English times to the present, writers and speakers have comprehensively disregarded it. Hugh Blair in *Rhetoric* (1848) dogmatized that "we should always avoid concluding with any of such particles as *of, to, from, with, by.*" Blair's book contains sentences concluding: "than we are accustomed to," "is to be carefully attended to," "which men had any occasion to take notice of," "the subject that is to be treated of." A. C. Ward,[3] who pointed out the paradox, says Blair's "sentences are proper; his rule is a sham." Few grammarians would whole-heartedly disagree.[4]

Particles: The Conjunction

The conjunction (Latin *conjunctus,* joined with) is a particle that conjoins or connects words or groups of words.[5] If the elements joined are of equal rank, the conjunction is called **co-ordinating;** if one element is dependent on another, the conjunction is called **subordinating.** In the Psalms and the earlier (Prayer Book) version of the Psalms, the difference is pointed up by two renderings of the same verse:

> Thou makest darkness, and it is night.
> Thou makest darkness that it may be night.

[1]Bryant and Asher, *Psychology of English.*

[2]Some, by analogy, extended the prohibition to clauses.

[3]*What Is English?*

[4]Of course this is not to say that the preposition is a desirable word with which to end a sentence, though it is frequently the natural and sometimes the inevitable word. In despair, grammarians have treated *reasoned with* (*laughed at, passed upon,* etc.) as a compound verb in sentences like He must be reasoned *with* (etc.). But sentences which strive for a prepositional ending—a classic instance is *Why did you bring this book to me to read out of from for?*— are not therefore admirable.

[5]In which it is like the preposition, the difference consisting of the exclusively connective function of the conjunction. It does not introduce a qualifying phrase and it does not take an object.

The first conjunction (*and*) pairs two co-ordinate expressions; consequently it is a *co-ordinating conjunction*. The second conjunction (*that*) binds together an independent and a subordinate expression; consequently it is a *subordinating conjunction*.[1] In both sentences God's making darkness is the antecedent cause of its being night. However, in one sentence, the elements are given equal grammatical rank; in the other they are not.

Conjunctions are not primitive parts of speech. Most were adverbs, some pronouns, and others prepositions, which developed special uses. Analysis is not always easy, particularly when the same word functions varyingly. In the following sentences, *since* is employed as three distinct parts of speech.

> As a Conjunction:—Since you persist, I shall leave.
> (*Since* links the principal and dependent expressions.)
> As an Adverb:—Since you went away, no birds sing.
> (*Since* modifies the verb.)
> As a Preposition—Since Spring, I have merely marked time.
> (*Since* takes *Spring* as object.)

The test for determining conjunctions is indecisive. Supposedly, if a word connects two sentence elements without itself being a part of either, it is a conjunction. But if it connects, and yet is part of the dependent expression—what then? Grammarians are uncertain. However, with the realization that logic and usage are often at odds, that no part of speech is a constant, a new grammatical concept has evolved —that of "hybrid" parts of speech. In *He defended those who attacked him, who* functions both as a relative pronoun and as a conjunction. In *He looked when he leaped, when* functions both as a relative adverb and as a conjunction. Majority opinion would be for this analysis. However, a respectable minority (respectable both as to quantity and quality) would favor regarding *who* as a relative pronoun only and *when* as a relative adverb only. Jesperson, in *The Philosophy of Grammar*, asserts that there is no "reason for making conjunctions a separate word class . . . if we retain

[1] Other names for the co-ordinating conjunction are *co-ordinate* or *weak;* for the subordinating conjunction, *subordinate* or *strong*.

the name, it is merely due to tradition not to any scientific necessity, and should not make us recognize conjunctions as a part of speech." Each attitude is defensible, and has been ably defended. Since, though, the connection with usage is remote, enough (and more) has been said here.

By dividing the conjunction—both subordinating and co-ordinating—into a variety of kinds, grammarians have multiplied confusion. There are several schemes of division, and in any given one the terminology apparently depends on the classical background of the schematist.

Based on the ways sentences and lesser word groups can be joined one to another, the co-ordinating conjunctions have been divided into **cumulative** or **copulative,** denoting addition (*both, and, also, moreover, further*); **disjunctive** or **alternative,** denoting choice or separation (*either, or, neither, nor, else, otherwise*); **adversative,** denoting contrast (*but, yet, still, notwithstanding, however*); **illative,** denoting inference or consequence (*therefore, wherefore, hence, whence, consequently, accordingly, thus, so, then*).[1] Any of the co-ordinating conjunctions used in pairs (*either . . . or, both . . . and, not only . . . but also*) for the purpose of correlating more closely, are called **correlative** conjunctions.

Subordinate conjunctions are also classified according to the modes of dependence they indicate; that is, by the way the subordinate is linked to the main expression. The following is an abridged list.

Time:	as, while, until, before, since, after.
Reason or *Cause:*	because, for, since, as, whereas.
Supposition or *Condition:*	if, provided, supposing, unless, except, otherwise.
Purpose or *Cause:*	that, in order that, lest, why.
Comparison:	as, than, as much as.
Extent or *Manner:*	as, according, as far as, so.

[1]The *illatives* are conjunctions because no one knows what else to call them. They join by continuing the thought from one word-group to another. But they do not conjoin the groups grammatically. They are essentially parenthetical

We have supplied the nomenclature, or part of it, because it seems an obligation of our office. However, Samuel Ramsey's acute comment[1] will serve as an antidote for "conjunctivitis."

> Grammarians have often divided conjunctions into a number of classes, according to the relations which they express or imply,—Copulatives, Disjunctives, Concessives, Continuatives, Illatives, etc., which classification seems to me to serve no useful purpose. A conjunction not only connects but indicates the character of the connection. It expresses a relation; and to tell what that relation is pertains to lexicography rather than grammar.

Particles: The Interjection

Any word uttered with sufficient force or emotion may be construed as an interjection (Latin *interjectum,* thrown between).[2] It is not a distinct part of speech, and it has no real relationship to other words in the sentence. Jesperson and most moderns exclude it from the parts of speech. *Bah! Ah! Quick! Ha! Heigh-ho!*—all interjections—are not even standard words. And words which function normally as other parts of speech—*Hell! Halt! Alas! Back! But—!*—may be called interjections. The only valid generalization is: If a word is a substitute for a cry of pain or anger or joy, it is interjectional. If the interjection did not so frequently appear in charged prose and in poetry, this brief paragraph would hardly be justified.

Double Parts of Speech: Verbals

How a word functions—as namer or actor or modifier—determines whether it is to be classified as noun, or verb, or adjective, or adverb. Some words (as we have seen) function now one way, now another: sometimes they are to be classified as one part of speech, sometimes another. Other words, however, have two functions simultaneously. These are the **verbals.**

elements. Unless there is another conjunction present, a semicolon must precede. (*I think; therefore, I am.*)

[1] In *The English Language and English Grammar.*

[2] An interjection is sometimes called an *exclamation.*

Verbals are double parts of speech. They combine all the noun or adjective or adverb functions with some of the functions of the verb from which they are formed. Retaining the essential asserting character of verbs, and like them modifiable by adverbs, they differ from verbs in being "non-finite" —that is, they are not limited to a particular person or number. Thus, they cannot take a subject and so cannot constitute the structural base of the sentence. This will become clear after we have considered the three verbals: the infinitive, the participle, and the gerund.

The Infinitive

Examine these three sentences:

> To conquer new worlds was Alexander's desire.
> The desire to conquer new worlds was Alexander's.
> Alexander desired to conquer new worlds.

In the first sentence, the **infinitive** (recognizable by *to*, called "the sign of the infinitive," which precedes it) acts as a noun: it is the subject of the sentence. In the second sentence, the infinitive acts like an adjective: it modifies the noun *desire*. In the third sentence, the infinitive acts like an adverb: it modifies the verb *desired*. In each of the sentences the infinitive takes an object: *new worlds*. In each of the sentences, too, a "finite verb"—one restricted to a particular person and number—is essential: the infinitive is not, by itself, able to bear the structure of the sentence.

The infinitive, though of no particular person or number, is yet capable of indicating two distinctions of tense, the present and the perfect.

> *Present:* to conquer
> *Perfect:* to have conquered

Tense sequence may be summarized briefly:

1. If the action of the infinitive is past in relation to the action of the finite verb or of another verbal, the perfect infinitive is employed.

2. If the action of the infinitive is present or future in re-

lation to the action of the finite verb or of another verbal, the present infinitive is employed.

The following sentence illustrates both sequences:

> Alexander seems [present] to have desired [perfect] to conquer [present] new worlds.

The "sign of the infinitive," *to,* is usually omitted after the active voice of the verbs *bid, see, feel, hear, let, make, dare, watch, behold* and others of similar meaning. Thus we may write, *Dare you, then, beard the lion in his den?* (As Scott wrote it, the sentence read, *Dar'st thou, then, to beard the lion in his den?*—the *to* being inserted for the sake of emphasis.)

The Participle

The **participle** is a verbal adjective: it must be attachable to a noun. Its functions and employment are like those of the infinitive as noun. There are two participles, the present and the past:

> *Present: Conquering* Alexander desired new worlds.
> *Past:* Alexander desired new, *unconquered* worlds.

The past participle regularly ends in *ed, d, t;* it may also end in *en* or *n,* or may undergo an internal vowel change (*abode, sung, swum*).

The Gerund

The **gerund** is a verbal noun (sometimes called a **participial noun**). Only in that it may take an object and be modified by an adverb does the gerund manifest its origin. Otherwise it is a complete noun and may function as subject, object, complement, or appositive:

> Conquering new worlds was Alexander's desire.

Note, in the foregoing sentence, that the gerund has been substituted for the infinitive, and is grammatically (though not stylistically) its equivalent. Sometimes the gerund is called the "infinitive in *ing.*"

Groups of Words: Phrases

A group of words may have the grammatic value of one word, that is, it may perform the offices of a single part of speech. If such a sense unit has neither subject nor predicate, it is called a phrase.

Usually phrases are considered prepositional, participial, gerund, or infinitive—according to the word they pivot on:

> *Prepositional:* "The Princess *with the Golden Hair*" did not appeal *to the censors.*
> *Participial: Desiring the better,* we must reject the worse.
> *Gerund: Wiggling his ears* constitutes his main talent.
> *Infinitive:* The ability *to draw a conclusion* is not indicative of artistic talent.

The functional classification, however, is more realistic. It considers a phrase as noun, verb, adverb, or adjective— according to the part of speech for which it does duty. Thus *with the golden hair,* in the first sentence cited, would be called an adjective phrase, since it modifies the noun *princess.* If we substituted the compound adjective *golden-haired* for the phrase, the meaning of the sentence would not differ significantly. Similarly, the gerund phrase is employed nominally, as subject of the sentence; and by calling it a noun phrase, we better indicate its job in the sentence.

Groups of Words: Clauses

Like the phrase, the clause acts as noun, adjective, or adverb. Unlike the phrase, the clause contains both subject and predicate.

> *Noun: That which is,* is.
> *Adjective:* Beware of all enterprises *that require new clothes.*
> *Adverb: When it rains,* it rains pennies from heaven.

Though each of the clauses in italics has a subject and a predicate, none is capable of supporting the sentence unaided. Consider the adverbial clause: *When it rains* is an incomplete statement without the words which follow. On the other hand, *it rains pennies from heaven* contains a complete predication. The adverbial (or adjective or noun) clause is therefore called the **dependent** or **subordinate** clause; and the words capable of making an independent assertion are called the **principal** or **main** clause.

The Sentence

This excursion into word groups brings us back to our starting point, the **sentence**. According to the number and arrangement of the clauses they contain, sentences are classified as **simple, compound,** and **complex.** Thus if a sentence contains only one main clause, it is a simple sentence:

It rains.

If it contains two or more main clauses connected co-ordinately the sentence is compound:

It rains and pennies fall.

If it contains one or more main clauses and one or more dependent clauses, the sentence is complex:

When it rains, it rains pennies from heaven.

Sentences, of course, may be both compound and complex: they may convey an indefinite number of statements, and these may be qualified by an indefinite number of clauses. One writer on style has asserted that "half the art of composition consists in keeping the subordinate parts of the sentence in proper relation to the principal parts."

BOOK TWO

Dictionary of Grammar

A

Ablative (Lat. *ablativus*, removed from).—The name of a case in Latin, and some other Indo-European languages, but not in English, which expresses removal or separation, origin, agent, instrument, etc. In Latin it appears regularly after certain prepositions (*ab*, from; *cum*, with; *ex*, from; etc.) which are sometimes called **signs of the ablative.** When independent of the rest of the sentence, an ablative with a participle in agreement is termed **ablative absolute.** The ablative is occasionally referred to as the *"wherefrom case."* The familiar phrases *ex libris, cum laude, ab ovo* are ablative constructions.

Ablaut (Ger. *ab*, off + *laut*, sound).—Term originated by Grimm to describe the substitution of one vowel for another within the same base, as a result not of the influences of the succeeding vowel—as in *Umlaut*—but rather as a result of the conditions and nature of original stress and intonation. Usually the vowel change is accompanied by a change in function or meaning. The process, which applies chiefly but not exclusively to verbs, is also called **Gradation.**

    ring, rang, rung;
    drive, drove, driven;
    bear, bore, born, borne, bairn, birth, bier.

Fruitful of new words as it once was, umlaut or gradation "has long since ceased to be an active principle in word formation" (Robertson).

Absolute (Lat. *absolutus,* loosened or freed from).—Standing apart from the usual relationship to other words; applied to a construction which is syntactically free from the rest of the sentence—in English, the **Absolute Nominative** (or the **Nominative Absolute**).

The words italicized below are absolute nominative, but the whole phrase or clause in which they appear is of absolute construction.

> "Your *fathers,* where are they? and the *prophets,* do they live forever?"—BIBLE

> "The *hour* concealed, and so remote the *fear,*
> Death still draws nearer, never seeming near."—POPE

> "*They* who serve me with adoration,—
> I am in them, and they are in me."—EMERSON

Absolute applies also to words which admit of no comparison: *perfect, round, universal, eternal, unique,* etc.

Abstract (Lat. *abstractus,* drawn off or away).—A term applied to substantives formed from adjectives (*ripeness* from *ripe, hardness* from *hard, bravery* from *brave*); or, more generally, to substantives naming that which is withdrawn or separate from the material, the practical, or the particular (*joy, literature, force, idea, capitalism*).

Opposed to *Concrete.*

> "An abstract name is a name which stands for an attribute of a thing."—J. S. MILL

> Nouns are abstract when "severed (not from Matter but) from the account of Matter."—HOBBES

Modern critics of language point out that all *words* are necessarily abstract; only *things* can be concrete. However, the term has been in grammar for about 700 years, and even the moderns find it useful in distinguishing degrees of remoteness from the actual.

Accidence (Lat. *accidentia,* things which befall).—That part of grammar which treats of the inflection of words.

Accusative (Lat. *accusativus,* caused or effected).—An alternate name for *Objective* (*q.v.*). *Accusative* is the term used in Greek, Latin, and German; though used in English too, the more common designation is *objective.*

Active Verb—One in the Active Voice. A verb is in the active voice when its subject denotes the doer or agent of the action.

> I *came,* I *saw,* I *conquered.*

Adjective (Latin *adjectivus,* added).—A part of speech limiting or describing a substantive. There are several ways of classifying adjectives as to kind. The following is by no means a complete list. (Note that the categories overlap in some instances.)

1. **Common:** applying to any of a class, not to a particular person or thing—*common, nominal, proper.*

2. **Proper:** restricting the noun to scope of a particular person or thing—*American, Marxian, Byronic, Newtonian, Gangetic.*

3. **Descriptive** or Qualitative: showing kind, state, or quality—*good, dead, clever.*

4. **Quantitative:** telling how much or in what degree—*little, much, all, enough, some.*

5. **Numeral:** denoting (a) how many things, or (b) in what order, or (c) how often repeated. If (a), they are termed **Cardinals**—*one, two, three,* etc.; if (b), **Ordinals**—*first, second, third;* if (c), **Multiplicatives**—*single, double, triple.*

6. **Demonstrative:** pointing out which or what is meant. They are further divided into **Definite**—*the, this, that, other;* and **Indefinite**—*a, any, certain, another.* The **Definite Article** (*the*) and the **Indefinite Article** (*a*) are both included in this class.

7. **Distributive:** indicating that the referent is to be taken singly or separately—*each, every, either, neither.*

8. **Possessive:** expressing ownership—*my, his, her, its, our, your, their.*

There is another system of classification, according to the part of speech from which the adjective is formed.

1. **Pronominal:** formed from a pronoun—*whose, my, which, what, our.* Usually, they have function only as possessives. But they may also aid in asking a question—*"What* manner of men are these who have as legs, parentheses?"*—in which circumstance they are classed as **Interrogative Adjectives.** Or they may be relative pronouns and still show possession. *"This* is the man whose might you mistook"—in which circumstance they are classed as **Relative Adjectives.**

2. **Verbal:** formed from verbs; also called **Participial Adjective.** (*See* entry under PARTICIPLES.)

> A *living, breathing,* though a *hated* man.

3. **Adverbial:** formed from an adverb and a participle, the latter often understood rather than stated.

> the then [presiding] president
> the up [going] escalator
> the late [living] poet

4. **Substantive** (or **Noun**): Some of the older grammarians designated every *adjective* as an *adjective substantive,* on the ground "that it is altogether as much the name of a thing as the Noun Substantive" (Tooke). Some restricted the term to adjectives which could double as substantives: *iron, captive, lunatic.*

Perhaps the most useful and certainly the least complex method of classification is according to function.

1. **Attributive:** *bad* break, *forty* days, *hopeful* Harry, *Bengal* lancer.

2. **Appositive:** His spirit, *mean in adversity, violent and inhuman in prosperity,* sank under the load of public abhorrence.

3. **Predicative:**

> a. The sea is *calm* tonight. (*Calm* in this construction is also called a **complement** [*q.v.*].)

b. I consider the thing *done*. (*Done* in this construction is also called a **factitive** [*q.v.*] adjective.)

(*See* also COMPARISON OF ADJECTIVES ; CLAUSE.)

Accent (Latin *accentus,* a singing).—The stress laid on a single syllable. It frequently shifts when a different part of speech is indicated.

> Re bel' (verb)
> Reb'el (noun)

The mark ' placed after the syllable means that the entire syllable is to be accented.

The distinction is often made between *accent* and *emphasis*. The latter denotes the stress placed upon the entire word.

> *Silver* and *gold* have I none.

Adjunct (Latin *adjunctus,* joined to).—A word, phrase, or clause which modifies one of the basic sentence elements.

The meanest *flower can* sometimes *invoke thoughts* too deep for tears.

The subject *flower,* the verb *can invoke,* and the object *thoughts* are the basic sentence elements. All the other words are adjuncts modifying either subject, verb, or object (Grouk).

Adjunct Object.—Same as **objective complement** (*q.v.*).

Adverb (Latin *adverbium,* adverb—from *ad* plus *verbum,* added to a word—a literal translation of the Greek word meaning "something additional to the predication").—A part of speech used to qualify a verb, an adjective, or another adverb. Nesfield proposes a definition more in accord with the functions of the adverb: ". . . a word used to qualify any part of speech except a noun or pronoun."

Adverbs are classified under three headings:

1. **Simple**
   a. **Time** (when?) : *now, instantly, late, tomorrow, afterwards.*
   b. **Place** (where?) : *here, there, within, above, far.*

  c. **Quality** (**Manner, State**) (how?): *thus, well, conveniently, probably, quickly.*

  d. **Number** (how many?): *again, seldom, secondly, never, once.*

  e. **Quantity** (**Measure, Degree**) (how much?): *much, little, half, scarce, exceedingly.*

  f. **Cause** (**Instrumentality**) (why?): *why, wherefore, whence.*

2. **Interrogative**

Adverbs employed in asking questions. The subdivisions correspond to those of the simple adverb: *When* (time)? *Where* (place)? *How* (quality)? *How many* (number)? *How much* (quantity)? *Why* (cause)?

3. **Relative**

Adverbs having a dual function: as conjunction and as adverb. Maintaining their adverbial status, they yet link sentences together: *I can tell* where *my own shoe pinches me.*

The relative adverbs are sometimes called **conjunctive adverbs.** (*See* also COMPARISON OF ADVERBS, CLAUSES.)

Adversative Conjunction.—*See* CONJUNCTION.

Affix (Latin *ad* plus *figere,* to fix or fasten).—A syllable or syllables fixed to a word and modifying its meaning. The affix may be joined to the beginning of a word, in which case it is called a *prefix* (*ad*—to; *post*—after; *pre*—before); or it may be joined to the end of a word, in which case it is called a *suffix* or *postfix* (*ful*—full; *ship*—state or quality; *or*—agent or person).—*See* also SUFFIX.

Agglutination (Latin *agglutinatus,* glued).—The combination of words into compounds in which the component words are unchanged, or only slightly changed.

> brick+yard=brickyard
> do+not=don't
> anti+fascist=anti-fascist

(*Cf.* AMALGAMATION.)

Languages in which such "gluing" is the rule (*e.g.,* Turkish, Finnish, Hungarian) are sometimes called **agglutinative languages.**

Agreement (French *agréer,* to receive with favor—from Latin *gratus,* pleasing).—"To be in concord; to take the same gender, number, case, or person; as happens in inflected language to words in apposition, and to substantives and their attributive words, whether adjective, verb, or relative" (*NED*).

Amalgamation (Greek *malagama,* a soft mass).—The act of welding words or their components together. Thus:

alone	— all one
Christmas	— Christ mass
nostril	— nose thirl (hole)
Norfolk	— North Folk

Ameliorative (Latin *amelioratus,* made better or more vigorous).—That tendency of words through which they undergo gradual elevation in meaning. Thus, *butler* once meant "bottle server"; *marshal,* "house servant"; *pastor,* "shepherd"; *minister,* "servant"; *steward,* "sty warden."
Opposed to *Pejorative.*

Anacoluthon (Greek *anakolouthos,* wanting sequence).— A construction which does not logically follow another. It constitutes a sort of grammatical "short circuit" (C. Alphonso Smith). Thus the indicative *are,* in the following sentence by Ruskin, is inconsistent with the subjunctive *be* (in a "contrary to fact" conditional clause):

> But if the mass of good things *be* inexhaustible, and there *are* horses for everybody,—then why is not every beggar on horseback?

Parallel construction would demand *be* in place of *are.*

Analysis (Greek *ana,* up; plus *lysis,* breaking).—Breaking up a whole into its components. There are several applications to grammar:

1. Breaking up a compound letter into its parts, as *x* into *k* and *s.*
2. Breaking up a syllable into its letters, or a word into its syllables.

3. Breaking up a word into prefix, root or stem, and suffix.

4. Breaking up a complex sentence into its clauses.

5. Breaking up a clause into its parts—subject, predicate, object, and adjuncts.

Modern English is sometimes referred to as an *analytic language*, to contrast with Old English which is considered a *synthetic language*.

Anomaly (Greek *anomalia*, unevenness of ground).—A departure from the norm in syntax or idiom.

Apheresis (Greek *aphairesis*, a taking from).—The loss of an unaccented initial letter or syllable:

> cheat for escheat
> spend for *dispendere*
> sample for ensample

(*See* also APHESIS, APOCOPE, SYNCOPE.)

Aphesis (Greek *aphesis*, a letting go).—The loss of an unaccented initial vowel.

> mend for amend
> vanguard for *avant-garde*
> sterling for Easterling

(*See* also APHERESIS, APOCOPE, SYNCOPE.)

Apocope (Greek *apokope*, a cutting off).—The loss of an unaccented final letter or syllable.

> beast for beste
> chivalry for chivalrye
> riches for richesse

The loss of the final *e* is one of the distinguishing marks of Modern English as against Middle English.

(*See* also APHERESIS, APOCOPE, SYNCOPE.)

Apodosis (Greek *apodosis*, conclusion).—The consequent clause, expressing the result, in a conditional sentence; its correlative is **protasis,** which is the introductory clause.

> [Protasis] *If thine enemy be hungry,*
> [Apodosis] *give him bread to eat;*
> [Protasis] *If he be thirsty,*
> [Apodosis] *give him water to drink.*

Apposition (Latin *appositus,* placed).—The placing of one sentence, or sentence element, against another for the purpose of explanation or emphasis.

A garden enclosed is my sister, *my spouse; a spring shut up, a fountain sealed.*

Argot (French *argot,* slang).—The secret or cant language of thieves. Also employed (inaccurately, Partridge says) to the technical or special vocabulary of any trade, profession, or other activity. As such, it is a synonym for *jargon* (*q.v.*), and should be employed only in writing about France (Fowler). In the sense of "secret language," *cant* is regarded as a synonym. However, *cant* is more generally applied to whining, affected, or hypocritical speech.

Article (Latin *articulus,* a joint or part).—*See* ADJECTIVE.

Aspect (Latin *aspectus,* look at attentively).—"One of the ways in which an action or state of condition is viewed" (Kantor). The term is generically used to cover those functions which do not come under mood, voice, or tense.

Curme analyzes the following phases of aspect:

1. Durative—indicating duration: *He is working in the garden.*
2. Point-Action—calling attention to only one point in the action.
   a. Ingressive—calling attention to the beginning of an action: *He woke up early.*
   b. Conclusive or Effective—calling attention to the end of an action: *His strength gave out.*
3. Terminative—emphasizing the act as a whole: *I worked in the garden this morning.*
4. Iterative—expressing repeated action: *He interrupted continually.*

Assimilation (Latin *ad,* to; plus *similis,* like).—The process by which one consonant changes, through the influence of contact, so that it sounds like another. Thus, instead of *adsimilation,* we have *assimilation.*

Attributive Complement.—*See* PREDICATE NOMINATIVE.

Auxiliary (Latin *auxiliaris,* helping, aiding).—A verb that helps principal or main verbs in forming their moods, voices, and tenses (*be, have, do; shall, will; ought, must; may, can; used, dare, let*).

B

Back formation.—The construction of a new word from one in use; frequently on the assumption that the one in use is derived from the one coined.

> Burgle from burglar
> Enthuse from enthusiasm
> Jell from jelly

Blending.—Mingling two distinct and separate words, the result either of confusion as to their meaning or of an attempt to be funny.

Kennedy quotes from *Word Lore* the comment of a man who regretted seeing two of his friends at "daggerlogs." He comments: "Doubtless at *daggers drawn* and at *logger-heads* had been confused by the gentleman." The words so formed are termed blends (*cf.* PORTMANTEAU WORDS).

Borrowings.—Words transferred from one language to another to supply some imagined or real deficiency (or, occasionally, for the sake of ostentation).

In 1531 Thomas Elyot published *The Governour.* From the brief dedication (to Henry VIII), Baugh extracts the following words, all new in Elyot's day and all borrowed: *devulgate, describe, attempate, benevolent, enterprise, studious, endeavor, protest, reproach, malignity, education, dedicate.* (The last two of this series are first recorded in Elyot's dedication.)

English, of course, is made up largely of borrowed words. But the exuberant borrowings during the Renaissance (1500–1650) from Latin (for most part), Greek, French, Italian, and Spanish were savagely attacked by many of the advocates of plain and pure English. Thomas Wilson, in the *Art of Rhetorique* (1553), inveighs against Inkhorn Terms:

> Among all other lessons this should first be learned, that wee never affect any straunge ynkhorne termes, but to speake as is commonly received . . .

C

Cant (Latin *cantus,* song, chant, or whine).—*See* ARGOT.

Cardinals: *See* ADJECTIVES.

Case (Latin *casus,* falling).—The changes of form a substantive undergoes to show its relation to another word.

Since in English there are only six or seven substantives, all of them pronouns, which have a distinctive case form when used objectively (*me, us, him, her, them, whom, thee*), some grammarians are disinclined to consider the accusative or objective case as having a real existence in English. The only other distinctive case form, if we exclude the possessive pronouns, is the genitive or possessive with *apostrophe s* (*'s*). Therefore, most modern grammarians maintain that there are, by the definition given above, only two cases in English: The common case and the possessive or genitive case. (Some, however, notably Sonnenschein, say that cases, in English, denote categories of *meaning,* not categories of *form.* Jesperson, who takes the position that form determines case, comments that Sonnenschein opens the door not only to the dative and ablative cases, but even to the instrumental and locative. He further points out that no grammarians ever meant what Sonnenschein means by case.)

See: NOMINATIVE, GENITIVE (POSSESSIVE), DATIVE, OBJECTIVE (ACCUSATIVE), and ABLATIVE.

Clause (Latin *clausus,* a thing concluded or closed up; an enclosure).—A group of related words forming part of a sentence and containing a subject and predicate.

a. A clause that contains a complete predication is called **independent:**

   Candy is dandy but *liquor is quicker.*—OGDEN NASH

In the compound sentence quoted above, the groups of related words (in italics) constitute two independent clauses. Each is grammatically independent of the other and of the same grammatical rank; each is consequently called a **co-ordinate clause.**

b. Now consider the following complex sentence:

The ability to make love frivolously is the chief characteristic *which distinguishes human beings from the beasts.*

The italicized portion of the sentence contains both a subject (*which*) and a verb (*distinguishes*). But the clause depends for its meaning on the rest of the sentence. It modifies *characteristic* in much the same way that *chief* does. Hence it is called a **dependent** or **subordinate clause.** The portion of the sentence not in italics makes the main statement. Hence it is called a **main** or **principal clause.**

c. **Dependent clauses** are classified according to the function—noun, adjective, or adverb—they perform in the sentence.

Noun: *What you don't know* would make a great book.—SIDNEY SMITH

Adjective: He is one of those wise philanthropists *who in time of famine would vote for nothing but toothpicks.*—JERROLD

Adverbial: *When I am dead,* I hope it may be said
"His sins were scarlet, but his books were read."
—BELLOC

Noun clauses may be introduced by (1) subordinating conjunctions; (2) relative (or conjunctive) and interrogative adverbs; (3) relative and interrogative pronouns.

(NOTE: Direct quotations are sometimes classed as noun clauses; indirect quotations always are.)

Adjective clauses are introduced by (1) relative pronouns; (2) relative (or conjunctive) adverbs.

Adverbial clauses are introduced by (1) relative (or conjunctive) adverbs; (2) interrogative pronouns; (3) interrogative adverbs.

(The introductory word is frequently omitted in all three types of clause.)

Adverbial clauses are sometimes named more particularly, with reference to the relations they indicate. Clauses of time, place, and degree; of purpose and result; of cause and effect; of condition and concession have been noted.

d. **Restrictive** and **nonrestrictive** clauses: Adjective clauses may modify their substantives by restricting their application, or by merely qualifying them. If the former, they are called *restrictive;* if the latter, they are called *nonrestrictive.* The following are examples of each type:

Restrictive: Clauses *that restrict* are usually, but not necessarily, introduced by *that* or *who.*

Nonrestrictive: Nonrestrictive clauses, *which are adjective clauses,* are usually, but not necessarily, introduced by *which* or *who.*

(Note that the restrictive clause is intimately attached to its substantive, and is not set off by commas; and that the nonrestrictive clause is almost parenthetical in nature and is set off by commas.)

Cognate Object:—*See* OBJECT.

Common Gender:—*See* GENDER.

Common Case:—*See* CASE.

Common Number:—*See* NUMBER.

Comparison (French *comparer,* to compare—from Latin *comparare,* to couple things together for judgment).—The inflection of an adjective or adverb to express degree.

Three degrees are distinguished: the **positive,** which is the uninflected form of the adjective or adverb; the **comparative,** which denotes a greater degree; and the **superlative,** which expresses maximum degree.

1. Comparison of Adjectives

a. Most monosyllables are compared by adding *r* or *er* to the positive to form the comparative and *st* or *est* to form the superlative.

brave	braver	bravest
bold	bolder	boldest
weak	weaker	weakest

A few frequently used monosyllables are compared irregularly.

bad (evil, ill)	worse	worst
far	farther	farthest
——	further	furthest
good	better	best
late	later (latter)	latest (last)
little	less (lesser)	least
much (many)	more	most
well (in health)	better	best

Some of the older forms (derived from adverbial roots of time and place) form the superlative by suffixing *most* to the positive.

east (eastern)	more eastern	easternmost
——	——	endmost
——	former	foremost
——	——	furthermost
hind	hinder	hindmost
——	inner	inmost (innermost)
——	nether	nethermost
north	——	northmost
northern	more northern	northernmost
south	——	southmost
southern	more southern	southernmost
top	——	topmost
west (western)	more western	westernmost

b. Most dissyllables and almost all polysyllables are compared with the use of *more* and *most*. (This mode of indicating degree is sometimes called comparison by adverbs.)

anxious	more anxious	most anxious
joyful	more joyful	most joyful
reluctant	more reluctant	most reluctant

c. Some adjectives are compared either way: by suffixing *er* and *est* to form the comparative and superlative; or by employing *more* and *most*.

lovely	{ lovelier { more lovely	{ loveliest { most lovely
handsome	{ handsomer { more handsome	{ handsomest { most handsome
remote	{ remoter { more remote	{ remotest { most remote

d. For the purpose of securing some rhythmical, emphatic, or other effect, departures from the standard modes of comparison are sanctioned.

> more white.—SPENSER
> honourablest.—BACON
> most true.—SHAKSPERE

2. Comparison of Adverbs

a. Almost all adverbs are compared by means of *more* and *most*.

bravely	more bravely	most bravely

b. Some adverbs are compared by suffixing *er* and *est*.

dear	dearer	dearest
high	higher	highest
loud	louder	loudest

c. A few are compared irregularly; usually they do double duty as adverbs and adjectives.

badly (ill)	worse	worst
far } forth }	{ farther { further	{ farthest { furthest
late	later	latest (last)
little	less	least
much	more	most
nigh	nigher	nighest, next
——	rather	——
well	better	best

d. Some adverbs have dual comparatives and superlatives.

often	{ oftener { more often	{ oftenest { most often

Complement (Latin *complementum,* that which fills up or completes).—The word or words which complete the predication. Though some grammarians would restrict the term to apply only to words following the copulative verb or verbs of *naming, choosing, calling,* etc., most distinguish four types of complement.

1. **Subject** (or **subjective**) **complement**; or **predicate nominative** or **attribute**: a substantive which is part of the predicate but which describes, defines, or equates with the subject.

> Love is *spinach.*
> Rose is *a rose* is *a rose* is *a rose.*
> Poetry is *what Milton saw* when he went blind.

2. **Predicate adjective**: an adjective which is part of the predicate but which describes, qualifies, or limits the subject.

> Grow *old* along with me!—BROWNING
>
> The masters of the subtle school
> Are *controversial, polymath.*
> —T. S. ELIOT

Strait is the gate, and *narrow* is the way that leadeth unto life . . .
—BIBLE

3. **Direct object** or **object of the verb.** (The older grammarians sometimes called it an **object(ive) complement**—a term now usually restricted to complements such as those listed under item 4.) A substantive which directly receives the action of a transitive verb.

> Pity the *Unicorn!*
> Delay breeds *danger.*

If the direct object is cognate (Latin *cognatus,* connected by birth) with the verb—having the same stem—it is called a **cognate object.**

> He fought the good *fight.*
> They lived their simple *lives.*

4. **Object** (or **objective**) **complement**, or **predicate objective**, or **adjunct object**, or **supplement**, or **factitive object**: a complement attached to an object and referring to the same person or thing; after verbs of *choosing, naming, calling, making, thinking,* and the like.

I think *him* (direct object) *honest* (predicate objective).

They made the eldest *son* (direct object) *slave* (predicate objective) in his father's stead.

(*See* also OBJECT.)

Complex Sentence (French *complexe,* complex—Latin *complexus,* entwined or encircled).—One which contains a principal (or main) clause and one or more subordinating (or dependent) clauses.

Clairvoyant, *n.* A person, commonly a woman, *who has the power of seeing that which is invisible to her patron*—namely, *that he is a blockhead.*—BIERCE

A **compound-complex** sentence is one compound in its structure and containing one or more subordinating clauses.

It would be dark *before he could reach the village,* and he heaved a heavy sigh *when he thought of encountering the terrors of Dame Van Winkle.*—IRVING

Compound (Latin *componere,* to set or place together).—

1. **Word:** two or more simple words joined together— *life-long, courts-martial, brothers-in-law, man-of-war.*

2. **Subject, Predicate, Object:** two or more subjects, predicates, or objects.

a. **Subject:** *Shadrach, Meshach,* and *Abednego* fell down bound into the midst of the burning fiery furnace.—BIBLE

b. **Predicate:** He *raved, ranted*—and *resigned.*—FELD

c. **Object:** He snatched the *lightning* from the sky and their *sceptre* from tyrants.—TURGOT

d. **Subject, Predicate,** and **Object:** The winds and the waves fiercely *tossed* and *buffeted* the frail *vessel* and its *passengers.*—KING

3. **Sentence:** two or more simple sentences joined together without subordination of the one to the other.

His moments were numbered; the strife was finished; the vision was closed.

> Only the game fish swims upstream,
> But the sensible fish swims down.

Conative Future (Latin *conationem,* endeavor, effort—hence, striving, willing).—The emphatic or compulsive future.

Achieved:

(1) by transposing the auxiliaries which normally indicate simple futurity, *shall* for the first person, *will* for the second and third persons. Thus:

> I will do it.
> He (you) shall do it.

(2) by simple emphasis, since the distinction made in (1) above is now apparent to very few. Thus:

> He *will* do it!
> I *shall* do it!

Concord (French *concorde*—from Latin *concordia,* agreement).—Same as AGREEMENT (*q.v.*).

Concrete.—*See* ABSTRACT.

Condition.—*See* MOOD; CLAUSE.

Conjugation (Latin *conjugatus,* united).—The inflections of a verb, giving its principal parts, and the forms of its numbers, persons, tenses, moods, and voices. The conjugation of the transitive verb *to love* follows. (NOTE: The forms of the subjunctive which differ from the corresponding forms of the indicative have been italicized.)

PRINCIPAL PARTS

Present Infinitive	*1st Person Singular of Past Tense*	*Past Participle*
to love	loved	loved

INDICATIVE MOOD

ACTIVE VOICE

Present Tense

Person	*Singular*	*Plural*
1st	I love	We love
2nd	You love	You love
3rd	He loves	They love

Past Tense

1st	I loved	We loved
2nd	You loved	You loved
3rd	He loved	They loved

Future Tense

1st	I shall love	We shall love
2nd	You will love	You will love
3rd	He will love	They will love

Present Perfect Tense

1st	I have loved	We have loved
2nd	You have loved	You have loved
3rd	He has loved	They have loved

Pluperfect or Past Perfect Tense

1st	I had loved	We had loved
2nd	You had loved	You had loved
3rd	He had loved	They had loved

Future Perfect Tense

1st	I shall have loved	We shall have loved
2nd	You will have loved	You will have loved
3rd	He will have loved	They will have loved

PASSIVE VOICE

Present Tense

1st	I am loved	We are loved
2nd	You are loved	You are loved
3rd	He is loved	They are loved

Past Tense

1st	I was loved	We were loved
2nd	You were loved	You were loved
3rd	He was loved	They were loved

Future Tense

1st	I shall be loved	We shall be loved
2nd	You will be loved	You will be loved
3rd	He will be loved	They will be loved

Present Perfect Tense

1st	I have been loved	We have been loved
2nd	You have been loved	You have been loved
3rd	He has been loved	They have been loved

Pluperfect or Past Perfect Tense

1st	I had been loved	We had been loved
2nd	You had been loved	You had been loved
3rd	He had been loved	They had been loved

Future Perfect Tense

1st	I shall have been loved	We shall have been loved
2nd	You will have been loved	You will have been loved
3rd	He will have been loved	They will have been loved

SUBJUNCTIVE MOOD

ACTIVE VOICE

Present Tense

1st	(If) I love	(If) We love
2nd	(If) You love	(If) You love
3rd	(If) He love or loves	(If) They love

Past Tense

1st	(If) I loved	(If) We loved
2nd	(If) You loved	(If) You loved
3rd	(If) He loved	(If) They loved

Present Perfect Tense

1st	(If) I have loved	(If) We have loved
2nd	(If) You have loved	(If) You have loved
3rd	(If) He *have loved* or has loved	(If) They have loved

Pluperfect or Past Perfect Tense

1st	(If) I had loved	(If) We had loved
2nd	(If) You had loved	(If) You had loved
3rd	(If) He had loved	(If) They had loved

PASSIVE VOICE

Present Tense

1st	*(If) I be loved*	*(If) We be loved*
2nd	*(If) You be loved*	*(If) You be loved*
3rd	*(If) He be loved*	*(If) They be loved*

Past Tense

1st	(*If*) *I were loved*	(If)	We were loved
2nd	(If) You were loved	(If)	You were loved
3rd	(*If*) *He were loved*	(If)	They were loved

Present Perfect Tense

1st	(If) I have been loved	(If)	We have been loved
2nd	(If) You have been loved	(If)	You have been loved
3rd	(*If*) *He have been loved*	(If)	They have been loved

Pluperfect or Past Perfect Tense

1st	(If) I had been loved	(If)	We had been loved
2nd	(If) You had been loved	(If)	You had been loved
3rd	(If) He had been loved	(If)	They had been loved

Conjunction.—A part of speech joining (but not qualifying) words or sentences.

If the conjunction joins co-ordinate elements—that is, those of equivalent grammatical rank—it is called **co-ordinating**. Depending on how they unite sentences or sentence elements co-ordinating conjunctions are classified in the following manner.

Type of Co-ordinating Conjunction	Denotation	Examples
Cumulative or Copulative	Addition	and, both, also, too, further
Disjunctive or Alternative	Choice	either, or, neither, nor, else, otherwise
Adversative	Contrast	but, yet, still, notwithstanding, however
Illative	Inference or Consequence	therefore, then, so, hence, consequently

Note that any of the co-ordinating conjunctions may be used in pairs for the purpose of correlating more closely:

> *Either* all *or* nought.

> A ful great fool is he, ywis
> That *both* rich *and* nigard is.—CHAUCER.

The subordinating conjunctions join a dependent clause to a principal clause. The dependent clause may be an ad-

jective or noun clause, linked to the principal clause by *that,*
whether, or, etc.; or it may be an adverbial clause, linked to
the principal clause by subordinating conjunctions indicating the following modes of dependence:

Time: *as, while, until, before, since, after*

Reason or Cause: *as, whereas, because, for, since*

Supposition or Condition: *if, unless, except, otherwise*

Purpose or Cause: *that, so, lest, in order that*

Comparison, Extent or Manner: *as, according, as far as, so*

Continuous.—A tense form denoting action still in progress.

I am, was, shall be loving.
I have been, had been, shall have been loving.

Conversion (French *conversion,* conversion—from Latin
conversionem, an alteration or change).—A functional
change in a word; a shift from one part of speech to another.

This is a very common occurrence in Modern English, and
all parts of speech are subject to it.

to *run*—to make a *run*
a *well* man—a man who does *well*
I, *but* not he—none *but* me—*but* me no *buts*

Copula (Latin *copula,* a couple, a tie).—A linking verb;
one which ties the subject to the predicate.

The pre-eminent copula, or copulative verb is *to be* in its
various forms. Others, though, are included by the term:
appear, seem, remain, look, become, grow; and occasionally,
smell, sound, taste, turn, prove, go, lie.

Correlative.—*See* CONJUNCTION.

D

Dative (Latin *dativus,* that which is given).—A case in
Indo-European languages signifying *to* or *for* someone or
something. In Modern English (as opposed to Old English
and the Indo-European languages generally) there are no
distinctive dative forms for the noun, or forms indistinguishable from those of the objective for the pronoun. The con-

struction called dative by some grammarians is better termed an indirect object. (*See* COMPLEMENT, OBJECT.)

> The bishop gave the *baboon* a bun.—BODMER

Dangling Participle.—*See* PARTICIPLE.

Declarative Sentence.—*See* SENTENCE.

Declension (Latin *declinationem,* a turning aside, a departure).—The inflection of nouns and pronouns to indicate gender, number, and case (*qq.v.*).

Defective (Latin *defectus,* a failure or lack).—Lacking one or more forms.

1. **Verb:** one lacking some mood, tense, or verbal (infinitive and participle) form. The six simple auxiliaries are the most defective of English verbs. *Can, may, shall, will, must, ought* have neither infinitive nor participle forms.

2. **Adjective:** one lacking a positive, comparative, or superlative form.

	former	foremost
top	——	topmost
round	——	——

3. **Noun:** one lacking either a singular (*eaves*) or a plural (*news*).

Deferred Word.—One which is postponed, placed after the word with which it is associated. The term is most frequently used with reference to prepositions (thus engendering something of an anomaly, since a preposition is, etymologically at least, a word *placed before* another):

> Whom have you reported to?

(Note that the deferred or postponed preposition is a frequent source of error. The inclination is to make its object, when a pronoun—as it normally is in this construction—nominative rather than objective: *Who* have you reported to?)

Degeneration (Latin *degeneratus,* departed from its kind).—The process by which words degenerate in meaning; that is, become depreciatory or pejorative.

The process is a frequent one in English: *Brats,* for example, was once used without any connotation of contempt to mean, simply, child:

> O Israel, O household of the Lord,
> O Abraham's *brats,* O brood of blessed seed,
> O chosen sheep that loved the Lord indeed.
> —GASCOIGNE

Similarly, *dunce* (a follower of Duns Scotus, a medieval schoolman), *fiend* (enemy), *insane* (unhealthy), *saloon* (hall), *villain* (serf), have degenerated in meaning.

Demonstrative (Latin *demonstratus,* pointed out, shown). —*See* ADJECTIVE, PRONOUN.

Derivative (French *dériver,* to turn off, as a stream—from Latin *derivare,* to draw off, to divert).—A word formed from a simple or primary word.

Derivatives are of two kinds: primary, or formed by a change in the root of the word (as *graze* from *grass*); and secondary, or formed by adding an affix to the stem (as *grassy* from *grass*).

Dialect (Greek *dialectos,* discourse, manner of speaking). —The speech of a community, district, or class; characterized by peculiarities of accent, pronunciation, and usage (*e.g.,* Yorkshire, Scots, American Negro, Yankee, and Southern dialects).

Nesfield comments: "Until some standard has become established, the different local varieties of kindred speech are dialects of coequal rank. But when a standard speech has been formed, the dialects or local varieties fall into a lower rank and are regarded as the speech of the unlearned."

Doublet (Latin *duplus,* twice as much).—One of two words having the same origin but different histories. Thus *wile* and *guile; antic* and *antique; chance* and *cadence; task* and *tax; etiquette* and *ticket; barb* and *beard* are all doublets.

Direct Address.—*See* NOMINATIVE.

E

Ellipsis (Latin *ellipsis;* Greek *elleipsis,* an omission).—The omission of a word or words necessary to complete the grammatical construction, but not necessary to make the meaning clear.

1. It is most apparent in imperative sentences. *Behold!* is an order with the subject *you* understood but not stated. Similarly, in *Lights! Action! Camera!* the predicate is omitted, and must be supplied from context.

2. The elliptical possessive (or genitive) is standard in English. *At a friend's* has *house* (or some other word) understood.

3. The elliptical clause has one or more of its elements understood: *He is as tall as I* [*am tall*].

4. Ellipsis causes adjectives to become substantives: *The quick and the dead* [*people*].

5. Verbs normally transitive may become intransitive through ellipsis: *He drives* [*his automobile*] *slowly.*

6. Ellipsis of the copula is frequent, particularly in idioms: *First come, first served.*

7. The relatives may be omitted for economy of expression. *I wish* [*that*] *I might.*

Emphatic Verb-Phrase:—One which registers emphasis by means of a verb-phrase composed of *do* or *did* plus the infinitive without *to*.

Compare the (italicized) emphatic form and the simple form:

I do fly.	I fly.
I did fly.	I flew.

In questions and negative statements the emphatic forms do not imply emphasis: *Did you fly? You did not fly.*

Ethic Dative.—A pronoun employed as an indirect object to indicate the person remotely concerned. (It might be defined as a *very* indirect object.)

He plucked *me* ope his doublet.

The pronoun is inserted "to emphasize the speaker's veracity."

Exclamatory Sentence.—*See* SENTENCE.

Expletive (Latin *expletivus,* filling up).—A word which serves only to introduce an intransitive verb; acting merely as a "filler," it communicates no meaning. Thus,

It is true that I lied

has expletive *it* functioning as the grammatical subject, but the real subject is the noun clause *that I lied.* Similarly in

There is no death

expletive *there* introduces the copula and acts as grammatical subject; the real subject is *death.*

Note that in both the instances cited the expletive introduced a sentence in the inverted order. It is commonly so employed.

Etymology (Greek *etymos,* true, *logos,* word).—The branch of philology which traces the origin of words and their derivation. Older grammars, however, used the term as a synonym for **accidence** (*q.v.*).

F

Factitive (Latin *factitus,* made or done frequently).—Applied to verbs in which the action expressed produces some change in the object, as He *made* the water wine. (The object is called factitive. *See* COMPLEMENT, 4, for a fuller discussion.)

Fading.—Weakening of the expressive force of a word. Thus it becomes a counter word, having a generalized or diluted meaning. *Epicure,* for example, which now is chiefly applied to those who devote themselves "with a certain elegance and refinement" to the pleasures of the table, once referred only to the followers of Epicurus:

> So the Epicures say of the Stoics' felicity placed in virtue, that it is like the felicity of a player, who if he were left out of his auditors and their applause, he would straight be out of heart and countenance.—BACON

Other words which are obviously in process of fading are *lousy, Conservative, Liberal, Communist, stink.*

Functional Change.—*See* CONVERSION.

Future in the Past.—The term applied by some grammarians to the tense in which past action is viewed as future: *I should love, I should be loving, I should have loved, I should have been loving* are respectively the indefinite, continuous, perfect, and perfect continuous forms.

Future Tense: *See* TENSE.

G

Gender (Latin *genus,* kind or sort).—That modification of a word which distinguishes objects with regard to sex.

In Modern English (though not in Old English) gender is completely logical—except for personifications. That is to say: gender in English follows sex and is not, as in most Indo-European languages, a grammatical convention. (For example: in Latin the word for *flower* is masculine; in French, feminine; in Spanish, feminine; in Italian, masculine. The word for *tooth* is masculine in Latin, Spanish, and Italian, but feminine in French. Endowed gender—which disregards sex—is termed grammatical gender.)

Four genders are distinguished in Modern English: masculine, if a male is signified (*John, father, cock, monk, he*); feminine, if a female is signified (*Jane, mother, hen, nun, she*); neuter, if a thing is signified (*bell, book, candle, wine, it*); and common, if the sex is indeterminate (*American, parent, poet, animal, they*).

Gender of substantives is shown in several ways.

1. By employing different words for the male and female of the species.

Masculine	Feminine	Masculine	Feminine
bachelor	maid (or spinster)	gentleman	lady
boar	sow	hart	roe
boy	girl	husband	wife
brother	sister	king	queen
buck	doe	lord	lady
bull (or ox)	cow	man	woman
cock	hen	nephew	niece
colt	filly	ram	ewe
dog	bitch (or slut)	sir	madam
drake	duck	sire	dam
drone	bee	sloven	slut
earl	countess	son	daughter
father	mother	stag	hind
fox	vixen	stallion	mare
friar (or monk)	nun	uncle	aunt
gander	goose	wizard	witch

2. By adding *ess* to the full masculine form to indicate feminine gender; or by adding *ess* after omitting the vowel of the last syllable; or by adding *ess* to the stem after modifying it so that it may be more easily pronounced.

Masculine	Feminine	Masculine	Feminine
abbot	abbess	heir	heiress
actor	actress	hunter	huntress
adulterer	adulteress	host	hostess
arbiter	arbitress	instructor	instructress
benefactor	benefactress	Jew	Jewess
caterer	cateress	marquis	marchioness
chanter	chantress	Negro	Negress
conductor	conductress	master	mistress
dauphin	dauphiness	Mr.	Mrs.
deacon	deaconess	poet	poetess
duke	duchess	prophet	prophetess
elector	electress	songster	songstress
emperor	empress	sorcerer	sorceress
founder	foundress	tiger	tigress
giant	giantess	traitor	traitress
god	goddess	viscount	viscountess
governor	governess		

(NOTE: This method of indicating gender, once quite customary, is still popular but on the decline. We do not normally speak of a *poetess,* or *instructress,* or *Jewess;* however, normally we still say *goddess, abbess, actress.*)

3. By adding to the full masculine form of some incompletely assimilated foreign words feminine endings characteristic of the language of their origin; or by modifying their stems and then adding the feminine endings.

Masculine	Feminine	Masculine	Feminine
administrator	administratrix	landgrave	landgravine
beau	belle	prosecutor	prosecutrix
czar	czarina	señor	señora
don	donna	signor	signora
executor	executrix	sultan	sultana
hero	heroine	testator	testatrix

4. By prefixing or suffixing a noun or pronoun to a word to indicate gender.

Masculine	Feminine	Masculine	Feminine
boy friend	girl friend	manservant	maidservant
bridegroom	bride	milkman	milkmaid
cash boy	cash girl	peacock	peahen
cock-sparrow	hen-sparrow	salesman	saleswoman
foreman	forewoman	tomcat	(tabby-) cat
he-goat	she-goat		

5. The suffix *ster* formerly indicated feminine gender. *Spinster* meant a woman who spins; *baxter,* a woman who baked; *webster,* a woman who wove. Now the termination is not thought of as feminine (*huckster* and *tipster* are hardly considered feminine). We have, consequently, created double feminines: *e.g., songstress, spinstress.* The *ster* suffix now denotes agent (*teamster, roadster*), or, more often, implies disparagement (*rhymester, punster, trickster*). None of these early feminines now remains with its medieval signification. The Norman-French *ess* has displaced the native English *ster* termination.

Genitive (Latin *genitivus,* pertaining to birth or generation).—A case denoting possession and relation. It is frequently termed the possessive, a designation which ignores the relational function of the case.

a. The genitive is the only case which has a distinctive termination in English: it adds *apostrophe s('s)* or *s apostrophe (s')* to the common case form: *John's, friend's, friends', people's, person's, Jesus'*. Otherwise, the substantive incorporating the genitive function is not accompanied by any change in form: *of John, of a friend, of friends, of people, of a person, of Jesus*. It merely prefixes the preposition *of*. Consequently, some grammarians, who hold that *case* implies a distinctive modification of form, refuse to grant case status to any but the form ending in *apostrophe s* or *s apostrophe*. For the half-dozen pronouns which retain distinct genitive forms, *see* PRONOUN.

b. The genitive case (with *'s* or *s'*) is now restricted chiefly to nouns referring to persons; but it still survives in its older, more inclusive employment, in certain idioms (*razor's edge, wit's end, goodness' sake, duty's call, God's will*).

c. All genitive forms with the apostrophe have an adjectional—that is, a descriptive, qualifying, or restrictive function; and sometimes they are classed as possessive adjectives.

d. The genitive case principally denotes:

1. *Ownership or possession:*
   a man's money, a woman's heart, the world's soul

2. *Origin, agent, or source:*
   Stevens and Malone's Shakspere,
   Auden's metrics, Einstein's theory

3. *Extent, measure, or duration:*
   a day's journey, a hair's breadth, water's depth

4. *Kind, quality, or characteristic:*
   knave's pate, fool's way, a printer's error

e. The meanings denoted by the case have been distinguished as follows:

1. *Subjective,* in which a person, an abstraction personified, is represented as carrying out one of the genitive functions (described in *d* above): *Shakspere's* imagery is unitary. I hear the *sea's* call.

2. *Objective,* in which a person or an object is represented as receiving the action the verb generates: *Caesar's murderers* were conquered at Philippi. They fiercely attacked *Johnson's position.*

Group Genitive: The genitive with *s* and an apostrophe added to a group of words with a unitary idea. Thus, *King of England's power; mother-in-law's perversity; Arthur Wellesley, Duke of Wellington, the Field Marshal's victory; Beaumont and Fletcher's plays* (but *Beaumont's and Fletcher's* prose—since the plays were in collaboration, but the prose was not).

Gerund (Latin *gerundus,* that which is to be done or carried on).—*See* VERBALS.

Government (Old French *governer*—from Latin *gubernare,* to direct, steer, govern; Greek *kybernan,* to handle the rudder, steer).—The influence or force that one word exerts on another, requiring it to "take" or be in a particular case. Thus, prepositions govern the objective case: *to, by, for, with, against* him.

Transitive verbs and their verbals govern the objective case: I *hit, bit, fought, saved, killed* him.

Gradation.—*See* ABLAUT.

Grammatical Gender.—*See* GENDER.

H

Hiatus (Latin *hiatus,* an opening, a cleft, a gap).—The following of one vowel by another, each distinctly sounded, without any intervening consonant (and also the "opening" of the mouth necessary for pronouncing such a conjunction of vowels): *hiatus, co-ordinate, trio, zoology, egoism.*

Historical Present.—The dramatic use of the present tense to describe past events.

(Its literary—as distinguished from its popular—use is declining; it is too obvious a device to appeal to writers striving for naturalness and simplicity.)

It is also called the dramatic present and the graphic

present; Jesperson suggests that the best name would be *unhistoric present.*

> It *is* not until the close of the Old English period that Scandinavian words *appear.*—SWEET

The historical present, as used in the quotation given above, is also called the *annalistic present.*

Hobson-Jobson.—The process by which Indian words are changed to make them fit more easily into English. The term illustrates the process: it is in the British soldier's version of the Mohammedan wail, "Ya Hasan! Ya Hosain!"

Hybrid (Latin *hybrida,* a mongrel—offspring of a wild boar and a tame sow; Greek *hubris,* a wanton act, an outrage).

1. *Words:* those formed of elements derived from different languages.

automobile	— Greek and Latin
marigold	— Hebrew and English
awkward	— Norse and English
asafetida	— Persian and Latin
surname	— French and English

2. *Parts of speech:* those in which the process of conversion (*q.v.*) is incomplete. Thus the genitive form *one man's meat* not only functions principally as an adjective (modifying the noun *meat*), but also as a noun (since it is modified by the adjective *one*). Participles and adverbs are particularly apt to be hybrid parts of speech.

3. *Constructions:* those which embody an irrational or anomalous meaning or syntax. Some are idiomatic (try *and* stop me), some colloquial (different *than*), and some the verbal manifestations of confused or inadequate thinking. (He runs *as fast or faster than* his brother.)

I

Identifying Adjective.—*See* ADJECTIVE.

Identifying Pronoun.—*See* PRONOUN.

Idiom (Greek *idioma,* peculiar phraseology).—A mode of expression or a form of speech peculiar to a language or a dialect; not usually susceptible to grammatical analysis.

Illative Conjunction.—*See* CONJUNCTION.

Imperative Mood.—*See* MOOD, SENTENCE.

Impersonal It.—*See* EXPLETIVE.

Indefinite Adjective, Article, Pronoun.—*See* ADJECTIVE, ARTICLE, PRONOUN.

Independent Clause.—*See* CLAUSE.

Independent Element.—A word or a group of words which is grammatically free from the rest of the sentence. Kennedy analyzes six *independent and introductory elements* of the sentence:

1. *Vocative*—the nominative of direct address:

> Hear, O *Caesar!*

2. *Exclamation:*

> *Damn!* I cut myself.

3. *Pleonasm*—when it entails unnecessary repetition of the subject or object (redundant subject or object):

> The nobles, *they* are fled,
>   the commons cold.—SHAKSPERE

> Who gaf Judith corage or hardinesse
> To sleen *him* Olofernus in his tente.—CHAUCER

4. *Nominative Absolute.*—*See* ABSOLUTE.

5. *Introductory word or phrase: yet,* we have come through.

6. *Parenthetical Expressions:* The facts, *it seems to me,* are not borne out by the figures.

Indicative Mood.—*See* MOOD.

Indirect Discourse.—An oblique means of quoting.

> *Direct Discourse:* John said, "*I do.*"
> *Indirect Discourse:* John said *that he did.*

Indirect Object.—*See* OBJECT.

Infinitive (Latin *infinitus*, unbounded).—*See* VERBALS.

Inflection (Latin *inflexis*, bending).—The variation in the form of a word to express a variation in function or in meaning. Substantive inflection is called declension (*q.v.*); verb inflection is called conjugation (*q.v.*).

Ingressive.—*See* ASPECT.

Intensive Adjective, Adverb, Pronoun.—*See* ADJECTIVE, ADVERB, PRONOUN.

Interjection (Latin *interjectus*, thrown between).—Any word "thrown in" to express some sudden emotion or passion.

> *Bah! Quick! But—! Gosh! Wow! Halt!*

may, if they are charged with the necessary emotion, be construed as interjections.

Interrogative Adjective, Adverb, Pronoun.—*See* ADJECTIVE, ADVERB, PRONOUN.

Intransitive Verb.—*See* VERB.

Inversion (Latin *inversus*, turned bottom upwards).—Reversing the natural order of words in a sentence, which (except in interrogative sentences) has the subject preceding the predicate.

> Wherever flagged his own, or failed the opposing force, *glittered his white robe,* and rose his bloody battle axe.—BULWER

> *Never were* such thrice magnificent carnival amusements.—CARLYLE

(Note that in negative affirmations the verb has greater weight, and consequently there is a tendency to use negative predicates in the inverted position.)

Irregular Comparison.—*See* ADJECTIVE, ADVERB.

Irregular Verbs.—Those, also called strong or gradation verbs, which undergo internal change, instead of *-ed* or *-t*, in forming their past tense. How many there are is a question variously answered. A fairly comprehensive list is given below. (*See* also VERB.)

Strong or Irregular Verbs

NOTE: Forms that also have regular flectional endings are marked R. Forms that are not used widely, or are not in the best modern usage, are italicized.

Pres.	Past.	Past. P.
Abide	abode, R.	abode
Am, be	was	been
Arise	arose	arisen
Awake	awoke, R.	awaked
Bake	baked	{ baked / *baken*
Bear	{ bore / *bare*	{ born
Bear (to carry)	{ bore / *bare*	{ borne
Beat	beat	{ beaten / beat
Begin	began	begun
Bend	bent, R.	bent, R.
Bereave	bereft, R.	bereft, R.
Beseech	besought	besought
Bet	bet, R.	bet, R.
Bless	blest, R.	blest, R.
Bid	bid, bade	bidden, bid
Bide	*bode*, R.	bided
Bind	bound	bound
Bite	bit	bitten, bit
Bleed	bled	bled
Blow	blew	blown
Break	{ broke / *brake*	{ broken
Breed	bred	bred
Bring	brought	brought
Build	built, R.	built, R.
Burn	burnt, R.	burnt, R.
Burst	burst	burst
Buy	bought	bought
Can	could	———
Cast	cast	cast
Catch	caught	caught
Chide	chid	{ chidden / chid

Pres.	Past.	Past. P.
Choose	chose	chosen
Cleave (to split)	clove, R. cleft *clave*	cloven, R. cleft
Cling	clung	clung
Clothe	clad, R.	clad, R.
Come	came	come
Cost	cost	cost
Creep	crept	crept
Crow	crew, R.	crowed
Cut	cut	cut
Dare	durst, R.	dared
Deal	dealt	dealt, R.
Dig	dug, R.	dug, R.
Dive	*dove,* R.	dived
Do	did	done
Draw	drew	drawn
Dream	dreamt, R.	dreamt, R.
Dress	drest, R.	drest, R.
Drink	drank	drank drunk
Drive	drove	driven
Dwell	dwelt, R.	dwelt, R.
Eat	ate	eaten
Fall	fell	fallen
Feed	fed	fed
Feel	felt	felt
Fight	fought	fought
Find	found	found
Flee	fled	fled
Fling	flung	flung
Fly	flew	flown
Forsake	forsook	forsaken
Freeze	froze	frozen
Get	got	got, gotten
Gild	gilt, R.	gilt, R.
Gird	girt, R.	girt, R.
Give	gave	given
Go	went	gone
Grave	graved	graven, R.
Grind	ground	ground
Grow	grew	grown
Hang	hung, R.	hung

Pres.	Past.	Past. P.
Have	had	had
Hear	heard	heard
Heave	hove, R.	hove, R.
Hew	hewed	hewn, R.
Hide	hid	hidden, hid
Hit	hit	hit
Hold	held	{held *holden*
Hurt	hurt	hurt
Keep	kept	kept
Kneel	knelt, R.	knelt, R.
Knit	knit, R.	knit, R.
Know	knew	known
Lade	laded	laden, R.
Lay	laid	laid
Lead	led	led
Lean	leant, R.	leant, R.
Leap	leapt, R.	leapt, R.
Leave	left	left
Lend	lent	lent
Let	let	let
Lie (recline)	lay	lain
Light	lit, R.	lit, R.
Lose	lost	lost
Make	made	made
May	might	——
Mean	meant	meant
Melt	melted	molten, R.
Meet	met	met
Mow	mowed	mown, R.
Pay	paid	paid
Pen (to inclose)	pent, R.	pent, R.
Put	put	put
Quit	quit, R.	quit, R.
Rap	rapt, R.	rapt, R.
Read	read	read
Rend	rent	rent
Rid	rid	rid
Ride	rode	ridden
Ring	{rang rung	{rung

Pres.	Past.	Past. P.
Rise	rose	risen
Rive	rived	riven, R.
Run	ran	run
Saw	sawed	sawn, R.
Say	said	said
See	saw	seen
Seek	sought	sought
Seethe	seethed	sodden, R.
Sell	sold	sold
Send	sent	sent
Set	set	set
Shake	shook	shaken
Shall	should	——
Shape	shaped	shapen, R.
Shave	shaved	shaven, R.
Shear	sheared	shorn, R.
Shed	shed	shed
Shine	shone, R.	shone, R.
Shoe	shod	shod
Shoot	shot	shot
Show	showed	shown, R.
Shred	shred	shred
Shrink	*shrunk* / shrank	shrunk / shrunken
Shrive	*shrove,* R.	shriven, R.
Shut	shut	shut
Sing	sang / *sung*	sung
Sink	sank / *sunk*	sunk
Sit	sat	sat
Slay	slew	slain
Sleep	slept	slept
Slide	slid	slidden / slid
Sling	slung	slung
Slink	slunk	slunk
Slit	slit	slit, R.
Smite	smote	smitten / *smit*
Sow	sowed	sown, R.
Speak	spoke / *spake*	spoken

Pres.	Past.	Past. P.
Speed	sped	sped
Spend	spent	spent
Spill	spilt, R.	spilt, R.
Spin	spun / *span*	spun
Spit	spit / *spat*	spit
Split	split	split
Spread	spread	spread
Spring	sprang	sprung
Stand	stood	stood
Stave	staved / stove	staved / stove
Stay	*staid* / stayed	*staid* / stayed
Steal	stole	stolen
Stick	stuck	stuck
Sting	stung	stung
Stride	strode	stridden
Strike	struck	struck / stricken
String	strung	strung
Strive	strove	striven
Strew	strewed	strown, R.
Swear	swore / *sware*	sworn
Sweat	sweat	sweat, R.
Sweep	swept	swept
Swell	swelled	swollen, R.
Swim	swam / *swum*	swum
Swing	swung	swung
Take	took	taken
Teach	taught	taught
Tear	tore, *tare*	torn
Tell	told	told
Think	thought	thought
Thrive	thrived / *throve*	thriven, R.
Throw	threw	thrown
Thrust	thrust	thrust
Tread	trod	trodden / trod

Pres.	Past.	Past. P.
Wax	waxed	waxen, R.
Wear	wore	worn
Weave	wove	woven
Weep	wept	wept
Wet	wet, R.	wet, R.
Whet	whet, R.	whet, R.
Will	would	——
Win	won	won
Wind	wound, R.	wound
Work	wrought, R.	wrought, R.
Wring	{ wrung, *wrang*	wrung
Write	wrote	written

Iterative.—*See* ASPECT.

J

Jargon (Old French *jargon,* gibberish. *Jargon,* it has been suggested, is connected with Gaelic *iarr,* to beg + *cainnt,* speech—thus denoting the canting, droning language of beggars).—A disparaging term applied to rude, harsh, difficult, or unintelligible speech; particularly to that which derives from a mixture of two or more discordant tongues (as Chinook, Pidgin-English, Beach-la-Mar). Partridge asserts that the term ought to be reserved for "the technicalities of science, the professions, the services, trades, crafts, sports and games, art, and Art"—thus making it a synonym for *shop-talk.* A synonym for *jargon* used in the sense of "hybrid language" is lingua franca, spoken chiefly in the coast towns of the Mediterranean, and consisting of Italian mixed with French, Spanish, Greek, and Arabic.

Junction (Latin *junctus,* joined, united).—The term (originated by Jesperson and employed by many grammarians after him) applied to a phrasal combination composed of grammatical elements on different levels. Thus, in the junction *a furiously barking dog, dog* is primary, *barking* secondary, *furiously* tertiary.

Opposed to *nexus* (*q.v.*).

L

Learned Word.—One employed in the speech or writing of the learned; opposed to **popular word,** one which has a mass currency.

The opposition (Greenough and Kittredge, who analyzed it, point out) is not an absolute one. "Learned words and popular words" are elements of a reversible reaction. Thus *atom, nucleus, fission*—once "learned"—are now "popular"; and *whilom, bate, weal*—once "popular"—are now "learned."

Lingua Franca (Italian *lingua franca,* Frankish tongue). —*See* JARGON.

Linguistics (Latin *lingua,* tongue, language).—The study of the origin and evolution of language, including its structure, sounds, forms, and meanings.

Some prefer to define it as "the study of language," and contrast it with philology (*q.v.*), "the science of a particular language." Others use it as a synonym for philology.

Linking Verb.—*See* COPULA.

Loan-Word.—One which has been "borrowed" by English from another language.

(More than 75 percent of the words in English are technically loan-words.)

Locution (Latin *locutio*—from *loquor,* to speak).— Speech or mode of speech. It is normally applied to any group of words functioning as a unit, as a phrase, or as a clause.

M

Metathesis (Greek *metathesis,* change—from *meta,* beyond, over, and *thesis,* a placing).—The transposition of successive letters or syllables in a word. It constitutes a frequent cause of linguistic change.

thrill	—	from *thirle*
third	—	from *thridde*
clasp	—	from *clapse*

Model Adverb.—One which asserts: *assuredly, certainly, yes, no.*

Modifiers (Old French, *modifier*—from Latin *modificare,* to measure or restrict).—Words, or groups of words, which qualify, describe, or restrict. Adjectives and adverbs (*qq.v.*) and phrases, clauses, and verbals (*qq.v.*) that function adjectivally or adverbially are classed as modifiers.

Mood (French *mode,* fashion, way—from Latin *modus,* a measure, manner).—That grammatical form pertaining to verbs which denotes "the style or manner of predication" (Curme).

Three moods are ordinarily distinguished:

1. *Imperative:* the mood of command or entreaty (called also the will-mood). The imperative mood has both an active and a passive voice (*q.v.*)—though only one form to indicate each. It has, however, only one tense (*q.v.*) and only one person (*q.v.*)—present tense and second person. Singular and Plural:

<blockquote>
Active: Warn him.
Passive: Be warned.
</blockquote>

2. *Indicative:* the mood of assertion or fact (called also the fact-mood). The indicative is the dominant mood in current English, and there is almost nothing that can be said subjunctively that cannot also be said indicatively. Statements both positive (*the sun rises*) and negative (*the sun does not rise*), questions (*does the sun rise?*), and predictions (*the sun will rise*)—in fact, *any* predication that is not supposititious takes the indicative mood.

3. *Subjunctive:* the mood of supposition, doubt, condition, contingency, and the like (called also the thought-mood). Once the specific form for a large number of constructions, its place has been pre-empted by the indicative. In only one construction—the *condition contrary to fact*—is the subjunctive a "live" mood. Other employments still met with, particularly in nineteenth-century literature and before, are listed below.

a. *Wishes or Exhortations:*

> Blessed *be* God that
> I have wedded five.—CHAUCER

b. *Doubt or Supposition:*

> It is one of the best bonds, both of chastity and obedience
> in the wife, if she *think* her husband wise, which she will
> never do if she *find* him jealous.—BACON

c. *Purpose or Expectation:*

> And lest she disobey, he left her.—AMY LOWELL

d. *Concession or Condition:*

> And *will* you, nill you,
> I will marry you.—SHAKSPERE

e. *Contrary to Fact Condition:*

> If "if's and an's" *were* pots and pans,
> There'd be no need of tinkers.

For all of these subjunctives, the indicative may be substituted. Occasionally, subjunctive and indicative appear in the same sentence, in parallel constructions:

> Whether it be owing to such poetical associations . . . or
> whether there is, as it were, a sympathetic revival.—IRVING

The switch is the more easily made since the forms for the subjunctive and indicative vary only slightly, and any subjunctive form has an indicative or imperative analogue. (*See:* TENSE, where variant forms of the subjunctive are italicized.)

(It should be noted that Jesperson holds that *subjunctive* ought to designate categories of form, not of meaning; or, more generally, the term *mood* must involve a difference of inflection.)

Mood is also spelled *mode,* and pronounced accordingly.

Morphology (Greek *morphe,* form + *logy,* study).—The study of the origin and evolution of inflectional forms and their functions.

Multiplicatives.—*See* ADJECTIVE.

Mutation.—*See* UMLAUT.

N

Neologism (Greek *neos,* new + *logos,* speech).—A new word or expression or an old one used with a new signification.

Among the new words listed in the fifth edition of Webster's *Collegiate Dictionary* are *Benzedrine, commentator, fifth column, heavy water, M Day, social credit.* Perhaps the next edition will include *dolorism, existentialism, flak, genocide, yard-bird, buzz bomb.*

Nexus (Latin *nexus,* connection).—The term (originated by Jesperson and employed by many grammarians after him) applied to the combination of subject or object and verb, as in *The dog barks furiously,* or *I see the dog.*

Opposed to junction (*q.v.*).

Nominative (French *nominatif*—from Latin *nominativus,* of a name).—The case which denotes that the substantive is the subject of a finite verb, or is equated with the subject.

In Modern English, there are no distinctions of form to indicate the nominative, except in the case of a few pronouns. There are four functions of the case usually distinguished:

1. *Subject of a Verb:*

    "When I use a word," *Humpty-Dumpty* said, "*it* means just what *I* choose it to mean—neither more nor less."— LEWIS CARROLL

2. *Predicate Nominative:*

    "The rule is, *jam to-morrow and jam yesterday—but never jam to-day.*"—CARROLL

3. *Vocative, or Nominative of Direct Address:*

    "You are old, *Father William,*" the young man said.— CARROLL

4. *Appositive with a Nominative:*

    The Good, the True, the Beautiful,—
    These are the things that pay!—CARROLL

See also ABSOLUTE, APPOSITION, COMPLEMENT, VOCATIVE.

Nonce (a corruption of the Old English phrase *to than anes,* for that only) **Word.**—One coined for a specific occasion, and used for that occasion only: *oiligarchy, wormify, splendiferous, whichcraft, yellocution, Peglerize.*

Notional (Latin *notus,* known).—

1. *Words:* Those that—unlike relational words—have meaning in themselves. Nouns, pronouns, all verbs but the auxiliary verbs, and most adjectives are *notional.* (The auxiliary verb becomes notional if no verbal form is dependent on it: thus *is* in *He is brave* may be termed *notional* whereas *is* in *He is braving the storm* may not be.)

2. *Categories:* Those "extra-lingual categories which are independent of the more or less accidental facts of existing language . . . Some of them relate to such facts of the world without as sex, others to mental states or to logic . . ." (Jesperson). The term, coined by Jesperson, is coming into general grammatical use, as opposed to *syntactic.*

Further it is very important to remember that we speak of "mood" only if the attitude of mind is shown in the form of the verb: mood is thus a syntactic, not a notional category.—JESPERSON

Noun (Latin *nomen,* name).—The name of a person, place or thing.

Nouns are classified as:

1. *Common,* if applicable to any of a class: *clerk, town, dictionary.*

2. *Proper,* if applicable to one particular person, place, or thing: *Byron, India, "The Raven."*

Another classification is *abstract* and *concrete* (*qq.v.*).

Noun inflection is termed *declension* (*q.v.*), and refers to the changes of form nouns undergo to indicate their properties of *gender, number,* and *case* (*qq.v.*).

Noun Clause.—*See* CLAUSE.

Noun Phrase.—*See* PHRASE.

Number (Old French *nombre*—from Latin *numerus,* number).—The distinction in the form of a word that shows whether it refers to one, in which instance it is termed *singular;* or to more than one, in which instance it is termed *plural.*

Number is a property of nouns, pronouns and verbs.

1. *Nouns:*

    a. Most form their plurals by adding *s* or *es* to the singular—*grammar, grammars; school, schools; folio, folios; class, classes; church, churches; fox, foxes.*

    b. Those ending in *y* preceded by a consonant change the *y* to *i* and add *es* to form their plurals—*city, cities; army, armies; dictionary, dictionaries.* (But: *valley, valleys; alloy, alloys.*)

    c. Those ending in *f* or *fe* change *f* to *v*, and add *es* or *s* to form their plurals—*half, halves; life, lives; wife, wives.*

    d. Four nouns in current usage add the old inflectional *n* to form their plurals—*ox, oxen; brother, brethren* (also *brothers*)*; child, children; cow, kine* (also *cows*).

    e. A few nouns change their root vowels to form their plurals. These are called mutation plurals—*man, men; foot, feet; louse, lice.*

    f. Some nouns have the same form for their singular and plural numbers. These are called uninflected plurals—*deer, sheep, hundredweight, fish, Japanese.*

    g. Some nouns have two forms for the plural, each with a slightly different meaning. These are called double plurals—*brothers, brethren; dies, dice; fish, fishes.*

    h. Some nouns have no plural number because their meaning does not admit of a plural idea—*fortitude, music, wheat.*

    i. Some nouns have no singular number because their meaning does not admit of a singular idea—*tongs, wages, billiards.*

2. *Pronouns:*

  a. The plural of *I* is (allegedly) *we* (—but obviously *I* has no plural, except if *I* should have a split personality).

  b. *You* is the pronominal form for the second person, whether singular or plural. (The old forms—*thou* and *thee* for the singular—are now found only in poetry, the "solemn style," and in the conversation of Quakers.)

  c. *They* is the plural for the third person: in the singular there are different forms indicative of gender—*he, she, it.*

3. *Verbs:*

  Number in the verb is now manifest only in the ending of the third person singular. Otherwise, number is shown by the subject of the verb. I run, you run, he *runs;* we run, you run, they run.

O

Object (Latin *objectus,* cast or thrown in the way, opposed).—The substantive toward which the action of a transitive verb is directed; also, the substantive that follows a preposition.

Five different kinds of objects used with verbs are distinguished.

  1. *Direct,* with transitive verbs:

  Love that *soap!*

  2. *Indirect,* with verbs of *allowing, bringing, denying, forbidding, giving, lending, paying, refusing, sending, teaching, telling, throwing,* and the like:

  His father gave *him* an allowance of nothing a year.

  3. *Retained,* with passive verbs:

  He was given an *allowance* of nothing a year by his father.

4. *Cognate,* with intransitive verbs:

He laughed his bitter *laugh.*

5. *Reflexive,* with intransitive verbs:

I'll sit *myself* down and write *myself* a letter.

See also COMPLEMENT, *3* and *4;* DATIVE.

Obsolescent (Latin *obsolescens,* going out of use).— Words that are going out of use, though not quite obsolete (*q.v.*): *e.g., blunderbuss, swain, wight.*

Obsolete (Latin *obsoletus,* gone out of use) **Words.**— Those once, but no longer, used; or used in a completely different sense than formerly: *kitchenry, sithen, Donet.*

Optative (French *optatif*—from Latin *optativus,* expressing a wish—from *optatus,* wished or desired).—The subjunctive denotative of desiring or wishing.

> God save you.
> Long live the king.

Order (French *ordre*—from Latin *ordinem,* an arranging).—Since, in English, the forms of words are a minor indication of their relations, the order or arrangement is of primary importance in determining meaning.

The usual order in declarative sentences is subject—predicate. This order is reversed in interrogative sentences, and in declarative sentences for the sake of euphony or emphasis. (Compare

> Diana of the Ephesians is great

with

> Great is Diana of the Ephesians.)

Of the many rules relative to order, only one has relative (though not absolute) validity: namely, "Things to be thought of together should be placed in close connection" (Bain). Thus "howlers," such as the following, may be avoided:

The deceased came to his death by excessive drinking causing apoplexy in the minds of the jury.

"Orismological Sesquipedalianism."—The exuberant employment of long technical terms.

P

Parse (Latin *pars,* a part—as *pars orationis,* a part of speech).—To resolve a sentence into its elements, naming the parts of speech and their relations.

Maxwell gives the following scheme for parsing. (Other possibilities, now in general disrepute, are the tabular and diagrammatic forms of analysis):

Where thou dwellest, I will dwell.

(A)

Complex Declarative Sentence	Subject	*I*
	Predicate Verb	*will dwell*
	Modifier	*where thou dwellest*
		(Adverbial clause of place)

(B)

Adverbial Clause	Connective	*where* (Conjunctive adverb)
	Subject (Pronoun)	*thou*
	Predicate Verb	*dwellest*

Participles.—*See* VERBALS.

Particle (Latin *particula,* a small part—the diminutive of *pars,* a part).—A class of uninflected relational words.

The relations they include give rise to the following classification of particles:

1. Directives: *to, with, for, on, by*
2. Link Words: *and, but when, because, or*
3. Uninflected Adverbs: *again, perhaps, soon, here, forward*

They are "essential words for clear statement, and are not the sort of words of which we can guess the meaning" out of context (Bodmer).

Passive (French *passif*—from Latin *passivus*—from *passus,* suffered).—

1. *Noun.* One which denotes the recipient rather than the agent of an action: *employee, trustee, draftee; porker, bunker, waiver.*
2. *Voice. See* VOICE.

Patois (French, but otherwise of unknown origin).—A synonym for dialect (*q.v.*), which Fowler suggests "should not be used except about France."

Perfect.—*See* TENSE, VERBAL.

Person (Old French *personne*—from Latin *persona,* a mask, character, person).—One of the three references of the verb as indicated by its nominative, denoting the speaker (first person), the one who or that which is spoken to (second person), and the one who or that which is spoken of (third person).

Only in the third person singular of the present tense is there a distinctive personal form. (*See* TENSE.)

Personification.—The act of investing things or abstractions with human qualities or characteristics; that is, endowing them with personality.

> Spring through death's iron guard
> Her million blades shall thrust;
> Love that was sleeping, not extinct,
> Throw off the nightmare crust.
> —CECIL DAY LEWIS

Philology (Greek *philos,* loving + *logos,* word).—The "study whose task is the interpretation of the literary monuments in which the spiritual life of a given period has found expression" (Pederson). It is more generally used as a synonym for linguistics (*q.v.*).

Phrase (Latin and Greek *phrasis,* speech, language—from Greek *phrazo,* I say).—A group of related words having no subject or predicate and employed as a single part of speech.

Phrase is used in two ways: either (1) as a group of words functioning in more or less unitary fashion, or (2) as a group of words constructed with prepositions, participles, infinitives, or gerunds.

1. *Phrases considered functionally:*

    a. *Adverbial:*

    The boy stood *on the burning deck.*

b. *Adjective:*

"The Princess *with the Golden Hair.*"

c. *Noun:*

Till, at last, it is Mississippi, *The Father of Waters* . . .

d. *Verb:*

It *might have been.*

e. *Preposition:*

For want of a nail the shoe was lost; *for want of* a shoe, the horse was lost; and *for want* of a horse the rider was lost.

f. *Conjunction:*

The man was a mental and moral monster—*as well as* a quite disagreeable person.

g. *Interjection:*

Well for crying out loud!

2. **Phrases considered genetically:**

a. *Prepositional:* One consisting of a preposition and its object (employed, for most part, as adverbs or adjective phrases) :

Licker talks mighty loud w'en it gits loose *from de jug.*— JOEL CHANDLER HARRIS

b. *Participial:* One consisting of a participle and its accompanying words (employed usually as an adjective) :

Rocked in the cradle of the deep,
I lay me down in peace to sleep.
—EMMA WILLARD

c. *Infinitive:* One formed by an infinitive and its accompanying words:

To split an infinitive frequently means *to clarify its purpose.*

d. *Gerund:* One formed by a gerund and its accompanying words (considered by some grammarians together with the infinitive with which it often equates) :

Splitting an infinitive frequently means *clarifying its purpose.*

Plural.—*See* NUMBER.

Popular Etymology: The derivation of a word, or an alteration in its spelling or pronunciation, as the result of mistaken identification with another, more familiar word. Also called *folk etymology.*

Thus: *acorn* derives from Old English *aecern,* which in turn derives from *aecre,* field. It is, etymologically, separate from both *oak* and *corn.* Yet the phonetic similarity has resulted in the notion that *aecern* meant an *oak-corn,* and people have changed the original suffix *ern* to *orn* to make the word conform to their mistaken etymology. Similarly, *Welsh rabbit* has been changed to *Welsh rarebit* (though the dictionary still marks this transformation *erroneous*). It should be remarked that popular etymology is a process not always restricted to the people. Scholars are also fallible. So Minsheu's derivation of *dismal* from *dies malus,* the unlucky or ill-omened day, is "exactly one of those plausible etymologies which one learns after a while to reject with contempt" (Trench).

Portmanteau Word.—The result of blending or fusing two words.

Lewis Carroll, who coined the term, said that portmanteau words were those "in which two meanings are packed as in a portmanteau." Walter Winchell is the chief creator of portmanteaus today—*Renovating, Chicagorilla, Bundit,* are a few of his amalgamations that have enjoyed more than temporary acclaim.

Possessive: *See* GENITIVE.

Potential (Latin *potens, entis,* having power).—Applied (by the older grammarians) to the mood which expresses possibility, liberty, power, will, or obligation by the use of the auxiliary verbs *may, can, must, might, could, would,* or *should.*

Most grammarians reject the designation of mood for the potential, since there are no potential constructions which cannot with logic be parsed as either indicative or subjunctive. If separate attention is given them, it is as *potential phrases,* or "phrases of possibility."

Predicate (Latin *predicatus,* declared).—That which is said of the subject of a sentence.

The predicates are italicized in the following compound sentence.

I *have alreddy given Two cousins to the war,* & I *stand reddy to sacrifice my wife's brother ruther 'n not see the rebelyin krusht.*
—ARTEMUS WARD

(For *predicate nominative* and *predicate adjective, see* COMPLEMENT.)

Prefix.—*See* AFFIX.

Preposition (Latin *praepositionem,* that which is put or placed before).—A part of speech that expresses the various relations of substantives to other words or groups of words in the sentence.

The relations may be of place (*at home*), cause (struck *by* lightning), instrumentality (*In* this sign we conquer), manner (*with* kind words and loving hearts), purpose (*for* God and Country), and a variety of others which defy classification.

Preterit(e) (Old French *preterit*—from Latin *praeteritus,* gone by or past).—An alternate name for the past tense. (*See* TENSE.)

Principal Parts.—*See* IRREGULAR VERB.

Progressive Verb.—*See* VERB.

Pronoun (French *pronom*—from Latin *pronomen,* in place of a noun). A word which refers to, or stands instead of, a noun.

It denotes without naming. "There is no possible noun for which some of them may not be used. Hence a pronoun has been termed *a name for everything*" (Ramsey).

Pronouns are inflected for case, gender, number, and person (*qq.v.*). However, there are only a few modifications of form (see below)—though more than those the noun undergoes.

The following classification, based on function, is that of The Joint Committee on Grammatical Nomenclature.

1. *Personal Pronoun:*

One which distinguishes person in each of its three relations. (*See* PERSON.) The declension that follows lists archaic forms in parentheses.

1st Person   *Masculine and Feminine*

Singular   *Plural*

	Singular		Plural
Nominative	I		we
Possessive	my *or* mine		our *or* ours
Objective	me		us

2nd Person   *Masculine and Feminine*

Nominative	you (thou)	you (ꝫe)
Possessive	your *or* yours (thy or thine)	your *or* yours
Objective	you (thee)	you (ꝫe)

3rd Person

	Masculine	Feminine	Neuter	All genders
Nominative	he	she	it	they
Possessive	his	her *or* hers	its	their *or* theirs
Objective	him	her	it	them

2. *Demonstrative Pronoun:*

One which *points out* or *points to* its antecedent definitely.

Singular	Plural
this	these
that	those

3. *Indefinite Pronoun:*

One which *points out* or *points to* its antecedent less definitely (than the demonstratives).

Examples: *one, none, some, any, aught, naught, each, every, either, neither, other, else, sundry, several, certain, all,* and their various compounds.

4. *Relative (or Conjunctive) Pronoun:*

One which connects a dependent to a main clause, and at the same time relates to an antecedent in the main clause.

Blessed is the man *that* walketh not in the counsel of the ungodly. —BIBLE

Who (for persons), *which* (for animals or things), *that* (for both), *as,* and *what* are the simple relatives. *Who* and *which* are declinable:

	Singular and Plural	*Singular and Plural*
Nominative	who	which
Possessive	whose	whose
Objective	whom	which

5. *Interrogative Pronoun:*

One that asks a question. It has been described as "a relative in search of an antecedent" (Nesfield), and its five forms do not differ from the relative: *Who? whom? what? whose? which?*

6. *Possessive Pronoun:*

One which signifies possession or an analogous relationship. (They are called absolute forms.)

Mine, ours, thine, yours, hers, theirs; whose, either's, neither's, other's, one's.

The pain is *mine* the pleasure *yours*.

7. *Reflexive Pronoun:*

One which signifies that the agent is also the recipient of an action.

He loves *himself*—with no discernible reason.

Self is the sign of the reflexive; *myself, yourself, himself, herself, itself; ourselves, yourselves, themselves.*

8. *Intensive (or Emphatic) Pronoun:*

One which enforces an expressed substantive:

I, *myself,* am the man.

Its forms are the same as those of the reflexive.

9. *Reciprocal Pronoun:*

One which denotes a mutual relation.

> Let us, then, be true to *one another*.

One another and *each other,* considered to be compound pronouns, are the reciprocals.

10. *Identifying Pronoun:*

One which signifies a unity.

> The *same* to you!

Same is the only identifying pronoun.

Purist.—Most generally the term applies to "any person who harasses himself or others by an unnecessary concern over the forms of speech" (Krapp).

More particularly it applies to one who believes that only words of native stock ought to be accredited. Since, according to Skeat, only 22.6 percent of the words in Modern English are of Anglo-Saxon origin (some linguists say less), the purist attitude evades linguistic reality. Yet from the time Edmund Spenser called "Dan" Chaucer "a well of English undefyled" to the present, a host of otherwise amiable people have embraced this mirage.

Q

Quality and Quantity.—*See* ADJECTIVE, ADVERB.

R

Reference (Latin *referens,* bearing or giving back).—As applied to the pronoun, the term denotes the clear and definite indication of its antecedent, as well as agreement of the pronoun with its antecedent in gender and number. (*See* AGREEMENT.)

Reflexive.—*See* PRONOUN.

Related or Syntactical Compound.—Same as compound word (*q.v.*).

Relative.—*See* PRONOUN, ADVERB.

Restrictive Clause.—*See* CLAUSE.

Retained Object.—*See* COMPLEMENT, OBJECT.

Root (Old English rōt, root).—The primitive element of a word, without affix of any kind, in which resides the core of its meaning, and from which other words are derived.

Thus, from the Teutonic root *būg* (Modern English *bow*), is derived *buxom*—literally, *bow-some,* pliant; *bow,* a weapon; *bight,* a coil. All these are from the Indo-European root *bleugh,* which appears in Latin as *fug*-ere, to flee; in Greek as *pheug*-ein, to flee; in Sanskrit as *bhuj,* to bend (Ncsficld).

(*See* STEM.)

S

Sentence (Old French *sentence*—from Latin *sententia,* an opinion or decision—from *sentio,* I perceive or feel).— A group of related words, containing a subject and predicate, which expresses a thought completely.

There are two ways of classifying sentences, according to form and according to meaning.

1. *Form:*

   a. *Simple Sentence:* Contains one subject and one predicate (though either subject or predicate, or both, may be compound).

      Naturally the *id* knows no values, no good and evil, no morality.—FREUD

   b. *Compound Sentence:* Contains two or more co-ordinate clauses joined by a conjunction.

      The *ego* has taken over the task of representing the external world for the *id,* and so of saving it; for the *id,* blindly striving to gratify its instincts in complete disregard of the superior strength of outside forces, could not otherwise escape annihilation.—FREUD

   c. *Complex Sentence:* Contains a subordinate clause employed as a modifier.

      It is the relation to the external world which is decisive for the ego.—FREUD

d. *Compound-Complex Sentence:* Contains two or more co-ordinate clauses, one or more of them complex.

We cannot do justice to the characteristics of the mind by means of linear contours, such as occur in a drawing or in a primitive painting, but we need rather the areas of color shading off into one another that are to be found in modern pictures.—FREUD

2. **Meaning:**

a. *Declarative Sentence:* One that makes an assertion.

You thank him.

b. *Interrogative:* One that asks a question.

Do you thank him?

c. *Imperative:* One which issues a command (or entreaty).

Thank him.

d. *Exclamatory:* One which expresses surprise (grief, joy, or some other sudden emotion).

Thank him! Rather damn him!

Sequence of Tenses.—The "principle in accordance with which the tense in a subordinate clause 'follows' or is adjusted to that of the principal clause" (Onions).

There are, says Nesfield, "two main rules about the Sequence of Tenses, and all special rules centre round these two."

1. If there is a *past tense* in the principal clause, it must be followed by a *past tense* in the subordinate clause (except that a present indefinite may also follow).

I knew
or
I had known
{that they would attack.
that they had surrounded us.
that they feared us.

(But:

I *knew* that God *is* on the side of the strongest battalions.)

2. If there is a *present* or *future* tense in the main clause, it may be followed by any tense in the subordinate clause.

I know
or
I shall know
{that they will attack.
that they surround us.
that they feared (or had feared) us.

The fixed sequence may be disregarded when it is desired to indicate habitual action (see parenthetical remark in [1] above), or when—in indirect discourse—"a more accurate expression suggests itself" (Curme). Thus, *He said that he'll be there* is considered an allowable usage.

Singular.—*See* NUMBER.

Solecism (Greek *Soloikos;* among the colonists of *Soloi* in *Cilicia,* that Attic dialect was barbarously corrupted).—A violation of idiom or syntax.

Stem (Old English *stemma,* stem or trunk of a tree).— The part of a word to which the inflectional endings are suffixed.

The stem of a word is sometimes its root, but more frequently it is the root *plus* a formative suffix (*see* SUFFIX). Thus the root of *loved* is *lov* (Old English *luf*), but the stem is *love* (Old English *lufo*).

Some writers prefer to restrict the term *root* to the primitive Indo-European words, and call the words which serve as the "base of inflection" *stems.*

(*See* ROOT.)

Suffix (Latin *suffixus,* fastened or fixed on).—The particle placed after a stem.

They are of two kinds.

1. *Formative:* One which forms the stem.

2. *Derivative:* One which, added to the stem, alters the function of the word.

Thus, in *loved,* the root is *lov,* the formative suffix -*e,* and the derivative suffix -*d.* From -*d,* the function—to indicate past time—derives. (It is sometimes declared that the prefix alters *meaning,* while the suffix alters *function.*)

Supine (Latin *supinus,* bent or thrown backwards).— *See* VERBALS 1.

Syllable (Greek *sullabe* [letters] taken together—from *sun,* together; *lambano,* I take).—A sound uttered with one effort of articulation.

The sound may be a word—a monosyllable: *Hand, good, bad, on, a.*

The sound and one other may unite to form a word—a dissyllable: *shameful, humor, return, above, beyond.*

The sound plus two or more others may constitute a word —a polysyllable: *syllable, separate, pragmatical, humorously, thremmatology.*

Syllepsis (Greek *syllepsis,* a taking together).—The figure of speech—or the error in grammar—which consists in having one word serve two purposes.

Syllepsis may be purposeful, as in

He took offense, a poke at his wife, his hat, his leave, and a vacation of several years before returning.

Or it may be erroneous, as in

> Here my sweet sons and daughters,
> all my bliss,
> Yonder my own dear husband
> buried is.

where "you see one singular verb supplying the singular and plural" (Puttenham).

(*See* ZEUGMA.)

Syncope (Greek *synkope,* a cutting up).—The loss of an unaccented medial vowel or syllable.

> butter for botiller
> proxy for procuracy
> sexton for sacristan

Synesis (Greek *sunesis,* coming together, union).—A construction in which there is a departure from syntax to follow meaning.

The departure may be purposeful as in

Then Philip went down to Samaria, and preached Christ unto them.

The antecedent of *them* is technically *Samaria;* but it was to the Samaritans that Philip preached.

The usage was normal in Vulgate English. Today the magnetic force of meaning that results, for example, in *these kind of things* or *those sort of things* is generally condemned.

Synonym (Greek *syn,* with + *onoma,* name).—A word having the same meaning as another word in the same language and capable of serving in the same context; as *same, identical.*

All synonyms, however, are imperfect. Thus, *same* and *identical* are as close to being synonymous as any two words in the language. Yet Joan would hardly have sung to Darby: "Always the *identical,* Darby, my own, Always the *identical* to your old wife Joan."

Syntax (Greek *syn,* with + *taxis,* arrangement).—That part of grammar which deals with the order, arrangement, and relations of the words in a sentence or other construction.

Synthesis (Greek *syn,* with + *thesis,* placing).—Constructing a whole from its components. It is "in all possible applications" the converse of analysis (*q.v.*).

T

Tense (Old French *tens,* time—from Latin *tempus,* time). —The form or modification of the verb by which time is expressed (Stormonth).

This definition would account for only three tenses—present, past, and future. However, there are other tenses customarily recognized. A modification of the definition given above seems essential: Tense is the form which a verb assumes, either by inflection or by the addition of auxiliary verbs, to locate the time at which an action took place, or to describe the degree of completeness of that action.

1. Tenses are called primary or simple if they refer to completed action; secondary, if they refer to continuing action.

2. Tenses are called indefinite if the action is not specified as complete.

3. Tenses are called imperfect (or continuous or progressive or definite) if the action is specified as incomplete.

4. Tenses are called perfect if the action is specified as complete.

Several kinds of combinations are possible: for example, *I have been loving*—which is the present form of the "Perfect Progressive Time"; or *I should love*—which is the indefinite form of the "Future in the Past" tense. But it is more profitable to consider such combinations (which can be made in profusion) as verb phrases. Thus, nine tenses may be distinguished. They are presented in tabular form for the sake of clarity:

Form	*Present*	*Past*	*Future*
Indefinite	I love	I loved	I shall love
Imperfect (or Progressive or Definite or Continuous)	I am loving	I was loving	I shall be loving
Perfect	I have loved	I had loved	I shall have loved

NOTE: 1. The past tense is also called the *preterit*.
2. The past perfect tense is also called the *pluperfect*.

V

Verb (Latin *verbum,* word).—A part of speech that denotes action, process, or state of being.

(Whitney says that all verbs originally suggested some form of mental or physical activity, but that after thousands of years of change some have lost their original force.)

Verbs are classified according to the following scheme:

Transitive and *Intransitive:*

If the action of the verb is received by an object, the verb is called transitive; if not, intransitive. (Incomplete intransitives or copulatives are verbs which equate subject and complement.)

<blockquote>
Transitive: I *love* life.
Intransitive: I *love*.
(Copulative: Life *is* love.)
</blockquote>

Verb conjugation (*q.v.*) includes inflection for voice, mood, tense, number, and person (*qq.v.*). (*See* also IRREGULAR VERB, COPULA, TRANSITIVE, NOTIONAL, AUXILIARY.)

Verbals.—Those forms of the verb that may be employed as nouns or as adjectives, while still retaining some of their verb functions.

There are three verbals.

1. *Infinitive* (Latin *in* + *finis,* without limit) : A verbal noun, adjective, or adverb.

a. The infinitive serves all the functions of a noun, but, additionally, it has three verbal features: it may take an object; it is qualified by an adverb; and it has two tense forms —the present and the perfect.

> She preferred *to store* her money in the stomachs of the needy than foolishly *hide* it in a purse.—ST. JEROME

b. *To* does not constitute the infinitive, though in Modern English it usually precedes it. (Sometimes the infinitive with *to* is called *supine.*) The infinitive coming after *may, can, shall, will, must, let, dare, do, bid, make, see, hear, feel, need,* and some others, usually omits the *to.*

> What man has done, I dare *do.*

c. The infinitive differs from a finite verb in three respects: it is not inflected for person or voice, and its subject is in the objective case (even if the verb is copulative). When the infinitive, preceded by a substantive in the objective case, is employed as the object of a verb, the infinitive group is sometimes termed an infinitive clause.

> I believe *him to be the fatal first cause.*

2. *Participle:* (Latin *participare,* to share) : A verbal adjective.

a. Like an adjective, the participle modifies a substantive, to which it is said to *belong;* and like a verb, it is modified by adverbs and (when derived from a transitive verb) governs the objective case.

b. There are three tenses of the participle: present or imperfect (*acting, asserting, being*), past (*acted, asserted, been*), and perfect (*having acted, having asserted, having been*).

c. A participial group, consisting of the participle, its modifiers, and its object (if it has one) is sometimes termed a participial phrase.

> Eurybiades *lifting up his staff as if he were going to strike,* Themistocles said, "Strike, if you will, but hear."

NOTE: the participle must "belong" to some substantive. If the relation is unclear or illogical, the dangling participle—the error that most "boners" exploit—will result:

> Approaching closer, the fact that it was a mirage became plain.

3. **Gerund** (Latin *gerere,* to carry) : A verbal noun (sometimes called a participial noun).

a. The form is identical with that of the present participle (*acting, asserting, being*), but whereas the participle functions as an adjective the gerund functions as a noun. The double nature of the verbals is perhaps most clearly illustrated by the gerund: like the other verbals it may take an object (if derived from a transitive verb and not preceded by an adjective); unlike the other verbals, it may be modified by either adjective or adverb.

> *Loud* talking is forbidden.
> Talking *loudly* is forbidden.

b. Gerunds resemble participles in form but resemble infinitives in function (and some of the older grammarians termed nouns ending in *ing* infinitives).

> To die is easy.
> Dying is easy.

c. Gerund or verbal noun phrases are those which contain a gerund and its related words.

> *Not being married* is one of man's most unfortunate conditions; another is *having a wife.*

Note that *having* and *being* denote time by the addition of a past participle.

d. The subject of a gerund is usually in the genitive case.

> I approve of his marrying.

However: if emphasis is desired, or if the number of the subject would otherwise be unclear, the subject of the gerund may be in the objective case.

> I approve of him marrying.
> I approve of my son marrying.

Voice (French *voix;* Old French *vois,* voice—from Latin *vox,* voice).—The property of a verb that indicates whether the subject is the agent or receiver of the action.

If the subject of the verb is the agent, as in *Louis beat Conn,* the voice is active. If the subject of the verb is the receiver of the action, as in *Conn was beaten by Louis,* the voice is passive. (*See* COMPLEMENT.)

Z

Zeugma (Greek *zeugma,* band; yoke).—A form of syllepsis (*q.v.*) in which a verb or an adjective relating to one noun is referred to another.

> He *runs* for pleasure, I for fear.

BOOK THREE

Spelling

The Spelling Situation

Thorstein Veblen, a trenchant critic of American life and letters, remarks, with characteristic perceptiveness, on our system of spelling:

As felicitous an instance of futile classicism as can well be found is the conventional spelling of the English language. English orthography[1] satisfies all the requirements of the canons of reputability under the law of conspicuous waste. It is archaic, cumbrous, and ineffective; its acquisition consumes much time and effort; failure to acquire it is easy of detection.

What would you say this "alphabetical monstrosity" spelled—*ghoughphtheightteeau?* Why, *potato* of course! By analogy: *gh* stands for *p*, as in *hiccough*; *ough* for *o*, as in *dough*; *phth* for *t*, as in *phthisis*; *eigh* for *a*, as in *neighbor*; *tte* for *t*, as in *gazette*; and *eau* for *o* as *beau*.

The little syllable *ough*, in particular, is the cause of great despair among inadequate spellers. Walsh quotes the following couplet as a partial illustration of its vagaries:

Though the tough cough and hiccough plough me through,
    O'er life's dark lough my way I still pursue.

Nor is *ough* the only sinner. Ellis points out that *e* in *mete* has forty equivalents; *a* in *mate*, thirty-four; and *e* in *net*

---

[1] Orthography (Greek *orthos,* straight; *grapho,* I write) deals with the spelling of words.

thirty-six. The word *scissors* could, by (over)working analogy, be spelled 58, 365, 440 different ways.

Among other limericks poking fun at the eccentricities of our outmoded spellings, this one is especially instructive:

> An old lady living in Worcester
> Had a gift of a handsome young rorcester.
> But the way that it crough,
> As 'twould never get through,
> Was more than the lady was uorcester.

Compare the foregoing with the following rimes:

> An old couple living in Gloucester
> Had a beautiful girl, but they loucester.
> She fell from a yacht,
> And never the spacht
> Could be found where the cold waves had toucester.

The Cause of the Condition

If we had only one letter for each sound, then spelling would be a very simple matter. In Italy and Spain there has never been any point in teaching spelling: instruction in the alphabet is enough because of the invariable sound and letter correspondence. But in America we are never quite sure that a *k* sound will be written *k*. It might be written *cc* (account), *cch* (Bacchus), *cq* (acquaint), *cu* (biscuit), *lk* (talk), *lke* (Folkestone), *q* (queen), *qu* (liquor), *que* (antique), *quh* (Urquhart), *sc* (viscount), *ugh* (hough), *x* (except), *k* (kite), *ke* (Burke), or *kh* (khan).

Our English alphabet has too few letters—and also too many.[1] There are twenty-six letters in our alphabet; there are at least forty-two different sounds in our language. Moreover, either *c* or *k* is unnecessary, and *x* and *q* are supernumerary. So really we have only twenty-three letters to represent about twice that number of sounds.

That is the beginning of the trouble—too few signs for the sounds. It is trouble enough; but we might get around it if we agreed on unchanging combinations: for example, if we agreed that the letter *k* should always represent the sound. However, as we have seen, the case is quite otherwise.

[1] This is what scholars mean when they say it is both "redundant and deficient."

How it came to be otherwise is an interesting story. The over-all explanation is suggested by one authority in the *Encyclopedia Americana:*

The modern English alphabet illustrates vividly the various changes through which the English tongue has passed since the days when the Germanic tribes first began to overrun the British islands. Saxon, Dane, Northman, Norman, French, Celt, and Latin have contributed to make it what it is today by giving it vowel and consonantal sounds and modifying those it primitively possessed when Saxon and Celt first met on English soil.

More specifically, three things have caused words to be spelled differently from the way they sound.

1. Their pronunciation has remained the same but their spelling has changed. Thus, *friend*—which the Anglo-Saxons probably pronounced as we do—was once spelled *frend*. (This is a comparatively rare cause.)

2. Their spelling has remained the same but their pronunciation has changed. Thus, *Pilate* was once pronounced *Peelahty*. (This is a common cause.)

3. Both spelling and pronunciation have changed—but in different directions. (This is generally the cause of the divergence between pronunciation and spelling.)

What to Do About It

Spelling is a conservative element. It would be better, of course, to adopt a system of simplified spelling. The logic Professor Lounsbury's question contains is unassailable:

If a man seriously believes that it is essential to the purity and perfection of the English language that *honor* should be spelled with a *u* and *horror* without it; that *honorable* should be spelled with a *u* and *honorary* without it; that meter should have its final syllable in *re* and *diameter* and *hexameter* in *er;* that *deign* should terminate in *eign* and its allied compound form *disdain* in *ain;* that *convey* should end in *ey* and *inveigh* in *eigh;* that *precede* should end in *ede* and *proceed* in *eed;* that *fancy* should begin with *f* and *phantom* with *ph;* that *deceit* should be written without *p* and *receipt* with it; if, in fine, spelling in different ways words which have the same origin brings him pleasure, why not leave him in the undisturbed enjoyment of this mild form of imbecility?

There is no answer to this—but nevertheless spelling obstinately refuses to accommodate itself to reason. There have been minor victories, of course: in America, at least, spellings like *centre* and *honour* (rather than *center* and *honor*) are affected; and spellings like *antick* or *comick* have long gone out of vogue, even in England. The spelling reformers have won all the battles but the last: spelling remains chaotic, confusing, and contradictory.

What to do about it? There are two possible answers. Some have decided to disregard the conventions of spelling utterly, and do as their ancestors did[1]—spell words as they sound. They have very respectable backing. Professor Childs (who knows how words are spelled) writes:

One of the most useful things just now is to break down the respect which a great foolish public has for the established spelling. Some have a religious awe and some have an earth-born passion for it. At present I don't much care how anybody spells, so he spells different from what is established. Any particular individual spelling is likely to be more rational than the ordinary.

The other answer rests on somewhat lower ground than the eradication of human folly. Granted that the spelling situation is a muddle, it nevertheless is possible to "muddle through" very satisfactorily. There are a few valid observations—"rules," if you will—concerning the dominant ways letters group themselves to form words: memorize them, and their "exceptions" (there is no other way, unfortunately), and you can become an almost perfect speller. *By applying the rules you will be able to wipe out 98 percent of your spelling errors.*

These observations, or generalizations, or rules, are easy to understand. And memorizing them will not be difficult either if you will always keep a few model forms in mind.[2]

[1]Their ancestors, until dictionaries more or less set the forms, spelled pretty much as they liked: however, they always kept close to the sound of the word. Chaucer was not really a "bad speller," as Mark Twain humorously intimated; he wrote words as he heard them. Sometimes he spelled the same word in three or four different ways, all being phonetically possible representations.

[2]There are always perfectionists—people who will not rest content with 98 but demand 100 percent accuracy. To reach that ideal needs continuous observation. Most of the "stumpers" (as they were called in old fashioned spelling bees) are listed in the "Dictionary of Spelling."

Rule 1.—*ei* and *ie* with the sound of *e:*—*c* is followed by *ei;* any other consonant is followed by *ie.*

(The old rime is helpful:

> *I* before *e*
> Except after *c,*
> Or when sounded like *a*
> As in *neighbor* or *weigh.*)

EXAMPLES

ei after *c*

conceive	receive	receipt
deceive	conceit	ceiling
perceive	deceit	ceil

ie after any consonant except *c*

achieve	grief	retrieve
belief	grieve	niece
believe	kerchief	piece
bier	lief	siege
brief	mien	thief
chief	reprieve	tier
field		

EXCEPTIONS

inveigle	nonpareil	teil
leisure	seine	weir
neither	seize	weird

NOTE: The rule does not cover cases where the sound of the *i* and *e* combination is $\bar{a}$ (as in *way* or *day*); or $\breve{i}$ (as in *hit* or *bit*); or $\bar{i}$ (as in *mine* or *rime*).

(a) If the sound is $\bar{a}$, the order is always *e* before *i.*

heinous	freight	rein
deign	vein	weight

(b) If the sound is $\breve{i}$, the order is *e* before *i.*

foreign	forfeit	sovereign

There are three exceptions to (b): *sieve, mischief, mischievous.*

(c) If the sound is $\bar{i}$, the order is *e* before *i.*

height	sleight	eider

In almost all other cases *i* precedes *e,* whatever the sound of the combination. In one case, when the sound is *e* (as in *bet* or *let*), the *i* goes before the *e* even after *c*: *ancient, deficient, friend*.

Note also that for the rule to be effective, the *i* and *e* must form a digraph—that is, they must represent a single sound, as in all the instances cited above; if the *i* and *e* represent two sounds, as in *science,* the rule does not apply.

Rule 2.—Final silent *e* is regularly dropped before a suffix beginning with a vowel.

EXAMPLES

gauge	gauging	wire	wiry
change	changing	plague	plaguy
give	giving	rogue	roguish
oblige	obliging	sense	sensible
write	writing	arrive	arrival
practice	practicing	desire	desirous
stone	stony	sponge	spongy
mire	miry	value	valuable

EXCEPTIONS

(a)   The *e* is retained after soft *c* and soft *g* (as in *race* and *rage*) when the suffixes *ous* or *able* are added. Reason: *g* and *c* are usually soft before *e, i,* and *y;* that is, *g* has the sound of *j* in *jet,* and *c* the sound of *s* in *sin.* But before *a, o,* and *u* both *g* and *c* are usually hard; that is, *g* has the sound of *g* in *gut,* and *c* has the sound of *k* in *Kodak.* In order to retain the soft sound of *g* and *c,* the final *e* is retained before a suffix beginning with *a, o,* or *u.*

advantage	advantaging	*but* advantageous
change	changing	*but* changeable
outrage	outraging	*but* outrageous
notice	noticing	*but* noticeable
trace	tracing	*but* traceable
service	servicing	*but* serviceable

(Compare: practice, practicing, and practicably.)

(b) In a few words, final silent *e* is retained before the suffix *ing,* in order to prevent ambiguity.

tinge	tingeing	— to color
singe	singeing	— to scorch
swinge	swingeing	— to whip

Compare:

ting	tinging	— to make a high-pitched sound
sing	singing	— to chant
swing	swinging	— movement to and fro

(c) Final silent *e* is retained in the endings *ye oe, ee* before adding the suffix *ing.*

dye	dyeing	see	seeing
eye	eyeing	agree	agreeing
hoe	hoeing	decree	decreeing
shoe	shoeing	guarantee	guaranteeing

(d) The ending *ie* is regularly changed to *y* before adding the suffix *ing.*

(Reason: to prevent two i's from coming together. Thus, if *lie* conformed to the general rule—that a final silent *e* is dropped before a suffix beginning with a vowel—we should have *liing.*)

tie	tying
vie	vying
hie	hying

(NOTE: Also allowable are *tieing* and *hieing.*)

Rule 3.—Final silent *e* is regularly retained before a suffix beginning with a consonant.

care	careful	careless
grace	graceful	graceless
fine	finely	finest
entire	entirely	entireness
sure	surety	sureness
state	stateroom	statecraft

NOTE: Words ending in *dge* preferably drop the final silent *e: judgment, abridgment, acknowledgment.* However, *judgement, abridgement, acknowledgement* are allowable.

Rule 4.—A final single consonant, preceded by a single vowel, is doubled before a suffix beginning with a vowel in words accented on the last syllable.

(NOTE: All monosyllables are included in the rule.)

EXAMPLES

beg	—	begged, begging, beggar
ship	—	shipped, shipping, shipper
acquit	—	acquitted, acquitting, acquittal, acquittance
commit	—	committee, committal, committable
transfer	—	transferred, transferring, transferrer

NOTE: If the accent in the derivative is displaced (thrown forward) by the addition of a suffix, the final consonant is not doubled.

EXAMPLES

confer	conference
parallel	parallelism
transfer	transference

The rule similarly does not apply (a) if the final consonant is already doubled or (b) if the final consonant is preceded by a double vowel or diphthong.

(a) rela*x*   rela*x*ed   rela*x*ing
(x is equivalent to ks)

(b) b*oi*l   b*oi*led   b*oi*ling
l*ea*d   l*ea*ding   l*ea*der

Rule 5.—Final y is regularly changed to i when a suffix (other than one beginning with i) is added.

EXAMPLES

rely	— reliance		modify	— modifier
crafty	— craftiness	(*but*	modify	— modifying
carry	— carriage		carry	— carrying)

EXCEPTIONS

(a) The *y* is usually retained if it is preceded by a vowel.

EXAMPLES

day	daylight	say	sayer
play	playable	enjoy	enjoyment
convey	conveyance	pay	payee

day — daily
pay — paid
say — said

(b) The *y* is retained when the suffix *ship* is added.

lady — ladyship

(c) The *y* is usually retained when the suffix *ness* is added to monosyllables (especially monosyllabic adjectives).

dry — dryness
sly — slyness
shy — shyness

NOTE: The final *y* of monosyllables is sometimes dropped and sometimes retained before the suffix *ly*. Either form is allowable.

dry   drily — dryly
sly   slily — slyly
shy   shily — shyly

Rule 6.—Derivatives formed by prefixing a syllable or syllables to words ending in a double consonant normally retain both consonants.

*under*sell   *down*fall   *un*well
*em*boss   *en*roll   *fore*tell

(a) Compounds of which *full* is the last part are apt to be curtailed.

fulfil   (*fulfill* optional)
*skil*ful
wilful   (*willful* optional)
cupful

Spelling Pointers

Some broad observations concerning spelling, not definite enough to be called "rules," may prove helpful in spite of the many "exceptions," the inevitable variations.

1. Plurals

(a) Normally nouns form the plurals by adding *s* to the singular.

| boys | joys | Americans | hopes |
| books | sorrows | Mussulmans | ottomans |

(b) Nouns form their plural by adding *es* to the singular:
(1) if the plural would otherwise be awkward to pronounce and therefore requires the extra syllable.

| lasses | watches |
| boxes | porches |

(2) If the singular ends in *o* preceded by a consonant.

| mosquitoes | Negroes |
| heroes | vetoes |

Exceptions

albinos	gauchos	magnetos	salvos
avocados	gringos	octavos	sextos
banjos	halos	octodecimos	solos
cantos	indigos	pianos	tobaccos
didos	juntos	piccolos	virtuosos
dynamos	lassos	provisos	zeros

(c) If the noun ends in *y* preceded by a consonant.

sky	skies
duty	duties
enemy	enemies

(Note that, in accordance with *Rule 5* quoted above, the *y* changes to *i* before suffixing *es*.)

(d) Nouns ending in *y* preceded by a vowel add *s*.

chimney	chimneys	buoy	buoys
money	moneys	play	plays
boy	boys	day	days

NOTE: Nouns ending in *quy* (*obloquy, soliloquy, colloquy*) change the *y* to *i* and add *es* to form their plurals (*obloquies*, *soliloquies, colloquies*). Reason: *qu* is the equivalent of *kw,* so that the final *y* is really preceded by a consonant.

(e) Compounds add the sign of the plural to the most important element.

brigadier generals	sergeants-at-arms
aides-de-camp	chargés d'affaire
courts-martial	men-of-war
court plasters	rights-of-way
courtyards	deputy chiefs of staff
vice-presidents	assistant attorneys general

NOTE: If both words are equally important, both are pluralized:

coats of arms   men servants   women writers

(f) Nouns ending in *ful* form the plural by adding *s* at the end; if it is necessary to express the idea that more than one container was filled, the two elements of the solid compound are printed as separate words and the plural is formed by adding *s* to the noun.

5 bucketfuls of the mixture (1 bucket filled five times)
5 buckets full of earth (separate buckets)
3 cupfuls of flour (1 cup filled three times)
3 cups full of coffee (separate cups)

(g) Foreign Plurals

(The spellings listed below are preferred for the plurals. Note that most of the words have entered English comparatively late, and are incompletely assimilated.)

agendum, agenda
addendum, addenda
alga, algae
alumnus, alumni (masc.); alumna, alumnae (fem.)
antenna, antennas (*antennae* in zoology)
appendix, appendixes (*appendices* in zoology)
axis, axes
basis, bases
chassis (singular and plural)

Co., Cos.
crisis, crises
criterion, criteria
datum, data
desideratum, desiderata
dilettante, dilettanti
ellipsis, ellipses
equilibrium, equilibriums (*equilibria,* technical)
erratum, errata
flambeau, flambeaus
folium, folia

formula, formulas (*formulae,* technical)

genius, geniuses

genus, genera

gladiolus (singular and plural— *gladioli* and *gladioluses* alternatives for plural)

hypothesis, hypotheses

index, indexes (*indices,* technical)

Kansas Citys

larva, larvae

lava, lavas

Marys

matrix, matrices

medium, mediums (*media,* technical)

memorandum, memorandums (*memoranda,* alternative)

minutia, minutiae

oasis, oases

parenthesis, parentheses

phenomenon, phenomena

procès-verbal, procès-verbaux

radius, radii

radix, radixes

septum, septa

stimulus, stimuli

stratum, strata

syllabus, syllabi

synopsis, synopses

tableau, tableaus (*tableaux,* theatrical)

terminus, termini

thesis, theses

vertebra, vertebras (*vertebrae,* technical)

2. Possessives

The possessive case of a singular or plural noun not ending in *s* is formed by adding an apostrophe and *s;* the possessive case of a singular or plural noun ending in *s* is formed by adding an apostrophe only.

man's, men's

prince's, princes'

Essex's, Essexes'

Co.'s, Cos.'

hostess', hostesses'

princess', princesses'

Jones', Joneses'

Jesus'

Mars'

Dumas'

(a) In compound nouns, the *'s* is added to the element nearest the object possessed.

> comptroller general's decision
> Mr. Brown of New York's motion
> attorney at law's fee
> John White, Jr.'s (no comma) account

(b) Joint possession is indicated by placing apostrophe on the last element of the series, while individual possession requires the use of apostrophe on each element of the series.

soldiers and sailors' home

Brown & Nelson's store

Mr. Smith's & Mrs. Nelson's children

The Army's and the Navy's work

(c) In the use of an apostrophe in geographic names, firm names, the names of organizations and institutions, and the titles of books, the authentic form is to be followed.

United States share
United Nations aims
Southern States industries
Harpers Ferry
Masters, Mates, & Pilots' Association

Court of St. James's
St. Peter's Church
St. Elizabeths Hospital
Johns Hopkins University
Hinds' Precedents

(d) Possessive pronouns do not take an apostrophe.

its   theirs

3. **Able** and **Ible**

These are extremely troublesome endings. No hard-and-fast rule can be quoted. But there are some practical hints which, if acted upon, can eliminate most of the trouble.

(a) If you are in doubt, and your dictionary is inaccessible, spell the ending *able:* Of the more than one thousand words terminating in *able* and *ible,* fewer than two hundred take the latter. Consequently, you have a better than 80 percent chance of being right by using *able*.

(b) If the word has been in the language for a long time, whatever its source, and is used frequently, *able* is probably the right ending. *Able* is a living suffix, the one almost invariably added to the verb in forming new adjectives.

(c) If the word has been derived from Latin (directly or indirectly)—except from Latin verbs of the first conjugation—the termination is *ible*. If derived from any other source, the ending is *able*.

(d) If you can't remember whether the adjective ends in *ible* or *able,* try to think of a related noun ending in *ation* or *ition*. There is an appreciable difference in the pronunciation of the noun endings, and they offer an almost infallible clue to the spelling of the adjective. If the corresponding noun ends in *ation,* the adjective ends in *able;* if the corresponding noun ends in *ition* (or its variants *tion, ion, sion*), the adjective ends in *ible.*

EXAMPLES
Able

Verb	*Noun*	*Adjective*
admire	admiration	admirable
excite	excitation	excitable
imagine	imagination	imaginable
inflame	inflammation	inflammable
terminate	termination	terminable
navigate	navigation	navigable

Ible

Verb	*Noun*	*Adjective*
admit	admission	(in) admissible
compress	compression	compressible
convert	conversion	(in) convertible
collect	collection	collectible
exhaust	exhaustion	(in) exhaustible
flex	flexion	flexible
instruct	instruction.	(un) instructible
reduce	reduction	reducible
vend	vendition	(in) vendible

4. Ise and Ize

Ize is the more normal termination for verbs ending with the sound the spelling indicates. It is also the better, whether the criterion be sound or source (verbs ending in *ize* are formed from Greek verbs ending in *izo,* or in imitation of such verbs). American usage rightly prefers to spell the ending *ize.* However, there are some exceptions; the more important are listed below.

advertise	compromise	exorcise
advise	demise	improvise
affranchise	despise	incise
apprise	devise	premise
arise	disguise	reprise
chastise	enterprise	supervise
circumcise	excise	surmise
comprise	exercise	surprise

5. **Sede, Ceed, and Cede**

These endings are the cause of innumerable misspellings. However, all the difficulties may be simply eliminated by remembering only four words.

(a) Only one word in English ends in *sede:*

> supersede

(b) Only three words in English end in *ceed:*

> exceed   proceed   succeed

(c) All other words having the sound indicated by any of the spellings end in *cede:*

> intercede   recede
> precede   secede

6. **Or or Our**

In America, the *our* termination has become obsolete, though it is still generally preferred in England. The only living ending in *our* is found in *Saviour* when the word refers to Jesus Christ. (Otherwise *savior* is employed.) The spelling *glamour* is occasionally thought more glamorous; but *glamor* is advisable for the less impressionable.

NOTE: The suffixes *or* and *er* both denote agency. However, *or* is normally appended to words of Latin origin (*distributor, factor, competitor*); whereas *er* is normally appended to words of English origin (*maker, doer, teacher*).

7. **Cy and Sy**

(a) *Cy* is a noun suffix meaning "state, quality, or condition." *Sy* is not a suffix. *Cy* frequently occurs in compound suffixes: *acy, ancy, ency, cracy, mancy.* *Sy* is not an added element; it is part of a primitive word—and probably a word derived from the Greek. (Compare *accuracy,* meaning "the state of being accurate," and composed of a root plus a suffix; with *hypocrisy,* meaning "a feigning to be what one is not," and composed of a prefix and a root.) Therefore, if you are able to recognize that the word in question has a suffix, use *cy*.

(b)   If an allied word terminates in *ate,* the spelling *acy* invariably replaces it.

advocate	advocacy
candidate	candidacy
pirate	piracy

(c)   If there is no recourse to a dictionary and none of the suggestions above may be acted upon, end the questionable word with *cy.* The *sy* termination occurs in but a very few common words. They are listed below:

apostasy	curtsy	heresy
autopsy	ecstasy	hypocrisy
argosy	embassy	idiosyncrasy
courtesy	epilepsy	minstrelsy
	pleurisy	

3. **Æ, Œ, and E**

E alone and *ae* and *oe* written separately have largely replaced the ligatures *æ* and *œ* in modern American spelling. Only in foreign words where national practice is followed and in a very few technical words are the ligatures retained. (Most dictionaries allow the ligatured forms, but they are thoroughly out of style.)

anemia	esophagus	homeopath
Caesar	esthetic	medieval
diarrhea	fetus	orthopedic
encyclopedia		

but:

Ælfric	*hors d'œuvre*	*Encyclopædia Britannica*
Cædmon	*pharmacopœia*	Æ [Russell]

All of these observations concerning spelling have proved helpful to poor spellers. They are, however, no substitute for careful observation of your persistent errors and for memorization of those words which fall outside the artificial limits of the generalizations. A good modern dictionary (and frequent recourse to it) is a necessary aid if spelling perfection is your goal—and if, as seems likely, we continue to use a needlessly difficult, hopelessly irrational, thoroughly outmoded, snobbish, and generally reprehensible system of spelling.

BOOK FOUR

Dictionary of Words Most Frequently Misspelled

A

ab'scess	Note that the spelling is *sc* though the *c* is silent.
ab'sence	The *ce* termination causes the difficulty.
ac cede'	Two syllables here, one ending, the other beginning with *c;* the *cede* root (rather than *sede* and *ceed*) is normal in English.
ac ces'so ry	"Aiding or assisting"—this spelling has prevailed over *accessary.*
ac"ci den'tal ly	Watch the *ally* at the end: do not abridge it to *ly.*
ac com'mo date	Two *c's* and two *m's;* do not scant either.
ac'cu ra cy	A "spelling demon": it rates only one *r.*
ac knowl'edg ment	Note the presence of the *k* (in *know*) and the absence of *e* after *g.*
a cross'	A "spelling demon": one *c,* one *r,* and two *s's* (*a + cross*).
ad dress'	Two *d's* and two *s's* (*ad + dress*).
ad ver'tise ment	The syllable before the last is *tise,* not *tize* or *tis.*
a line'	*Align* is also sanctioned; but *aline* is the simpler and more rational spelling.
al lege'	Note that there are two *l's* and not even one *d* in *allege.*
all right	*All right* is two words; *alright* is not a word at all.
al'most	One word and one *l.*
a lu'mi num	This is the spelling preferred in America. (The British spell and pronounce it *aluminium.*)
am bas'sa dor	Like *embassy,* spelled with one *b* and two *s's.*

an'a loy	This is a simple and reasonable way to spell the word: and an approved way, too. However, most dictionaries prefer *analogue*.
an'gel	The celestial personage.
an'gle	The fishhook.
an'y way	No *s* at the end when you mean "in any case"— unless you want a dialectal term.
a piece'	One word, and *pie* in the middle.
ap par'ent	The *ent* of the last syllable—as in *parent*—is the stumbling block.
a pol'o gize	*Ze* not *se* is the ending.
ar''che ol'o gy	A simpler spelling than its variant *archaeology* —and just as correct.
arc'tic	The *c* in the first syllable is often omitted—incorrectly—in both pronunciation and spelling.
ar'ti cle	The ending is *le* not *al*.
ar'ti san	Resist the temptation to place an *i* between the *s* and the *a* of the last syllable.
as cend'ance	Also possible: *ascendence*. But both forms have *sc* as their second and third letters.
as par'a gus	Note the *agus* ending: the vowels are frequently transposed—and other errors are possible too, if you try.
as sas'sin	The sin of the misspeller is the irrational *sain*.
ath'lete	The misspelling *athalete* stems from the mispronunciation.
au'di tor	Not *auditer*—think of *editor, creditor,* etc.
au''to gi'ro	This is the spelling of the trade-mark.
ax	Chop the superfluous *e* of *axe* off—though it is allowable to keep it on.
aye	The adverb meaning "yes" is spelled this way preferably; the interjection meaning "Alas!" is spelled *ay*.
av'e nue	Not *avanue;* and above all, not *avenyue*.

B

bag'ging	Double the final consonant of *bag* when adding a suffix beginning with a vowel.
bal'ance	The *lance* (not *lence*) ending is easy to remember when you think of the difficulty of balancing a lance.
bank'rupt cy	If the *t* were pronounced, as it ought to be, it would not be omitted in the spelling.

bar'i tone	*I* is a distinctive quality of baritones: do not substitute an *a*.
bas tille'	The French prefer this spelling for their prison-fortress, the Bastille; but *bastile* is also sanctioned.
beau'ti ful	No matter how full of beauty—only one *l* at the end.
be fore'	The preposition *for* is not relevant here; the adverb *fore* is. Do not omit the final *e*.
be hoove'	This is the verb form (also spelled *behove*); do not confuse with the noun *behoof*.
bloc	Distinguish *bloc,* a "political combination," from *block,* a "hindrance or obstruction"—in spite of their numerous points of identity.
blond	This spelling may be used whether the person referred to is male or female. However, purists prefer: *blond* man, *blonde* woman.
blu'ing	*Blueing* is also possible; but prefer the given spelling.
boul'der	Use either this spelling or *bowlder* indifferently.
boun'te ous	Remember that the *y* of bounty changes to *e* before the suffix *ous*.
bron'co	Also acceptable: *broncho*.
bruised	The *ui* element causes the trouble here: think of *cruised*.
bun'ion	No *onion* in this word.
buoy	Nothing but examination and memorization will help.
bus, bus'ses	One *s* in the singular, two in the plural.
busi'ness	The *y* of *busy* is changed to *i* before adding the suffix *ness*.
by'-and-by'	Hyphenate or not, as you choose.

C

cad'die	Spell the title of the boy who carries your golf clubs this way; a *caddy* is a small tea-chest.
cad'dy ing	The present participle of the verb related to *caddie* is spelled with a *y*.
cal'en dar	Distinguish from *calender,* which is a pressing machine.
calk	Either *calk* or *caulk:* but prefer the former.
can"cel la'tion	Either *canceled* or *cancelled; canceling* or *cancelling;* but only *cancellation*.

can'not	One word. Purists, however, insist on writing it *can not* because it is the negative of *can*. The contraction is *can't*.
can'yon	If you want to spell the Spanish way write *cañon;* the pronunciation is the same in either case.
cat'a log	This is a simple and thoroughly acceptable spelling. However, *catalogue* is still the more frequent spelling.
ca tarrh'	One *t* and two *r*'s for this "spelling demon"; the adjective is *catarrhal* or *catarrhous*.
cat'sup	Variant spellings of the same item are *catchup* and *ketchup*. (The last spelling corresponds most closely to the usual pronunciation.)
cav''i ar'	Or *caviare*, if you will.
cel'lar	Two hazards here; both in the last syllable: either the *l* is omitted, or an *e* replaces the *a:* avoid both.
cen'ter	This is the preferred American spelling; the British still stick to *centre*.
chan'cel lor	Two *l*'s; note also the caps in *Lord Chancellor*.
check	The English spell the banking term *cheque*.
chili (pepper)	*Chilli* and *chile* are also sanctioned.
chock'full	Either write separately or hyphenate (*chock-full*).
choice	The *oi* in the middle of the word and the *ce* at the end are sources of difficulty.
choir	*Quire* is best restricted to mean "a collection of folded sheets" not of singers (for which prefer *choir*).
chop' su'ey	Two words *chop sooy* is the alternate spelling.
cig''a rette'	The preferred spelling; but *cigaret*, though further from the French, is the more logical (because more phonetic) spelling.
clew (nautical) **clue (other meanings)**	The *Style Manual* of the Government Printing Office prefers *clew* for the nautical term, but *clue* for all other significations.
co'co nut''	This is the sounder as well as the simpler spelling; but *cocoanut* is also allowable.
cole'slaw''	*Coleslaw* stems from the Dutch words meaning "cabbage salad." The fact that it is served cold ought to mislead no one concerning its spelling.
col'lar	The final syllable *lar* is unaccented; and like many other unaccented syllables, it is subjected to some weird misspellings.

col'lege — Many—including some college graduates—erroneously insert a *d* in the final syllable.

col'umn — Columnists humorously spell it *colyum;* others seriously spell it *colum;* but the (unsounded) final *n* is still required.

com mit'tee — Two *m's,* two *t's,* two *e's:* watch this "spelling demon."

com mod'i ty — Two *m's.*

com mu'ni cate — Two *m's.*

com'ple ment — That which completes.

com'pli ment — Praise, flattery, congratulation.

con ceive' — This word conforms to the same pattern as *deceive, receive, perceive;* yet, it seems to cause more spelling stumbles than the others.

con"de scend' — The silent *c* in the last syllable tends to be omitted.

con'science — Think of *science,* which is the base spelling of this word, and you will spell it wrong only if you try.

con'scious — The second syllable *scious* is derived from *scio,* "I know"; think of the derivation and the *i* concealed in the pronunciation will be present in the spelling.

con sign'ment — The middle syllable is *sign*—a word rarely misspelled when it is by itself; but frequently misspelled when it is part of a larger word.

coo'lie — A variant spelling is *cooly.*

co quet' — This is the preferred spelling for the verb meaning "to flirt." (It may also mean "a male who flirts." The female flirt, of course, is spelled *coquette.* The special activity of both is *coquetting.*)

cor"re spond'ence — There are two *r's* here—as also in *correct, correlate, corrode,* and most words formed from *co* + a stem beginning with *r.*

coun'ci lor — The word spelled thus indicates "a member of a council." (Two *l's* are allowable.) Often confused with *counselor,* "an advisor, particularly a legal advisor."

coun se lor — *Counsellor* is also sanctioned. See COUNCILOR.

crit'i cism — The soft *c* conceals its origin: *critic* + *ism.*

cruise — This word and its homophone *crews* are often confounded. Both have something to do with ships, but their origins are quite different:

cruise derives from the Dutch *kruissen,* "to cross"; *crews* from the Old French *creue,* "an increase."

crys'tal   There is only one *l* in this basic form: the derivatives all have two: *crystallize, crystalline, crystallite.* (Note that there is no *h* after the *c* in the first syllable: the analogy with *chromatic, chronology, Christ,* etc., often causes an *h* to be erroneously inserted.)

cu"ri os'i ty   The adjective *curious* causes the misspelling *curiousity.*

cyn'i cism   The Cynics were members of a school of philosophy and believed in nothing but doubt. Their *ism* is *cynic-ism.*

D

debt'or   The *b* should be absent when the word is pronounced, but present when it is spelled.

de'cen cy   The adjective is *decent;* but no *t* ought be present in the noun form.

de fense'   This is the preferred spelling for the noun in America; the British prefer *defence* (and *offence*).

def'i nite   If you pronounce the vowel in the second syllable as you do the vowel in the first, you are likely to misspell the word: neither say nor write *defenite.*

de riv'a tive   *A* is the penultimate syllable, not *i.* (Again, be careful of the unaccented syllables.)

de scend'ant   Two invitations to error here: the *sc* of the second syllable, and the *ant* of the last. Decline both.

des'ic cated   There is only one *s;* there are two *c's.* The dominant error is mistaking the number of each.

de vel'op   No terminal *e* in this word; and *development* is simply *develop + ment.*

dex'trous   Many dictionaries prefer *dex-ter-ous.* But since the *e* is rarely sounded in current American speech, it seems better to omit it.

di'a log   The simplified spelling for the more formal *dialogue.*

di"ar rhe'a   One of the "spelling demons." Note the two *r's* and the one *h.* An old-fashioned but still sanctioned spelling is *diarrhoea.*

di'a ry	This spelling refers to "the book in which events are recorded," not to "the place where milk is converted." (The latter is a dairy.)
di"e ti'tian	Just as acceptable and perhaps more frequent (in spite of Government preference) is *dietician*.
dike	*Dyke* is a variant spelling.
din'gey	(The boat.) Also spelled *dinghy* and *dingy*.
dis"ap pear'	One more *s* than is warranted tends to appear and one of the necessary *p's* tends to disappear. Guard against each tendency.
dis as'trous	The last three letters sound like and are sometimes erroneously written *us*. Sometimes, too, in excessive zeal to avoid that error, an uncalled for *u* (*disastruous*) is inserted.
disk	This is the preferred spelling. *Disc*, though acceptable, does not suggest the pronunciation so well.
dis syl'la ble	When *di* is prefixed to a stem beginning with *s*, almost invariably it adds another *s* for euphony.
dis trib'u tor	The suffixes *er* and *or* frequently denote the agent of the action; but *or* is usually added to words of Latin origin (as in this instance), *er* to words of English origin (*e.g., maker*)
di vine'	The affected and false pronunciation *de-vine* is the cause of the frequent misspelling of this word.
di vor"cee'	This spelling is valid whether a divorced man or woman is referred to. However, if you choose, *divorcé* (masculine) and *divorcée* (feminine) may be employed.
doesn't	The apostrophe is necessary: and so is the *e*. Avoid both *doesnt* and *dosn't*.
dor'mi to"ry	The unaccented *i*—like other unaccented vowels —tends to be displaced. In this case, an *a* often does the displacing.
drought	Prefer this spelling to *drouth*.
drunk'en ness	*Drunken + ness:* supply a full measure of *n's*.
du'el	Avoid confusing *duel*, "combat" and *dual*, "twofold."
du'ly	*Duly* means "properly" and *dully* means "stupidly." Avoid confusing them.
dum"found'	Omit the functionless *b* of *dumbfound* (though you may keep it if you prefer to). Unfortunately, it is still necessary to retain the equally functionless *b* of *dumb*.

dy'ing	Distinguish *dying,* "perishing," from *dyeing,* "staining."

E

ec'sta sy	So generally is this word misspelled that the misspelling (*ecstacy*) threatens to become the approved form. It is not as yet, though.
ed'i ble	The *ible* ending, since the word is of Latin origin. *Eat*able, on the other hand, is of Anglo-Saxon origin.
em bar'rass	A "spelling demon": two *r's* and two *s's* in all its forms: *embarrassed, embarrassing, embarrassment.*
em' i nent	Distinguish *eminent,* "prominent," from *imminent,* "threatening," and *immanent,* "indwelling."
en cage'	More frequently used than its variant, *incage.*
en case'	*Encase* and *incase* are both in good usage.
en close'	Unless the reference is legal, prefer *enclose* to *inclose.*
en cum'ber	Prefer the *en* to the *in* spelling (*encumber* to *incumber*).
en cum'brance	The *e* of the *encumber* is superfluous to both the spelling and pronunciation of the noun *encumbrance.*
en dorse'	*Endorse* is more general than *indorse,* but both are correct.
en'e my	Neither *enimy* nor *enamy.* The unaccented middle syllable is the source of error—here as elsewhere.
en roll'ment	*Enroll + ment:* do not drop an *l.*
en trench'	*Intrench* is a variant, employed, usually, where the reference is military.
en trust'	*Entrust* and *intrust* are forms on parity with regard to usage.
en vel'op	The verb meaning "to wrap."
en've lope	The noun meaning "wrapper."
é pée'	Note the two (acute) accent marks; they are still required by the dictionaries.
e'qualed, -ing	The *l* of *equal* is preferably not doubled in spelling the past tense or present participle of the verb. (So also: *equality, equalization, equalitarian;* but: *equally.*)

Es'ki mo   Prefer this spelling to the French form *Esquimau*. (For the plural, add only *s: Eskimos*.)

es thet'ic   *Esthetic* and *aesthetic* are both in general use; the former, though, tends to be preferred in America, the latter in England.

ex ceed'   One of the three words in English with *ceed* (the other two being *proceed* and *succeed*).

ex hib'i tor   The *h* should not be in evidence in the pronunciation, but should in the spelling.

ex ist'ence   The terminal syllable ends in *ence*, not *ance*.

ex pense'   The *se* ending, here as elsewhere, gives trouble: avoid *expence*.

F

fan'ta sy   The *sy* ending is occasionally the source of error. Avoid *phantasy*, a spelling which has been out-of-date for a long time.

far'ther   Carelessly rather than ignorantly written *father*. This word connotes "more distant." (*Compare* FURTHER.)

fas'ci nate   Note the *s* ending the first syllable and the *c* beginning the second. Avoid both *fasinate* and *facinate*.

fa'vor   Write *favor* rather than *favour*, which is a British spelling.

fea'si ble   Not *feasable*, as it is often (erroneously) spelled.

Feb'ru ary"   The *r* of the second syllable ought be included in both pronunciation and spelling. Avoid saying or writing *Febuary*.

fe'tus   Prefer to *foetus*. The latter is sanctioned, though.

fi'er y   Often misspelled *firey*.

flex   Sometimes confused with *flecks*.

fli'er   Both *flier* and *flyer* are correct, the latter being, perhaps, the more frequent form.

flight   Sometimes misspelled *fleight* by false analogy with *height*. (Paradoxically, *height* is sometimes misspelled *hight* by false analogy with *flight*.)

for bade'   Both *forbade* and *forbad* are sanctioned.

for'bear   The word spelled this way (containing the prefix *for*) means "to endure" (*See* FOREBEAR).

fore'bear   The word spelled this way (containing the prefix *fore*) means "ancestor."

for'eign   The *g* is silent but spelled.

for'mal ly   Do not confuse with *formerly*, a careless error.

for'mer ly	Do not confuse with *formally* (*q.v.*).
for'ty	Note that *forty*, unlike *four* and *fourteen*, has
four, four'teen	no *u*.
ful fill'	*Fulfil* is equally correct. But the difficulties are decreased with regard to the derivative forms if you spell it *fulfill*.
ful fill'ment	Either *fulfillment* or *fulfilment* is allowable.
fun'gus	Prefer to *fungous* for both the noun and adjective, though *fungous* is a sanctioned spelling for the adjective. (The plural of the noun is *fungi*.)
fur'ther	Distinguish *further* which connotes "something additional" from *farther* which connotes "more distant."

G

gage	This is a simplified spelling of *gauge*. Prefer it.
gai'ly	Either *gayly* or *gaily;* so too, either *gayety* or *gaiety*.
ga losh'	May also be spelled *galoshe*, but the given spelling is more usual.
gas'o line	Prefer to *gasolene*.
gen'er al	Note that there are three syllables in the word. Neither write nor say *genral*.
glam'or	*Glamour* is still preferred in most American dictionaries. However *glamor* is also sanctioned; and since the *our* termination is in general disuse everywhere else in American spelling, there seems to be no reason to insist on *glamour*.
god'dess	The feminine suffix *ess* is added to *god*, and the *d* of *god* doubles according to rule (monosyllable ending in a consonant preceded by a vowel).
good'-by'	*Good-bye* is the alternate form. Retain the hyphen with each.
go ril'la	Distinguish *gorilla*, "the ape," from *guerrilla*, "the irregular fighter."
gov'ern ment	Neither pronounce nor spell the word without *n*.
grue'some	The word derives from the Danish *gru*, "horror." The *e* keeps the sound of *u* long. Guard against transposing the *u* and the *e*.
guar"an tee'	The verb ends in *ee;* the noun in *y*. The pronunciation frequently motivates the misspelling *garantee* or *garanty*.

gui tar'	The *u* in the first syllable is essential for the correct spelling, though not the pronunciation of the word.
gyp'sy	Also sanctioned is *gipsy*. But avoid *gypsey* and *gipsey*.

H

hal''le lu'jah	*Halleluiah* is a variant spelling. (The word means "praise ye Yah"—that is, Jehova.)
hand'fuls	This is the plural of *handful,* rather than *handsful.*
ha rangue'	Misspelled—and very frequently—*harrangue.* The silent *ue* does not seem to be an especial source of difficulty.
har'ass	A "spelling demon." The tendency to spell it with two *r's* and one *s* must be guarded against.
hark'en	The older form, still in good usage, is *hearken.*
hei'nous	If you remember that the first syllable rimes with *weigh,* and that *e* precedes *i* when the combination is "sounded like ā," you should have no difficulty with this frequently misspelled word.
hic'cup	Spell the word *hiccup* rather than *hiccough* and you will not be inclined to mispronounce the last syllable so that it would rime with *off.*
hor'ri ble	The *ible* ending causes the difficulty.
ho'sier y	This word is not *hose* plus *ery,* but *hosier* plus the *y* suffix.
hu'mor ous	The suffix *ous* means "full of." Do not curtail it.

I

idyl	The spelling *idyll* is a variant; but prefer the short form.
im me'di ate ly	Two *m's:* the final *e* of *immediate* is retained when a suffix beginning with a consonant is added.
im per'iled, -ing	Either a single or double *l* for the past tense and present participle. Like many other words ending in *l, imperil* allows the option.
in ci den'tal ly	A "spelling demon." Note that there are five syllables. Do not spell it *incidently.*
in dict'	Distinguish *indict* "to accuse," and *indite* "to write."

in quir′y   The British prefer *enquiry* (and *enquire*).

in struc′tor   Like most words of Latin origin, this has the *or* rather than the *er* suffix to indicate "one who."

in sure′   *Insure* has displaced *ensure* almost entirely in the U. S. because insurance companies employ the former spelling. The final *e* is dropped when suffixes beginning with a vowel are added (*insurance, insurable, insurer, insuring*).

its   *Its* does not take the apostrophe when functioning as the possessive case of *it* (*e.g., such is* its *nature*); *it's* as a contraction of *it is* (*say* it's *so*) does. The error, a very frequent one, may be overcome by a moment's analysis.

J

jew′el ry   Not *jewlery*, as the mispronunciation of the word indicates. And, in America, not *jewellery*.

judg′ment   *Judgement*, though sanctioned, has gone out of fashion.

K

kha′ki   A Hindustani word meaning, literally, "dust colored." Avoid transposing the *h* and *a* of the first syllable.

kin′der gar″ten   This is a German word adopted without change by English. (It means "child's garden.") Both of the *r's* tend to be slurred in pronunciation and omitted in spelling.

knowl′edge   The *k* of *knowledge*, as always in the digraph *kn*, is silent; but should not, therefore, be unwritten.

Ku Klux Klan   An unwarranted alliteration causes the misspelling *Klu Klux Klan*.

L

lab′o ra to″ry   There are five syllables in this word, though in careless speech only four are usually heard, and in careless spelling only four are written (*labratory*). Remember that *labor* is an essential part of the laboratory.

las civ'i ous	When *c* follows *s* and the combination is pronounced *s*, either the *s* or *c* tends to disappear in spelling. Guard against the omission of either.
le'ni ent	Avoid spelling it *lenyent* or *lienient*—both spellings being false deductions from pronunciation.
li'brar y	If the *r* in the second syllable is slurred, *libary*—an illiterate spelling—often results.
li'cence	Also sanctioned: *license,* but avoid *lisence* (*sense* is no part of the spelling).
lic'or ice	*Licorice,* preferably; *liquorice,* allowably. But not *likerish* (as *licorice* is sometimes pronounced), which is another word.
lik'a ble	*Likeable* is the alternate spelling, and is preferred by British but not by American dictionaries.
lis'ten	You should not hear the *t* in this word when it is spoken; but you should see it when it is written.
lit'er a ture	One *t* in the first syllable, and in all its derivatives (*literary, literate, literati*).
lla'ma	As Ogden Nash said: "The one *l* lama is a priest; the two *l* llama is a beast."
loath	The adjective form has no terminal *e;* the verb form has (*loathe*).
loose	Distinguish *loose,* "unattached," and *lose,* "to miss or mislay."
ly'ing	The *ie* of *lie* changes to *y* before adding *ing,* the sign of the present participle, to avoid the piling up of vowels which would otherwise result.

M

mar'i tal	If you transpose the *i* and *t* you will have *martial*—a quite different word.
mea'ger	*Meagre,* though more indicative of its French origin, has been largely displaced in America by *meager.*
mean'ness	*Mean* + suffix *ness.* Do not scant the *n's.*
med'i cine	Note particularly the *i* in the middle syllable of this "spelling demon." Poor spellers have a penchant for substituting an *e* in its place.
me di e'val	*Mediaeval* is an alternate but less popular spelling.

me′ter	*Metre* is also sanctioned if the reference is to the rhythmical structure of either verse or music. Otherwise, write *meter*.
min′ute	The noun meaning "a unit of time or space" and the adjective meaning "small" are both spelled this way; but the latter is differently accented (*mi′ nute*).
mis′cel la′ne ous	A "spelling demon," because of its length primarily; note the five syllables, and remember that the first ends with *s* and the second begins with *c*.
mis spell′	It is ironic that this word is so frequently misspelled. It is a simple combination of *mis* ("not") and *spell*—neither a difficult element.
Mo ham′med an	*Mahometan* is the variant form.
mold	Prefer this spelling to *mould*.
mon′o log	The simplified and thoroughly acceptable spelling of *monologue,* the form most dictionaries still prefer.
mo rale′	Distinguish *morale,* "mental state," from *moral,* "ethical."
mort′gage	The *t* is silent but spelled.
mus tache′	The spelling *moustache* went out with side whiskers.

N

nec es sa ry	A "spelling demon": note the one *c* and the two *s's.*
nick′el	Not *nickle,* as often misspelled.
nine′ty	Note that the *e* of *nine* is retained when the suffix *ty* is added.
ninth	Note that the *e* of the cardinal *nine* is dropped in the ordinal *ninth.*
no′tice a ble	The *e* of notice is retained before *able* to preserve the soft sound of *c.*

O

oc ca′sion	A "spelling demon": note the two *c's* and one *s.*
oc ca′sion al ly	The adverb is formed by adding *ly* to the adjective occasional.
oc cur red′, -ing	A "spelling demon": two *c's* and two *r's;* also: *occurred, occurrence, occurrent.*

of fense'	*Offense* rather than *offence* is still preferred by most dictionaries—but both are allowable.
ours	The possessive of *our;* it is not written with an apostrophe.

P

pa ja'mas	You may also spell it *pyjamas,* but that is asking for trouble.
par'al lel, par'al leled, par'al leling	The profusion of *l's* in the past tense and present participle causes much unhappiness among inadequate spellers: *paralleled* and *paralleling.* Final *l,* as in most words ending in single *l* preceded by a vowel, may also be doubled: *parallelled, parallelling.* In the one system, the number of *l's* separated by the *e* are parallel; in the other, unparallel.
pas'time"	One *t.* When written solid, *pastime* is a noun meaning "diversion."
pe cul'iar	The *liar* at the end is to be noted here.
ped'ler, ped'dler ped'lar	The first spelling is to be preferred by Americans; the second is an alternative spelling; the third is in general use in England.
pen'e trate	For the unaccented middle syllable, *a* or *i* is often incorrectly substituted.
per cent'	The Chicago *Manual of Style* prefers *per cent;* the Government Printing Office *Style Manual* prefers *percent.* Dictionaries are similarly divided. So take your choice.
per'ma nent	The vowels of the last two syllables are frequently transposed. Avoid *permenant.*
phase	Do not confuse *phase,* "aspect," with *faze,* "to puzzle."
piece	*Pie* is contained in *piece.* Do not confuse with *peace.*
pit'e ous	Sometimes spelled *pitious,* by analogy with *pitiful.*
pleas'ant	The *a* of the digraph *ae* is sometimes omitted—avoid *plesant.*
plow	Prefer this simple spelling to *plough.*
poi'son	Shun *poisen.*
por ten'tous	Partly through analogy and partly through mispronunciation the final syllable is sometimes misspelled *teous.*
pos'si bly	Two *s's* and no *a's.*

prac'ti cal ly   The syllable before the last is usually slurred when pronouncing the word, but must be included when spelling it.

prac'tice   Prefer *practice* to *practise* for the verb; for the noun, *practice* is mandatory.

prep"a ra'tion   Not *preperation*.

prim'i tive   The unaccented middle syllable is the primary cause of trouble: avoid *primative*.

prin'ci pal   Do not confuse *principal*, "chief," and *principle*, "rule."

prin'ci ple   Do not confuse *principle*, "rule," and *principal*, "chief."

priv'i lege   Do not substitute *a* or *e* for the unaccented middle syllable.

pro ceed'   This word is one of the three in English which contains the stem *ceed* (*exceed* and *succeed* being the other two).

proc'ess   The conjunction of *s* sounds creates spelling difficulties here: note the one *c* and two *s's*. (The plural is *processes*.)

pro fes'sor   One *f* and two *s's*, not the reverse.

proph'e cy   This noun ends in *cy*; the verb ends in *sy*.

proph'e sy   This verb ends in *sy*; the noun ends in *cy*.

pto'maine   The initial *p* is not pronounced but must be written.

pur sue'   A "spelling demon": *persue* is understandable but not allowable.

Q

quan'ti ty   Not *quantaty*: be careful of short vowels, here as elsewhere.

qui'et   Distinguish *quiet* and *quite*: each has the same letters, but differently placed.

R

rac coon'   Both *racoon* and *raccoon* are acceptable spellings.

re ceipt'   *E* comes before *i* after *c* when the sound of the digraph is long *e*. (The *p* is silent but spelled.)

re ceive'   *See* RECEIPT.

rec"om mend'   A "spelling demon": one *c* and two *m's*.

re con'nais sance   Note the two *n's* and two *s's* separated by the digraph *ai*.

ref"er ee'   Only one *f* in the word.

reg'is trar   The person who keeps the register is a *registrar* not *registrer*.

re li'gious   There are two excellent possibilities of error: *religous* and *riligious*. Avoid both.

rem"i nisce'   The *sc* is often incorrectly abridged to *s* or *c*, since the *s* sound is the only one heard in pronunciation.

res'tau rant   Note the *u* of the second syllable and do not omit it. (In pronunciation, it combines with the *a* which precedes it to produce an *o* sound.)

ret'i cence   There is no *sense* in the word.

rhythm   It is easy to omit the functionless *h* or to substitute an *i* for the *y*. Do neither.

rime   Prefer *rime* to its variant *rhyme*. The latter was formed by false analogy with *rhythm,* and, though otherwise reasonless, has survived. *Rime* is the ascendant spelling and will prevail.

route   Distinguish *route,* "direction," and *rout,* "a confused flight."

S

sal'a ble   Drop the *e* of *sale* in spelling the adjective form; however, *saleable* is also sanctioned.

sar'casm   American pronunciation tends to supply the word with three syllables (*sar cas um*). However, since there is not the necessary vowel immediately before the *m*, the word is a dissyllable.

Sav'iour   When the word refers to Jesus Christ, capitalize it and spell the final syllable with a *u*. In all other contexts, write *savior*.

se ces'sion   This noun is formed from the verb *secede:* remember the verb spelling and you will not be inclined to misspell the noun *sesession*.

sec're tar"y   The unaccented second syllable causes the trouble: neither *secetary* nor *secertary* is literate.

sen'si ble   Perhaps because this word is so frequently used the *able* ending (which is usual with commonly employed adjectives) is appended instead of the *ible* (which is correct).

sep'a rate   Study the middle syllable long and earnestly: it is *a*. The substitution of another vowel is one of the most frequent errors in the whole list.

Shak'spere	Samuel Tennenbaum, the chief authority on Shakspere's signatures, asserts that the dramatist spelled it as given—without the *e* after the *k* or the *a* before the *r*. However, three-quarters of the Shaksperean authorities consulted in a recent study spell the name *Shakespeare*.
shep'herd	The *h* is silent but do not omit it in writing the word.
sig nif'i cant	Two unaccented syllables cause twice as much trouble as one: avoid both *signifacant* and *significent*.
sim'ile	Not *simale*. (Think of *similar*.)
sin cere'ly	Frequently misspelled *sincerly*: the *e* of *sincere* is retained before the suffix *ly*.
smol'der	*Smoulder* is also sanctioned, but the given spelling is preferable.
sol'emn	The terminal *n* is useless but must be included in the spelling.
some'time"	The word spelled without a final *s* means "formerly." (*See* SOMETIMES.)
some'times'	The word spelled with a final *s* means "at times." (*See* SOMETIME.)
sta'tion ar"y	The word thus spelled (—*ary*) means "unmoving." (*See* STATIONERY.)
sta'tion er"y	The word thus spelled (—*ery*) means "writing equipment." (*See* STATIONARY.)
stu pen'dous	The spelling (and pronunciation conforming to it) *stupendious* smacks of the carnival. Avoid it.
sub pe'na	*Subpoena* is sometimes preferred because it is closer to the Latin; but *subpena* is far more frequent.
suc ceed'	Note *ceed:* this is one of the three words in the English language containing that root (the other two being *proceed* and *exceed*).
su'i cide	The *cide* root is often misspelled. It means "kill" and appears in such words as *homicide, fratricide, patricide*.
su per sede'	This is the only English word containing the root *sede*.
sure'ly	Do not omit the *e* of *sure* when adding the suffix *ly* or a very different word will result.
sur prise'	*Suprise* and *surprize* are misspellings resulting from the pronunciation of the word. The former is infantile, the latter obsolete.

syl'la ble
The vowel of the first syllable has the sound of *i* but is represented by *y*. And note that the *y* is followed by two *l's*.

T

ta boo'
Tabu is the alternative spelling.

tax'i
Prefer this spelling to *taxy* for the contraction of *taxicab*.

taxy'ing
The present participle of *taxi* is preferably spelled this way to prevent a conjunction of *i's*.

teas'able
The suffix *able* is almost invariably employed in obviously constructed adjectives, such as this.

the'a ter
Prefer to the British spelling *theatre*.

their
Spelled thus, *their* is a possessive adjective (*their* rights).

there
Spelled thus, *there* is an adverb (*there* goes nothing).

tied, ty'ing
The *ie* of *tie* is retained in the past tense of the verb but changes to *y* in the present participle to avoid a conjunction of *i's*.

till
Two *l's:* The spelling of *until* is not relevant.

trag'e dy
The first syllable has no *d* when written.

tre men'dous
The *dous* termination is infrequent: only two other commonly used words end in *dous: stupendous* and *horrendous*. For that reason it looks somewhat strange, and the attempt to render it more familiar by inserting an *i* (*dious*) is made. Guard against it.

tru'ly
The same secretaries who insert a superfluous *e* in *truly* tend to omit a necessary *e* from *sincerely*.

tur'quoise
The *qu* in the second syllable may have the sound of *kw*. (The word is of French origin, and initially meant "Turkish": the gem was first brought to France from Turkey.)

tyr'an ny
One *r* and two *n's* in this word. There is, apparently, something about *tyranny* that motivates a double *r*. Psychological spellings are interesting but unauthorized.

U

un til'
Only one *l* in this word. *Till* does not, properly, constitute an analogy.

V

val'u a ble
There are four syllables in this word. If you are under the illusion that there are three, the misspelling *valuble* is almost inevitable.

venge'ance
Both the *e* ending one syllable and the *a* beginning the other are necessary. Neither *vengence* nor *vengance* will do.

vict'ual
The pronunciation of this word (*victual* rimes with *whittle*) indicates its spelling only faintly. *Vittle* is a humorous or dialectal spelling. (A knowledge of the word's derivation—it is from the Latin *victum,* "nourishment"—may help in the spelling.)

vil'lain
Some, who triumph over the twofold difficulty of this word and remember to retain all the *l's* and *i's* necessary, nevertheless spell the abstract noun derived from it *villany* (instead of *villainy*).

W

weath'er
There are three homophones: *weather, wether,* and *whether.* The first means "atmospheric conditions"; the second, "a castrated ram"; the third, "in case that."

Wednes'day
This word in itself almost constitutes the argument for simplified spelling: The six letters of the first syllable are pronounced *wenz.* Perhaps remembering that the name of the God *Woden* or *Wodnes,* to whom the day is dedicated, appears in the word in modified form will help the spelling.

weird
This violates the *i* before *e* rule: recognize and remember.

whis'key
Whiskey and *whisky* are both used by the people who make the stuff. American distillers, however, seem to prefer *whiskey,* whereas British distillers like *whisky.* (NOTE: The plural of *whisky* is *whiskies;* the plural of *whiskey* is *whiskeys.*)

Y

your

Distinguish between the possessive adjective *your* (*your* trick) and *you're*, the contraction of you are (*you're* the tops).

Z

zig'zag"

Write solid. The past tense and present participle forms are *zigzagged* and *zigzagging*.

zo-ol'o gy

Take your choice of *zo-ology*, *zoölogy*, or *zoology*. But shun *zoo-ology*.

BOOK FIVE

Punctuation

The Importance of Punctuation

Modern punctuation has a variety of important functions. One of the most fundamental is that of insuring clarity. Consider one of Halliwell's *Nursery Rhymes:*

> Every lady in this land
> Has twenty nails upon each hand
> Five and twenty on hands and feet
> All this is true without deceit.

The only statement which is not plainly nonsense is the last; and that is plainly untrue. Yet the insertion of a couple of small points makes the verse not quite a monument to man's reasoning powers, but at least relatively sensible:

> Every lady in this land
> Has twenty nails; upon each hand
> Five; and twenty on hands and feet.
> All this is true without deceit.

The lack of a clear and comprehensive system of punctuation has resulted in all kinds of scholarly feuds, some of them still active and acrimonious. Lawyers pounce avidly on any constructions rendered dubious by improper punctuation. And once the uncalled-for insertion of a comma cost the United States about two million dollars. In a tariff bill, a number of articles were enumerated as being admissible free of duty. Among them were "foreign fruit-plants." The clerk who transcribed the bill changed the hyphen to a comma, inadvertently, thus changing the reading to "foreign fruit, plants," etc. For the next year all oranges, lemons, grapes, bananas, and coconuts were allowed in without import taxes being levied on them.

Brief History of Punctuation

The history of punctuation consists largely of a series of guesses. Still, it illuminates much. We should not, for example, advise you to bet money on the conjecture that the exclamation point derives from an accented period. But— whether an item of romance or history—it does shed light on the real nature of the exclamation point.

It was formerly customary to trace punctuation to Aldus Manutius, a sixteenth-century Venetian printer. However, manuscripts dating as far back as the fourth century B.C. have rudimentary pointing. The period is even older: in the earliest stone inscriptions a dot is sometimes placed after each word to separate it from the one following. After some degree of sophistication had been reached, the period was placed after each separable fragment; and finally (in about the eighth century A.D.) the modern use of the period as a full stop evolved.[1]

Aldus Manutius, though he did not invent punctuation, certainly did more than anyone to systematize it. Printers adopted his improvisations, and added others of their own. The comma, at first a 7, then a slash (/), eventually became altered to its present form. The semicolon, which Skelton calls "a sort of master comma," was adapted from the Greek question mark. Our own question mark probably has the semicolon as its source. It has been suggested that printers, "finding that the inverted semicolon broke the alignment of the type, substituted an upright comma over the period and so created the question mark."[2]

[1] It was sometimes placed on a level with the top of the last word of the sentence, sometimes with the center, sometimes with the base.

[2] Another possibility: that the early manuscript writers put a Q (for question) over the period; later, to speed matters up, they wrote the letter with a single stroke and evolved our present question mark.

The quotation marks in English, it seems likely, derive from the parallel markings (like elongated accents) which set off quotations in German. Probably commas, the first set inverted, were substituted since they were immediately at hand.[1] A similar expediency may have dictated the use of the raised comma for the apostrophe.

The only thing certain about this vastly hypothetical history is that punctuation has developed in haphazard fashion. Printers improvised. Other printers borrowed the improvisations and added some of their own. When the systematizers got to work, they were confronted with contradictory practices. They resolved them as best they could, but never quite achieved order. While less chaotic, the present state of punctuation is hardly as definite as the "rules" to be found in most manuals would seem to indicate.

The Two Conventions of Punctuation

Mason, in his *Elocution* (1748), may not have started the trouble, but he certainly increased it by his unambiguous declaration: "A comma," he wrote, "stops the voice while we may privately tell one; a semicolon, two; a colon, three; and a period, four." This "elocutionary" or "rhetorical" pointing corresponds somewhat to practice, and it has been accepted widely by the uncritical. John Wilson's *Treatise on Punctuation* (1884) stated the more modern view, that punctuation indicates the relationship of one sentence element to another and of sentences to each other: ". . . on the whole, it will be found that the art of Punctuation is founded rather on grammar than on rhetoric; that its chief aim is to unfold the meaning of sentences, with the least trouble to the reader; and that it aids the delivery, only in so far as it tends to bring out the sense of the writer to the best advantage."

That punctuation is essentially grammatical may easily be demonstrated by employing a notation suited for the platform rather than the page:

> Men of superior genius; while they see the rest of mankind,
> painfully struggling, to comprehend obvious truths; glance,

[1] Guillaume Morel, King's Printer of Paris, is credited with first deploying the commas as quotes.

themselves, through the remote consequences; like lightning, through a path, that cannot be traced; they see the beauties of nature, with light and warmth, and paint them forcibly, without effort; as the morning sun, does the scenes he rises upon, communicate to objects, a morning freshness, and unaccountable lustre, that is not seen in the creations of nature. The poet, the statuary, the painter, have produced images, that left nature far behind.

Perhaps a modern speaker (assuming he would construct such a paragraph) would regard "the real pauses demanded by an accurate and effective delivery" to be not quite so extensive nor so prolonged. Nevertheless, the vocal pauses and the written pauses would, under any circumstances, exhibit wide differences.

All this is true without deceit: do not let us, therefore, undermine the rhetorical base which exists for some punctuation. The question mark and the exclamation mark, for example, cue the speaker (always somewhere in the background of all discourse). The one informs him that the voice is to assume a questioning tone; the other that a degree of emotion is to be infused in the utterance.

Essential Punctuation: Clarity

The *New English Dictionary* defines punctuation as "the practice, art, method, or system of inserting points or 'stops' to aid the sense in writing or printing." *To aid the sense* is a composite phrase. Most obviously it means "to help attain maximum clarity"—"to fulfil that aim which George Meredith beautifully states of a clear style, that it 'may be read out currently at a first glance.' "[1] This may be saying a fraction too much; but it is, at any rate, undeniable that an important function is to prevent misreading "at a first glance." Consequently, we consider it advisable to place a warning comma after introductory elements—even if they are short. Thus, in *Though I wander, home is my haven,* without the comma to warn the eye, one might initially read *Though I wander home.* Upon rereading, of course, the meaning becomes manifest. But the necessity of rereading would be

[1]S. A. Leonard, *The Rationale of Punctuation: A Criticism.*

obviated by a "warning comma."[1] Therefore, though "the less punctuation, the better" is a good guide, and though most authorities regard the comma after short introductory clauses and phrases as optional, we nevertheless hold that the option should often be exercised by placing the comma after such introductory elements.

Similarly, all punctuation which renders immediately plain what might otherwise be even temporarily dubious is more than merely sanctionable. We ought to have no hesitation about taking sides in the old debate about the placement of a comma before the last item of a series with *and*. *Paint, pomade, and eau de rose* is preferable to *paint, pomade and eau de rose* because the comma indicates that the series is about to terminate. Proper punctuation lubricates reading. *At OCS he learned a little—a very little—about each of these subjects: First Aid and Sanitation, Military Mathematics, Surveying, Military Strategy and Tactics* may really include one subject less than . . . *Surveying, Military Strategy, and Tactics.*

Essential Punctuation: Emphasis

Punctuation "to aid the sense," though, includes more than inserting stops for the sake of clarity. Emphasis is not less important. "Pointing," one authority declares, "must be conditioned by the immediate and often complex substance of . . . meaning."[2] A simpler statement of the same principle is that punctuation should denote the "quality of connection"; that is, "show in what relation to one another sentences, or parts of sentences, are intended to stand."[3]

Consider the rather complex punctuation of that last sentence. The semicolon was employed to point the large break in the argument of the sentence rather than the colon, dash, comma, or period—all of which were possibilities—because the connection was felt to be intimate and co-ordinate. Be-

[1] A more obvious example: *If the cannibals eat John, Henry, her father, will be displeased.* Everybody would agree that the comma after *John* is necessary to prevent the reading of *John Henry.*

[2] Constance Rourke, *The Rationale of Punctuation.*

[3] Robert Graves and Allen Hodge, *The Reader Over Your Shoulder.*

cause intimate, the period was not employed; because co-ordinate, neither the dash nor the colon was employed. Then why not the comma? Because the other commas in the sentence might cause the emphasis to be misplaced.

"Essential punctuation" implies the proper relation of ideas. Subordination and equality; contrast and apposition; what is parenthetical and what is primary—all these are to be considered when placing a point. The significance of these alternative punctuations ought to convince those still unconvinced:

> Woman—without her, man would be a savage.
> Woman, without her man, would be a savage.

The Flexibility of Punctuation

The Government Printing Office *Style Manual* states:

> Punctuation is a device to clarify the meaning of written or printed language. Well-planned word order requires a minimum of punctuation. The trend toward less punctuation calls for skillful phrasing to avoid ambiguity and insure exact interpretation.
>
> The general principles governing the use of punctuation are (1) that if it does not clarify the text it should be omitted and (2) that in the choice and placing of punctuation marks the sole aim should be to bring out more clearly the author's thought.

Clarity is not, as we have seen, the only operating principle. Emphatic and rhetorical pointing are also to be taken into account. And even "the kind of paper, the size and kind of text type, the presswork, the binding, and design," according to one authority,[1] must be considered.

These, of course, are matters for the printer. He is an important man in the development of punctuation. The rules which most publishing houses work by have been formulated by him. Since he is chiefly concerned with the consistency of the style and the appearance of the type-page, his rules are not those which the writer can always employ happily. When the circumstance is such—then the writer may employ whatever punctuation he chooses.

[1] George Summey, Jr., *Modern Punctuation.*

edward estlin cummings (who does not capitalize the initial letters of his name) has created a startling system of punctuation which accords with his (apparent) purposes. Once, poetry was read aloud; and the reader accelerated or retarded his reading pace to conform to meaning. Today, unfortunately, poetry is read silently. Cummings, by dislocating standard punctuation, can make the silent reader hurry or halt:

> by jingo by gee by gosh by gum
> why talk of beauty what could be more beautiful
> than the heroic happy dead . . .

James Joyce, Robert Bridges, Ezra Pound, John Dos Passos, and a host of others have felt themselves constrained to depart from the norms of punctuation. (More power to them!) Nor is their revolt unprecedented. Whitman, who supervised the type-setting of *Leaves of Grass,* decided upon a system of punctuation as heterodox as his poetry. If it was self-contradictory, very well: it contradicted itself. More important, though, it advanced his stated aims; it conduced to a larger, freer expression.

These instances are cited as encouragement for the timid. If any mechanical rule of punctuation limits full expression, that rule should unhesitatingly be rejected. But—a large *but* —it is important to know the rules before rejecting them. The reader does not consciously examine punctuation; he is interested, rather, in what is being punctuated. Violations of standard usage, however, cause him to take notice of the secondary (punctuation) at the expense of the primary (communication). This "diffusion of concentration," as Spencer called it, may be necessary; it ought never be thought a good in itself.

The Tendency of Modern Punctuation

As little punctuation as intelligible communication demands—that is the guiding principle of modern punctuation. George Summey, Jr., has counted the number of points per sentence for a number of authors, past and present. The lushest punctuator of all is Walter Pater who averages more than seven points a sentence.[1] Henry James is very nearly as luxuriant in his employment of punctuation marks: he uses almost seven per sentence. Thomas Carlyle ranks third, with about four and a half points per sentence. H. G. Wells, G. K. Chesterton, and Arnold Bennett—moderns all—have about a two and a half sentence-point average. Ernest Hemingway has the lowest average we have been able to discover: he needs less than one and one-half marks of punctuation per sentence.

Newspapers, which influence punctuation tendencies to the greatest extent, average about two points per sentence. Magazines such as *Time* and *Life* punctuate less sparingly, employing about three marks per sentence.

These statistics are significant. They prove that punctuation (like diction, grammar, or even spelling) evolves in the direction of simplicity. The "rules" become less rigid, the areas of choice larger.

The Logic of Punctuation

American punctuation finds its sanction in custom rather than in logic. There is no good reason for placing the period and comma within quotes; and the colon, the semicolon, the dash, the question mark, and the exclamation point outside except when they are part of the quoted matter. It would certainly be more reasonable to put *all* marks within quotes *only* when they are integral parts of the quotation, and to punctuate the portion of the sentence outside the quotes as if it had a separate existence. Thus we might write

Who asked "What plays?"?

or even

Who asked "Who asked 'What plays?'?"?

[1] It was Pater, incidentally, who declared for the pruning of all surplusage in punctuation. This is how he made the declaration:

"Say what you have to say, what you have a will to say, in the simplest, the most direct and exact manner possible, with no surplusage:—there, is the justification of the sentence so fortunately born, 'entire, smooth, and round,' that it needs no punctuation, and also (that is the point!) of the most elaborate period, if it be right in its elaboration."

This happens to be "the most elaborately pointed" passage which came under Mr. Summey's scrutiny.

instead of, as standard usage would require,

> Who asked "What plays?"

or

> Who asked "Who asked 'What plays?' "

It would not be a too difficult job to construct a logical system of punctuation. Of course, such a system would cause a substantial increase in the number of type-setters having nervous breakdowns. But that is not the big reason for avoiding originality in punctuation. The big reason is the one we have already indicated (along with the conditions warranting exception): that the reader has accepted a convention, and that by upsetting the convention you upset the reader. Scene designers are content to have audiences accept the convention of a three-walled room; they do not feel that logic compels them to construct rooms with four walls.

Henry W. Fowler in *The King's English* offers the following instances of logical punctuation. (Note that English usage prefers the single quotes.)

1. It is enough for us to reflect that 'Such shortlived wits do wither as they grow'.
2. We hear that 'whom the gods love die young'.
3. 'Certainly not;' he exclaimed 'I would have died rather'.
4. 'I cannot guess' he retorted 'what you mean'.
5. How absurd to ask 'Can a thing both be and not be?'!

The third and fourth sentences omit the punctuation, because "Words that interrupt quotations should never be allowed stops to part them from the quotation"—the quotation marks themselves are sufficient indication of the points at which the quotation breaks and is resumed. The other punctuation of these two sentences seems somewhat deficient in logic. Since *rather* and *mean* end their respective quotations, they ought each to be followed by a period: '. . . rather.'. ; '. . . mean.'.

The sentences, if we want to conform to almost completely accepted American practice,[1] should be rewritten as follows:

1. It is enough for us to reflect that "Such shortlived wits do wither as they grow."

[1] The chief exception is in scholarly quotation. There a system resembling Fowler's is generally employed.

2. We hear that "whom the gods love die young."
3. "Certainly not," he exclaimed; "I would have died rather."
4. "I cannot guess," he retorted, "what you mean."
5. How absurd to ask "Can a thing both be and not be?"

The punctuation of the last sentence could allowably correspond to Fowler's. It would, though, as he suggests, be better to rewrite it. (*"Can a thing both be and not be?" The question is absurd.*)

We have devoted this much space to Fowler's system because all tendencies indicate that it will triumph in the end. However: the end is not yet. Pope's advice is relevant:

> In words, as fashions, the same rule will hold,
> Alike fantastic if too new or old:
> Be not the first by whom the new are tried,
> Nor yet the last to lay the old aside.

Open and Close Punctuation

Open punctuation is the name given to the modern tendency of punctuating lightly—going easy on the marks. It is also, as a consequence, called **light** or **easy punctuation**. The opposite tendency, gleefully pointing wherever possible, is called **close punctuation**. The ultimate of open punctuation is perhaps achieved in the last chapter of James Joyce's *Ulysses* where the reader may find eighty or so punctuationless pages. The reverse extreme was popular in the seventeenth century and later: John Donne in his *Sermons* sets off each phrase by means of one or another mark.

Samuel Johnson used what we should today call an extremely close style in *Taxation No Tyranny*. Here is a specimen sentence:

> The necessary connexion of representatives with taxes, seems to have sunk deep into many of those minds, that admit sounds, without their meaning.

Clarence Stratton's version of the same sentence includes only one mark: the period at the end. But Samuel Johnson knew what he was about—in relation to punctuation if not to taxation. Every mark is thoroughly justifiable by his system: the comma after *taxes* because long subjects were thus separated from their predicates; the comma after *minds* because subordinate clauses were thus detached from their main clauses; the comma after *sounds* because a phrasal modifier that came after the word modified was thus set off.

Whether you should adopt a close or open system (and either is possible within the limits of the current code of punctuation) depends on your style and your subject. Sentence movement is the controlling consideration. A long and heavily freighted sentence requires more points than a short and simple sentence. Henry James's complex style demands a relatively close system of punctuation; Ernest Hemingway's forthright style determines the light system he employs.

This much modern authorities are agreed upon: that most people employ a much heavier and tighter system than their sentences warrant. They are less interested in communicating their thoughts as directly as may be than they are in avoiding the appearance of ignorance in regard to the conventions of punctuation.

The Options of Punctuation

The National Council of Teachers of English submitted eighty-one questions on punctuation to the leading publishing houses, magazines, and newspapers in the country. The answers of the judges prove that to speak of "standard punctuation" is very nearly meaningless.[1] Almost all of our rules are challenged by the men from whose practice the rules are supposed to stem.

You were taught that the elements of a compound sentence must be separated by a comma if they are linked by a co-ordinating conjunction. The judges favored a comma when the clauses are long, but no comma when they are short.[2]

You were taught to put a semicolon before *so, for, yet, however, hence* with co-ordinate clauses. The judges favor

---

[1]*Current English Usage.* The volume appeared in 1932, but we have not caught up to many of its usages in punctuation yet.

[2]Except, as in this instance, where the elements are joined by *but*.

the comma before *so* and *for* overwhelmingly; they are equally divided between the comma and the semicolon before *yet;* they favor the semicolon before *hence* by two to one. Only before *however* do they insist on the semicolon— and even in this instance there are dissenting voices.

You were taught that an introductory adverbial clause had to be set off by commas. If it is long or if misinterpretation would result were the comma omitted—certainly, the judges agree. But if the clause is short—not necessarily.

You were taught that the sin of sins in punctuation was the "comma splice" (placing a comma instead of a period between sentences). Yet the judges rank the comma as an established usage when there are "special circumstances of [sentence] structure or momentum."[1]

The conclusions that the National Council of Teachers of English came to and the recommendations that they made will powerfully influence both the theory and practice of punctuation for a long time to come. The study already has had definite and observable effects in liberalizing both. This is noteworthy because teachers are notably (not to say notoriously) conservative in adopting new and discarding old linguistic forms. They are, understandably, afraid of floods if the dam is weakened, however slightly. Allow an occasional, even an exceptional, comma where the period is normally required and the period will become obsolete, they fear. Miss Weeks, in her highly intelligent introduction to *Current English Usage* does much to dispel the fear: "Freed . . . from the crushing load of outworn formalities," the teacher shall perhaps have time to stimulate in his students "the clarified thought from which alone a composition worth punctuating results."

The three clear and practical findings of the study are:

1. That few points are "required." Options are plentifully present. The meaning and movement of the sentence is to be considered above all else in preferring one point to another.

[1]The sentence the judges approved by a large majority, though there was a good deal of disagreement: *This book is valueless, that one has more to recommend it.*

2. That there is a marked tendency toward open punctuation. Other things being equal, the fewer the marks the better.

3. That where punctuation depends on meaning, agreement as to usage is general among experts; but where punctuation depends not on principles but on formal rules, the doctors disagree greatly.

Punctuation for the Plain Man

Enough theory. Let us become basic. Let us try to see what each specific mark means. Let us attempt a streamlined, simplified analysis. There are nine marks of punctuation generally employed: the period, comma, semicolon, colon, dash, parentheses, brackets, exclamation point, and question (or interrogation) mark. These are the substitutes in writing for pause, pitch, tone, accent, inflection, stress, and gesture in talking. Some "cue the ear; others guide the eye."

Imagine a sentence—a complete thought—trying to make the distance from writer to reader. These are what the following marks indicate concerning the stages of its progress. (Each of the descriptions illustrates the relevant point.)

1. **The period:** the thought is completed. The progress is accomplished, and so the sentence comes to a full stop. (The period is also called a **full stop.**)

2. **The comma:** the thought is joined by another, somewhat separate thought. The comma sets it off, indicates its separateness, and then carries it along.

3. **The semicolon:** the thought is joined by a separate but co-ordinate thought; the two proceed together, arm in arm, toward the goal.

4. **The colon:** the thought has subdivisions which must be indicated: an explanation, perhaps, or an example, or a listing, or a restatement in parallel fashion of the main thought.

5. **The dash:** the thought is interrupted—*dashes* off its main course—and then is resumed. Or the dash introduces

a summary word (acts like a colon in reverse)—in which case it may be called a *summation dash*.

6. **The parentheses:** the thought is interrupted by another thought, not unconnected (or it would not be included within the body of the sentence) but not immediately relevant.

7. **The brackets:** the thought is commented on, or an omission or a correction is indicated frequently [compare this instance] in such a way that a footnote would be a suitable substitute, since the matter added is not properly part of the text.

8. **The exclamation point:** the thought is completed. And a startling thought it is! Conveyed with what emotional charge!

9. **The question mark:** the thought is completed, but how is it conveyed? Positively? Then the period ought to stop it. Emotionally? Then the exclamation point ought to stop it. So that it seems to require an answer? Then the question mark ought to stop it.

There are other marks, of course, which do not aid the movement of the sentence—at least not in quite the same way. The *hyphen,* the *apostrophe,* the *brace,* the *caret,* the *ellipsis,* and the *quotation marks* may be called "notational marks": they enable the writer to note in shorthand fashion what his intentions are.

1. **The hyphen:** tells the reader that a particular word-group has the force of a single word.

2. **The apostrophe:** tells the reader that there's a word that's been contracted.

3. **The brace:** tells the reader that (a) words ⎫ have a
(b) ideas ⎬ common
(c) facts ⎭ element.

4. **The ellipsis:** tells the reader that "something . . . has been omitted." (The words omitted between *something* and *has* in the preceding quotation were: "which could not be supplied, or which it was thought unnecessary to supply.")

l   word

5. **The caret:** tells the reader to insert the ^etter or ^which is placed directly above it.

6. **The quotation marks (quotes):** tell the reader that, as one authority puts it, "the words quoted are not those of the present writer."

Once more: the above analysis is not complete. It does not attempt to list all the uses of the various points. It does, however, give what—both historically and currently—are the fundamental uses, those from which the confusing variety of other uses have developed. If these few essential functions are understood, it will be difficult to go far wrong in punctuating; and the other functions, which are extensions of these, will become easy as π is to the mathematician.

BOOK SIX

Dictionary of Punctuation

A

Abbreviations

1. Abbreviations are used to save space and to avoid distracting the mind of the reader by a repetition of long, cumbersome words or phrases.

The nature of the publication governs the extent to which abbreviations are used. In text of technical and legal publications and in parentheses, footnotes, sidenotes, tables, leader work, and bibliographies, many words are commonly abbreviated; but in ordinary text, especially in formal writing, few abbreviations are used.

Some scientific, technical, and industrial groups have adopted definite forms of abbreviations for terms in their specialized fields, and these forms are acceptable for use in publications falling within the respective classes.

The same forms of abbreviations should be used throughout a job. Standard and easily understood forms are preferable. Abbreviations not generally known should be followed in the text by the spelled-out forms in parentheses the first time they occur; in tabular work such explanatory matter should be supplied in a footnote. As the printer cannot rewrite the copy, the author should supply these explanatory forms.

Abbreviations of measure should be used only with figures; similarly many other abbreviations should not appear in isolation; for example: *Pressure is measured in foot-pounds,* not *Pressure is measured in ft.-lb.; John was graduated with a bachelor of arts degree,* not *John was graduated with a B.A. degree; Boise is on mountain standard time,* not *Boise is on m.s.t.*

Avoid dividing the elements of a single abbreviation, such as *a.m., kw.-hr., f.o.b.,* and *G.m.a.t.,* at the end of a line.

2. The following abbreviations are in general use:

A.B. or **B.A.,** bachelor of arts
ab ex. (*ab extra*), from without
ab init. (*ab initio*) from the beginning
abs. re (*absente reo*), the defendant being absent
a.c., alternating current
A.D. (*anno Domini*), in the year of our Lord
ad fin. (*ad finem*), to the end
ad h. l. (*ad hunc locum*), at the place
ad inf. (*ad infinitum*), to infinity
ad init. (*ad initium*), at the beginning
ad int. (*ad interim*), in the interim
ad lib. (*ad libitum*), at pleasure
ad loc. (*ad locum*), at the place
ad us. (*ad usum*), according to custom
ad val. (*ad valorem*), according to the value
AEF, American Expeditionary Forces
a.k.a., also known as
A.M. (*anno mundi*), the year of the world
A.M. or **M.A.** (*Artium Magister*), master of arts
a.m. (*ante meridiem*), before noon
antilog (no period) antilogarithm

approx., approximately
A.S.N., Army serial number (assigned each man)
A.s.t., Atlantic standard time
A.t., Atlantic time
A.U.C. (*anno urbis conditae*), in the year the city (Rome) was founded
AUS, Army of the United States
Ave., avenue
a.w.l., absent with leave (over leave)
a.w.o.l., absent without (official) leave
B.C., before Christ
b. hp., brake horsepower
Bldg., building
B. Lit(t). or **Lit(t). B.,** bachelor of literature
Blvd., boulevard
b.o., buyer's option
b.p., boiling point
b.p.d., barrels per day
B.S. or **B. Sc.,** bachelor of science
B. t. u., British thermal units
ca. (*circa*), about
cc., cubic centimeter
C. Cls., Court of Claims
C. Cls. R., Court of Claims Reports
cd.-ft., cord-foot
cf. (confer), compare
c.f.m., cubic feet per minute

c.f.s., cubic feet per second

c.-h., candle-hour

c.i.f., cost, insurance, and freight

c.m., circular mil (wire measure)

c.o.d., cash on delivery

cos (no period), cosine

cot (no period), cotangent

c.p., chemically pure

c.p.a., certified public accountant

csc (no period), cosecant

c.s.t., central standard time

Ct., court

c.t., central time

db (no period), decibel

d.b.a., doing business as

d.c., direct current

D.D. (*Divinitatis Doctor*), doctor of divinity

D.D.S., doctor of dental surgery

D. Lit(t). or Lit(t).D., doctor of literature

D.V.M., doctor of veterinary medicine

do. (*ditto*), the same

D.P.H., doctor of public health

D.P. Hy., doctor of public hygiene

Dr., doctor; drive

e.d.t., eastern daylight time

e.g. (*exempli gratia*), for example

8°, octavo

e.m.f., electromotive force

e.o.m., end of month

e.s.t., eastern standard time

e.s.u., electrostatic unit

e.t., eastern time

et al. (*et alii, et aliae*), and others

etc. (*et cetera*), and so forth

et seq. (*et sequentes, et sequientia*), and the following

et ux. (*et uxor*), and wife

et vir. (*et viri*), and husband

f., ff., and following page (pages)

f.a.s., free along ship

f.o.b., free on board

F.R.S., Fellow of the Royal Society

f°, folio

4°, quarto

G.A.R., Grand Army of the Republic

g.c.d., greatest common divisor

G. c.t., Greenwich civil time

G.m.a.t., Greenwich mean astronomical time

G.m.t., Greenwich mean time

HE (no periods), high explosive

hp., horsepower

ibid. (*ibidem*), in the same place

id. (*idem*), the same

i.e. (*id est*), that is

i.h.p., indicated horsepower

infra dig. (*infra dignitatem*), undignified

in lim. (*in limine*), at the outset

in.² or sq. in., square inch

in.³ or cu. in., cubic inch

I O U (no periods), I owe you

i.q. (*idem quod*), the same as

I.Q., intelligence quotient

jg (no periods), junior grade

K. C. B., Knight Commander of the Bath

kv.-a., kilovolt-ampere

kw.-hr., kilowatt-hour

lat., latitude

lb. ap., pound, apothecary's

lb. av., pound, avoirdupois

l.c.l., less than carload lot

l.c.m., least common multiple

LL. B. (*Legum Baccalaureus*), bachelor of laws

LL. D. (*Legum Doctor*), doctor of laws

loc. cit. (*loco citato*), in the place cited

log (no period), logarithm

long., longitude

l.t., local time

l.s.t., local standard time

M (no period), thousand

m (*meridies*), noon

M.b.m., thousand (feet) board measure

memo (no period), memorandum

m.m.f., magnetomotive force

m.p., melting point

ms. mss., manuscript, manuscripts

m.s.t., mountain standard time

m.t., mountain time

n.b. (*nota bene*), note well, take notice

NED, *New English Dictionary* (Oxford)

n.e.s., not elsewhere specified

n.l. (*non licet*), it is not permitted; (*non liquet*), it is not clear

No., Nos., no., nos., number, numbers

n.o.i.b.n., not otherwise indexed by name

nol-pros (*nolle prosequi*), to be unwilling to prosecute

non-pros (*non prosequi*), to be unwilling to prosecute

non seq. (*non sequitur*), it does not follow

n.o.p., not otherwise provided for

N.S., New Style (after 1752)

n.s.p.f., not specifically provided for

o.c., on center

O. K., O. K.'d, O. K.'ing, O. K.'s, correct

op. cit. (*opere citato*), in the work cited

O.S., Old Style (before 1752)

pct., percent (no period), per centum

p.ex. (*par example*), for example

Pfc (no periods), private first class

Phar. D., doctor of pharmacy

Ph.B. or B.Ph., bachelor of philosophy

Ph.D. or D.Ph., doctor of philosophy

Ph.G., graduate in pharmacy

Pl., place

p.m. (*post meridiem*), afternoon

PMLA, *Publications of the Modern Language Association*

p.o.d., pay on delivery

p.o.r., pay on return

p.p.i., policy proof of interest

pp.m., parts per million

p., pp., page, pages

p.q., previous question

pro tem. (*pro tempore*), temporarily

P.S. (*post scriptum*), postcript

p.s.i., pounds per square inch

P.s.t., Pacific standard time

P.t., Pacific time

p.t.o., please turn over

q., qq., question, questions

Q. E. D. (*quod erat demonstrandum*), which was to be demonstrated

q.v. (*quod vide*), which see

radar (no periods), radio aircraft discovery and recognition

Rd., road

r.f., radio frequency

r.p.m., revolutions per minute

r.p.s., revolutions per second

R. R., railroad

Ry., railway

sc. (*scilicet*), namely (*see also* ss)

sd (*sine die*), without date

sec (no period), secant

sec-ft., second-foot

2d, second

ser., series

sic (no period), thus

sin (no period), sine

s.l. (*sine loco*), without place

s.o., seller's option

S1c (no periods), seaman first class

S O S (no periods), wireless distress signal

s.p. (*sine prole*), without issue

sp. gr., specific gravity

Sq., square

ss (no period) (*scilicet*), namely (in law) (*see also* SC.)

S.S., steamship

St., Ste., SS., Saint, Sainte, Saints

St., street

T., Tps., township, townships

tan (no period), tangent

TB (no periods), tuberculosis

Ter., terrace

3d, third

t.l.o., total loss only

t.m., true mean

TNT (no periods), trinitrotoluol

U. S. A., United States of America

U. S. Army, United States Army

U S 40 (no periods), U.S. No. 40 (with periods), United States Highway No. 40

U.S.S.R., Union of Soviet Socialist Republics

u.t., universal time

v. or **vs.** (*versus*), against

viz (no period) (*videlicet*), namely

wf (no periods), wrong font

WMAL, etc. (no periods), radio station

Titles

In other than formal usage, a civil, military, or naval title preceding a name is abbreviated if followed by Christian name or initial; but *Mr., Mrs., M., MM., Messrs., Mlle., Mme.,* and *Dr.* are abbreviated with or without Christian name or initial.

Adjt.	Insp. Gen.	Prof.
Adjt. Gen.	Judge Adv. Gen.	Pvt.
Asst. Surg.	Lt.	Q. M. Gen.
Brig. Gen.	Lt. Col.	Q. M. Sgt.
Capt.	Lt. Comdr.	Rear Adm.
Col.	Lt. Gen.	Sic (no periods)
Com. Sgt.	Lt. Gov.	Second Lt.
Corp.	Lt. (jg)	Sgt.
First Lt.	Maj.	Sgt. Maj.
First Sgt.	Maj. Gen.	Supt.
Gen.	Orderly Sgt.	SURG.
Gov.	Ord. Sgt. (Ordnance Sergeant)	Surg. Gen.
Hosp. Sgt.	Pfc (no periods)	Surg. Maj.

The following abbreviations are authorized by the Government Printing Office:

(1) **Days of the Week**

Mon.	Wed.	Fri.	Sun.
Tues.	Thurs.	Sat.	

(2) Compass Direction

N.	S.	ESE.
NE.	NNW.	10° N. 25° W.
E.	W.	NW. by N. ¼ W.
SW.		

(3) Temperature and Gravity

C., centigrade	R., Réaumur	B., Baumé
F., Fahrenheit	K., Kelvin	API, American Petroleum
Cel., Celsius	Abs., absolute	Institute

(4) Parts of Publications

art., arts. (article, articles)
bull., bulls. (bulletin, bulletins)
ch., chs. (chapter, chapters)
fig., figs. (figure, figures)
No., Nos. (number, numbers)
p., pp. (page, pages)
par., pars. (paragraph, paragraphs)
pl., pls. (plate, plates)

pt., pts. (part, parts)
sec., secs. (section, sections)
subpar., subpars. (subparagraph,
  subparagraphs)
subsec., subsecs. (subsection, sub-
  sections)
supp., supps. (supplement, sup-
  plements)
vol., vols. (volume, volumes)

(5) Months of the Year

Jan.	Mar.	Aug.	Oct.	Dec.
Feb.	Apr.	Sept.	Nov.	

(6) Latitude and Longitude

lat. 52° 33′ 05″ N.   long. 13° 21′ 10″ E.

(7) Length

in., inch   ft., foot   yd., yard   mile(s), not abbreviated

(8) Weight

gr., grain	oz., ounce	cwt., hundredweight
dr., dram	lb., pound	dwt., pennyweight
		ton(s), not abbreviated

(9) Area and Volume

sq. in., in.^{2}, square inch   sq. mile (s), square mile (s)
cu. in., in.^{3}, cubic inch   cu. ft., cubic foot

(10) Time

yr., year	min., minute
mo., month	sec., second
day, not abbreviated	(10 a.m. 2:30 p.m.
hr., hour	12 a.m.—noon 12 p.m.—midnight)

(11) Capacity

gill (s), not abbreviated	gal., gallon	bu., bushel
pt., pint	pk., peck	bbl., barrel
qt., quart		

(12) Abbreviations for States, Territories, and Insular Possessions

Ala.	Ga.	Miss.	N. Y.	Tex.
Ariz.	Ill.	Mo.	Okla.	T. H.
Ark.	Ind.	Mont.	Oreg.	Va.
Calif.	Kans.	N. C.	Pa.	V. I.
Colo.	Ky.	N. Dak.	P. I.	Vt.
Conn.	La.	Nebr.	P. R.	Wash.
C. Z.	Mass.	Nev.	R. I.	Wis.
D. C.	Md.	N. H.	S. C.	W. Va.
Del.	Mich.	N. J.	S. Dak.	Wyo.
Fla.	Minn.	N. Mex.	Tenn.	

Apostrophe

1. The apostrophe is used—

   (a) To indicate a contraction.

   it's, e'er, shouldn't

   (b) To form the coined plurals of letters, figures, symbols, and of words referred to as words.

   W. C. T. U.'s p's and q's 2 by 4's and's, if's, and but's.

   (c) To form the possessive case.

   John's Joneses' Burns' Schmitz'
   The Speaker of the House's ruling (The last word of a phrasal group or of a compound expression takes the apostrophe.)

NOTE: Normally, the apostrophe and *s* are added even if the word ends with *s* —as indicated. However, if the syllable before the last ends with an *s*, most authorities agree that only the apostrophe ought be added: *e.g., Moses'*,

Jesus'. Again, if the word ending in *s* is polysyllabic, or if it is accented on the last syllable, it is better to add only the apostrophe: *e.g., Aristophanes', Sophocles'*.

2. The apostrophe in such Irish names as *O'Neil* and *O'Connor* is allied to the possessive apostrophe. (A single turned comma, not an apostrophe, is frequently used in the abbreviation of the Scotch *Mac; e.g., M'Gregor*.)

3. The apostrophe is omitted in abbreviations.

Dr. Mr. Danl. Sgr.

NOTE: Unlike the contraction, the abbreviation retains the original sound-values of the word—that is, *Dr.* and *Doctor* are pronounced the same way.

B

Bibliography

Except that the surname is placed before the Christian name, each item in the bibliography is identical with the footnote citation for the initial reference to a book. (*See* FOOTNOTE.)

Brace

The brace is used to show the relation of one line or group of lines to another group of lines. The point is placed toward the fewer number of lines; or, if the number of lines is the same, toward the single group.

Supervision of timber sales
{
  1-hour jobs {
    District 1
    " 7
    " 6 } $1\frac{1}{2}$ hours' travel time
  2-hour jobs {
    " 4 } 1 hour's travel time
  3-hour jobs {
    " 2
    " 3
    " 5 } 2 hours' travel time
} Sales conducted monthly from May to June

Three Johns
{
1. The real John; known only to his Maker.
2. John's ideal John; never the real one, and often very unlike him.
3. Thomas's ideal John; never the real John, nor John's John, but often very unlike either.

$$\text{Three Thomases} \begin{cases} 1. \text{ The real Thomas} \\ 2. \text{ Thomas's ideal Thomas} \\ 3. \text{ John's ideal Thomas} \end{cases}$$

Brackets

1. **Brackets** (or **crotchets**), in pairs, **are used—**

   (a) To indicate a correction, a supplied omission, or an interpolation.

   > He died on the 3d [2d] of July.
   > The general [Washington] ordered him to leave.
   > The paper was as follows [read]:
   > They fooled only themselves. [Laughter.]
   > Our party will always serve the people [applause], in spite of the opposition [loud applause].
   > The bill has *not* been paid. [Italics ours.]

   (b) In bills, contracts, etc., to indicate matter that is to be omitted.

   (c) In math, to denote that enclosed matter is to be treated as a unit.

   (d) A **single bracket** may be used to indicate matter overrun into an adjoining blank space.

   > [of all.
   > Till one man's weakness grows the strength

2. When matter in brackets makes more than one paragraph, start each paragraph with a bracket and place the closing bracket at the end of last paragraph.

3. In sentences where both brackets and parentheses occur, it is preferable that the main digression be placed in brackets, the subordinate in parentheses.

   > "[but I have fully explained my position (see particularly my 'Notes for Nonentities')]."

Breve

1. **The breve is used** to indicate that the vowel over which it is placed is short, as in ăt and fĭt

C

Capitalization

1. The initial letter is capitalized in—

(a) Proper names.

Rome John England

(b) Derivatives of proper names.

Roman Johannean English

NOTE: If the proper names have acquired independent common meaning, or are no longer identified with their source, they are lower cased—*i.e.*, not capitalized: *roman type, brussels sprouts, italics, anglicize.*

(c) Common nouns used alone as a well-known short form of a specific proper name.

the Canal (Panama Canal)
The Channel (English Channel)
the District (District of Columbia)

NOTE: A common noun or adjective used alone as a substitute for the name of a place or thing is not capitalized.

Massachusetts Avenue; the avenue
Cape of Good Hope; the cape

(d) Particles such as *d', da, della, van, von* (unless preceded by a forename or title).

D'Orbigny; *but* Alcide d'Orbigny
Da Ponte; Cardinal da Ponte
Van Rensselaer; Stephen van Rensselaer.

NOTE: Individual usage may vary; then individual usage, where ascertainable, should be followed: *Henry van Dyke; Samuel F. Du Pont; Irénée du Pont.*

(e) Names of organized bodies and their adherents or members.

Communist Party; a Communist
U. S. Congress; a Representative
K. C.; a Knight

(f) Names of regions, localities, and geographic features.

the North Atlantic States
the Orient
the East Side
the Badlands

(g) Name of calendar divisions.

January; February; Monday
(but spring, summer, autumn or fall, winter).

(h) Names of holidays, ecclesiastical feasts and fast days, and historic events or epochs.

Fourth of July
Easter
Yom Kippur
Battle of Bunker Hill
Reformation

(i) Personifications.

The Chair recognizes the gentleman from New York.
For Nature wields her scepter mercilessly.

(j) Fanciful appellations.

the Big Four
the Hub
the New Deal

(k) All words denoting the Deity except *who, whose,* and *whom;* all names for the Bible and other sacred writings; all names of confessions of faith and of religious bodies and their adherents; the words specifically denoting Satan.

Heavenly Father; the Almighty;
Thee, Thou; He, Him;
Bible; Scriptures; Koran;
Apostles' Creed; Augsburg Confession;
Episcopal Church; Episcopalian;
Satan; Father of Lies; the Devil (*but*
a devil; the devils).

(l) Titles of persons.

President Roosevelt
King George

Nurse Cavell
Captain John Smith
Professor Bevington

(m) Titles of publications, papers, documents, acts, laws, etc.

The Outline of History
Saturday Evening Post
Address of President Roosevelt on Unemployment Relief
Statutes at Large
British White Paper

NOTE: Particles—*of, at, on,* etc.—are not capitalized in titles.

(n) The first words of sentences, of independent clauses or phrases, of direct quotations, of lines of poetry, or of formally introduced series following a colon.

The question is, Shall the bill pass?
I will say of the Lord, He is my refuge
and my fortress. . .—BIBLE.

  I have forgot much, Cynara!
    gone with the wind,
  Flung roses, roses, riotously
    with the throng.—DOWSON.

The duchess said "Hell!" when the amorous plumber bit her on the leg.—ANON.
The voting was as follows: In the affirmative, 23; in the negative, 11; not voting, 3.

(o) Addresses, salutations, and signatures.
         (*See* LETTERS.)

2. Where historic or documentary accuracy is required, capitalization and other features of style of the original text should be followed.

NOTE: Formerly, all important words, or all words deemed important, were capitalized. Later, only nouns were capitalized. Today, capitalization is very much more restricted.

Caret

The caret (^) is used—

To show where words are to be inserted among other words already written. (Its use outside of manuscript is rare.)

Cobbet calls ^the caret the "blunder mark."

Cedilla

The cedilla is used—

To indicate that the letter *c* under which it is placed has a "soft" or *s* sound, as in *façade*.

Colon

The colon is used—

(a) To introduce a clause that summarizes the preceding clause or contrasts with it.

Railroading is not a variety of outdoor sport: it is service.

(b) Before a final clause that summarizes preceding details.

Keep your mouth shut; keep your eyes open: those are the best pieces of advice I can give you.

(c) After a salutation.

My dear Sir:

(d) To introduce formally any matter that follows.

He said: [long quotation]

(e) In expressing clock time.

2:40 p.m.

(f) After introductory lines in lists, tables, and leader work, if subentries follow.

Seward Peninsula:
    Council District:
        Northern Light Mining Co.
        Wild Goose Trading Co.
    Fairhaven District:
        Alaska Dredging Assn.

(g) In Biblical and other citations [there ought to be a full space after the colon].

> Luke 4: 3
> I Corinthians xiii: 13
> Journal of Education 3: 342–358

(h) In bibliographical references, between the place of publication and the name of the publisher.

> Congressional Directory. Washington:
> U. S. Government Printing Office.
> [For alternative punctuation, *see* BIBLIOGRAPHY.]

(i) In imprints before the year.

> United States Government Printing Office
> Washington: 1947

(j) In proportions.

> 1 : 2 = 5 : 10
> 3 : 5 :: 12 : 20

NOTE: the double colon serves as a ratio sign.

(k) Between the main title and the subtitle.

> *Daisy Miller: A Study*

Colon-Dash

The colon-dash is now not so frequently used as formerly, the period generally being preferred; but it is hardly obsolete. The colon-dash is still an approved way of formally introducing a list, especially if the list is long or complex.

Comma

1. The comma is used—

(a) To separate two words or figures that might otherwise be misunderstood.

> Instead of hundreds, thousands came.
> Instead of 20, 50 came.
> February 1, 1900.
> To John, Smith was very kind.

(b) Before a direct quotation of only a few words following an introductory phrase.

> Says he, "I am a handsome man, but I'm a gay deceiver."

(c) To indicate the omission of a word or words.

> Mr. X was a moron; his sister, not quite so bright.
> Histories make men wise; poets, witty; the mathematics, subtle; natural philosophy, deep; moral, grave; logic and rhetoric, able to contend.—BACON

(d) After each of a series of co-ordinate qualifying words.

> short, swift streams; *but* short tributary streams

(e) Between an introductory modifying phrase or clause and the subject modified.

> Beset by the enemy, they retreated.

(f) To set off parenthetical words, phrases, or clauses.

NOTE: Adverbial clauses and phrases are considered parenthetical when they precede the main clause. However, if they are short, or if they are intimately connected with the rest of the sentence, the comma is sometimes omitted.

> I had grown to my desk, as it were, and the wood had entered my soul.
> When a stupid man is doing something he is ashamed of, he always declares that it is his duty.
> (*But:* In Thomas Henry Huxley Darwinism had a champion in invincible "armor.")

(g) Before *Jr., Sr., Esq., Ph. D., F.R.S.,* etc., and initials following a surname.

> John Henry Smith, Jr.
> Smith, J. H.

(h) To separate thousands, millions, etc., in numbers of four or more digits.

> 4,230   50,491   1,000,000

(i) After each member within a series of three or more words, phrases, clauses, letters, or figures used with *and* or *or*.

NOTE: The comma precedes the conjunction, not the final member of a series. If there is no conjunction, the comma precedes the last member of the series. In either case the comma follows the final member of the series only if it would be required were the series one word.

> Jutes, Saxons, and Angles invaded England.
> Jutes, Saxons, Angles invaded England.
> (*But:* Deep, intense, ominous, the silence pervaded all.)
> 2 days, 3 hours, and 4 minutes (series);
> *but* 2 days 3 hours 4 minutes (age).
> Know'st thou the land where the lemon-trees bloom,
> Where the gold orange glows in the deep thicket's gloom,
> Where a wind ever soft from the blue heaven blows,
> And the groves are of laurel, and myrtle and rose?
>
> —GOETHE

NOTE: Brief, closely connected sentences are occasionally joined by commas. Lelio's epitaph sums up his history in this fashion:

> He was born, he lived, he died.

(j)   Before the conjunction in a compound sentence if the second clause is complete. (If the second clause is short the comma may be omitted.)

> Ovid wrote an *Art of Love,* but it is all untrue. Love and poetry do not satisfy by their art, for poets are born, and lovers are made by love.—DE MOLINA

NOTE: The second clause may be elliptical. The comma, then, is optional.

> From his imagination he derived his facts, and from his memory his phrases.

(k)   After a substantive or phrase in direct address.

> Now, Macaulay, when I am gone, you'll be sorry that you never heard me speak.—SYDNEY SMITH

NOTE: When strong emotion is expressed, an exclamation point is generally used.

> O Hamlet! thou hast cleft my heart in twain!

(l)   To set off a nonrestrictive clause or phrase.

> Rome, the city of the Emperors, became the city of the Popes.
> Rome, which had been the city of the Emperors, became the city of the Popes.

NOTE: A nonrestrictive sentence element is essentially parenthetical. A restrictive sentence element defines, limits, isolates; it is *not* set off by commas.

> . . . The glory that was Greece,
> And the grandeur that was Rome.—POE

(m)   Between the title and the name of organization in the absence of the words *of* or *of the*.

> Chief, Division of Finance
> Colonel, Seventh Cavalry
> president, Columbia University
> editor, Caxton House

(n)   Between the name and number of an organization.

> General U. S. Grant Post, No. 25.

(o)   Inside closing quotation mark.

NOTE: The practice of a sizable number of authorities— particularly, but not exclusively, British authorities—is at variance with this stricture. They would prefer to be consistent and place the comma (as they place the semicolon) inside the closing quotation mark only if it is an integral part of the quotation. Much may be said for their practice. But the *Style Manual* of the Government Printing Office, from which the rule is quoted, the *Manual of Style* of the University of Chicago Press, and the style manuals of almost all magazines and newspapers recommend the more illogical practice.

> "A man could not set his foot down," says Cortes, "unless on the corpse of an Indian."—PRESCOTT

(p)   To set off words or phrases in apposition—unless a name and descriptive title are blended together.

> Paul, the apostle of the Gentiles, was eminent for his zeal and knowledge.—BEADNELL

But: Paul the Apostle was, before his conversion, a vigorous opponent of Christianity.—JONES

(q)   To set off contrasted statements.

Angels, not Angles.
Of the other two men, one was a species of giant, the other a sort of dwarf.—HUGO

(r)   After the year in dates within a sentence.

The reported dates of September 11, 1943, to June 12, 1944, were proved erroneous.

(s)   After postal-delivery zone numbers.

Cleveland 21, Ohio.
Washington 11, D. C.

(t)   After the complimentary close of a letter.

Yours sincerely,
Cordially yours,

2. The comma is omitted—

(a)   Between month and year in dates.

May 1938; 22d of May 1938 (*but* May 22, 1938).
May 22 A. D. 1938; 22 May 1938.

(b)   In built-up fractions, decimals, and in serial numbers, except patent numbers.

page 2632
Circle 5-4989 (telephone number)
1721–1727 St. Clair Avenue
Army Serial Number O–1081730

(c)   Wherever possible without danger of ambiguity.

My age is 30 years 6 months 12 days.
John Lewis 2d
$2.50 Mexican
General Order No. 12
(*but:* General Orders, No. 12)
Henry of Navarre
(*but:* President Hadley, of Yale)

(d)   Between two nouns, one of which identifies the other.

The Labor Department's booklet *Infant Care* is a best seller.

(e)   Before ampersand (&).

Brown, Wilson & Co.

(f)   Before a dash. (This is quoted from the Government *Style Manual*. But *see* COMMA-DASH.)

(g)   In Bibliographies between name of publication and volume or similar number.

American Library Association Bulletin 34:238, April 1946.

Comma-Dash

Most style manuals object to the use of the comma-dash on the grounds that there is nothing the combination can do which cannot be as well done by the dash alone. However, the comma-dash has generally been employed as a "strong or intensive" dash, and is still, though decreasingly, so employed.

> Your manners are always under examination, and by committees little suspected,—a police in citizens' clothes,—but are awarding or denying you very high prizes when you least think of it.—EMERSON

NOTE: The (obsolete) rule for the employment of the comma-dash reads: No grammatical point is used with the dash if none would be required had the sentence been finished without a break. "But if the parts of the sentence, between which the pause of suspension is to be made are susceptible of being grammatically divided, their proper point should be inserted; as *He sometimes counsel takes, —and sometimes snuff*" (Wilson). If there were no dash after *takes,* the comma would nevertheless be in order. (This rule is quoted as a gloss for the punctuation found in much literature; it is no longer applicable to modern punctuation.)

D

Dash

1.   **The dash is used—**

(a)   To mark a sudden break or abrupt change in thought.

(b) To indicate an interruption or an unfinished word or sentence. (A 2-em dash—that is, a dash two units or squares of type in size—will be used by the compositor to indicate that the interruption is made by a person other than the speaker; a 1-em dash will be used to show self-interruption.)

"But——" "No 'buts'!"
Well d— I almost said "Damn!"

(c) Instead of commas or parentheses, if the meaning may thus be clarified.

There are shore deposits—gravel, sand, and clay—but marine sediments underlie them.

(d) Before a final clause that summarizes a series.

Freedom of speech, freedom of worship, freedom from want, freedom from fear—these are the fundamentals of a moral world order.—F. D. ROOSEVELT

(e) After a word or group of words set in a separate line, if followed by elements at the beginning of each line which complete the original word or group of words.

He suggested—
1. That we accept the rules.
2. That we publish them.

(f) With a preceding question mark, in lieu of a colon.

How can you explain this?—"Fee paid, $5.00."

(g) Sometimes in lieu of opening quotation marks, in French, Spanish, and Italian dialog.

(h) To precede a credit line or a run-in credit or signature.

Angling is always to be considered as a stick on a string, with a fly at one end and a fool at the other.—SWIFT

(i) To separate run-in questions and answers in testimony.

Q. Did he go?—A. No.

(j) En dashes—that is, dashes one-half the width of a unit of type—are used in connected combinations of figures, letters, or figures and letters; they are also used in the absence of *to* when denoting a period of time.

exhibit 6–A
$15–$20
5–20 bonds
1935–37

2. **The dash is not used—**

(a) At the beginning of any line of type, except as indicated in paragraphs (g) and (h) on page 176.

(b) Immediately after a comma (but *see* COMMA-DASH), colon (*see* COLON-DASH), semicolon (*see* SEMICOLON-DASH).

Dieresis

The dieresis is used—

To indicate that the second of two identical vowels in succession belongs to a different syllable.

   zoölogy coördinate

NOTE: Frequently, the hyphen is placed after the first vowel and the dieresis omitted. Less frequently, no punctuation at all indicates the separation. Thus, Webster lists *co-ordinate* and *coordinate* along with *coördinate*.

Ditto Mark

The ditto mark is used—

To indicate that the word or letter above it is to be repeated.

   Modern literature
    "   " and language

NOTE: The ditto mark is not a formal mark of punctuation; and even informally it ought not to be used to indicate the repetition of proper names.

E

Ellipsis

1. Marks of ellipsis indicate the omission of letters, words, or sentences.

2. The rule (or dash), asterisks, and periods constitute the marks of ellipsis. The periods have rendered the asterisks nearly obsolete as marks of ellipsis.

> I was the true descendant of those old W—s.—LAMB
> The president suggests that "an early occasion be sought * * *."
> The Persian messengers travel with a velocity . . . nothing human can equal. . . . Neither snow, nor rain, nor heat, nor darkness, are permitted to obstruct their speed.—HERODOTUS

NOTE: A dash is customary where part of a word—usually one in half-hearted disguise—is omitted: N—Y— (for New York); E—a P—d (for Ezra Pound); or D—n! (for Damn!). Three asterisks have the same function as a like number of periods to indicate elision. Practice is far from standardized, but there seems little doubt that the series of periods (three) will win out over the asterisks for denoting elision. A whole line of periods is sometimes used in place of an omitted line of poetry. *Three* periods, it will be noted, indicate the ellipsis normally; however, if the preceding sentence has been brought to a close, *four* periods are employed.

Exclamation point

The **exclamation point** (or **note of admiration** or **exclamation**) is used to mark surprise, incredulity, admiration, or appeal.

> "Great!" he shouted.
> Who shouted "Great!"

Note that the question mark is omitted in the second sentence cited. Some writers, particularly some British writers, would prefer: Who shouted "Great!"? But this piling up of punctuation is generally rejected—probably due to the influence of the over-worked compositor.

(a) In direct address, either to a person or a personified object, *O* is used without an exclamation point; but if strong feeling is expressed, an exclamation point is placed at the end of the expression.

O Lord, save Thy people!

(This rule is not invariable: it is the procedure employed at the Government Printing Office at Washington, but practice varies greatly.)

(b) In exclamations without direct address or appeal *oh* is used instead of *O,* and the exclamation point is omitted.

Oh dear; the time is so short.

(Again, the Government Printing Office and general practice are somewhat at variance.)

F

Footnotes

A footnote is used—

(a) To set forth explanatory or incidental matter. Thus used it constitutes a formal parenthesis to the text.

(b) To cite sources. (It is not only with direct quotations that footnotes are used.)

NOTE: Footnotes may be informal or formal. Informal footnotes merely cite the source generally:

Thomas Wilson, *Arte of Rhetorique.*

Formal footnotes cite the source specifically. The documentation is derived from the title page and its *verso.* Where a title page is faulty, any corrections or additions should be supplied in square brackets.

[Thomas] Wilson, *Arte of Rhetorique* (1560), edited by G. H. Mair, Tudor and Stuart Library, Oxford, Clarendon Press, 1909, pp. 39 ff.

The form quoted is recommended by Columbia University. There are other possibilities; consistency is the chief criterion of any scheme of documentation. The *Manual of Style* of the University of Chicago Press recommends:

> A Manual of Style (10th ed.; Chicago: University of Chicago Press, 1925), p. 10.

Citations from periodicals are slightly more complex:

> Henry Barret Hinckley, "Science and Folk-Lore in *The Owl and the Nightingale*," *Publications of the Modern Language Association of America*, Vol. XLVII, pp. 303–314 (June, 1932).

(*See* also MARKS OF REFERENCE.)

After the first citation of a work the title should be shortened:

> [T.] Wilson, *Arte of Rhetorique*, pp. 39 ff.
> H. B. Hinckley, *P. M. L. A.*, p. 310.

The following is a list of abbreviations used in footnote documentation.

ibid.	*ibidem,* in the same work
idem or *id.*	the same (if the same page of the same work is cited)
op. cit.	*opere citato,* the work cited
loc. cit.	*loco citato,* the place cited (if the same passage is cited immediately)
l. (ll.)	line (lines)
p. (pp.)	page (pages)
vol. (vols.)	volume (volumes)
ch. (chs.) or chap. (chaps.)	chapter (chapters)
v. (vv.)	verse (verses)
ante	before
supra	above
infra	below
art.	article
sec. (secs.)	section (sections)
n. (nn.)	note (notes)

H

Hyphen

1. The hyphen is used—

(a) To avoid ambiguity. (This is the most general principle of hyphenation. Thus, Fowler counsels that *walking-stick* or *walkingstick* be used when a stick used for walking is intended; otherwise a *walking stick,* or a "stick that walks," might be construed as referring to a "stiffly behaved person.")

competent shoemaker   tomato-canning factories
wooden-shoe maker   field canning factories

(b) To avoid doubling a vowel (except after the short prefixes *co, de, pre, pro, re*) or tripling a consonant.

thimble-eye   brass-smith   shell-like
anti-imperial   micro-organism   ultra-atomic

(c) To prevent mispronunciation or to insure a definite accent on each element of the compound.

contra-indicated
non-civil-service position
re-treat (*treat again*)
anti-hog-cholera serum
blow-out-proof
co-op (short for *cooperative,* also *written coöperative* and *co-operative*)
at-homes

(d) To join the elements of an improvised compound.

make-believe (noun)
blue-pencil (verb)
know-it-all (noun)

(e) In compounds formed of duplicating or conflicting terms, and in compounds naming the same person or thing under two aspects.

devil-devil   pitter-patter
comedy-ballet   treasurer-manager

(f) In (1) a compound noun containing an adverb or a preposition as its second element; and (2) in a compound noun consisting of three or more words.

(1) flare-*back*   (2) forget-me-not
    go-*between*   man-of-war
    hold-*up*   mother-in-law
    looker-*on*   jack-in-the-box

(g) In compound numbers, in technical compound units of measurement, in complex terms of compass direction, and in other complex compounds.

twenty-one   light-year
twenty-first (*but* one hundred and twenty-first)
horsepower-hour   north-northeast
a 6-footer   great-grandfather

(h) In a compound containing an apostrophe in one of its elements.

bull's-eye   mare's-nest

(i) In a compound predicate adjective, the second element of which is a past participle.

The material is fire-tested
The slopes are wind-blown
The area was drought-stricken

NOTE: If the second element is a present participle, the hyphen is not used: *They withstood the ever increasing opposition.*

(j) In a derivation of a compound word.

cold-bloodedness   ill-advisedly

NOTE: If the original word was written without a hyphen, the derivative is too—*praiseworthiness, outlawry.*

(k) In unit modifiers immediately preceding the word or words modified.

no-par-value stock
Latin-American countries
life-insurance companies
most-favored-nation clause
heavy-laden ship

NOTE: If (1) the first word of such a unit modifier is an adverb, ending in *ly* or (2) if the first word of a three-word modifier is an adverb modifying the second, the hyphen is omitted.

> (1) heavily laden ship (2) very well defined curve

(1) In a unit modifier following the word or words it modifies and referring back to it.

> motors, alternating-current, 3-phase, 60-cycle, 115-volt.

NOTE: The unit modifier is always printed in the singular.

(m) In fractions, between the numerator and denominator.

> two-thirds   one-thousandth

NOTE: If the hyphen appears either in the numerator or in the denominator, it is omitted between numerator and denominator.

> two one-thousandths   twenty-three thirty-seconds

(n) Where two or more hyphened compounds have a common basic element and this element is omitted in all but the last term, the hyphens are retained.

> 2- or 3-em quads
> 2- by 4-inch boards
> (*but* 2 to 6 inches wide)
> long- and short-term loans
> (*but* twofold or threefold; goat, sheep, and calf skins)

2. **The hyphen is not used—**

(a) In color terms unless used as unit modifiers.

> blue green
> orange red
> milk white
> (*but* pea-green boat)

(b) In Latin forms

> *ex officio* member
> *ante bellum* days
> *prima facie* evidence

(c) In unit modifiers enclosed by quotation marks.

"blue sky" law
"good neighbor" policy

NOTE: This rule does not apply if the term is normally a hyphened one—as *"mark-off" galleys.*

(d) In proper names used as unit modifiers.

United States laws

NOTE: If the original form was hyphened, the hyphen is retained in the unit modifier: *Wilkes-Barre streets.*

(e) In civil and military titles denoting a single office.

commander in chief
vice president
major general

(f) With combining forms, prefixes, and suffixes.

*Anglo*mania	*non*neutral	*ultra*violet
*ante*date	*plano*convex	*un*necessary
*anti*slavery	*post*script	clock*wise*
*by*law	*pre*exist	lily*like*
*counter*case	*pro*optic	Lincoln*like*
*de*energize	*re*enact	man*hood*
*ex*communicate	*semi*official	north*ward*
*extra*curricular	*step*father	self*ish*
*hero*icomic	*sub*secretary	spoon*ful*
*infra*red	*super*fine	stain*less*
*inter*view	*trans*ship	twenty*fold*
*mis*state	*tri*color	

NOTE: The prefixes *ex* (former) and *self* (reflexive) and the adjective *elect* require a hyphen:

ex-governor
self-interest
vice-president-elect

Duplicating prefixes also require the hyphen:

re-redirect
sub-subcommittee
sub-sub-subcommittee

The prefix or combining form takes a hyphen when it is joined to a capitalized word.

> pan-American
> Anglo-American
> trans-Atlantic
> (*but:* Pan American Union, the official name)

I

Italics

Italics (indicated in typescript by a straight line drawn under a word) **are used—**

(a) For emphasis, for contrast, or for words or phrases considered as such.

> *Crazy* (literally "cracked") and *insane* ("unsound") were at first milder terms for *mad,* but they now carry the full force of the idea in question.—GREENOUGH and KITTREDGE

NOTE: Italics for the sake of emphasis are to be used sparingly: they are the mark of "the school-girl style."

(b) For indicating the titles of books, magazines, and newspapers. *The Postman Always Rings Twice,* The *Saturday Evening Post,* The New York *Post.*

NOTE: An article or story or chapter in a magazine or book would be indicated by quotes: James Rowland Angell's "The University in a Time of Change" appeared in *Harpers Magazine.*

(c) For foreign words or their abbreviations if they have been incompletely naturalized.

> *ante meridiem* (but a.m.)
> *anno domini* (but A.D.)
> *et cetera* (The tendency is to leave the abbreviation etc. unitalicized, and most style manuals are in favor of the tendency.)

L

Leaders

Leaders (or dots) are used—

To help the eye bridge the gap between words, letters, or numerals at the beginning and end of a line.

Vocabulary.....................page 3

Letters

1. The parts of a letter are:

(a) The **heading,** (b) the **introduction** (or **inside address**), (c) the **greeting** (or **salutation**), (d) the **body,** (e) the **complimentary close,** (f) the **signature,** and (g) the **superscription** (or **address on the envelope**). These seven parts would normally appear in all business letters. In personal letters any of them may be omitted—except, of course, the address, the body, and the signature. The mechanics recommended in the following paragraphs apply with full force only to business letters.

(a) The **heading:** There are two main ways to punctuate and space the items:

(1) Close and indented

9 Rockefeller Plaza,
New York City,
June 1, 1947.

(2) Open and block

9 Rockefeller Plaza
New York City
June 1, 1947

NOTE: The open and block form is employed by most business organizations. The close and indented form ranks second in popularity. Less common, but nevertheless permissible, is the open and indented form. Whatever style is adopted should be employed consistently: if the heading is open and block, the introduction and the outside address should be also. (If the letterhead supplies the address, only the date need be typed. It may be placed either under the letterhead or flush with the right-hand margin.)

(b)   The **introduction** (or **inside address**) should be the same as the address which appears on the envelope (or outside address). It should also be consistent in form with the heading—open and block, close and indented, or open and indented.

(c)   The **greeting** (or **salutation**) should vary with the formality of the letter. *My dear sir:* is recognized as being more formal than *Dear Sir:* and *Sir:* more formal than either. Similarly *My dear Mr. X:* is, according to American conventions of letter writing, rather more formal than *Dear Mr. X.* As for abbreviations, avoid all but *Mr., Mrs.,* and *Dr.*

(d)   The **body** of the letter ought to be single spaced, with double spacing between paragraphs. The paragraphs themselves may be equally indented (five spaces from the left-hand margin is the rule) or may begin flush with the left-hand margin.

(e)   The **complimentary close** may be quite formal, as *Respectfully yours,* or almost informal, as *Cordially yours,* (note that the complimentary close begins with a capital letter and terminates with a comma). *Yours truly* is the formula most generally employed. In any case, the complimentary close should begin about halfway between the left- and right-hand margins.

(f)   The **signature** should be written by hand. It should be placed several spaces below the complimentary close and immediately above the typewritten name. The official position of the writer may be included

—should be, if he is functioning for his organization.

(g) The **superscription** (or **outside address**) should be identical with the introduction (or inside address).

M

Macron

The macron is used—

To indicate that the vowel over which it is placed has a long sound, as in *āle* and *fīre*.

Marks of Reference

1. **Marks of Reference are used** to refer to notes at the bottom of the page or to remarks in the margin. They include:

   (a) The *star* (*)   (d) The *section* (§)
   (b) The *dagger* (†)   (e) Parallel lines (‖)
   (c) The *double dagger* (‡)   (f) The paragraph (¶)

2. The six marks of reference are employed in the order listed above. If the number of notes exceeds six, the signs are doubled. The seventh note is marked **, the eighth ††, and so on.

3. Figures, raised or in parentheses, are more normal in current practice. If there are many footnotes, they are usually numbered consecutively through the chapter or the section. If few, the numbering usually begins anew with every page. Modern footnote citation is invariably made by arabic numbers; letters were formerly used.

(*See* FOOTNOTES.)

N

Numbers

1. **Numbers are spelled out—**

   (a) When they can be expressed in one or two words.

   two   twenty-two   two billion

(b)   When they come at the beginning of a sentence.

>   Three hundred and thirty-three, 777, and 999 were considered magical numbers by the Cabalists.

(c)   When they are mentioned in a dignified, serious, or formal connection.

>   The three hundred and fifty-third meeting of the parliament.

(d)   When they are fractions (in formal writing).

>   three-fifths   thirty-three fiftieths
>   thirty-three   fifty-fifths

(e)   When they refer to a formal time division.

>   the feminine fifties
>   the third decade
>   the twentieth century

(f)   When they are in even units of hundreds or thousands ("round numbers").

>   five hundred   five thousand   thirteen hundred
>   one and one-half million
>   one million five hundred thousand
>   (or 1½ million)

2.   Numbers are written in figures—

(a)   When they occur frequently in the text.

(b)   When they refer to dates or pages or addresses.

>   May 1, 1900 (*not* May 1st, 1900)
>   page 4000
>   100 West 10 Street (*or* 100 West 10th St.)

(c)   When they express quantities or measurements.

>   *Age:* a 3-year old
>
>   *Clock time:* 4:30 p.m.
>   2300 hours
>   10 o'clock
>
>   *Dates:* June 1947
>   June 29, 1947
>
>   *Decimals:* 0.25 inch
>   .30 caliber
>   gage height 10.0 feet

Degrees: an angle of 57°
longitude 77° 04′ 06″
45.5° to 49.5° below zero

Market quotations: 4½–percent bonds
sugar, .03
wheat at 42
gold is 109

Measurements: 110 meter
20/20 vision
40 bushels

Money: $3.65; $0.75; 75 cents
$3.00 per 200 pounds
2.5 francs (*or* fr. 2.5)

Percentage: 0.5 percent (or one-half of 1 percent)
50–50 (colloquial)
3–65 bonds

Proportion: 1:62,500
1–3–5
1 to 4

Time: 6 hours 8 minutes 20 seconds
10 years 3 months 29 days

Unit modifiers: 5-day week
8-year-old wine
½-inch pipe

NOTE: Consistency is the important caution with regard to usage. Styles may vary according to needs; but whatever style is adopted should be adhered to throughout. Otherwise, confusion is inevitable.

P

Parentheses

Parentheses are used—

(a)   To set off matter not intended to be part of the main argument of the text or not a grammatical element of the sentence, yet important enough to be included.

The Chairman (to Mr. Smith):
The Chairman (reading):
The result (*see* fig. 2) is most surprising.

(b)   To enclose a parenthetical phrase or clause where the interruption is too great to be indicated by commas.

> You can find it neither in French dictionaries (at any rate, not in *Littré*) nor in English.

(c)   To enclose an explanatory word not part of the statement.

> Portland (Oreg.) Chamber of Commerce;
> *but* Washington, D. C., schools.

(d)   To enclose letters or numbers designating items in a series.

> The order of delivery will be: (a) food; (b) clothing; and (c) tents and other housing equipment.
> You will observe that the sword is (1) old-fashioned, (2) still sharp, and (3) unusually light for its size.

(e)   To enclose a figure inserted to confirm a statement given in words. (The use of this double form is on the wane, and the Government *Style Manual* approves it only if specifically requested.)

> The contract shall be completed in sixty (60) days.
> Sixty dollars ($60)

NOTE: The reference in parentheses at the end of a sentence is placed before the period, unless it is a complete sentence in itself or unless there is some special reason (emphasis, for example) for excluding it from the sentence proper.

> The specimen exhibits both phases (p. 14, *A, B*).
> The individual cavities show great variation. (*See* p. 4.)

(a)   If a sentence contains more than one parenthetic reference the one at the end is placed before the period.

> The sandstone (*see* p. 6) occurs in every county of the State (*see* p. 12).

(b)   When matter in parentheses makes more than one paragraph, start each paragraph with a parenthesis and place the closing parenthesis at the end of the last paragraph.

Period

1. **The period is used—**

(a) After a declarative or an imperative sentence.

> Stars are suns.
> He was employed by Sampson & Co.
> Tell me how he did it.
> They love him most for the enemies he made.

(b) In place of parentheses after a letter or number denoting a series.

> a. Bread well baked
> b. Meat cooked rare
> c. Cubed apples stewed
>
> 1. Punctuate freely.
> 2. Compound sparingly.
> 3. Index thoroughly.

(c) After a question intended as a suggestion and not requiring an answer.

> May we hear from you.

(d) To indicate ellipsis (three periods; use four periods when preceding sentence has been brought to a close).

> He called . . . and left. . . . He returned next day.
> (*See* ELLIPSIS.)

(e) To separate integers from decimals in a single expression.

> 3.75 percent
> 3.50   1.25 yards

(f) In continental European languages to indicate thousands.

> 1.317 (1,317)
> 72.190.175 (72,190,175)

(g) After abbreviations, unless otherwise specified. (*See* ABBREVIATIONS.)

> gal. N.E. m. (meter)
> qt.   N.Y. kc. (kilocycle)

(h)   After legends and explanatory matter beneath illustrations.

(i)   Rarely, to indicate multiplication; the multiplication sign is preferable for the purpose.

a.b. (a$\times$b *or* ab)

2. **The period is omitted—**

(a)   After Roman numerals used as ordinals.

George V

(b)   In general, at the ends of lines in title pages, after scientific, chemical, or other symbols.

(c)   After a quotation mark that is preceded by a period.

He said, "Now or never."

(d)   After letters used as names without specific designation.

He's a Mr. X—a complete mystery.
but Mr. X. (for Mr. Xerxes).

(e)   After a middle initial in a name—when the initial is not an abbreviation but the entire middle "name."

Ross T McIntire
but Franklin D. Roosevelt

(f)   After short names that are not abbreviations.

Ed   Sam   Alec

(g)   After words and incomplete statements listed.

Period-dash

The period-dash is used—

(a)   After quoted matter, to indicate its author.

(b)   To mark an abrupt break in the communication or an abrupt resumption.

Treason doth never prosper.—What's the reason?
Why, if it prospers, none dare call it treason.

NOTE: The question mark-dash and the exclamation point-dash are similarly employed.

But do we discover dissenting voices in England at the time?—England to which so many panegyrics of liberty have been dedicated?

"Oh! I have been robbed!"—"I pity your grief."
"Of all my verses!"—"I pity the thief."

Q

Question Mark

The question mark (or **interrogation point**, or **note of interrogation**) **is used—**

(a) To indicate a direct query, even if not in the form of a question.

Did he do it?
He did what?
Can the money be raised? is the question.

(Note that the question mark may interrupt a sentence. It is not necessary to capitalize the first letter after resuming the sentence.)

Who asked, "Who's that?"

(Note the single question mark.)

(b) To express more than one query in the same sentence.

Can he do it? or you? or anyone?

(c) To express doubt.

He said the boy was 8 (?) feet tall.

Quotation Marks

Quotation marks (or **quotes**) **are used—**

(a) To enclose direct quotations. (Each part of an interrupted quotation begins and ends with quotation marks.)

Humpty-Dumpty said: "There's glory for you." "I don't know what you mean by 'glory,'" Alice said. Humpty-Dumpty smiled contemptuously. "Of course you don't—till I tell you. I meant, 'There's a nice knock-down argument for you.'" "But 'glory' doesn't mean 'a nice knock-down argument,'" Alice objected. "When I use a word," Humpty-Dumpty said in a rather scornful tone, "it means just what I choose it to mean, neither more nor less."

Note: Employ single quotes for a quotation within a quotation. Remark particularly the position of the period and the comma in such constructions: the comma comes *before* both the single and the double quotation marks. All other marks of punctuation are placed inside the quotation marks *only* if they are intrinsic parts of the quotation:

> The question they considered carefully was: Is there enough available protection for "commercial Banks"?

(This is the practice recommended by Joseph Lasky in *Proofreading and Copy-Preparation*, by the *Manual of Style* of the University of Chicago Press, and by most standard authorities. Unfortunately, the *Style Manual* of the Government Printing Office adopts the thoroughly confusing practice of placing the period inside the double but outside the single quotes: He answered, "John said, 'No'." The mechanics, in this instance, are difficult to justify.)

If another quotation goes within the single quotes—"a quotation within a quotation within a quotation"—double quotes are used; and the alternation is continued if additional quotations are introduced:

> "Who asked 'Who asked "Why?" ' "

(b) To enclose any matter following the terms *entitled, the word, the term, marked, endorsed,* or *signed;* but are not used to enclose expressions following the terms *known as, called, so-called,* etc., unless such expressions are misnomers or slang.

Of what does the item "miscellaneous debts" consist?

Note: If specific attention is to be given the words, if they are to be considered as words, or if emphasis or contrast is the effect desired, then *italics* are preferable.

(c) At the beginning of each paragraph of a quotation, but at the end of the last paragraph only. (If the quotation is extensive it is, normally, preferable to set it off from the body of the text. If in typescript, the quoted matter ought to be single spaced; if in manuscript, plainly indented. No quotation marks are employed.)

(d) To enclose misnomers, slang expressions, or ordinary words used in arbitrary fashion. (Employ sparingly, however.)

"lame duck" amendment   "Bobo" Jones

S

Semicolon

The semicoln is used—

(a) To separate two independent clauses.

Man proposes; God disposes.

(b) To separate groups of words that include commas.

Among Latin abbreviations that introduce explanations and enumerations are *e.g. (exempli gratia),* "for the sake of example"; *i.e. (id est),* "that is"; *viz. (videlicet), namely."*

(c) To set off words and abbreviations that introduce explanations, enumerations, and the like.

He has no friends; that is, none who like him.

Semicolon-dash

1. The semicolon-dash is nearly obsolete, and it was never much in vogue. The rules for its employment are analogous to those for the employment of the comma-dash (*q.v.*).

His religion, at best, is an anxious wish;—like that of Rabelais, "a great Perhaps."

T

Tilde

The tilde is used—

To indicate that the letter *n* over which it is placed has the sound of *n* and *y* combined, as in *cañon.*

BOOK SEVEN

Pronunciation

Standard Speech

STANDARD SPEECH is "that which is least likely to attract attention to itself as being peculiar to any class or locality."[1] In reality, the standard is never attained. "Probably no intelligent person actually expects cultivated people in the South, the East, and the West to pronounce alike."[2] *Standard speech* too often implies *uniform speech*. The greatest authorities on pronunciation—Daniel Jones, George Philip Krapp, Henry Morgan Ayres, Henry Sweet, Henry Cecil Wyld—agree that it is neither feasible nor desirable to set up any one form of pronunciation, and declare it the standard to which all must adhere.

In America there are three distinct norms of pronunciation: the Eastern, the Southern, and the Western-Northern or General American. About 10 percent of Americans speak the Eastern type, about 20 percent the Southern, and about 70 percent the General American. The attitude of Prof. Kenyon, who "admits no rivalry in his admiration of that clear, intelligent pronunciation of the best types of Southern and Northern British, of Scottish standard English, of Eastern, Southern, and General American, which is the best index of personality, that most interesting of all facts," is the attitude of most intelligent critics today.

[1] Elwood Murray, *The Speech Personality.*
[2] John Samuel Kenyon, *American Pronunciation.*

Any valid system of pronunciation, therefore, must take account of sectional differences. No block of communication will ensue. As Letitia Raubicheck points out, "The differences between cultured speech in London, San Francisco, and Australia are as nothing compared to the differences between the dialects of Lancashire and Inverness."

Within any group, the pronunciation employed by "the main proportion of effective and cultured speakers is the only standard." The adoption of a liberal standard does not, however, mean that all is allowed. Illiterate, foreign, and affected pronunciations are of course rejected. But a liberal standard does mean a practicable standard, one attainable by the mass of men.

The Authority of the Dictionary

Every dictionary records pronunciation: it neither originates nor prescribes. "Correctness of pronunciation," the editors of a foremost dictionary warn us, must be a flexible term. A pronunciation is deemed correct when a sufficient number of cultivated speakers employ it. But how many equal a sufficient number? And how are they to be counted? There have been no satisfactory answers to either question. Moreover, as Dr. Lounsbury observes, "the pronunciation of every dictionary expresses the preferences and prejudices of the particular person and persons who have been concerned in its compilation. At best it represents the taste of a select coterie to whose members the accidents of birth and training and circumstance have made familiar certain ways of pronouncing words."[1] And again, dictionary-makers do not always go to the people, or even to the experts, to ascertain pronunciations: they sometimes go to other dictionaries— thus maintaining an outmoded pronunciation.

One more qualification must be noted. The spoken language changes far more rapidly than the written language. Many pronunciations which were repudiated as vulgar a few years ago are now accepted and sometimes even preferred. The complaint of William Caxton, a fifteenth-cen-

[1] *The Standard of Pronunciation in English.*

tury printer and publisher, "Our language now used varieth far from that used when I was born," has been often echoed. The passage of time has rendered many a once-perfect rime something less. Could he see it, Pope would be aghast at what has happened to the rime in this famous triplet:

> Waller was smooth; but Dryden taught to join
> The varying verse, the full resounding line,
> The long majestic march, and energy divine.

Yet, Pope would also be prepared, for he wrote—and it is as true today as it was then:

> Our sons their father's failing language see,
> And such as Chaucer is, shall Dryden be.

The dictionary, then, is an imperfect guide to pronunciation; the only nearly-perfect guide is the cultivated speech of one's section. And a devoted listening to that speech is the best way of learning and improving pronunciation.

However, the spoken word lasts only as long as a breath and the written word as long as the paper it is written on. Therefore, it is repeatedly necessary to go to the dictionary to supplement oral memory, as well as to check on particular pronunciations. Besides, it becomes necessary at times to say a word that one has never heard pronounced, and, of course, the dictionary is the most feasible place to find out how to say it.

Consequently, it is important to know thoroughly the system by which pronunciation is indicated. Some dictionaries employ diacritical marks for the purpose; others respell words so that their letters approximate their sounds; and still others represent pronunciation by means of phonetic symbols. Each system has its limitations. For example, the dictionary cannot indicate whether the *r* at the end of the words (*far, bar, aster*) or before consonants (*barber, lard, Argentina*) should be pronounced or not. The choice belongs to each man. All that can be said is that in some sections the *r* is pronounced, in others it is not. The dictionary becomes a valuable aid to pronunciation only when the limitations of the dictionary are fully understood.

The Formal and Familiar Styles

Different conventions exist in formal speech and in conversation. In the familiar style, but not in the formal style, words are often curtailed, sounds are not given their full value; and psychological stress is the rule. In conversation, for example, slightly accented words, such as prepositions, frequently lose their final consonant: a phrase group like *a pot of gold* may be converted to *a pot o' gold*. Sometimes, also, *gold* will become simply *gol'*. Again, the *to* in a phrase like *going to town* may shed its final vowel almost completely and be sounded more like *t'* than *too*. Once more, the force of emotion may cause a word like *im*-POSS-*ib'l* to shift its stress and become IM-*poss-ib'l*. The dictionary cannot indicate such modifications. They are, nevertheless, thoroughly legitimate.

Some Definitions

A few definitions of terms are necessary before we start a more specific study of pronunciation.

Voiced sound: one uttered with vibration of the vocal cords (*k, t, p*).

Voiceless sound: one uttered with the breath only (*b, d, g*).

Vowel: A voiced sound made with the mouth-passage open and free from obstructions (*a, e, i, o, u* and occasionally—as in *rhythm*—*y*).

Consonant: A sound made by obstructing the breath in some part of the mouth or throat (*b, c, d, f, g, h, j, k, l, m, n, p, q, r, s, t, v, w, x, y, z*).

Diphthong: A combination of two vowels, sounded one after the other in a syllable, without a break between them (the *yoo* sound in *beauty*, the *ow* sound in *owl*, the *oy* sound in *boy*).

Digraph: A combination of two letters which represents only one sound (*ea* in *beat* is sounded *e; ch* in *loch* is sounded *k; ph* in *phiz* is sounded *f*).

Syllable: A unit of pronunciation containing at least one vowel (*u-nit, syl-la-ble, pro-nun-ci-a-tion*).

SUGGESTIONS FOR PRONUNCIATION

This observation by Thomas R. Lounsbury ought to be noted and remembered along with every "rule" for pronunciation:

. . . in English orthoepy[1] rules exist mainly for the purpose of furnishing opportunities for the creation of exceptions.

Syllabication

1. Every syllable, by definition, must be a pronounceable unit; and every syllable ought to be given its full pronunciation. The following *words* are frequently *pronounced minus one necessary syllable.*

barbarous	history
boisterous	interesting
comfortable	library
desperate	memory
difference	misery
February	poem
geography	really
government	zodiac

2. The following *words* are frequently *pronounced with a syllable wrongly inserted.*

athlete	ordnance
business	mischievous
grievous	safety
naïve	tremendous

Accent

1. Simple words of two syllables have only one accent: do not place full stress on each syllable in words like *combat, exile, convert.*

2. In compound words each part retains its own accent:

morn'ing-glo'ry
emp'ty-hand'ed

[1]*Orthoepy* comes from two Greek words and means simply "the study or science of correct pronunciation."

a. When the compound words are monosyllables each part retains its clear utterance, as when taken alone, but the greater stress is laid on that which is descriptive or restrictive of the other:

seed'-coin
wheel'-horse

b. When a compound has come into such common use as to drop the hyphen, it is often accented like a simple word:

cup'board
high'land

3. Words which serve as verbs and also as nouns and adjectives usually have the accent on the last syllable when verbs, on the first syllable when nouns or adjectives:

VERB	NOUN OR ADJECTIVE
ab sent'	ab'sent
af fix'	af'fix
com pound'	com'pound
dis count'	dis'count
in crease'	in'crease
ob ject'	ob'ject
per mit'	per'mit

4. Words ending in *sion* or *tion* have the accent on the syllable next to the last (the penultimate syllable), as in *presenta'tion.*

5. Words ending in *acal* or *ical* generally have the accent on the syllable just preceding:

demoni'acal
fin'ical

6. The tendency to shift accent to the beginning of a word is characteristic of American speech and has triumphed in a number of cases. But it should be recognized that some words still resist the tendency. *Inquiry, opponent, museum,* for example, are not accented on the first syllable.

NOTE: Some words, as *ad dress', ex press',* do not change the accent to denote the part of speech. Exceptions such as these are mispronounced through the force of analogy.

WORDS STRESSED ON THE FIRST SYLLABLE

ancestors	eczema	inventory
Andes	engine	Iowa
admirable	envoy	lamentable
adverse	excellent	mischievous
applicable	explicable	opposite
armistice	exquisite	orator
assets	favorite	orchestra
cemetery	formidable	positively
cerebrum	genuine	preferable
champion	gondola	relative
chastisement	hospitable	reputable
combatant	hygiene	requisite
conversant	impious	syringe
deficit	industry	theater
despicable	inference	theory
desultory	integral	vegetable
disputant	interesting	vehement

WORDS STRESSED ON THE SECOND SYLLABLE

acclimate	divan	nocturnal
address	enthusiasm	plebeian
adept	estate	portray
annex	excess	pretense
antipodes	executive	remediable
appellant	finance	remiss
autumnal	giraffe	research
burlesque	horizon	resource
cadet	hotel	reverse
calliope	idea	robust
cement	inquiry	romance
cognomen	lyceum	routine
condolence	maternal	superb
curator	municipal	transact
defect	museum	triumphal
demonstrative	mustache	umbrella

Running Words Together

When sounds occur in a series not only are they modified by stress, but also neighboring sounds tend to influence one another. A certain amount of this is fairly inevitable and hardly objectionable. *Four en twenty* (Four and twenty),

Tom uh Jerry (Tom or Jerry), *horeshoo* (horseshoe) are natural pronunciations. Occasionally, however, sounds are so united in pronunciation that their original values become debased. When *d* or *t* or *v* ends a word, or when *y* begins one, the tendency toward an unfortunate fusion is enhanced.

SAY	AVOID
Did you eat	Jeet
Give me	Gimee
Used to	Yustuh
Must have	Muhstuh
Thousand years	Thousan djeers
First year	Firs tcheer

THE CONSONANTS

C

1. *C* when followed by *e*, *i*, or *y* has the sound of *s*, as in *cede*, *city*, *cycle*.

2. *C* when followed by *a*, *o*, *u*, *l*, or *r*, or when it ends in a syllable, usually has the sound of *k*, as in *placate*, *raucous*, *occult*, *incline*, *recreation*.

G

1. *G* when followed by *e*, *i*, or *y* has the soft sound of *j*, as in *Jack* or *Jill:*

> *German, gist, gyrate*
> *gestate, gin, gyve*

There are innumerable exceptions to this rule: *get, gear, gild, gift, giggle*. Almost all are of Teutonic origin, and retain their native hard sound. But they are easy to discern and, moreover, rarely offer any problem in pronunciation.

2. *G* when followed by *a*, *o*, *u*, *l*, or *r*, and when at the end of a word, has the native or hard sound:

game	garden	garret
good	golden	gorgon
gun	guttural	gusto
glory	glossary	global
greet	gradual	Grail
drug	crag	jig

Only the obsolescent word *gaol* (spelled *jail* in America) constitutes an exception.

T and D

T and *D* are both formed the same way: by pressing "the tip of the tongue to the top of the teeth." BUT: *t* is a voiceless or breathed consonant, produced by quickly expelling the breath; whereas *d* is a voiced consonant produced by vibration of the vocal cords. The substitution of one sound for the other is characteristic of foreign accents. The substitution is particularly apt to occur when *t* comes between vowels or other voiced sounds.

Note that in the past tense of verbs ending in voiceless consonants, such as *k, p, s, f, ch* in *chief, th* in *thin,* and sometimes *l* and *n,* the suffix-*ed* represents the sound of *t:*

wrecked	packed	spanked
dropped	ripped	harped
hissed	passed	sassed
laughed	puffed	huffed
launched	reached	notched
girthed	frothed	pithed
dwelled	spilled	burned

S and Z

S and *Z* are cognate sounds, the one voiceless, the other voiced. Both are *sibilants,* or *hissing* sounds and both are produced in the same manner. With upper and lower teeth almost touching, place the tip of the tongue (which should be curled upwards slightly) near—but not against!—the upper teeth where they join the gums. Force the breath over the tip of the tongue through the teeth. The soft hissing sound must be under control always. (*Z,* of course, is sounded with vibration of the vocal cords.)

Two widespread faults in pronouncing s must be noted.

1. **Hissing:** The breath must be expelled with sufficient force to yield the soft sibilant sound of *s;* but it must not be expelled with such force that a whistling sound is emitted. Practice in breath control helps eliminate the hissing *s.*

2. Lisping. Lisping is the substitution of a *th* (as in *thin*) for the *s* sound. If not the result of some organic condition (such as faulty alignment of teeth), lisping can be cured by keeping the tongue from touching the teeth during the production of the *s* sound.

Practice with tongue twisters, such as *She sells sea shells by the sea shore,* is an excellent way to correct the faults analyzed above. These lines by Swinburne, also, are models for practice sentences:

> Surely no spirit or sense of a soul
> that was soft to the spirit and
> soul of our senses
> Sweetens the stress of suspiring sus-
> picion that sobs in the semblance
> and sound of a sigh . . .

There is no fixed rule as to when to pronounce *s* as *z,* when as *s.* Spelling is an unsure guide. The following pairs, however, are suggestive. They represent a definite tendency.

VERB (*z*)	NOUN OR ADJECTIVE (*s*)
use	use
close	close
lose	loose

Q

Q always has the sound of *k.* It is always followed by *u,* which has the sound of *w,* as in *quart,* unless silent, as in *mosque* and *liquor.*

X

1. *X* has the sound of *gz* when followed by an accented vowel, as in *exact', exer'tion.*

2. *X* at the beginning of a word has the sound of *z* as in *Xerxes, xylem, xyster.*

Y

Y has its own sound at the beginning of a syllable, as in *yes, beyond.* In other situations, and when it constitutes a syllable, it has the vowel function, as in *my, abyss, yclept.*

N and Ng

N has a semi-vowel character, often constituting a syllable of itself, as in *heaven, cotton, garden,* where the preceding vowel is silent.[1]

Ng in such words as *bring, song, twang* represents one sound. The representation of that sound by two letters is confusing. It has a nasal resonance like *n* and a tongue position like *g:* but these are simultaneous, not successive. The blended sound is produced by bringing the soft palate and the back part of the tongue into complete contact and compelling the breath to escape through the nose (as in *m* and *n*) with accompanying vibration of the vocal cords. The tongue and the palate should remain in the position indicated until all sound has stopped: otherwise a *k* or *g* sound (*ngk* or *ngg*) will be incorrectly attached. Just as bad, however, is a simple *m* or *n* sound instead of the *ng* sound—a substitution once fashionable but no longer.

The letters *ng* represent four sounds, namely, *ng, ngg, ngk,* and *nj.* The following observations will perhaps make the distinction clearer.

1. *Ng* coming at the end of a word has the single sound described above, as in *king, bring, sung, running, tongue.*

2. *Ng* followed by a suffix that may be eliminated and yet leave a meaningful stem has the single sound described above, as in *sing-er, sing-ing, long-ing, harangu-ing, hang-er.*

    a. *Exceptions: Ng* is pronounced *ngg* if the suffix is *al, ate,* or *ation;* or if the suffix is *er* or *est* signifying the comparative or superlative degree: *diphthong-al, elong-ate, prolong-ation; long-er, strong-er; long-est, strong-est.*

    b. Note that the *ng* spelling represents the sound of *ngg* where the removal of the suffix renders the stem meaningless: *fing-er, hung-er, lang-uor, tang-o, English.*

3. The *nge* spelling represents the sound of *nj* where *nge*

---

[1] The *l* sound has the same semi-vowel characteristic in *able, shovel, camel, devil, funnel,* etc.

either ends a word or a stem, as in *strange, strange-r; binge, binge-ing; stringe-nt, larynge-al, syringe*.

R

When *r* is final or before a consonant (*star, poor, our, hard, heart, further*), it is pronounced in General American speech—the speech of the North and West—but not in Southern or Eastern speech. No uniform direction for including or omitting the *r* sound may validly be given. Both *ah* and *arr* are correct for *are*.

However, the intrusive *r*—sounding an *r* when none is indicated—rests without a defense. No *r* should be heard when any of these words are pronounced:

dog	*not*	dorg
idea	*not*	idear
Utah	*not*	Utahr
Martha	*not*	Marthar
saw	*not*	sawr

The tendency to sound a nonexistent *r* is especially marked (and should be especially guarded against) when two vowel sounds are in conjunction, though in separate words. The *r* serves as an easy glide from one vowel to the other:

The idea of it *not* The idear of it.
The India Office *not* The Indiar Office.
I saw it *not* I sawr it.

W and Wh

W tends to become silent in some accented syllables. In a number of names, too, especially British names, the *w* is not sounded. The italicized *w* is omitted in the following words:

to*w*ards	Green*w*ich
ans*w*er	Nor*w*ich
s*w*ord	War*w*ick
t*w*o	Bruns*w*ick

The *wh* sound coming at the beginning of a word is generally breathed in American speech; the reverse is true in English speech. The sound, better represented by the spelling *hw*, is made by pronouncing *h* with rounded lips. Words containing the sound include: *whoa, what, where, when, whang, why.*

Silent Consonants

The following consonants are usually silent:

1. *b* before *t*.
    debt   subtle
2. *b* after *m*.
    bomb   crumb   dumb
3. *g* before *n* or *m*.
    gnat   sign   phlegm
4. *k* before *n*.
    knew   knight
5. *t* after *f* or *s* and when followed by the sounds *l* or *n*.
    often   soften
    chestnut   listen
6. *n* after *m*.
    autumn   solemn

NOTE: Frequently the addition of a suffix will cause silent letters to be sounded: the silent *g* of *phlegm* is sounded in *phlegmatic;* the silent *n* of *autumn* is sounded in *autumnal;* the silent *b* of *crumb* is sounded in *crumble.*

VOWELS

Classification of Vowels

The vowels are generally classified in the following manner:

a: long, as in *mate*
    short, as in *mat*
    circumflex, as in *care*
    Italian, as in *ah, far*
    Short Italian or intermediate,
    as in *ash*[1]
    broad, as in *awe*

e: long, as in *me*
    short, as in *met*
    tilde, as in *verse*

[1]This sound is intermediate between the *a* in *at* and the *a* in *ah*.

ī: long, as in *time*
short, as in *tin*

ō: long, as in *bone*
short, as in *not*

ū: long, as in *use*
short, as in *up*
circumflex, as in *urge*

Vowels in Monosyllables and Accented Syllables

1. An accented vowel at the close of a syllable usually has its long or name sound: *za'ny, pa'triot.*

2. An accented vowel followed by a single consonant (except *r*) in the same syllable generally has its regular short sound: *man'ly, lin'en.*

3. An accented vowel in a syllable ending in silent *e* preceded by a single consonant (except *r*) has its regular long sound: *mice, debate.*

4. In accented syllables ending in *r* final or *r* followed by another consonant, and in derivatives of such words—

   a. *A* has its full Italian sound; *bar, barn, debarred.*
   b. *E* has its tilde sound: *fern, infer, inferred.*
   c. *I* has the sound of tilde *e*: *sir, stir, stirring.*
   d. *O* commonly has the sound of broad *a*, as in *nor, storm;* but sometimes equals circumflex *u*, as in *word.*
   e. *U* has its circumflex sound: *cur, curt, incurred.*
   f. *Y* has the sound of tilde *e*: *myrtle, Myrmidon.*

5. An accented syllable ending in *r* doubled or *r* followed by a vowel has the regular short sound of its vowel: *mirror, heroine.*

6. In most monosyllables, and some other words, *a* has its short Italian or intermediate sound when followed by *ff, ft, ss, st, sk, sp,* and sometimes *nt* and *nce: pass, after, dance.*

7. *U* has the sound of long *oo* when preceded by *r: rule, ruin, rube.*

A few familiar monosyllables and their derivatives take short *u: run, rush, rub.*

A

The question "Shall words like *raft, class, chance, gasp, basket* take the Italian *a* of *ah* or the short *a* of *mat* or the intermediate *a* of *ask?*" cannot be categorically answered, except by reference to the prevailing sectional practice: The Italian *a*, though, usually sounds affected when used by Americans. The intermediate *a* is perhaps the American ideal; but as Krapp points out "the sound used by the majority of speakers is either that of *a* in *arm* or *a* in *at*." The main thing to avoid in words such as those listed above is drawling the short *a* so that it sounds like the *ai* of *air*.

E

1. *E* is usually silent in the termination *ed*—usually, but not always. EXCEPTIONS:

a. When preceded by *d* or *t*, the *e* is necessarily sounded: *blasted, deeded*.

b. When *ed* is followed by *ly* or *ness*, the *e* has its regular short sound: *assuredly, blessedness*.

c. A number of adjectives, mostly participles, have short *e: aged, beloved, blessed, cursed*. As verbs, however, they drop the sound of *e*.

2. Perhaps the main error in pronouncing *e* is giving it an undue accent in words such as *equator, elusive, elixir*. The initial *e* should receive only the faintest stress: it should be sounded like the *a* in *sofa*. But because American accent is recessive, that is, it tends to carry back to the first syllable, the *e* in words like those cited above is frequently mispronounced *ee*.

3. An error to which foreign speakers seem addicted is the substitution of short *a* for short *e*—*I mat him* for *I met him*.

I

1. Long *i* as in *time* is subjected to several mispronunciations, all due to faulty production of the sound. It is a combination of two sounds: Italian *a* and long *e*. Thus it is a diphthong. If the first element (Italian *a*) is not properly rounded, a dialectal pronunciation like *foine* or *moine* re-

sults. If the second element is omitted, another dialectal pronunciation results—*ah, trah.*

2. Substituting long *e* for short *i* is a mark of the foreign
accent: *e.g.,* I'll *sleet* his throat for I'll *slit* his throat; or He
deed it for he *did* it.

O

1. In a large number of words the choice lies with the
speaker as to whether he will use short *o* (as in *not*), broad
a (as in *awe*), or some sound between. This is especially true
when *o* is followed by *f, n, ng, th* (as in *thin*), *s.*

coffee	often
gone	wrong
cloth	sloth
Boston	loss

Most careful speakers, it is probable, prefer a sound intermediate to short *o* and broad *a*—since the first tends to
sound precious and the second is easily corrupted.
NOTE: Of course, in most words there is a clear distinction
between short *o* and broad *a:* it is incorrect to say *geawg-
raphy* for *geography, lawg* for *log,* or *dotter* for *daughter,
squoll* for *squall.*

2. Shortening and advancing long *o* until it approxi-
mates the sound of *o* in *above* is an old New England custom and, according to Professor Grandgent, still prevails in
the region. Most authorities, though, persist in regarding the
substitution as dialectal.

U

U has, for some time, been a battleground between the
pundits and the people. Two sounds which it symbolizes, *oo*
and *yoo,* are the cause of the contention.

In some words, the pronunciation is clear enough. After
r, for example, *u* always has the sound of *oo: rue, rule, ruin,
bruit.* And the distinction relative to sound is patent between such pairs as *pure* and *poor, feud* and *food, mute* and
moot, hue and *who, ooze* and *use.* Nor does anyone doubt

that the *yoo* sound is contained in these words: *beauty, fuse, bureau, mutual, furious, acute, huge;* or that the *oo* sound is contained in these: *Susan, Jupiter, solution, lure, conclude.* It would be difficult to pronounce the vowel sound in either group other than correctly.

The problem of *oo* and *yoo* has been greatly simplified, moreover, by the successive victories of the *oo* pronouncers. Formerly *u* after the letters *bl, fl,* and *pl* (as in *blue, fluent, plume*) was regularly pronounced *yoo;* now it is rarely pronounced anything but *oo.* Even the simple consonants *l* and *s* generally take the *oo* rather than the *yoo* sound after them: *luminous, lunar, lupine, lure,* and *lute; suicide, supreme, super, Suez, suture.* Only a few years ago, the *yoo* sound would have been prescribed after *l* or *s;* it is now almost the exclusive property of a select coterie.

What, then, is the status of *yoo* as against *oo?* Kennedy reports that the *yoo* pronunciation "is commonly favored by lexicographers and teachers of speech in the case of words spelled with *u, eu,* and *ew*" after the sounds *d, t, th* as in *thin; n, z, s, j* as in *judge; sh,* and *ch* as in *chew.* Thus, the pronunciation *yoo* is favored by lexicographers and teachers of speech for the *u* sound in the following words:

d*u*ke	d*u*ration
t*u*be	t*u*mor
enth*u*siasm	th*ew*s
n*ew*	n*u*merous
res*u*me	s*u*it
s*ew*er	s*u*itable
J*u*ne	J*ew*
s*u*rety	ch*ew*

Yet, in every one of these words, the dictionary either authorizes or prefers the *oo* pronunciation to the *yoo* pronunciation. There is no doubt that the *oo* pronunciation is winning out in all moot cases. After *t, d, n,* and *th* the *yoo* sound is still generally preferred: Professor Kenyon estimates that only about 40 percent of Americans use *oo* after these letters. But even after these, it would take a brave phonetician to declare that the *oo* sound is wrong.

PRONUNCIATION LISTS

Pronounce these words, paying attention to the underlined vowel sounds.

alma mater	gala
amenable	heinous
apparatus	jocund
civilization	oblique
culinary	onyx
drama	pathos
fief	route

Pronounce these words, paying attention to the underlined consonant sounds.

absurd	England
arctic	February
blackguard	government
breadth	height
chaos	only
chiropodist	orgy
depths	width

Do not transpose the underlined sounds.

bronchial	perspiration	perhaps
eastern	pharynx	represent
irrelevant	modern	southern
larynx	northern	western

Do not confuse the following groups.

accent	area	envelope	pillar
assent	aria	envelop	pillow
	era		
access		hospital	statue
assess	dias	hospitable	stature
excess	dies		statute
	dice		
affect		prerequisite	
effect		perquisite	
	desert		
	dessert		
	dissert		

BOOK EIGHT

Dictionary of Words
Most Frequently Mispronounced

THE PRONUNCIATION SYSTEM employed is that developed by the editors of *Words: The New Dictionary*, published by Grosset and Dunlap, and is reproduced with their permission. It "eliminates completely the bothersome diacritical marks found in many dictionaries. Each word for which pronunciation is necessary is respelled in the closest approximation to the most common values of English vowels and consonants. The stressed syllable is printed in italic type. Thus, for the word **inhibition** the following pronunciation is given:

in-hih-*bish*-'n.

Say it aloud and place emphasis on the *bish* syllable. The word pronounces itself."

A

abdomen	*ab*-duh-m'n	accounter	uh-*kownt*-er
	ab-*doh*-men	accumulate	uh-*kyoo*-myuh-layt
abject	*ab*-jekt	accurate	*ak*-yoo-rut
absolutely	ab-suh-*lute*-ly	acetylene	uh-*set*-uh-leen
absolve	ab-*solv*	acoustics	uh-*koo*-stiks
absorb	ab-*sorb*	acquiesce	ak-wee-*ess*
abstemious	ab-*stee*-mee-us	acrid	*ak*-rid
abstractly	ab-*strakt*-ly	acumen	uh-*kyoo*-m'n
absurd	ub-*serd*	adagio	uh-*dah*-joh
abysmal	ab-*iz*-m'l	address	uh-*dres*
academician	uh-kad-uh-*mish*-'n	adept	uh-*dept*
accent	*ak*-sent	admirable	*ad*-mer-uh-b'l
acclimate	uh-*kly*-m't	adobe	uh-*doh*-bee
	ak-luh-mayt	Adonis	uh-*dohn*-iss
accolade	ak-uh-*layd*	adulatory	*ad*-yoo-luh-tor-ee

adult	uh-*dult*	answer	*an*-ser
	ad-ult	antarctic	ant-*ark*-tik
adversary	*ad*-ver-ser-ee	antipode	an-*tip*-uh-dee
advertisement	ad-*ver*-tiz-ment	apiary	*ay*-pee-ehr-ee
aerial	ay-*eer*-ee-ul	apish	*ayp*-ish
	ayr-ee-'l (radio antenna)	apotheosis	uh-poth-ee-*oh*-sis
			uh-poth-ee-oh-*ses*
aeroplane	*air*-uh-playn		uh-*poth*-ee-uh-syz
aesthetic	es-*thet*-ik	apparatus	ap-uh-*ray*-tus
after	*aft*-er		ap-pa-*rat*-us
again	uh-*gen*	apparently	uh-*pair*-n't-lee
against	uh-*genst*	appendicitis	uh-pen-dih-*sy*-tis
aged	*ay*-jed		uh-pen-dih-*sy*-tus
agenda	uh-*jen*-duh	applicable	*ap*-lih-kuh-b'l
agile	*aj*-il	appreciation	uh-*pree*-shee-ay-shun
albumen	al-*byoo*-min		
algebra	*al*-jeh-bruh	apropos	ap-ruh-*poh*
alias	*ay*-lee-us	aquatic	uh-*kwat*-ik
alleged	uh-*lejd*	arbiter	*ahr*-bih-ter
allies	*al*-ize	archangel	*ahrk*-ayn-j'l
alloy	*al*-oi	architect	*ar*-kih-tekt
ally	*al*-y	aristocrat	uh-*riss*-tuh-krat
	uh-*ly*	aristocratic	uh-riss-tuh-*krat*-ik
alma mater	al-muh *may*-ter	armistice	*arm*-iss-tiss
	ahl-muh *mah*-ter	artificer	ar-*tif*-ih-ser
aloof	uh-*loof*	artistically	ar-*tis*-tik-uh-lee
alternating	awl-ter-*nayt*-ing	askance	uh-*skanss*
ameliorate	uh-*meel*-yuh-rayt	askew	uh-*skyoo*
amen	ay-*men*	asphalt	*ass*-fawlt
	ah-*men*	assiduity	ass-sih-*dyoo*-ih-tee
amenity	uh-*men*-ih-tee	assiduously	uh-*sid*-yoo-us-lee
amicable	*am*-ih-kuh-b'l	assimilate	uh-*sim*-'l-ayt
anathema	uh-*nath*-uh-muh	assume	uh-*syoom*
anchovy	an-*choh*-vee		uh-*soom*
	an-choh-vee	asthma	*az*-muh
angel	*ayn*-j'l	attaché	at-ash-*ay*
angle	*ang*-g'l	attacked	at-*takt*
annex	uh-*neks*	attitude	at-uh-*tyood*

attribute	uh-*trib*-yoot	automobile	*aw*-tuh-muh-beel
audacious	aw-*day*-shus		aw-tuh-*moh*-bil
audience	*aw*-dee-ens	avenue	*av*-uh-nyoo
auditorium	aw-dih-*tor*-ee-um		*av*-uh-noo
aunt	*ant*	avoirdupois	av-er-du-*poyz*
	ahnt	awful	*aw*-ful
au revoir	*oh* rih-*vwahr*	aye	*ay*
authoritative	aw-*thor*-ih-tay-tiv	azure	*azh*-er

B

bacillus	buh-*sil*-us	blasphemy	*blas*-fuh-mee
backgammon	bak-gam-'n	blessed	*bles*-ed
badinage	*bad*-'n-ij	boatswain	*boh*-s'n
	bad-ih-*nahzh*	bologna	buh-*lohn*-uh
banana	buh-*nan*-uh	bona fide	*boh*-nuh-*fy*-dee
bathe	*bayth*	bourgeois	boor-*zhwah*
baton	bat-*ahn*	bovine	*boh*-vyne
battery	*bat*-er-ee	braggadocio	brag-uh-*doh*-shee-
bayou	*by*-oo		oh
beatific	bee-uh-*tif*-ik	bravado	bruh-*vah*-doh
beauty	*byoo*-tee	brigand	*brig*-und
before	bih-*fore*	bringer	*bring*-er
bellows	*bel*-lohs	brochure	broh-*shoor*
benign	bih-*nyne*	brogans	*broh*-g'ns
bibliophile	*bib*-lee-uh-fyl	bronchial	*bronk*-ee-ul
	bib-lih-uh-fil	brusque	*brusk*
bigamy	*big*-uh-mee	buccaneer	buhk-uh-*nihr*
biography	by-*og*-rah-phee	buoyant	*boy*-unt
bivouacked	*biv*-ou-akt	bureau	*byoor*-oh
blancmange	bluh-*mahnzh*	bureaucracy	byoor-*ok*-ruh-see

C

cabal	kuh-*bal*	candidate	*kan*-dih-dayt
cadaver	kuh-*dav*-er	canine	*kay*-nyne
caffeine	*kaf*-een	canon	*kan*-un
caldron	*kawl*-dr'n	cantaloupe	*kan*-tuh-lohp
calliope	kuh-ly-*uh*-pee		*kan*-tuh-loop
caloric	kuh-*lor*-ik	carbine	*kahr*-byne

caricature	*kair*-ih-kuh-cher	clearly	*kleer*-lee
carte blanche	*kahrt blahnsh*	clientele	kly-en-*tel*
cartridge	*kahr*-trij	clothe	*klohth*
casualty	*kaz*-yoo-ul-tee	cognac	*kohn*-yak
cayenne	ky-*en*	cognomen	kog-*noh*-m'n
	kay-*en*	coiffure	kwah-*fyoor*
centimeter	*sen*-tih-mee-ter	colossal	kuh-*los*-'l
cerebral	*seh*-ruh-brul	column	*kol*-um
cerebrum	*seh*-ruh-brum	colt	*kohlt*
chagrin	shuh-*grin*	combatant	*kom*-bat-'nt
chameleon	kuh-*meel*-yun	commandant	kom-un-*dant*
champion	*champ*-ee-un	comment	*kom*-ent
chaos	*kay*-ahss	comparable	*kom*-p'r-uh-b'l
chaperon	*shap*-uh-rohn	comptroller	k'n-*trohl*-er
charade	shuh-*rayd*	concave	kon-*kayv*
	shuh-*rahd*	concentrate	*kon*-sen-trayt
chargé d'af-	*shahr-zhay* duh-	concerto	kun-*chehr*-toh
faires	*fair*	confidant	*kon*-fih-dent
charwoman	*char*-wom-an	confiscatory	kon-*fis*-kuh-tor-ee
chasten	*chays*-'n	conjecture	kun-*jek*-cher
chauffeur	*shoh*-fer	conjugal	*kon*-joo-g'l
chestnut	*ches*-nut	constable	*kon*-stuh-b'l
chic	*sheek*	constitution	kon-stih-*too*-shun
chicanery	chih-*kayn*-er-ee	construe	kun-*stroo*
chimera	kuh-*mihr*-uh	contemplate	*kon*-tem-playt
chimney	*chim*-nee	contemplative	kon-tem-*pluh*-tiv
chimpanzee	chim-pan-*zee*	contemptuous	kun-*tempt*-yoo-us
chiropodist	ky-*rop*-uh-dist	contour	*kon*-toor
chocolate	*chawk*-lit	contrary	*kon*-trer-ee
	chok-uh-lit	contumely	*kon*-tyoo-mee-lee
chorus	*kor*-us	conversant	kun-*ver*-s'nt
cigarette	sig-uh-*ret*	coquette	koh-*ket*
	sig-uh-ret	coral	*kor*-ul
circulation	serk-yuh-*lay*-shun	corps	*kor*
circumstances	*ser*-kum-stanss-es	corral	kuh-*ral*
civilization	siv-ih-lih-*zay*-shun	cosmetics	koz-*met*-iks
clandestine	klan-*des*-t'n	costume	*kos*-tyoom
cleanly	*kleen*-lee	coterie	*koh*-tuh-ree

couchant	*kow*-ch'nt	credulity	kruh-*dyoo*-luh-tee
courtesy	*ker*-tuh-see	creek	*kreek*
courtier	*kor*-tee-er		*krik*
cowardice	*kow*-er-dis	curator	kyoo-*ray*-ter
creature	*kree*-cher	cynosure	*sy*-noh-shoor

D

dahlia	*dal*-yuh	deshabille	des-uh-*beel*
	dahl-yuh	design	deh-*zyne*
	dayl-yuh	despaired	dis-*payrd*
dairy	*dayr*-ee	desperado	des-per-*ay*-doh
daub	*dawb*		des-per-*ah*-doh
daughter	*daw*-ter	despicable	*des*-pik-uh-b'l
daunt	*dawnt*	desultory	*des*-ul-tor-ee
dazzling	*daz*-ling	devotee	dev-oh-*tee*
deaf	*def*	diameter	dy-*am*-uh-ter
debt	*det*	diapason	dy-uh-*pay*-z'n
debut	*day*-byoo	dietary	*dy*-uh-tehr-ee
decade	*dek*-ayd	different	*dif*-runt
decadent	duh-*kay*-dunt	dilatory	*dil*-uh-toh-ree
	dek-uh-dunt	dilettante	dil-uh-*tan*-tee
deceases	deh-*sees*-us	diminution	dim-ih-*nyoo*-shun
décolletté	day-kol-*tay*	diocesan	dy-*os*-eh-s'n
decorative	*dek*-er-ay-tiv	dirigible	dihr-*ij*-ih-b'l
decrease	dee-*krees*	disadvan-	dis-ad-van-*tay*-jus
deduce	dih-*dyoos*	tageous	
deficit	*def*-uh-sit	discernible	dih-*zern*-ih-b'l
definitive	deh-*fin*-it-iv		dih-*sern*-ih-b'l
deign	*dayn*	disciplinarian	dis-ih-plin-*air*-ee-
delinquent	deh-*lin*-kw'nt		un
demagogy	*dem*-uh-goh-jec	discordant	dis-*kawrd*-'nt
demesne	deh-*mayn*	discursive	dis-*ker*-siv
demoniacal	duh-moh-*ny*-uh-k'l	disparage	dis-*pair*-ij
		disreputable	dis-*rep*-yoo-tuh-b'l
demur	deh-*mer*	dissolute	*dis*-uh-loot
dénouement	day-*noo*-mahn	dissonance	*dis*-uh-n'ns
depot	*dee*-poh	distingué	dis-tang-*gay*
derisive	deh-*ry*-siv	distrait	dis-*tray*

diva	*dee*-vuh	drama	*drah*-muh
divagate	*dy*-vuh-gayt		*dram*-muh
domicile	*dom*-uh-s'l	dramatis per-	*dram*-uh-tis per-
Dominican	duh-*min*-ih-k'n	sonae	*soh*-nee
Don Quixote	don-kee-*hoh*-tee	duce	*doo*-cheh
	don-*kwik*-sut	ductile	*duk*-t'l
dossier	*doss*-ee-ay	dulcinea	dul-*sin*-ee-uh
	doss-ee-er	duodenum	doo-oh-*dee*-num
doughty	*dow*-tee	dynasty	*dy*-nus-tee
dragoon	druh-*goon*		

E

ebullience	eh-*bul*-y'ns	entente	ahn-*tahnt*
ecarté	ay-kahr-*tay*	envelop	en-*vel*-up
Ecclesiasticus	uh-klee-zee-*ass*-tih-kus	envelope	*en*-vuh-lohp
		epicurean	ep-ih-kyoor-*ee*-un
eclectic	ek-*lek*-tik	Epiphany	eh-*pif*-uh-nee
eclogue	*ek*-log	episcopacy	eh-*pis*-kuh-puh-see
education	ej-oo-*kay*-shun	epithalamium	ep-ih-thuh-*lay*-mee-um
effect	eh-*fekt*		
effluvium	eh-*floo*-vee-um	epode	*ep*-ohd
either	*ee*-ther	equator	eh-*quay*-ter
	eye-ther	equatorial	eek-wuh-*tor*-ee-ul
elite	eh-*leet*	equinoctial	ee-kwih-*nok*-shul
	ay-*leet*	equivocal	eh-*kwiv*-uh-k'l
Elizabethan	eh-liz-uh-*bee*-thun	Eros	*eer*-os
	eh-liz-uh-*beth*'n	erotic	uh-*rot*-ik
embosom	em-*booz*'m	Esau	*ee*-saw
emir, emeer	uh-*meer*	esplanade	es-pluh-*nayd*
emu	*ee*-myoo	estuary	*es*-choo-ehr-ee
emulate	*em*-yuh-layt	Ethiopic	ee-thee-*op*-ik
encyclical	en-*sy*-klih-k'l	ethnology	eth-*nol*-uh-jee
endive	*en*-dyve	etiology	ee-tee-*ol*-uh-jee
	on-deev	evolution	ev-uh-*loo*-shun
endocrine	*en*-duh-kryne		ev-uh-*lyoo*-shun
endurable	en-*dyocr*-uh-b'l	exacerbate	eg-*zass*-er-bayt
ensanguine	en-*sang*-gwin	ex cathedra	eks kuh-*thee*-druh
ensconce	en-*skonss*	excrement	*eks*-krih-m'nt

excreta	eks-*kree*-tuh	ex post facto	eks pohst *fak*-toh
execrable	*eks*-ih-kruh-b'l	expostulate	eks-*poss*-chuh-layt
exigency	*eks*-uh-jun-see	expressionism	eks-*presh*-un-izm
exiguous	ig-*zig*-yoo-us	extortionate	ek-*stawr*-sh'n-it
expatriate	eks-*pay*-tree-ayt	extravaganza	ek-strav-uh-*gan*-
expiate	*ek*-spee-ayt		zah
exposé	eks-poh-*zay*		

F

Fabian	*fay*-bee-'n	financier	fin-un-*seer*
fabulous	*fab*-yuh-lus		fy-nan-*seer*
factitious	fak-*tih*-shus	flaccid	*flak*-sid
Fahrenheit	*far*-un-hyte	flâneur	flah-*ner*
faker	*fayk*-er	flautist	*flawt*-ist
fakir	fuh-*keer*	fleur-de-lis	fler-duh-*lee*
	fayk-er	fluoresce	floo-er-*ess*
falderal	*fahl*-duh-rahl	fluorine	*floo*-er-een
fasces	*fass*-eez		*floo*-er-in
Fascisti	fah-*sheess*-tee	forecastle	*fohk*-s'l
Fatima	*fat*-ih-muh	forestall	for-*stawl*
Faust	*fowst*	forfeit	*for*-fit
faux pas	foh *pah*	formula	*for*-myuh-lah
febrile	*fee*-bril	forsythia	fer-*sith*-ee-uh
	feb-ril	fortissimo	for-*teess*-uh-moh
February	*feb*-roo-er-ee	Frankenstein	*frank*-'n-styne
fedora	feh-*dor*-uh	frappé	frap-*pay*
feline	*fee*-lyne	Fraulein	*froy*-lyne
fellah	*fel*-uh	freight	*frayt*
fer-de-lance	fehr-duh-*lahnss*	fuchsia	*fyoo*-shuh
festoon	fess-*toon*	fulcrum	*ful*-kr'm
fete, fête	*fayt*	funereal	fyoo-*nihr*-ee-ul
feudal	*fyoo*-d'l	furbelow	*fer*-buh-loh
fiancé	fee-ahn-*say*	furor, furore	*fyoor*-or
	fee-*ahn*-say	fuselage	*fyoo*-z'l-ij
fiasco	fee-*ass*-koh		*fyoo*-z'l-ahj
fiducial	fih-*dyoo*-shee-ul	fustian	*fuss*-chun

G

Galen	*gay*-len	gonad	*gon*-ad
Galilean	gal-ih-*lee*-un	gondolier	gon-duh-*leer*
Gallic	*gal*-ik	Gorgonzola	gor-gon-*zoh*-luh
garrulity	guh-*rool*-uh-tee	gossamer	*goss*-uh-mer
gaucho	*gow*-choh	gourmand	*goor*-mand
gendarme	*zhahn*-dahrm	gourmet	*goor*-may
geniality	jeen-*ee*-al-uh-tee	gradation	gray-*day*-shun
genre	*zhahn*-ruh	gradual	*grad*-joo-ul
gentian	*jen*-sh'n	gratuitous	gruh-*too*-ih-tus
gentile	*jen*-tyle	gravure	*grayv*-yer
genuine	*jen*-yoo-in	Greenwich	*gren*-ij
Gestalt	geh-*shtahlt*		*grin*-ij
Gestapo	geh-*stah*-poh	grievous	*greev*-us
gestation	jess-*tay*-shun	grippe	*grip*
Gethsemane	geth-*sem*-uh-nee	grovel	*gruv*'l
glacier	*glay*-sher	gruel	*groo*-ul
glaucoma	glaw-*koh*-muh	Gruyère	groo-*yehr*
glazier	*glay*-zher	gubernatorial	goo-ber-nuh-*tor*-
glucinum	gloo-*sy*-num		ee-ul
Gnostic	*noss*-tik	guerrilla	ger-*il*-uh
gnu	*noo*	guillotine	*gil*-uh-teen
	nyoo	gynecology	gyne-uh-*kol*-uh-jee
golgotha	*gol*-guh-thuh		jyne-uh-*kol*-uh-jee
Goliath	guh-*ly*-uth	gyrate	*jy*-rayt

H

habeas corpus	*hay*-bee-us *kor*-pus	Harlequin	*hahr*-luh-kwin
		hasenpfeffer	*hah*-zen-fef-er
habitué	huh-*bich*-oo-ay	hateful	*hate*-ful
handicraft	*han*-dih-kraft	hauteur	haw-*ter*
hangar	*hang*-er	hedonism	*hee*-dun-izm
hara kiri	hair-uh *keer*-ee	hegira, hejira	heh-*jy*-ruh
harangue	huh-*rang*	height	*hyte*
harass	*hair*-us	helicopter	*hel*-ih-kop-ter
	huh-*rass*	helium	*hee*-lee-um
harbinger	*hahr*-bin-jer	Hellenic	hel-*en*-ik

hematoma	hem-uh-*toh*-muh	holocaust	*hol*-uh-kost
hemoglobin,	*hee*-moh-gloh-bin	homeopathy	hoh-mee-*op*-uh-thee
haemoglobin			
herbaceous	her-*bay*-shus	homogeneity	hoh-moh-jen-*ee*-uh-tee
Hereford	*hehr*-uh-ferd		
heterogeneous	het-er-oh-*jee*-nee-us	Homo sapiens	*hoh*-moh *say*-pee-unz
hiatus	hy-*ay*-tus	hosiery	*hoh*-zher-ee
Hiawatha	hy-uh-*woth*-uh	humus	*hyoo*-mus
hiccup	*hik*-up	hussar	huh-*zahr*
hierarch	*hy*-er-ahrk	hussy	*huz*-ee
hindrance	*hin*-drunss	hydropathy	hy-*drop*-uh-thee
Hippocratic	hip-uh-*krat*-ik	hygiene	*hy*-jeen
historic	*hiss*-tor-ik	hygienic	hy-jee-*en*-ik
history	*hiss*-ter-ee	hypothesis	hy-*poth*-uh-siss

I

iamb	*eye*-am	incriminate	in-*krim*-uh-nayt
ibex	*eye*-beks	incunabula	in-kyoo-*nab*-yoo-luh
Icarus	*ik*-uh-rus		
idea	eye-*dee*-uh	indefatigable	in-deh-*fat*-ig-uh-b'l
ideology	eye-dee-*ol*-uh-jee		
idyl, idyll	*eye*-d'l	indubitable	in-*dyoo*-bih-tuh-b'l
ignominious	ig-nuh-*min*-ee-us	indurate	*in*-dyoo-rit
ignoramus	ig-nuh-*ray*-mus	inexplicable	in-*eks*-plik-uh-b'l
illusive	il-*oo*-siv	infamous	*in*-fuh-mus
immanence	*im*-uh-nunss	informant	in-*form*-ent
imminent	*im*-ih-nunt	ingenious	in-*jeen*-yus
impecunious	im-peh-*kyoo*-nee-us	ingénue	*an*-juh-noo
impermeable	im-*per*-mee-uh-b'l	inherent	in-*heer*-'nt
imperturbable	im-per-*terb*-uh-b'l	inhibition	in-hih-*bish*-'n
importunate	im-*por*-choo-nit	innocuous	in-*ok*-yoo-us
imprimatur	im-prim-*ay*-ter	insatiable	in-*say*-shuh-b'l
impugn	im-*pyoon*	insouciance	in-*soo*-see-unss
inane	in-*ayn*	insular	*in*-suh-ler
inaugurate	in-*aw*-gyoo-rayt	insulin	*in*-suh-lin
incognito	in-*kog*-nit-oh	integral	*in*-teh-grul
		integrity	in-*teg*-rit-ee

intellectual	in-t'l-*ek*-choo-ul	ion	*eye*-un
intelligentsia	in-tel-uh-*jent*-see-	Iroquois	*ihr*-uh-kwoy
	uh	irreparable	ih-*rep*-er-uh-b'l
intermezzo	in-ter-*met*-soh	Iscariot	iss-*kair*-ee-ut
intestate	in-*tess*-tit	Ishmael	*ish*-mee-ul
inveigle	in-*vee*-g'l	isolate	*eye*-suh-layt
	in-*vay*-g'l	isthmus	*iss*-muss
iodine	*eye*-uh-dyne	itinerary	eye-*tin*-er-ehr-ee
	eye-uh-din	ivory	*eye*-ver-ee

J

jabot	zhah-*boh*	jewel	*joo*-ul
jackanapes	*jak*-uh-nayps	jocose	joh-*kohss*
Jacobean	jak-uh-*bee*-un	Judaism	*joo*-duh-izm
jaguar	*jag*-wahr	Judea	joo-*dee*-uh
Jehovah	jeh-*hoh*-vuh	judiciary	joo-*dish*-ee-ehr-ee
jejune	jeh-*joon*	ju jitsu	joo *jit*-soo
Jesuit	*jez*-yoo-it	juridical	joo-*rid*-ih-k'l

K

kaleidoscope	kuh-*ly*-duh-skohp	kilogram	*kil*-uh-gram
kapok	*kay*-pok	kimono	kuh-*moh*-nuh
khaki	*kak*-ee	kindred	*kin*-drid
	kah-kee	kohlrabi	*kohl*-rah-bee
kiln	*kil*	Ku-Klux	*koo*-kluks
	kiln	Kuomintang	kwoh-min-*tahng*
kilo	*kee*-loh		

L

laboratory	*lab*-ruh-tor-ee	lapis lazuli	*lap*-iss *laz*-yuh-lee
laborious	luh-*bor*-ee-us	larder	*lard*-er
labyrinthine	lab-er-*in*-thin	lascivious	luh-*siv*-ee-us
lacerate	*lass*-er-ayt	latent	*layt*-'nt
lacquer	*lak*-er	Lebensraum	*lay*-b'nz-rowm
lager	*lah*-ger	lenient	*lee*-nee-unt
laissez faire	leh-say *fair*		*lee*-nee-yunt
lamé	lam-*ay*	lese majesty	leez *maj*-ess-tee
languid	*lang*-gwid		leez mah-zhess-*tay*
languor	*lang*-er	Levant	leh-*vant*
lanolin	*lan*-uh-lin	liaison	lee-*ay*-zun

libido	iih-*by*-doh	liqueur	lee-*ker*
licorice	*lik*-er-iss	lissom	*liss*-um
	lik-er-ish	literature	*lit*-er-uh-cher
Lidice	lih-*deech*-eh	locale	loh-*kal*
lieu	*loo*	loch	*lok*
ligature	*lig*-uh-cher	loggia	*loj*-ee-uh
Lilliputian	lil-ih-*pyoo*-shun	Lorelei	*lor*-uh-lye
limn	*lim*	Louvre	*loov*-'r
lineament	*lin*-ee-uh-ment	lozenge	*loz*-enj
lingerie	*lan*-jeh-ree	lyceum	ly-*see*-um
	lahn-jeh-*ray*	lyonnaise	ly-uh-*nayz*

M

macabre	muh-*kah*-brah	matrix	*may*-triks
Machiavellian	mak-ee-uh-*vel*-ee-un	matzoth	*mat*-sohth
		mausoleum	maw-soh-*lee*-um
machination	mak-ih-*nay*-shun	mayhem	*may*-hem
machinist	muh-*sheen*-ist	medieval,	med-ih-*ee*-vul
madam	*mad*-'m	mediaeval	mee-dee-*ee*-vul
madame	muh-*dam*	medulla	meh-*duhl*-uh
Madeira	muh-*deer*-uh	meerschaum	*meer*-shum
mademoiselle	mad-'m-wuh-*zel*	mensuration	men-sher-*ay*-sh'n
Magdalen	*mag*-duh-lin	Mephistophe-	mef-iss-*tof*-uh-leez
Magna Carta	*mag*-nuh kahr-tuh	les	
maître d'hôtel	meh-truh doh-*tel*	Mephistophe-	meh-fiss-toh-*fee*-lee-an
malaise	muh-*layz*	lian	
malevolent	muh-*lev*-uh-l'nt	mercantile	*mer*-k'n-til
malinger	muh-*ling*-ger	meringue	mer-*ang*
Malthusian	mal-*thoo*-zhun	Mesozoic	mess-uh-*zoh*-ik
Maori	*mow*-ree	messieurs	*mess*-erz
	mah-uh-ree	mezzo	*met*-zoh
marijuana	mair-uh-*wah*-nuh	milieu	meel-*yer*
marquis	*mahr*-kwiss	minestrone	min-ess-*troh*-nee
marquise	mahr-*keez*	miniature	*min*-ee-uh-cher
Marseillaise	mahr-suh-*layz*	miscegena-	miss-seh-jeh-*nay*-shun
	mahr-seh-*yez*	tion	
masochism	*mass*-uh-kizm	mischievous	*miss*-chiv-us
matériel	muh-teer-ee-*el*	miscreant	*miss*-kree-ent

misogyny	mih-*soj*-in-ee	mousse	*mooss*
Mocha	*moh*-kuh	muezzin	myoo-*ez*-in
monarchic	muh-*nahr*-kik	Munich	*myoo*-nik
monger	*mung*-ger	museum	myoo-*zee*-um
monitory	*mon*-ih-tor-ee	mustache,	*mus*-tash
monogamy	muh-*nog*-uh-mee	moustache	muss-*tash*
monsieur	meh-*syer*	mutual	*myoo*-choo-ul
monsignor	mon-*seen*-yer	myopia	my-*oh*-pee-uh
mores	*mor*-eez	myrrh	*mer*
mortuary	*mor*-choo-air-ee		

N

naïve	nah-*eev*	nephew	*nef*-yoo
narcissism	nahr-*siss*-izm	Niagara	ny-*ag*-ruh
nascent	*nass*-n't	Nibelungen-	*nee*-buh-lung-un-
	nayss-n't	lied	leed
nasturtium	nuhss-*ter*-shum	Niger	*ny*-jer
nausea	*naw*-shuh	nihilism	*ny*-ul-izm
Navaho,	*nah*-vuh-hoh	Nisei	*nee*-say
Navajo		Nobel	noh-*bel*
Nazi	*naht*-see	nom de plume	nom duh *ploom*
	nat-see	nonentity	non-*en*-tuh-tee
Neanderthal	nee-*an*-der-tahl	non sequitur	non *sek*-wih-ter
Nebuchad-	neb-yuh-kud-*nez*-	Nostradamus	noss-truh-*day*-mus
nezzar	er	noxious	*nok*-shus
negotiable	neh-*goh*-shee-uh-	numismatics	noo-miz-*mat*-iks
	b'l	nuptial	*nup*-shul

O

obbligato	ob-lih-*gah*-toh	omniscient	om-*nish*-'nt
obdurate	*ob*-dyoor-rit	onomato-	on-uh-mat-uh-*pee*-
oblique	ob-*leek*	poeia	yuh
obstreperous	ob-*strep*-er-us	oratorio	or-uh-*tawr*-ee-oh
Occident	*ok*-sih-d'nt	oread	*or*-ee-ad
octave	*ok*-tayv	orientation	oh-ree-en-*tay*-shun
Odysseus	oh-*diss*-yooss	Orion	oh-*ry*-un
Oedipus	*ed*-ih-pus	orthodontia	or-thuh-*don*-shuh
ogre	*oh*-ger	osteopathy	oss-tee-*op*-uh-thee
oleaginous	oh-lee-*aj*-ih-nus	Ouija	*wee*-juh

P

padre	*pah*-dray	pince-nez	*panss*-nay
pall-mall	*pel-mel*	pique	*peek*
panegyric	pan-eh-*jihr*-ik	pistachio	piss-*tah*-shee-oh
panoply	*pan*-uh-plee		piss-*tash*-oh
papier-mâché	pay-per-muh-*shay*	piteous	*pit*-ee-us
paradigm	*pair*-uh-dim	pizzicato	pit-seh-*kah*-toh
	pair-uh-dyme	placate	*play*-kayt
paranoia	pair-uh-*noy*-uh	plaque	*plak*
paraphernalia	pair-uh-fer-*nayl*-	Platonic	pluh-*ton*-ik
	yuh	plebeian	pleh-*bee*-un
parfait	pahr-*fay*	pneumonia	nyoo-*moh*-nee-uh
pariah	puh-*ry*-uh	pogrom	*pog*-rum
parliament	*pahr*-lih-m'nt	poignant	*poyn*-yunt
parvenu	*pahr*-veh-nyoo	poilu	*pwah*-loo
pater noster	*pay*-ter *noss*-ter	poinsettia	poyn-*set*-ee-uh
pathos	*pay*-thoss	polygamy	puh-*lig*-uh-mee
patio	*pah*-tee-oh	polynomial	pol-ih-*noh*-mee-al
patois	*pat*-wah	polyphony	puh-*lif*-uh-nee
pediatrics	pee-dee-*at*-riks	polysyllabic	pol-ee-sih-*lab*-ik
Pegasus	*peg*-uh-sus	porous	*por*-us
penalize	*peen*-uh-lyze	portmanteau	port-*man*-toh
	pen-uh-lyze	posthumous	*poss*-choo-mus
penicillin	pen-ih-*sil*-in	precarious	preh-*kayr*-ee-us
Pentateuch	*pen*-tuh-took	preciosity	presh-ee-*oss*-ih-tee
peon	*pee*-un	predecessor	pred-eh-*ses*-er
	pay-on	preferential	pref-uh-*ren*-sh'l
pernicious	per-*nish*-us	prelude	*prel*-yood
perpendicular	per-pen-*dik*-yoo-	prescience	*pree*-shee-enss
	ler	presidium	preh-*sid*-ee-um
peso	*pay*-soh	prestidigita-	press-tih-dij-ih-
phalanx	*fay*-langks	tion	*tay*-shun
phallus	*fal*-us	preterit,	*pret*-er-it
Phillistine	fih-*liss*-teen	preterite	
phlegm	*flem*	preternatural	pree-ter-*nach*-er-al
phraseology	fray-zee-*ol*-uh-jee	prima donna	*pree*-muh *don*-uh
phthisis	*thy*-siss	Primates	pry-*may*-teez
piety	*py*-eh-tee	proboscis	proh-*boss*-iss

prodigy	*prod*-ih-jee	Ptolemy	*tol*-eh-mee
promenade	*prom*-uh-nahd	ptomain,	toh-*mayn*
	prom-uh-nayd	ptomaine	
Prometheus	proh-*mee*-thus	puberty	*pyoo*-ber-tee
pronounce	proh-*nownss*	pueblo	*pweb*-loh
prophecy	*prof*-eh-see	pugilism	*pyoo*-jil-izm
prophesy	*prof*-eh-sy	pursuance	per-*syoo*-unss
propitiate	proh-*pish*-ee-ayt		per-*soo*-unss
proselyte	*pros*-eh-lyte	putsch	*putch*
prosody	*pros*-uh-dee	pyrites	py-*ry*-teez
prostrate	*pros*-trayt	pyromania	py-roh-*may*-nee-
psittacosis	sit-uh-*koh*-siss		uh
Psyche	*sy*-kee	Pythagorean	pih-thag-uh-*ree*-un
psychiatry	sy-*ky*-uh-tree	python	*py*-thon

Q

quadrennial	kwah-*dren*-ee-al	quiver	*quiv*-er
quinine	*kwy*-nyne		

R

Rabelais	*rab*-eh-lay	repatriate	ree-*pay*-tree-ayt
raconteur	rak-on-*ter*	repercussion	ree-per-*kush*-un
rapier	*ray*-pee-er	residual	reh-*zid*-yoo-ul
ratio	*ray*-shoh	resonance	*rez*-uh-nenss
ration	*ray*-shun	résumé	ray-zoo-*may*
	rash-un	rococo	ruh-*koh*-koh
raucous	*raw*-kus	rodeo	*roh*-dee-oh
ravine	ruh-*veen*		roh-*day*-oh
recalcitrant	rih-*kal*-sih-tr'nt	Roentgen	*rent*-g'n
recession	reh-*sesh*-un	roseate	*roh*-zee-it
reformation	ref-or-*may*-shun	roué	rooh-*ay*
regress	reh-*gress*	rumba, rhum-	*rum*-buh
remembrance	reh-*mem*-brenss	ba	
renaissance	ren-uh-*sahnss*		

S

sacerdotal	sass-er-*doh*-tal	sadism	*sad*-izm
sachem	*say*-chem		*sayd*-izm
Sadducee	*sad*-yoo-see	safari	suh-*fah*-ree

sagacious	suh-*gay*-shus	silage	*sy*-lij
Sagittarius	saj-ih-*tair*-ee-us	Sioux	*soo*
sake	*sah*-kee (Japanese	sirocco	sih-*rok*-oh
	wine)	sluice	*slooss*
salient	*say*-lee-ent	Somme	*sum*
samaritan	suh-*mair*-ih-t'n	somnambu-	som-*nam*-byoo-
sang-froid	sang-*frwa*	lism	lizm
sanguinary	*sang*-guih-nehr-ee	Sorbonne	sor-*bun*
sarsaparilla	sahrss-puh-*ril*-uh	soubrette	soo-*bret*
satyr	*sat*'r	soufflé	soo-*flay*
	sayt-'r	spermatozoon	sper-muh-tuh-
sauté	soh-*tay*		*zoh*-un
scallop	*skol*-up	stentorian	sten-*toh*-ree-un
scaramouch	*skair*-uh-mowch	stipend	*sty*-pend
schism	*siz*-'m	stratum	*stray*-t'm
sciatica	sy-*at*-ik-uh		*strat*'m
scour	*skow*-'r	streptococcus	strep-tuh-*kok*-us
scrupulous	*skroop*-yoo-lus	strontium	*stron*-shee-um
Seine	*sayn*	styptic	*stip*-tik
seismic	*syze*-mik	succinct	suk-*sinkt*
semen	*see*-m'n	suki yaki	soo-kee *yah*-kee
sentience	*sen*-shunss	sundae	*sun*-dee
septicemia	sep-tuh-*see*-mee-	supernumer-	soo-per-*noo*-mer-
	uh	ary	ehr-ee
septuage-	sep-choo-uh-juh-	sycophant	*sik*-uh-f'nt
narian	*nair*-ee-un	systole	*siss*-tuh-lee

T

tacit	*tass*-it	tortilla	tor-*tee*-yuh
tedious	*tee*-dee-us	totalitarian	toh-tal-ih-*tair*-
teetotaler	tee-*toh*-t'l-er		ee-un
tepid	*tep*-id	tourniquet	*toor*-nih-ket
terpsichorean	terp-sih-kuh-*ree*-	transigent	*tran*-sih-jent
	un	triad	*try*-ad
thesaurus	theh-*saw*-rus	triptych	*trip*-tik
titan	*ty*-t'n	troll	*trohl*
titanium	ty-*tay*-nee-um	tsetse	*tset*-suh
tomato	tuh-*may*-toh	Tuileries	*twee*-ler-eez
	tuh-*mah*-toh	tyro	*ty*-roh

U

ubiquitous	yoo-*bik*-wih-tus	urinalysis	yoo-ruh-*nal*-ih-siss
unconscionable	un-*kon*-shun-uh-b'l	usury	*yoo*-zhoo-ree

V

vacuum	*vak*-yoo-um	viands	*vy*-'ndz
valence	*vay*-lunss	vice versa	*vy*-suh *ver*-suh
variorum	vair-ee-*or*-um	vicissitude	vih-*siss*-ih-tyood
Veda	*vay*-duh		vih-*siss*-ih-tood
	vee-duh	victual	*vit*-'l
vehicle	*vee*-uh-k'l	vignette	vin-*yet*
venial	*veen*-yul	virago	vih-*ray*-goh
venue	*ven*-yoo	virtuoso	ver-choo-*oh*-soh
verily	*vehr*-ih-lee	viscid	*viss*-id
Versailles	ver-*sy*	vizier	vih-*zeer*

W

walrus	*wawl*-rus	whorl	*hwerl*
warp	*worp*	wizened	*wiz*-'nd
wassail	*woss*'l	worsted	*wus*-ted
wharf	*hworf*		

X

xanthein	*zan*-thee-in	xenophobia	zen-oh-*foh*-bee-uh
Xanthippe,	zan-*tip*-ee	xylem	*zy*-l'm
Xantippe		xylophone	*zyle*-uh-fohn
xebec	*zee*-bek	xyster	*ziss*-ter

Y

yacht	*yot*	y-clept	ee-*klept*
Yahweh	*yah*-weh	Yosemite	yoh-*sem*-ih-tee
Yangtze	yahng-*tsee*	younker	*yung*-ker

Z

zenith	*zee*-nith	Zoroastrian	zor-oh-*ass*-tree-un
zephyr	*zef*-er	Zouave	zoo-*ahv*
Zeus	*zooss*	Zwinglian	*zwing*-glee-un

BOOK NINE

Usage

"To usage," Horace wrote, "belongs the rule, the law, and the government of language." But *whose* usage? That of the students of language? Our level of usage would be higher—more precise and less chaotic—if the language habits of the people who knew most about languages formed the standard. Unfortunately, the level would also be unattainable by the great mass of men. And language belongs to them, not to any "small, select coterie." The standard of usage in a democratic society, it has been well said, ought to be "the highest level likely to be operative as an example." When a recommended usage is not accepted by the generality of people, the better part of intelligence is not to insist on it. Conversely, when a usage frowned upon by the experts is regularly employed by everyone else, the intelligent expert stops frowning.

Levels of Usage

Standard English is defined by Krapp as that "use of the language least marked by local or other special peculiarities, which is regarded as regular and customary use wherever the language is spoken." In America, the standard is an ideal one: the speech of any locality differs (sometimes extensively) from the speech of any other. **Standard English**—also called **formal** or **literary** English—is the English of literature, of dictionaries, of grammars: it is not the language of the mass of the people.

A **dialect** is a language characterized by peculiarities of accent, pronunciation, or usage, common to a particular community or class. A dialect, says Bodmer, is associated "with local variations of pronunciation and minor differences of vocabulary within a single political unit." All national languages were once dialects; they gained ascendancy and are now standard speeches. Once the standard speech had been formed and had been given literary recognition, the local varieties of kindred speech, which were of equal rank till then, fell in linguistic estimation. Today they are regarded "as the speech of the unlearned." Yorkshire, Devonshire, Lancashire all have dialects peculiar to themselves. Among American dialects are Negro, Yankee, and Southern —and each of these exhibits wide variations from the individual dialectal norm.

Dialectal words—also called **localisms** or **provincialisms**— are suitable for a variety of legitimate purposes: creating "local color," lending an air of informality to discourse, giving a homely touch to speech or writing. However, they are not generally suitable for formal or studied speech. *Reckon* for *think, tote* for *carry, poke* for *bag* are dialectal usages; and the books on usage bristle with warnings against their indiscriminate employment.

Colloquial English is not necessarily the speech of the unlearned: rather it is unstudied expression, the English of familiar conversation—right and proper for ordinary, everyday speech. *Don't, I'd, we'll,* and contractions generally are colloquialisms, as are words and phrases like *fixed* (for *bribed*), *pretty* (for *very*), *funny* (for *peculiar*), *take stock in* (for *believe*) and *O.K.*

Colloquial speech at its lowest level shades into **slang**. Slang is disreputable language, made up of coined words, or of legitimate words employed grotesquely. H. L. Mencken declares that behind it lies "simply a kind of linguistic exuberance, and an excess of word-making energy." Slang has its impassioned defenders and its vehement antagonists. Perhaps the range of opinion may be indicated by these two quotations:

> Slang is language that takes off its coat, spits on its hands, and gets to work.—SANDBURG
>
> Slang is the speech of him who robs the literary garbage carts on their way to the dumps.—BIERCE

All that can be definitely said here is that slang is evanescent language, usually out of place in formal writing or speaking. Yet, it is undeniable that slang terms like the following are compellingly graphic: *rubberneck, hoosegow, flimflam, bozo, hot-shot*.

No one, however, can say much for the **vulgarism**. Vulgarisms are the grosser violations of the proprieties of usage and they exist at the bottom level of slang. Words like *gents, babe* (for *girl*), *bust* (for *burst*) are instances.

The **barbarism** is an expression which is not legitimately part of the language. *Hisself, ain't, drownded* are egregious examples.

Of a different order than these violations of usage are **technical terms,** those peculiar to a specialized activity (*Gothic bold, liliaceous, indene*); **foreign** terms, those, unlike *garage* or *fiancée*, not assimilated into the body of our language (*ab extra, n'est-ce pas, wanderjahr*); and **obsolete** or **archaic** terms, those not in current use (*whilom, yclept, thine*). None of these terms is to be condemned; but all are to be avoided in writing intended for the general reader. Suitable for some special contexts, they are thoroughly out of place in standard speech or writing.

PRINCIPLES OF USAGE

The Choice of Words

Fundamentally then, good usage is the choice of words suitable for the situation. Colloquialisms, technical words, slang—all are on occasion fit and proper. Walt Whitman held that "The Real Grammar will be that which declares itself a nucleus of the spirit of the laws, with liberty to all to carry out the spirit of the laws, even by violating them, if necessary." He took "pleasure in the use, on fit occasions, of —*traitor, coward, liar, shyster, skulk, doughface, trickster, mean, cuss, backslider, thief, impotent, lickspittle.*" Advocates of the King's English, the more than 99 98/100 percent purists, would, if they had their way, make ours a polite, limited, and consequently lifeless speech.

Idiom

The native cast of a language, the structure peculiar to it and its fixed modes of expression, must not be violated. Idiom is a paramount consideration in writing and speaking well. Unfortunately, idiom defies the rules. Only the habit of observing how words are consistently combined can insure against errors in idiom. The Frenchman who says *I return to the France* will be instructed that he is translating a French idiom into un-idiomatic English: the structure of the two languages is different. He supposes, then, that the article before France is superfluous and to be eliminated. He tries again with: *I leave United States.* And again he is subject to correction, since the article before *United States* is required this time. Why retain the *the* in one instance and not the other? Only because it is normally done by English-speaking people. Foreigners find that the most difficult part of English is to avoid tripping over the idioms. Only use will improve idiomatic usage.

Endowing inanimate objects with gender is another error of idiom to which foreigners are prone:

I took the pen.   She was blue.

The American pen is of neuter gender, though French pens are feminine.

The *'s* method of indicating possession similarly gives trouble to foreigners used to a different way of indicating possession. *His master's voice* may become *The voice of the master of him,* which, among other faults, would hardly do as an advertising slogan.

The normal word order of English (subject-verb-object)

undergoes some interesting, and occasionally attractive, transpositions when foreigners who have a wavering command of English idiom speak the language. They tend to rearrange, and sometimes reverse, the normal English sequence, as a result of the pull exerted by the word order inhering in their native tongue. Mark Twain cites an exaggerated instance, which, however, makes the point clear.

> But when he, upon the street, the (in satin-and-silk-covered - now - very - unconstrainedly - after - the - newest - fashion - dressed) government counselor's wife met, etc., etc.

The relations between certain prepositions and the words they follow are fairly definite, though the prepositions themselves show many shifts in meaning and use. The idiomatic linking of word and preposition cannot be reduced to rule, and any list is bound to be incomplete. Only study and practice will be of value in suggesting the appropriate preposition for a specific word. We say:

> *She agrees with him* and *to it.*
>
> *It is convenient to her place* and *for her purpose.*
>
> *The belief was grounded in error* and *upon fact.*
>
> *He was lavish of praise* and *in everything.*
>
> *Mr. A was reconciled to Mrs. A*
> and *Proposition A with Proposition B.*

Why? Because "usage wills it so." Rending asunder the preposition and other word that usage has joined together is a sin against idiom to which we are all prone and against which we must all guard.

Omission of Necessary Words

No necessary words may be omitted if the demands of clear unambiguous expression are to be fully met. The articles *a, an,* and *the* are small enough elements; yet, leaving them out sometimes renders the meaning of the sentence dubious. Compare

> The chief cook and bottle washer quit

with

> The chief cook and *the* bottle washer quit.

The first sentence indicates that one man, who held two offices, quit; the second, that two men, each of whom held one office, quit.

Omitting necessary prepositions frequently undermines the logic of a sentence. Such a sentence as:

> He has no interest or knowledge of Assyrian cuneiforms

is better revised to read:

> He has no interest in [,] or knowledge of [,] Assyrian cuneiforms.

(Better still would be:

> He has no interest in Assyrian cuneiforms or knowledge of them.)

NOTE: The commas in the brackets are optional.

Omitting necessary verbs or parts of verbs similarly impairs the consistency of a sentence. Revise:

> The plot was discovered and the plotters *were* executed.

to read:

> The plot was discovered and the plotters *were* executed.

Note that this error—one easy to make and difficult to discern—results from forcing a single verb to act in a double capacity. The following sentence:

> She never has and never will enjoy preserved turnips

should be changed to read:

> She never has *enjoyed* preserved turnips and never will *enjoy* them.

Closely related to the foregoing error is that of forcing a noun to assume two roles, only one of which is warranted:

> He is among the likeliest, if not the likeliest candidate for the gallows.

Here, the singular noun *candidate* completes two constructions; but the first construction demands a plural noun:

> He is among the *likeliest* candidates for the gallows, if not the likeliest candidate.

A certain license, however, is generally allowed in sentences like these. If the noun immediately follows and properly completes the first of the constructions, it will do for the second—even though rigid analysis would seem to require another form. This sentence is unexceptionable:

> He is among the likeliest candidates for the gallows, if not the likeliest.

Omitting a word or words necessary to complete a comparison often renders the meaning of a sentence doubtful:

> John likes Joan better than Jim

may mean either

> John likes Joan better than Jim does

or

> John likes Joan better than he does Jim.

The meaning is clear enough in the following sentence, but its faulty structure implies sloppy thinking:

> He is as brave or braver than anyone.

Better would be:

> He is as brave as, or braver than, anyone else.

Or better yet:

> He is as brave *as* anyone *else,* or braver.

Note, too, that *else,* has been added to the sentence. Otherwise, say some, the comparison must logically extend to the subject: *He is . . . braver* than anyone, including himself. This seems to be an overnice dictinction; but the rule (quoted for potential purists) is: Comparatives with *than,* completed by *any, all, everyone, anyone,* etc., must be followed by *else, other,* or some word which excludes the subject of the comparison. This rule applies of course only to comparisons within a specific class: it is perfectly logical to say

> I like my beret better than any fez.

Omitting the completing phrase or clause after *so, such, too,* and similar words is suggestive of "schoolgirl diction"— a kind of writing widely abhorred and better suppressed.

He is too divine

might, perhaps, be altered to read

> He is too divine to live.

At any rate, the activity, function, or whatever he is too divine for ought to be supplied.

Reference of Pronouns

The substantive to which a pronoun refers is called its *antecedent*. If the reference is unclear, if the antecedent is obscure, the pronoun is misplaced. Consider this sentence:

> Pat introduced Mike to his father.

Mike's father or Pat's? Normally, one would expect the reference to be to the nearer noun; but, in the sentence cited, that Mike had to be introduced to his father seems unlikely. The revision probably in order is:

> Mike was introduced by Pat to his father.

Precisionists might object to the sentence even as rephrased, though to most it would seem clear enough that Pat's father was introduced to Mike. An alternative way of putting the sentence

> Pat introduced Mike to his (Pat's) father

is occasionally taken, in spite of its clumsiness. In general, unless the sense of the sentence is against the interpretation, the antecedent nearer the pronoun is the referent.

Remote reference is usually inadvisable. It sends the reader scurrying back for the antecedent:

> The witchcraft trials are central in any consideration of the relation of Cotton Mather to his time. Remember that Cotton Mather was a theocrat, and that the new charter threatened theocratic supremacy. They took place in Salem, Massachusetts.

They in the last sentence refers to *trials* in the first, as the reader can discover by a bit of diligent search. Simply repeating *trials,* however, would have eliminated the necessity for search.

Broad reference when it results in a real ambiguity is to

be avoided. The reference of pronouns should, as a rule, be to specific words or groups of words, rather than to the general ideas contained in them. What, in the following sentence, is regrettable?

> He was found stone-cold dead in the market, a fact which was regrettable.

That he was found in the market? That he was found dead? That he was found stone-cold dead? Such questions have an apparent plausibility, but they must not be too much insisted on. The context would make it plain enough, in most cases, that his being found dead is central to the sense of the sentence—not the location at which he was found nor yet the quality of his deadness. Revision would dissipate much of the naïve charm of the sentence: for example:

> He was dead, a fact which was regrettable. His stone-cold body was found in the market.

Broad reference is bad if it results in real ambiguity, certainly; but a certain amount of latitude is granted by usage even in formal English.

However, the employment of indefinite pronouns like *it*,[1] *they,* and *you* to refer to antecedents that are unexpressed may not be defended in the same way—at least, not for formal writing.

> The legislature passed such bad laws that you could not be good.

For you, substitute *people,* or *one,* or some similar word.

An even more fertile source of confusion is the repetition of the same pronoun when it refers to a different antecedent.

> If the horse makes a superequine effort and *it* is successful, *it* may win the race.

The first *it* refers to *effort;* the second, to *horse.* One possible revision is:

> The horse, if it makes a superequine effort which is successful, may win the race.

---

[1] The indefinite it in *It is generally believed* is idiomatic, and hence a perfectly acceptable usage.

Dangling Modifiers

A modifier—it needs no great feat of logic to deduce—requires something to modify. Participles, gerunds, and infinitives are sometimes left "dangling"—that is, unattached or wrongly attached to the word or words they are to modify. The result is almost inevitably a "boner" or "howler." Correction is easy: simply relate the verbal to the logical substantive, the agent that really performs the action inherent in the verbal:

DANGLING PARTICIPLE:
Having misspent his youth, age found him bankrupt.
(*Having misspent* modifies *age*.)

REVISED:
Having misspent his youth, he was found bankrupt by age.
(*Having misspent* modifies *he*.)

REVISED:
Because his youth had been misspent, age found him bankrupt.
(The participial phrase has been expanded into a clause.)

DANGLING GERUND:
By solving the case, the money was recovered by Philo.

REVISED:
By solving the case, Philo recovered the money.

REVISED:
The money was recovered by Philo's solving of the case.

DANGLING INFINITIVE:
To avoid folly, fools must be avoided.

REVISED:
To avoid folly, one must avoid fools.

REVISED:
To avoid folly, avoid fools.

Dangling Phrases and Clauses

Phrases and clauses that modify must be placed as close as possible to the words they are to modify. Otherwise, the relation of modifier and word modified may readily be mistaken. Douglas Jerrold was once asked, "Does a gentleman belong to your club with one eye named Walker?" "What is the name of the other eye?" returned Jerrold. If the phrase *with one eye* had been placed in logical relation to the word the speaker intended it to modify, *gentleman,* Jerrold's purposeful misconstruction would have been out of order.

Or again, if the lady who advertised for "A husband with a Roman nose that has strong religious tendencies," had placed the clause *that has strong religious tendencies* and the noun *husband* in conjunction, she would have avoided William Walsh's query: "Did she wish those tendencies to be Roman also?"

The Split Infinitive

The infinitive ought, normally, to be kept intact—that is, no word ought to be placed between *to* and the verbal. The reason for the injunction is that related words are best kept together. But split infinitives are sometimes more natural than unsplit: the inserted word may secure for the sentence a clearness or an emphasis or a rhythm otherwise unobtainable. Expert writers who are thoroughly aware of the rule do not hesitate to break it:

> Send five souls more to just precede his own.—BROWNING

> In the critical commentary which accompanies the pictures we . . . have tried—and it has been hard at times!—to not too strongly show our prejudices.—ROCKWELL KENT

Try rewriting the first sentence cited:

> Send five more souls just to precede his own.
> Send five more souls to precede just his own.

Either rewriting misses the meaning. The split infinitive is, beyond debate, necessary to the sentence. In the second sentence cited, three words come between *to* and its infinitive— and yet any other placement of the modifying words would violate either the meaning or the movement of the sentence.

The Terminal Preposition

Since it is good prose practice to end clauses and sentences by a relatively strong word, and since prepositions are relatively weak words, the restraining injunction has been made:

"Never allow a preposition to stand at the end of a clause or sentence." Yet, very often, the terminal preposition is completely natural; and recasting the sentence so that the preposition will precede its object makes for artificial and awkward expression. Whenever a stylistic point can be gained, the preposition may unhesitatingly be placed at the end of the clause or sentence. Compare

> What do you stand for?

with

> For what do you stand?

Sometimes, in fact, the terminal preposition is inevitable:

> He was laughed at.[1]

"Squinting" Constructions

Look at the following sentence:

> The author consented unsmilingly to take a bow.

Did the author unsmilingly consent? or did he consent to unsmilingly take a bow (or, if the infinitive is to remain unsplit, to take a bow unsmilingly)? The adverb may refer to either the verb preceding or the infinitive following. Avoid such squinting constructions: they make for a needless ambiguity.

Agreement

The *New English Dictionary* has this definition of *Agreement:* "To be in accord; to take the same gender, number, case, or person; as happens in inflected languages to words in apposition, and to substantives and their attributive words, whether adjective, verb, or relative."

Since modern English is largely an uninflected language, many of the above notations concerning agreement are superfluous. The few that follow comprise the rules of agreement applicable to English—and even they are not universally applicable.

1. **Verb and Subject.** The verb agrees with its subject in number and person:

> I *am* the man.

[1]Some grammarians consider *at,* in such constructions, to be part of the verb.

Where the subject consists of two or more words differing in number, person, or both, and connected by a pair of alternative conjunctions, the verb agrees with the nearer.

Neither my friends nor I *am* content.

The usage, however, ought to be avoided.

2. **Nouns and Pronouns.** The pronoun agrees with its antecedent in gender, number, and person.

Each boy (girl, thing) remained in *his* (*her, its*) place.

3. **Substantive and Adjective.** The adjective agrees in number with the substantive it modifies—if the adjective has a distinctive modification to indicate numbers. Only the two demonstratives have.

This or that kind.

These or *those* kinds.

The Intensive or Reflexive Pronoun

Pronouns like *myself, yourself, himself, ourselves, yourselves, themselves* ought not to be indiscriminately employed as substitutes for the personal pronouns. Instead of writing

They scorned Mary and *myself*

write

They scorned Mary and *me*.

Conjunctions

Three conjunctions, particularly, give trouble:

1. *So* is a conjunction by courtesy. Employed sparingly, *so* may impart an informal air to discourse; employed excessively, *so* renders it rather childish. *Since, because, accordingly,* are possible—and recommended—substitutes.

2. *While* implies a time element: *The seven dwarfs whistled while they worked.* As a substitute for words like *though, whereas,* and *but*—words which imply contrast—*while* is better avoided.

3. *Like* may be used as a conjunction only in special circumstances; essentially, *like* is a preposition. *As,* a conjunction, almost always is to be preferred.

Beauty is *as* (not *like*) beauty does.

Placing of Adverbs

Adverbs like *almost, always, ever, merely, quite,* and *only* should be placed as close as possible to the word or word group that they limit. There is plainly a large difference between

>   Only the brave deserve the fair

and

>   The brave deserve only the fair

and

>   The brave deserve the fair only.

Yet, for several centuries, both in speech and writing, men who knew very well what they were about have placed the adverb away from the sentence element it modified, if they thought the rhythm of the sentence could be improved:

>   And now I only hear
>   Its melancholy, long, withdrawing roar.—ARNOLD

With a like motive, one is justified in following their example.

Misconstructions

In each of the following sentences, an adverbial clause is employed where a noun clause is required:

> The reason is *because he is unreasonable.*
>
> Prejudice is *where you decide you don't like someone* before knowing him.
>
> Fear, according to one psychological theory, is *when you run away.*

Righting the wrong is easy: simply convert the adverbial clause to a noun clause, a noun, or a noun equivalent.

> The reason is that he is unreasonable.
>
> Prejudice is deciding that you don't like someone before knowing him.
>
> Fear, according to one psychological theory, is the act of running away.

The Double Negative

If two negatives interweave, the result is construed affirmatively. Thus,

None is immortal

is logically taken to mean

All are mortal.

The situation is not quite the same when two negative adverbs modify the same sentence element. Few would suppose

They will not never die

to mean

They will die.

Logically, the two sentences just quoted are equivalent; but the process of solving the negatives is difficult, and most conclude that *None should not die* is merely an illiterate attempt to achieve emphasis—as commonly it is. No blanket order to refrain from employing double negatives can be issued by the grammarian, because too many literary masters from Chaucer to the present have used double (and triple) negatives; but the grammarian ought strongly to advise great circumspection.

Co-ordination

The harmony of the sentence requires that like be joined to like. For example, it is bad usage to co-ordinate a gerund and an infinitive, or a phrase and a clause, or a passive and an active construction.

NOT: Mark Twain learned to fear God and dreading the Sunday School.

BUT: Mark Twain learned to fear God and to dread the Sunday School.

OR: Mark Twain learned fearing God and dreading the Sunday School.

NOT: A man of taste and who has no objects to gratify it must be a malcontent.

BUT: A man of taste who has no objects to gratify it must be a malcontent.

OR: A man who has taste and (who has) no object to gratify it, must be a malcontent.

NOT: He wishes to write well, and therefore great pains must be taken by him.

BUT: He wishes to write well, and therefore he must take great pains.

BOOK TEN

Dictionary of Usage

A

A—an

Ayres remarks concerning *a* and *an:* "The second form of the indefinite article is used for the sake of euphony only. Herein everybody agrees, but what everybody does not agree in is, that it is euphonious to use *an* before a word beginning with an aspirated ("breathed") *h,* when the accented syllable of the word is the second. For myself, so long as I continue to aspirate the *h's* in such words as *heroic, harangue,* and *historical,* I shall continue to use *a* before them; and when I adopt the Cockney mode of pronouncing such words, then I shall use an *an* before them." This is sound (in both senses of the word) theory: but what is our practice? Do we aspirate the *h* in *historical?* Very few of us do; and therefore *an historical* is perfectly right. However, we do aspirate the *h* of *history;* and therefore *a history* is the preferable form.

Affect and effect

Affect, as a verb, means "to act upon or influence"; as a noun, *affect* signifies "an emotion or feeling." *Effect,* as a verb, means "to produce, to bring to pass, to accomplish"; as a noun, *effect* signifies "a result or consequence." The dif-

ference is definite enough, but the words continue to be confounded.

> Little things affect little minds.—DISRAELI
> An affect must stretch into thought.—GOLDSCHMIDT

(NOTE: *Affect* (the noun) is used primarily in psychological contexts.)

> All he effects is defective.—RATNER
> Every cause produces more than one effect.—HERBERT
> SPENCER

Aggravate

Aggravate is a very inadequate synonym for *annoy, pro-
voke,* or *irritate.* Properly it signifies "to increase" or "to intensify" (French *aggraver,* to make worse: Latin *aggravatus,*
make heavy). The noun *aggravation* has an analogous meaning:

> The effect of power and publicity on all men is the aggra-
> vation of self, a sort of tumor that ends by killing the victim's
> sympathies.—HENRY ADAMS

Alright

Alright is gaining currency, though it has not yet been
recognized. It was, probably, formed by analogy with *already.* Properly, the elements are separate words: *all right.*

Amount and number

Amount applies to a sum or mass or quantity; *number,* to
units. With *amount* use *less;* with *number, fewer.* This "harmony," as the older grammarians called it, ought to be observed whether the amount or the number is implied or
expressed.

> The rare Few, who, early in Life, have rid Themselves of the
> Friendship of the Many.—WHISTLER.

> Give all thou canst; high Heaven rejects the lore
> Of nicely-calculated less or more.—WORDSWORTH

Also

Also is an adverb—a word that modifies; it is not a conjunction—a word that joins. Consequently it is no substitute

for *and* (except in colloquial speech). *For it was the first time, also the last,* write . . . *and the last.*

It is considered "inelegant" to begin sentences with *also*. Nevertheless, the sentence situation may warrant it: *Also* used initially may enhance paragraph movement and emphasize sentence relation.

> He is a cutthroat, liar, and thief. Also, he is my friend.

Alternative

Alternative means, strictly, "a choice between two things"; and strict grammarians hold that we cannot speak of "two alternatives," there being only "one alternative or choice. When that choice has been made, there remains no other." The force of usage, however, has rendered *alternative* acceptable even when more than two things are offered for choice. "Two alternatives" is, in fact, more frequent than "the alternative."

Aren't and ain't

Every contraction for *am not* grates. *I aren't,* though good form in England, sounds awkward and artificial to Americans; further, it violates both grammar and idiom. *I ain't* is hardly better—not even Mencken considers it a standard American substitute for *am not.* And *ain't* as a contraction of *is not, are not, has not,* or *have not* is without a defense, since there exist suitable contractions for all four:

> He is not—He isn't
> They are not—They aren't
> He has not—He hasn't
> They have not—They haven't

Let us face it: There is not any acceptable contraction for *am not* in cultivated colloquial speech.

Around and about

Around, in the sense of "approximately," is sanctioned as a colloquial usage. But for more formal expression, prefer *about:*

> At the top of his form he could run the hundred in about ten minutes.

Awake, awaken, wake, waken

Awake and *awaken* may be employed either transitively or intransitively. As an intransitive verb, *awaked,* or *awoke* are the forms for the past tense and *awaked* is the form for the past participle. As a transitive verb, *awaked* is the form for both the past tense and past participle.

The past tense of *wake* is either *waked* or *woke;* the past participle is *waked* or, occasionally, *woken. Wakened* is the form for both the past tense and past participle of *waken. Wake* and *waken* may be employed either transitively or intransitively.

There are a few distinctions still insisted upon relative to the use of these verbs:

1. *Wake* is what Fowler calls "the ordinary working verb" and it has been used as such from the beginnings. (Chaucer, for example, writes of being "waked with small foules a gret hepe.")

2. *Waken* and *awaken* are employed more frequently as transitive verbs than as intransitives. *Awakened,* either as a simple past or as a past participle, is the regular transitive form:

> I awake (*or* awaken) with difficulty and with regret.

But:

> I awakened him with difficulty and without regret.

3. *Awake* and *awaken* are employed figuratively more often than *wake* or *waken:*

> Awake, my soul!—DODDRIDGE
> A sense of glad awakening—MILLAY

B

Behind and in back of

Since *in front of* is unimpeachable, why not *in back of?* The question admits of no really rational answer, and consequently *in back of* is frequently employed, in spite of the strictures of the grammarians. Moreover, *Behind the house* may not refer to the same location as *in back of* the house: *in back of* is a constant, as definite (and opposed to) as *in front of; behind* varies with the locus of the speaker.

Beside and besides

Historically these words have been employed interchangeably. In current usage, they are fairly distinct. *Beside* means "by the side of" and is a preposition; *besides* means "in addition to, moreover" and is both a preposition and an adverb. You can be "beside yourself" and, besides, "be yourself."

Between and among

Between is used in relation to two objects, both of which may be plural in form. *Among* is used in relation to more than two objects. However, the *NED* approves *between* in sentences like *The treaty between the three powers was worth the paper it was written on—but not much more.*

Burst and bust

The chief employment of *bust* is as a noun; as a verb, its proper application is confined to broncos. In the sense of *burst,* it is "inelegant, dialectal, or vulgar."

But

1. *But* as a preposition meaning "except" should take the objective case:

> All but him had fled.

However, some authorities construe *but,* in sentences like the one quoted, as a conjunction in an elliptical construction. Consequently they would defend

> All but he had fled,

regarding it as equivalent to

> All had fled, but he had not.

The logic is not a little questionable; but the usage is permitted (though not preferred).

2. *But* as an adverb means "only," or "merely." Beware of its use in negative constructions. *Stay but a little longer,* and *Don't stay but a little longer* have opposite significations. *But that* and *but what* are also to be guarded against. *There is little doubt that Jack the Ripper was no gentleman* is a neater, less involved, and more exact sentence than *There is little doubt but what* (or *but that*) *Jack the Ripper was no gentleman.*

C

Can and may

Can implies power or possibility; *may,* permission or sanction. *Could* and *might* are similarly distinguished. Originally *can* and *may* were interchangeable, as were their past forms, *could* and *might.* The Bible speaks of the maniac in the tombs of Gadara whose ferocity was so great "that no man *might* pass that way." The revised version, in conformity with our altered usage, substitutes *could* for *might.*

Come and . . .

Come and get it, Try and do it, Go and see it, and parallel constructions are good American speech—idiomatic, forceful, unambiguous. Purists, who regard them as ungrammatical, fail to see that they are the psychological equivalents of *Come to get it, Try to do it, Go to see it.*

Complected

Complected is dialectal for *complexioned.*

> Saxe says that the lesson young ladies ought learn from *Othello* is to beware of swarthy-complexioned (*not* complected) suitors.

Continuous and continual

Time is continuous; but the periodic striking of a clock is, at most, continual. *Continuous* implies "that which is unbroken, never ceasing"; *continual,* "that which is constantly renewed and recurring, with, it may be, frequent stops and interruptions." Such, at any rate, is the usage of (perhaps excessively) discriminating writers, though in the speech of most *continuous* and *continual* are continually (*not* continuously) confounded.

Couple

"Couple: two of the same species or kind"—thus Stormonth and most authorities. However colloquial usage frequently makes *couple* mean "a few, several." The authorities frown, but the usage persists.

D

Data

Data is a plural noun, and it takes a plural verb: *data are* not *data is.* The form is frequently felt to be singular because the singular form *datum* is rarely used. But there is no dictionary justification for its employment as a singular, and even the liberal judgment of *Current English Usage* ranks such employment as "illiterate."

Date

Except colloquially, *date* is not a happy substitute for *appointment.*

Die with

People die *with* their boots on, but *of* pneumonia, consumption, or, simply, old age.

Differ and different

Writers differ from one another with regard to the particle to be used with this verb. "Some say they differ *with,* others that they differ *from,* their neighbors in opinion." What is clear is that *differ from* and *differ with* are not very different in most significations. The distinction, that *differ from* more emphatically connotes dissimilarity whereas *differ with* better implies unlike opinion, does not stand up under scrutiny. Sentence rhythm will dictate the one or the other usage.

Different from, however, is the standard American idiom. *Different than* is sanctioned if awkward phrasing would result from the employment of the standard idiom. *Different to* is British and is best avoided by Americans.

Done

Done for *did* is dialectal or illiterate.

I saw my duty and I *did* it (*not* done it).

Don't and doesn't

Don't and *doesn't* are both colloquial contractions—unexceptionable when they are used with proper reference. But *He don't* is as incorrect as *He do not,* which is its expanded form. *We doesn't* is hardly adult, and is perhaps no more common than *We does not.*

Doubt whether and doubt that

Doubt whether connotes uncertainty; *doubt that,* improbability. If you say "I doubt whether it will rain or not," the implication is that you are no weather prophet. If, on the other hand, you say "I doubt that it will rain," the implication is that you are predicting it will not.

Due to and because of

Due to is an adjective phrase; *because of* is an adverbial phrase. The notes beginning *Due to a cold, John was absent on Monday* which generations of mothers have written to generations of teachers should have begun: *Because he had a cold, John was absent on Monday* or *John's absence on Monday was due to a cold. Due to* used adverbally is acceptable for conversation—in fact, it is almost unavoidable. But, in writing, remember that *due to* must always be attachable to a noun. (A practical suggestion: Never begin a sentence with *due to* unless you have a firm grammatical footing.)

E

Each other and one another

The overscrupulous insist that *each other* must apply to two only; and that *one another* must be used if the number considered exceeds two. When Buckle wrote that the great authors of Germany "address themselves, not to their country, but to each other," he was taken to task. One authority comments: "Buckle should have written *one another* and not *each other,* unless he meant to intimate that the Germans had only two great authors, which is not probable." However, this distinction is finical; *each other* and *one another* are used interchangeably by almost everyone.

Everybody

Everybody attempts to climb the heavenly staircase in his own way rather than *their own way.*

The usage recommended above is not a happy one, but it is better than the alternative. For some reason *everyone* (*q.v.*) is regarded as being either singular or plural—according to context—while *everybody* is regarded as being only singular. There is no logic in condoning one and condemning the other: but people's preferences in things other than language have never been notably logical.

In informal conversation, though, *everybody . . . their* is quite permissible.

Everyone

Everyone is a singular form, but it has the force of *all*. Thus, sentences like *Everyone came, and they were all sorry* are defensible in spite of the apparent departure from the grammatical straight-and-narrow. The *NED* says: "The pronoun referring to *everyone* is often plural; the absence of a singular pronoun of common gender rendering this violation of grammatical concord sometimes necessary." The purists, however, still are violently opposed to condoning the "violation." But Samuel Johnson, "no functionalist he," wrote:

> Everyone sacrifices a cow or more, according to *their* different degrees of wealth or devotion.

Except and accept

Accept means "to take what is offered"; *except,* "to exclude." The similarity of sound causes these clearly different verbs to be confused. The following are very nearly opposite enjoinders: *accept him* and *except him.*

F

Fixed

In America, as in England, fixed means "fastened into position." In America, the word may, with entire propriety, also be used as a synonym for "repaired."

Folk

The plural of *folk* is *folk,* and consequently purists oppose the coined plural *folks.* But the senses of the two plurals differ. When speaking of groups of people that have their own distinctive cultures and traditions, the preferred plural is *folk.* When speaking of people in general (*folks say*) and especially when speaking of the members of one's family (*my folks*), *folks* is incontestably more fitting and more natural.

Former and latter

Former should refer to the first named of two things, and *latter* to the second named. If more than two things are named, *first* and *last* should be used instead of *former* and *latter.*

Further and farther

Further and *farther* have become identified in popular speech and are used interchangeably. Lovers of nice distinctions, however, are still careful to employ them distinctly:

further is preferred with reference to degree or extent; *farther,* with reference to physical distance. But:

> Might have gone *further* and fared worse.—HEYWOOD

> But now it's little joy
> To know I'm *farther* off from heaven
> Than when I was a boy.—HOOD

Actually *further* and *farther* are almost synonymous. Only one distinction is really valid: *further* rather than *farther* is the figurative word:

> He is a fool; *further,* he is a tedious and egotistical fool.

G

Got—gotten

In sentences expressing simple possession (*I've got some news*), *got* is superfluous as the *ten* sometimes tacked on to it. In a few idiomatic expressions, of course, *got* is fitting and proper—and so is *gotten:*

> I've got plenty of nothing.
> She's got what it takes.
> We've got the men.
> Ill-gotten gains.

Peculiarly, though *gotten* is considered archaic and dialectal, *forgotten, begotten,* which have the same stem, are the preferred forms of the perfect participle.

> Misbegotten knaves.
> Forgotten dreams.

H

Hadn't ought, hadn't of

Hadn't ought and *hadn't of* are illiterate combinations. In Steinbeck's *Of Mice and Men,* there is a character addicted to these locutions; he suffers from arrested development.

Ought not to have and *had not* are infinitely better.

Had rather

Had rather signifying "would prefer"—now an established colloquial usage—exemplifies an interesting bit of popular etymologizing. *I'd* is a contraction of both *had rather* and *would rather*. *Would rather* is, of course, synonomous with *would prefer*. Wordsworth writes, *Great God! I'd rather be a Pagan suckled in a creed outworn,* employing the perfectly legitimate contraction for *would rather*. At this point, a "semantic switch" occurs—the result of a false identification If *I'd rather* is correct, why, then, so is *I had rather,* since one merely expands the other. In this context, the only justifiable expansion is, plainly, *would rather;* but because the expansion has so frequently been *had rather,* the latter has become accepted.

His or he, he or she

Unless there is some particular point of discrimination to be achieved, expressions like *Each will do what he or she can,* or *Each will do his or her best,* are needlessly stilted. Through long custom, *he* and *his* are considered sufficiently explicit, *even* if the antecedent indicates both male and female genders. Note that Pope does not say "he or she":

> For modes of faith let graceless zealots fight,
> He can't be wrong whose life is in the right.

I

I'd

I'd is a contraction of *I would* as well as *I had*. It is acceptable colloquial English to use *I'd* as the contraction for *I should*. *I'd like, I'd rather, I'd go* are all established colloquialisms.

If and whether

After such verbs as *ask, learn, say, know, understand, doubt,* and the like, modern usage tends to prefer (but does not demand) *whether:*

> Who knows whether tomorrow we die.
> Who cares if tomorrow we die.

(Note that the *or* to indicate an alternative does not necessarily follow *whether*.)

Imply and infer

The difference between *imply* and *infer* is the difference between hinting and getting the hint. The speaker *implies* and the hearer *infers*.

L

Lay and lie

These verbs are irregular—but regularly misused.

Lie is an intransitive verb and means *to recline;* it also means *to tell a falsehood.*

Lay is a transitive verb and means *to put in position,* to place.

Principal Parts

	Present	*Past*	*Present Participle*	*Perfect Participle*
Lie (to recline)	Lie	Lay	Lying	Lain
Lie (to tell a falsehood)	Lie	Lied	Lying	Lied
Lay (to place)	Lay	Laid	Laying	Laid

The chief difficulties seem to be that the past tense of *lie* (to recline) is the same as the present of *lay* (to place); and that *lie* (to tell a falsehood) and *lie* (to recline) have the same forms for both present tense and present participle.

Perhaps these instances will make the matter clearer:

A ship lies at anchor.
He lies as other men tell the truth—a matter of principle.
A mason lays bricks.

He lay on the grass.
He lied with admirable consistency.
He laid his toys away.

The lion is lying down with the lamb.
He keeps lying about the affair.
Father is laying down the law.

They have lain in bed long enough.
He has lied for the last time.
The hen has laid an egg.

Leave—let

Leave means "depart"; *let* means "permit." Their confusion is unwarranted and easily eradicated by keeping their distinct significations in mind.

> Let (*not* leave) me be.
> Let (*not* leave) it alone.
> Let (*not* leave) me see it.

Like and as

Like is a preposition; *as,* a conjunction.

Where the clause-verb is suppressed, *like* is preferable if the meaning is "in the manner of." *As* in such a context would connote "when he was." Compare

> He sang like a child

with

> He sang as a child.

The first sentence means ". . . in the manner of a child"; the second, ". . . when he was a child."

When the clause-verb is present, it is obviously better to use *as,* which has the function of linking co-ordinate elements:

> He sang as a child sings.

Loan

Loan as a verb is established in financial parlance and for colloquial usage. Elsewhere, it is better to use *loan* as the noun, *lend* as the verb.

> Lend me your ears.
> Make me a loan of your ears.

M

Mad and angry

Mad is not properly a synonym of *angry;* used as such, it ranks as a vulgarism.

> It's wiser being good than bad.
> It's safer being meek than fierce.
> It's fitter being sane than mad.—BROWNING

I was angry with my friend:
I told my wrath, my wrath did end.
I was angry with my foe:
I told it not, my wrath did grow.—BLAKE

Majority and plurality

If three candidates run for office and one thousand ballots are cast, the successful candidate must garner more than five hundred votes in order to claim (honestly) a *majority,* since *majority* denotes a "portion greater than half." The number by which his votes exceed those of the runner-up constitutes his plurality.

Mutual

Purists insist that *mutual* refers to "that which is reciprocally given and received." Therefore, they say, a friend cannot ordinarily be mutual—though friendship may be. Dickens, notably, disagreed: he called his novel *Our Mutual Friend.* Perhaps putting *mutual* into the form of an equation will make the purists' point clear:

$$A:B::B:A$$

not

$$A:B::A:C$$

or: Al's attitude toward Ben is the same as Ben's toward Al. *Not:* Al's attitude toward Ben is the same as Ben's toward Charles.

Thus, the title of Dickens' novel ought to be (the purists affirm) *Our Common Friend,* since *common* denotes "that which two or more share equally or alike." But the popular vote—and the vote of the authorities, too—is against the distinction.

Myself, himself, yourself

In formal English, *myself, himself,* and *yourself* are not used as substitutes for *I* or *me, he* or *him,* and *you.* They are, properly, intensive and reflexive pronouns:

His affection for himself will rank as one of the great love affairs of history.

Avoid, in writing,

> They suggested Monroe and myself,

though in informal conversation this sentence would be sufficiently correct. Less defensible, even as colloquial English, is

> Yourself and I are suggested.

Least acceptable is

> I suggested Monroe and himself.

(Yet, to prove once again the futility of rule-making, let it be remembered that Omar writes:

Myself when young did eagerly frequent Doctor and Saint. . . .)

N

Neither

Neither, like *none,* is a singular pronoun, but one frequently plural in effect. *Neither* with a plural verb is not so well established as *none* in the similar construction. While it ought not to be used for formal expression, it is nevertheless good colloquial English.

> And the best and worst of this is
> That *neither is* most to blame,
> If you have forgotten my kisses
> And I have forgotten your name.—SWINBURNE

None

None is a singular pronoun and requires a singular verb —in theory. In practice, *none* frequently exerts a plural force and pulls a plural verb into its orbit. Consider, on the one hand,

> None but the brave *deserves* the fair,

and on the other,

> None *are* quite so single in intent. . .

Either a singular or plural verb is indicated with *none;* in fact, if either expresses the sense as well as the other, the plural is more commonly used.

O

One

A series of *ones* strikes the average reader, unless he has been conditioned to the convention, as pedantry. Few can accept "with unmixed pleasure" this instance from Browning:

> Alack! one lies oneself
> Even in the stating that one's end was truth,
> Truth only, if one states so much in words.

P

Proved

Proven is marked *archaic and dialectal* in most dictionaries. It persists in popular speech (and in law courts) but elsewhere *proved* is the preferred form for both the past participle and adjective.

R

Reason

The reason was because has no champions. *The reason why* has some stanch defenders, and they can bolster their position by quotation:

> All beauteous things for which we live
> By laws of time and space decay.
> But oh, the very *reason why*
> I clasp them is because they die.—CORY

However, that *the reason is* should preferably be followed not by a causal clause but by a predicate nominative, all authorities agree. *The reason* for their unanimity *is* that the latter constitutes a simpler, more direct, and more economical locution.

S

Shall and will

Macaulay once said that while few university graduates could supply the rules for using *shall* and *will*, none would misuse them. If *shall* and *will* are governed by rules, the rules are consistently violated. In spoken English, the distinctions between these two auxiliary verbs have about disappeared; in written English, they are disappearing. When the point of a sentence depends on the reader's recognition of the distinction between *shall* and *will*, the author may be confident that the point will be missed. The conventional rules for employment of *shall* and *will* are not especially complex, though —if we discard those which have never really been relevant.

1. To denote simple futurity, expectation, prediction, use *shall* in the first person, *will* in the second and third person.

2. To denote promise, purpose, determination, obligation, or inevitable action, use *will* in the first person, *shall* in the second and third persons.

> Shall I, wasting in despair,
> Die because a woman's fair?—WITHER
> We will be avenged . . . we'll hear him,
> We'll follow him, we'll die with him.—SHAKSPERE

> They shall beat their swords into plowshares; and their spears into pruning hooks; nation shall not lift up sword against nation, neither shall they learn war any more.—BIBLE

> In the first person, simply *shall* foretells,
> In *will* a threat or else a promise dwells.
> *Shall* in the second and third does threat,
> *Will* then simply foretells a future feat.—GRAMMAR, *Irish National Schools*

So . . . as and as . . . as

The theory is that *so* is to be used correlatively with *as* in negative expressions, but that *as* is its own correlative in affirmative statements. Thus, Shakspere has Mercutio, even in death, observe the grammatical amenities:

> No, 'tis not so deep as a well, nor so wide as a church-door; but 'tis enough, 't'will serve.

The familiar saw, *It's as broad as it's long,* illustrates the obverse use of the correlatives.

Current practice, however, refuses to accommodate itself

to this nice discrimination. *Not as far as I know,* for example, is as common as *not so far as I know.* Except as it applies in formal composition, the theory is outmoded.

Slow

Slow is an established adverb, and objections to expressions like *Drive slow* are groundless. As a matter of fact, in referring to auto-driving, *slow* rather than *slowly* is the preferred form.

T

Than

"*Than* implying comparison has the same case after as before it":—so runs the rule. This is manifestly not so. *I gave you more than he* implies *gave you* after *he;* while *I gave you more than him* implies *I gave* before *him.* The ellipsis or gap in each sentence is differently situated and requires a different reconstruction. In conversation the distinction, which is an important one, is not generally observed; in writing it should be.

Than whom may or may not be grammatical: the proposition is much debated. Cobbett says that, following *than,* "*who* should be made use of: for it is nominative, not objective."

Lowth flatly contradicts him: "The relative *who, . . .* when it follows *than, is always in the objective case."* On the one hand, it is stated that the full construction of a sentence like *Cromwell, than whom no man was better skilled in artifice . . .* would prove the error of putting *who* in the objective case: *Cromwell—no man was more skilled in artifice than he was.* On the other hand, it is claimed that *than* frequently exerts a prepositional force. Thus Milton says:

> Beelzebub, than whom, Satan except, none higher sat.

Logic is with Cobbett; idiom with Lowth. However we decide, though, it is certain that *than whom* is artificial, stilted, awkward. It is far better to avoid it than to justify it.

This here and that there

This here and *that there* are needlessly repetitive. *That* and *this* fulfill the demonstrative function perfectly.

This kind of

This and *that* are singular demonstrative pronouns; *these* and *those,* plural. *Kind* and *sort* are singular nouns; *kinds* and *sorts,* plural. Associate the singular pronouns with the singular nouns, the plural pronouns with the plural nouns.

This (*or* that) kind (*or* sort)
These (*or* those) kinds (*or* sorts)

Kind of and *sort of* are adjective phrases, and are used adverbially only in colloquial speech.

I rather like raw meat. (Not: I *kind of* (or *sort of*) like raw meat.)

Kind of a and *sort of a* (though adjective phrases) are also colloquial. Suppress the pleonastic *a.* Emulate Poe rather than Kipling in formal expression:

'E's *a sort of a* 'blooming cosmopolous—soldier an' sailor too.—KIPLING

Keeping time, time, time,
In a *sort of* Runic rhyme.—POE

Transpire

Transpire (from Latin *trans,* through, and *spirare,* to breathe) means "to emit through the pores of the skin"; hence, by extension, "to escape from secrecy, to become known." In the sense of "happen, occur," *transpire* is on most indexes of condemned words. Yet, as Webster remarks, "it is found in the writings of authors of good standing." It is, nevertheless, a pompous word and it would be better to avoid it.

W

Who and whom

The *NED* says that *who* is "common in colloquial use as object of a verb or preposition following at the end of a clause."

The established word-order of the English sentence is: Subject—Verb—Object. Dislocations of this pattern produce sentences like *Who did you say?* Status of the usage: admissible in conversation, inadmissible in a formal literary style.

Whoever and whomever

Whoever and *whomever* are compound relatives, that is, each contains its antecedent in itself. Case depends on the relative clause in which it appears, not on the main clause. Is this sentence grammatical?

> I consider myself beholden to whoever corrects my mistakes.

Whoever equals the *one who;* and the case is decided by the *who,* not by the *one. Who,* in this construction, is the subject of the relative clause *whoever shows me my mistakes.* Therefore, the sentence is perfectly correct. How about this sentence?

> I consider myself beholden to whomever my mistakes are corrected by.

Whomever equals the *one whom;* and *whom,* in this construction, is the object of the preposition by. Therefore, *whomever* is correct in the given context.

Whose

Whose as equal to *of which* is a perfectly established usage for both formal literary and colloquial expression. The use of *whose* as the possessive of *which,* "where the antecedent is not only irrational but inanimate, has had the support of high authority for several hundred years" (Hall).

As a matter of fact, when the purpose is restrictive, *whose* is frequently better than *of which:*

Propositions of whose truth we have no certain knowledge.—LOCKE

Y

You

Generic *"you,"* as in, *In most scientific schools* you *get a diploma which certifies only that you are completely ignorant of literature,* is good colloquial English, but you had better eschew it for formal literary expression.

BOOK ELEVEN

Vocabulary, Word Study, Etymology

The Average Vocabulary

How many words does the average man command—how big is his vocabulary? Dr. Vizetelly, the editor of Funk & Wagnalls *New Standard Dictionary,* offers a well-founded guess by way of answer:

> The plain people, as Lincoln liked to call them, use or read understandingly from 8,000 to 10,000 words according to their general intelligence and conversational power, while a person who cannot read, but who has a good degree of native mental ability, will command about 5,000.

Other guesses put the number as low as 3,000 and as high as 12,000. The New York State Department of Education at one time chose 4,000 words as the basis for its literacy test.

Well-read or specially trained men and women have, of course, a much larger vocabulary. They can recognize perhaps 50,000 words and can use at least 15,000, and maybe as many as 25,000, in conversation and writing. Shakspere is variously said to have used between 15,000 and 24,000 words; and Milton, between 8,000 and 14,000. These figures are not particularly relevant, because the English vocabulary has expanded enormously since they wrote. Woodrow Wilson has been credited with over 60,000 words, but his vocabulary, relative to the number of words current in the twentieth and seventeenth centuries, was not greater than Shakspere's.

Three kinds of vocabulary must be distinguished: one for speaking, a second for writing, and a third for reading. Obviously, everyone recognizes more words than he uses; and, just as obviously, everyone uses more words in writing than in speaking. Probably the recognition vocabulary is about two or three times larger than the active vocabulary; but it is extremely difficult to measure the proportion exactly, and next to impossible to determine the relative size of the speaking and writing vocabularies.

Determining the Size of Your Vocabulary

If you want a rough estimate of your own vocabulary, here is the way to make the count:

1. Take a large abridged dictionary—one containing about 150,000 words. It is not likely that a significant number of words you know will not be included in such a dictionary.

2. Count the number of words whose meaning you know on the page after each successive letter of the alphabet: thus, if the *a's* begin on page 3, count the number of words whose meaning you know on page 4; if the *b's* begin on page 100, count the number of words whose meanings you know on page 101; and so on. This will enable you to get a fair sampling. You may eliminate the *x's* from consideration: too few words begin with *x* to matter for our purposes.

3. Assume your dictionary has a thousand pages. You have recorded the number of words that you recognize on twenty-five pages, or on one-fortieth of the total number of pages. Let us say that the sum of words whose meanings you know is 500. Multiply by 40. The result, 20,000 words, is a rough approximation of your recognition vocabulary.[1]

Improving Your Vocabulary

Vocabulary has often been called the clue to personality. It is also the key to success. Having conned the results of

[1] Of course, a more accurate way to determine the extent of your vocabulary is to record all the words that you recognize on all the pages of the dictionary. However, that method is perhaps a bit too painstaking to commend itself generally.

thousands of scientifically constructed vocabulary tests, Johnson O'Connor does not hesitate to affirm that "An extensive knowledge of the exact meaning of English words accompanies success in this country more often than any other single characteristic."

How to acquire that extensive and exact knowledge? Memorizing the dictionary is hardly a feasible project. Webster's *New International Dictionary* contains more than 600,000 terms—rather too many for convenient memorization. Smaller dictionaries present proportionally smaller problems; but even a "pocket dictionary" contains more words than the average man can keep in memory. Besides, an *increased* vocabulary does not necessarily equal an *improved* vocabulary. It is a doubtful advantage to know the meanings of words we never use. An increased *active* vocabulary—for speaking, writing, and reading—ought to be the goal.

The Roots of Language

The method of attaining an increased active vocabulary was suggested two centuries ago by Lord Chesterfield. "The shortest and best way of learning a language," he wrote, "is to know the roots of it; that is, those original primitive words of which other words are formed." These roots are central; other words cluster about them—sometimes by the hundreds.

A Detour into Language History

Before we can profitably continue along the road to word mastery, we have to make a short detour into language history. From the sixteenth century on, scholars have pointed to strange similarities in languages as apparently unrelated as Persian and German, or Lithuanian and Latin. Only recently, though, have they formulated a sound explanation for the similarities:

1. That the relationship between Lithuanian and Latin, or Persian and German, or Icelandic and Greek, or Sanskrit and Russian is really a family relationship.

2. That these languages, and many others, derived from a single earlier language which, sometime, someplace, was spoken by some group. (*When, where,* and *which* cannot be answered with certainty.)

The Indo-European Family

This family of languages has been variously named the *Indo-European* (by the French), the *Aryan*[1] (by the English), and the *Indo-Germanic* (by, needless to say, the Germans). *Indo-European* is generally accepted to be the most accurate designation—though the family stretches beyond the boundaries indicated. Most people from Central Asia to westernmost Europe speak one or another of the Indo-European languages. The chart below lists most of the Indo-European languages:

A. **The Asiatic**

1. Sanskrit, and the neo-Sanskrit languages of India (Bengali, Hindi, Punjabi, etc.)
2. Zend, or old Persian; modern Persian
3. Armenian, ancient and modern

B. **The European**

4. Greek, ancient and modern
5. Romanic, including Latin and the neo-Latin or Romance languages (Italian, French, Provençal, Spanish, Portuguese, Romanian)
6. Lettic: Old Prussian (dead); Lithuanian, Lettish
7. Slavonic: Old Russian, modern Russian, Polish, Bohemian, Bulgarian, Serbian
8. Celtic: Welsh or Cymric: Cornish (nearly dead, but not extinct), Gaelic; Erse, Manx, Breton
9. Teutonic: Dutch, German, English, Scandanavian

Root, Stem, and Affix

A more extended definition of root now becomes possible. A **root** is the core of a word, the part which contains its essential meaning. Indo-European roots are the elements of all the Indo-European languages. Thus, the Indo-European

---

[1]Aryan, it ought to be emphasized, properly applies *only* to languages, not to races.

root PA, "father," gives us Anglo-Saxon *faeder,* Icelandic *fathir,* Dutch *vader,* Gothic *fadar,* Swedish *fader,* German *vater,* Greek *pater,* Latin *pater,* Persian *pidar,* Sanskrit *pitar.*[1]

However, we are here primarily concerned with *English roots,* the forms these Indo-European roots take in English. The elementary or *root* meaning of *tru-th-ful-ness* is conveyed by the root *tru;* of *man-li-ness* by the root *man;* of *lov-e-d* by the root *lov.*

The **stem** is often defined as "the derivative of a root"—or "that which *stems* from a root." But a stem "may consist of a simple root, as *fa* (Latin *fari,* to say) in *fable, fame, fate, preface.*" More commonly, however, the stem is "a root with certain relational elements added, yet not so as to constitute it an independent word, as *struct* in *structure, instruct, construction, destructive,* from root *stru,* seen in Latin *stro,* to arrange to build."[2]

An **affix** is a syllable or syllables *fixed* to a word and modifying its meaning. The affix may be placed at the beginning of a word, in which case it is called a **prefix** (as *ad,* to; *pre,* before; *un,* not); or it may be placed at the end of a word, in which case it is called a **postfix** or a **suffix** (as *art,* one who; *ish,* like; *ior,* more). Suffixes are of two kinds: *formative,* those which form the stem; and *derivative,* those which alter the function of a word when added to the stem. Thus in *loved,* the root is *lov;* the formative suffix is *-e,* and by attaching it to the root, the stem *lov-e* is formed; the derivative suffix is *-d* (the sign of the past tense), and by attaching it to the stem, the word *loved* is derived.

The analysis given in the foregoing three paragraphs has been exceedingly refined—perhaps excessively refined. Actually, the distinctions between stem and root, and between formative prefix and derivative prefix, need not be insisted on for practical purposes. For practical purposes, it is quite enough to say that the root or stem—we shall use the words interchangeably—is *lov;* and the suffix—we shall disregard

[1] All these are cognate words—that is, they have the same root.
[2] S. S. Haldeman, *Word-Building.*

the kinds—is *-ed*. Our purpose (and in spite of the seeming byways, the purpose is really being held in mind) is chiefly a practical one: to increase our command of words.

Indo-European Roots

The words in English derive, ultimately, from the Indo-European roots. A great etymologist,[1] W. W. Skeat, has extracted 461 Indo-European roots[2] from which the total vocabulary of English may theoretically be traced. However, to trace it would require very nearly the etymological genius of Dr. Skeat. We must content ourselves with a humbler aim and a simpler method.

Still, it is both interesting and instructive to dabble with Indo-European roots. For example: the root AK unveils a cousinly relationship (distant, to be sure) between *acrobat* and *aconite*. Both derive from AK, which means "to pierce; to be pointed or sharp; to be quick." *Aconite* is a poisonous herb. It was given its name, Pliny said, because it grew on "steep, sharp rocks." An *acrobat* initially meant "one who walks with toes pointed"—on the tips of his toes. Similarly: —*acme* means "the highest point." An *acid* is sharp to the taste. *Acute* denotes "sharp." An *aglet* is a sharp needle. Other cognate words are *edge, egg* (in the sense of "egg on to action"), *ague, equine*—and even *hippopotamus!* But to uncover their histories requires etymological detective work for which we are not yet ready.

The Cluster Method of Vocabulary-Building (1)

There are a few hundred English roots and stems around which thousands of English words cluster. Consider the root *fac,* "make, form, do." From it are derived *affect, affecta-*

---

[1]An etymologist is a student of languages who concentrates on the origin and formation of words (from Greek *etumos,* true, and *logos,* word).

[2]Other scholars have been even more intensive: "Max Müller lists 121 original Sanskrit roots, which lie at the base of all Indo-European languages. There was a Dr. Murray who imagined that he could derive our language from nine roots, AG, BAG, CWAG, DWAG, LAG, MAG, NAG, RAG, SWAG; an even more thoroughgoing Dr. Schmidt traced the whole Greek dictionary back to the root E, and the whole Latin dictionary back to the root I. . . ." (Wood.)

tion, affection, beatific, beautify, certify, clarify, classify, codify, defection, deficient, deify, difficult, dignify, edify, efficient, facile, fact, faction, factor, factory, faculty, fiat, glorify, gratify, horrify, identify, indemnify, intensify. . . . These entries by no means exhaust the list. More than two hundred other derivatives might be cited.

From the root *ced* (and its variant form *cess*), "go, yield," are derived *abscess, accede, accessory, ancestry, antecedent, cease, cede, concession, decease, exceed, excessive, incessant, intercede, precede, predecessor, proceed, recede, recess, secede, succeed* . . . and about seventy-five more.

From the root *pon* (and its variant form *pos*), "place, put," are derived *apposite, apposition, component, compose, composite, composition, compositor, compost, deponent, depose, deposit, deposition, depositor, depot, expose, im—, inter—, op—, pre—, pro—, pur—, post—, re—, super—.* These are fewer than one-tenth of the total number of derivatives of *pon* (*pos*) that might be cited.

The advantage of the "cluster method" of vocabulary building ought, then, to be plain. It supplies an organic center around which you can build your vocabulary. Knowing the root *fac* and the meaning, you can now probably make an accurate guess as to the meaning of, say, *factor,* if that word is not already in your vocabulary.

The Cluster Method of Vocabulary-Building (2)

Let us look at prefixes and suffixes, roots and stems once again. Suppose we choose a word like *contradictory* for analysis. It breaks up into three parts:

PREFIX: *contra,* against
STEM: *dict,* speak, say
SUFFIX: *ory* (an adjective-forming suffix), pertaining to

Both prefix and suffix stringently modify the stem. But whereas the prefix changes its meaning, the suffix changes its grammatical function. A few instances will make the point clearer. There is a basic change of meaning between *man* and *unman;* or *cede* and *antecede;* or *chromatic* and *achromatic;* or *obverse* and *converse;* or *precede* and *succeed.* In fact, sometimes the prefix reverses the meaning of the root or stem, as in *man* and *unman*. The suffix, on the other hand, changes the grammatical function without much altering the meaning. Thus *dark* becomes an adverb when *ly* is suffixed (*darkly*); *eat* becomes an adjective when *able* is suffixed (*eatable*); *bright* becomes a *verb* when *en* is suffixed (*brighten*).

The stem *dict* can form a variety of words by joining different prefixes and suffixes to itself. Always, it will have the root meaning of *say*, though sometimes that meaning will be disguised (for what reasons we shall soon see). Note, in the following series, what alterations the prefixes effect:

pre, before + *dict*=*predict*, say beforehand
inter, between + *dict*=*interdict*, "speak between" or prohibit
e, from, out of + *dict*=*edict*, a speaking from "or proclamation"

Now note the alterations the suffixes effect.

dict + *ate*, to make, to put, to take=*dictate*, "make said" or command
dict + *ion*, act of=*diction*, "act of speaking" or manner of speech
dict + *ate*, to make, put, take + *or*, one who=*dictator*, one who commands.

Obviously some of the meanings we have attached to the combination of stem and affix are distorted. A word is more than the simple sum of stem and affix. But the *clue* to the meaning is present. Moreover, a knowledge of the component parts of a word will enable us not only to define it, but also to remember it.

Again, two roots or stems sometimes combine to form a new word:

vale, good-by + *diction*, act of=*valediction*, the act of saying + good-by
ver, true + *dict*=*verdict*, "a true saying" a judgment
dict (+ *a*) + *phone*, sound, voice="*a saying of the voice*," the trade-mark for a phonographic instrument that records and reproduces

The same prefix often assumes various forms for the sake of euphony. The prefix *ad*, to, for example, becomes *a, ac, af, ag, al, an, ap, ar, as, at,* depending on the initial letters of the root. Thus *ad* retains its original form in *ad*duce and *ad*here, but *ad* becomes *a* before *s,* as in *a*scend, "to climb to"; *ac* before *c,* as in *ac*cede, "to yield to"; *af* before *f,* as in *af*fix, "to fix to"; *ag* before *g,* as in *ag*gravate, "to make heavy to"; *al* before *l,* as in *al*lot, "to apportion to"; *an* before *n,* as in *an*nex, "to tie to"; *ap* before *p,* as in *ap*pend, "to hang to"; *ar* before *r,* as in *ar*range, "to put into a row"; *as* before *s,* as in *as*sist, "to stand to"; *at* before *t,* as in *at*test, "to bear witness to."

Suffixes vary for euphonic reasons too; but, for the most part, when suffixes have the same meaning and different forms, it is because they came into English from different languages. Thus *or* and *er* both mean "one who." The former, however, came into English from Latin (through French), and it is appended to words of Latin origin: act*or,* audit*or,* aviat*or,* benefact*or,* profess*or.* The latter is of Anglo-Saxon origin, and it is appended to words of native origin: do*er,* listen*er,* fly*er,* wish*er,* talk*er.*

Roots and stems exhibit changes that will require some detailed attention. First, though, look through the "Dictionary of Roots" and note how many come from Latin, how few from Old English. The reason is not that the Old English element is scarce in Modern English. Quite the contrary. But words of native origin—*many, lady, loaf, head, year, world, day, over, road, daisy, woman, lord, yes,* etc.—are so thoroughly familiar that there is little point in citing them. Our purpose is to increase our command of words, and listing the elements of words we already know serves the purpose only slightly.

In Skeat's *Etymological Dictionary,* there is a breakdown of English words according to origin. It is enlightening:

33% of English words are of Germanic origin
56% of English words are of Greek and Latin origin
2% of English words are of Celtic origin
3% of English words are of hybrid origin
6% of English words are of Oriental, African, and Amerindian origin

S. Stephenson Smith points out that "if only the Germanic and classical origin is considered, 37% are from the first source, 63% from the second."

The staple words of the language are of Germanic origin, and though they are fewer than words of classical origin, they appear far more frequently in writing and speech.

The words of classical origin—particularly of Latin origin (whether they came into English directly, or through French or one of the other Romance languages—are, then, the words we are more apt not to know. In the following passage from the preamble to the Constitution of the United States the words of Latin origin are italicized; observe how much less familiar they are than the words in roman:

> We, the *people* of the *United States,* in *order* to *form* a more *perfect union, establish justice, insure domestic tranquillity, provide* for the *common defense, promote* the *general* welfare, and *secure* the *blessings* of *liberty* to ourselves and our *posterity,* do *ordain* and *establish* this *constitution* for the *United States* of *America.*

Of course our command of words does not depend on our knowledge of languages. John Kennedy makes this valuable observation:

> Roots and Stems have been ignored in many cases because of the prevalent fallacy that knowledge of the value of a stem implies a knowledge of Greek, Latin, French, Portuguese, and every other language that has contributed to the formation of the English language. This is a remarkable fallacy, as the English language does not resolve into Greek, Latin, Scandinavian, or anything else than English. The stem and its value are the basis of the English language . . . If the English language does not resolve into English, then the English language is a myth.

That is very true. Nevertheless, it is also true that if we are aware of how they change, we will sense relationships between words that previously we had thought utter strangers. Thus we will see why *dual* and *twain, pedal* and *foot, century* and *hundred* are cousins not distantly removed. The business of tracing these relationships—"word-genealogy"—is called *etymology.* It is a fascinating and instructive study, once the initial difficulties are overcome. However, it is not basically necessary to our scheme of vocabulary-building, and, if you like, you may omit the pages in reduced type that follow.

The Why and How of Linguistic Change

Two pointed questions concerning linguistic change are thoroughly in order at this juncture.

1. How does language change?
2. Why does language change?

1. How language changes

A little specialized knowledge is required to explain *how*. A simple definition of language will supply the basis for the answer: *Language is man's method of communicating to other men his thoughts, feelings, and desires.* As man develops, he needs to tell other men more. So he combines sounds a little differently and thus increases his supply of words, the counter of communication. Again, as we have learned, every sound is the product of a series of muscular actions involving lungs, larynx, and lips, among other organs; and every muscular action, when repeated often enough, becomes modified. The changes especially important in English are those which affected the consonants. Technically this is termed the *consonantal shift.* In order to understand it fully, a few preliminary definitions are necessary.

Consonants Defined and Classified

A consonant is the sound produced when a column of air is stopped in some part of the mouth and throat. In vowel sounds no such stoppage takes place. Try saying *d*, for example; note that the sound is stopped by the tip of the tongue pressing against the upper front teeth. Now try saying *a, e, i, o, u*—the vowel sounds; the column of air meets with no friction at all in its outward progress.

1. Voiced and voiceless consonants: If the vocal cords vibrate, the consonant is said to be *voiced;* if not, it is said to be voiceless. (All vowels are voiced.) Try putting your fingers against your larynx (Adam's apple) while saying first *k* (or *p*, or *ch* as in *chin*, or *t*) and then *g* (or *b*, or *dg* as in *ridge*, or *d*); note that in the former sounds there is no vibration felt; in the latter the vibration is definite and unmistakable.

2. Labials, dentals, etc.: Consonants are further classified according to the part of the mouth or nasal passage which is chiefly operative during their formation. The names have been already supplied

to these consonants, but you can check on the accuracy of the nomenclature merely by watching someone speak or by analyzing the mechanics of your own speech.

Labials: The sounds *g, p, b, m, w, f,* and *v* are formed chiefly by the lips—hence they are called *labials* (Latin *labium,* lip).

Dentals: The teeth and gums are most active in sounding *t* and *d; th(in)* and *th(at); s* and *z; n* and *l*—hence they are called dentals (Latin *dentes,* teeth).

Gutturals: The sounds *k, g, ch* (as in the German *nacht*), and *ng* are throat sounds, produced by raising the back of the tongue against the soft palate—hence they are called *gutturals* (Latin *guttur,* throat).

Palatals: In forming *ch* (as in *chair*), *sh, j, y, zh* the front of the tongue touches or else comes near the hard palate (the bony roof of the mouth)—hence they are called *palatals* (Latin *palatum,* palate).

Glottals: The aspirate *h*—that is, the *h* which is pronounced with an audible emission of breath (as in *horse*)—is called a *glottal* (Greek *glottis,* mouth of the windpipe).

It is possible, of course, for a sound to be made by a combination of organs: both the lips and the teeth are active in pronouncing *f* and *v*. They are therefore termed *labio-dentals*. For a parallel reason *wh* and *w* are named *labio-gutturals*. The *th* sounds (as in *thin* or *this*) are called *interdentals* because the tip of the tongue is placed between the teeth in forming them.

3. Stops or Continuants: There is another way of classifying the consonants, depending on the manner in which the breath is expelled. If, in sounding a consonant, the current of air is completely stopped (as in *k, t, p*), then released with a mild explosion of breath, the consonant formed is a *stop* or *mute*. If the breath is narrowed or squeezed so that the sound can be prolonged, the consonant formed is a *continuant* or *spirant* (*ch, th, f, w, s, sh*). If (as in *l, m, n, ng, r*) the breath has neither a free passage, as in sounding the continuants, nor is closed entirely, as in sounding the stops, the consonant formed is a *liquid*.

This excursion into "Phonetics"[1] is probably the most difficult you will be called upon to make. However, its importance for properly understanding the "Dictionary of Roots" makes it thoroughly worth-while. If you are slightly confused, take a glance at the synoptic chart below.[2] You will find the various relationships we have been emphasizing neatly summarized.

[1] "Phonetics" (Greek *phone,* "voice") is the study of speech sounds.
[2] From J. C. Nesfield, *English Grammar, Past and Present.*

VOCABULARY 281

The Consonantal Shift

The change in consonant sounds ("the consonantal shift") from the classical languages to the Germanic was first described in 1822 by a German philologist named Grimm. The law itself is quite complicated; however, Fick and Skeat simplified it greatly by emphasizing its application to English.

Here is the scheme of sound changes which you will have to learn. It is the simplest presentation of Grimm's Law possible.

DENTALS: d→t→th→d
LABIALS: b→p→f →b
GUTTURALS: g→k→h →g

The explanation of this apparently cryptic series of letters is not at all difficult, once the letters themselves have been memorized in order: Any sound in any group is represented in English by the sound that immediately follows it. First, let us look at the dental sounds: if a Greek or Latin word began with *d,* it is represented in English by a word beginning with *t.* The *d,* after having been spoken for many years by many different groups of men, became *t.* Similarly, a *t* sound in Greek or Latin was transformed into a *th* sound in English. The labials and gutturals are to be read in a like manner. The labial Greek and Latin *b* became the labial English *p.* The guttural Greek and Latin *g* became the guttural English *k.*

A few examples may make the process clearer. Remember that the classical languages may, for our purposes, be regarded as a unity. That is, an illustration from Greek or Latin is equally to the point in demonstrating sound-change.

	Latin *duo*→English *two*
DENTALS	Latin *tres*→English *three*
(d→t→th→d)	Greek *thugater*→English *daughter*
	Latin *labium*→English *lip*
LABIALS	Greek *pos*→ English *foot*
(b→p→f→b)	Latin *frater*→ English *brother*
	Latin *genu*→ English *knee*
GUTTURALS	Latin *centum*[1]→English *hundred*
(g→k→h→g)	Latin *hostis*→ English *guest*

Significance of the Consonantal Shift

In going through the "Dictionary of Roots" and the "Dictionary of Affixes" you will find many entries that are immediately familiar, some that are only vaguely recognizable. There is, however, a def-

[1] The *c* in *centum* is hard (*kentum*).

inite pattern of sound-change, and Grimm's Law helps you to recognize it. Many factors have interfered with the change, but the clear and regular tendency can be discerned. And once discerned, the number of words which burst into meaning justify our slight efforts in learning the pattern.

2. Why Language Changes

Words, like men, inevitably carry traces of the road they have traveled. But also, they frequently signify quite other things at the end of the road than at the start. To say that *hussy* means *housewife,* or *buxom* means *pliant,* is plainly nonsense. To say that originally *hussy* meant *housewife* and *buxom* meant *pliant* is good etymology. In the world of words, as in the world of men, change is constant. These are a few of the ways in which the meanings of words change:

Words go up in the world. *Marshal* is now a title of honor, and denotes "an army officer of high rank"; the original sense of the word was "horse-servant" or "groom." *Nice,* which at one time meant "ignorant," and later "foolish," now means "fastidious" or (colloquially) "pleasant." *Paradise,* which denotes a "park" etymologically, is employed to signify "heaven." The process by which words go up is termed **elevation** or **amelioration.** (As we might expect from the nature of things, it does not happen as often as the reverse process.)

Words go down in the world. *Villain* (because of its supposed connection with *vile*) denotes "a scoundrel"; formerly a villain was a serf. *Specious* once meant "beautiful," now means "plausible but false." *Lewd* meant simply "ignorant," but now means "licentious." This process is called **degeneration** or **pejoration.**

Words narrow their domain. *Deer* meant "animal" (Shakspere speaks of "rats and mice and such small deer"). *Girl* referred to a young person, either male or female. *Corn,* which meant "grain," now means a specific kind of grain—in America, at least (and the word is at present being restricted still further—someday it may mean an unfortunate brand of humor). This process is called **specialization.**

Words widen their domain. The *butcher* once killed goats. A *picture* was once a painted (not photographed) representation. A *frock* was the coarse gown monks wore, but now it is a gown if made of satin and trimmed with ermine. This process is called **generalization.**

Words are formed on basis of analogy. *Sang* is a past tense of *sing; rang* of *ring;* why not *brang* of *bring? Brang* has not yet triumphed,

TABLE OF CONSONANTS

	GUTTURAL	PALATAL		DENTAL (Dental)	DENTAL (Inter-Dental)	LABIAL (Labial)	LABIAL (Labio-Dental)	LABIAL (Labio-Guttural)	GLOTTAL
I STOPS {Voiceless	k			t		p			
I STOPS {Voiced	g			d		b			
II CONTINUANTS {Voiceless		ch	sh	s	th(in)		f	wh	h
II CONTINUANTS {Voiced		j, y	zh	z	th(is)		v	w	
III LIQUIDS (ALL VOICED) {Nasal	ng			n		m			
III LIQUIDS (ALL VOICED) {Lingual		r		l					

but many words formed like it on the basis of analogy have: *book,* which once changed a vowel to indicate plural number, now merely adds an *s*—like most of our nouns. This process is called **analogy**.

Words fade: At one time *astonish* meant "stun"; now it denotes "surprise." To *mortify* has been reduced from its original signification "to make dead"; now it means "humiliate." No daring is any longer involved in "I *dare* say." This process (by which words weaken their original force) is called **fading**.

The Cluster Method of Vocabulary-Building (3)

The "Dictionary of Roots" and the "Dictionary of Affixes" may be used in two ways—one passive, the other active. Each gets results; but the second holds the greater promise as it entails the greater effort.

The Passive Method

Use the "Dictionary of Roots" and the "Dictionary of Affixes" in intimate connection with your reading. When an unfamiliar word occurs—say, *arable*—see if the meaning can be determined by the context, supplemented by the relevant root and affix. You remember (or you look up if you do not) the root *ar* and the suffix *able.* You ought not be far from the dictionary definition of *arable,* "able to be cultivated by ploughing." This "contextual method"[1] of improving vocabulary fully accords with modern psychological theory, and has been proved the most permanently effective *passive* method by many controlled experiments.

Knowing Grimm's Law, you will be able to discern many new word relationships; much of what was previously dark will become luminous. You will realize why the root *duk* gives us not only *duke, educate,* and *adduce,* but *doge, tug,* and *tuck* as well.

The Active Method

This method requires work, and as a consequence will be unpopular. However, it is the surest way to that "extensive

[1]Sometimes, as in a word like *occiput,* "the back of the head," two roots will seem equally relevant, so far as similarity of form is concerned. In this case the root *cap, capt,* "take," and the root *capit, cipit,* "head," might both apply. But, almost invariably, the context will rule one out.

knowledge of the exact meaning of English words" which—
in spite of seeming by-paths—is the steadfast goal. The list
of English derivatives given in the "Dictionary of Roots"
and "Dictionary of Affixes" is purposely abridged; but those
central for vocabulary-building are included. Look up each
—find out how it got that way. You will discover the procedure to be not only illuminating but also fascinating: For
example: *lustrum* (or *lustre*) derives from the root *lustr* "to
wash," but now means "a period of five years." Why? Because that was the interval between the *lustralia,* the ancient
Roman ceremonies of purification by water. *Furlough, gnos-
tic, logic, mistletoe, theism*—these and hundreds of others
will reveal the truth of the dictum that words begin as poetry
though they end as prose. The concrete conception degener-
ates, and we are left with one more abstraction. However,
even the abstraction will become memorable if you investi-
gate its genesis.

Cautions

1. Do not attempt to deduce word-histories from similarities in word-form. Consult a good etymological dictionary
if you are in doubt concerning the evolution of a word.

2. Do not attempt to force a primitive meaning on a modern word. Words, like men, bear traces of their ancestry;
but you can no more define a word than you can describe
a man by constructing genealogies. Sometimes, as we have
seen, root and derived word have widely divergent, even opposite, significations. The definitions given for many words
in the "Dictionary of Roots" and the "Dictionary of Affixes"
are distorted to indicate better their derivations. Do not follow suit, unless you have the same purpose in mind.

BOOK TWELVE

Dictionary of Roots

ROOT OR STEM	MEANING	EXAMPLES
abb (Syr., *abba*)	father	*abbott.*
abol (L. *abolere*)	do away with	*abolish.*
ac (L. *acus*)	needle	*aciform.*
accip (L. *accipere*)	seize	*accipitres,* an order of rapacious birds.
acerb (L. *acerbus*)	bitter	*acerbity.*
acm (Gr. *acme*)	top, summit	*acme.*
acon (Gr. *acone*)	whetstone, sharp stone	*aconite,* the herb monk's-hood, which grows on steep, sharp rocks.
acro (Gr. *acros*)	pointed, upper, top, first	*acrobat,* an athlete or a contortionist, one who can go on the points of his toes.
acu (L. *acurere*)	sharpen	*acumen,* sharpness, a keenness of intellect.
aesth (Gr. *aisthomai*)	perceive, feel	*aesthetic* (or *esthetic*); perceiving the beautiful; *anesthetic,* that which destroys feeling.

Root or Stem	Meaning	Examples
ag (L. *agere*)	drive, urge, act	*agent,* one who acts; *coagulate,* curdle, or drive together—as rennet does to milk.
agger (L. *agger*)	heap, excess	*exaggerate,* to overstate, or state in excess of the truth.
agog (Gr. *agogos,* *agoge*)	leading, bringing	*demagogue,* a false leader; *synagogue,* a congregation, a "bringing together."
agon (Gr. *agon*)	contest, struggle	*antagonist.*
agr (L. *ager*)	field, land	*agrarian.*
alb (L. *albus*)	white	*albumen,* the white of an egg; *Albion,* England, the land of white chalk cliffs.
ali (L. *alius*)	another	*alien,* strange, from another land; *alias,* otherwise; *alibi,* the plea of being in another place; *aliquot,* an exact part or measure of another, as in dividing.
all (Gr. *albos*)	other	*allopathy,* a system of cure producing symptoms other than those of the disease; *allegory,* a description of one thing in terms of another.
alt (L. *altus*)	high	*altitude,* height; *altar,* a high table for religious service.
am (L. *amare, amatus*)	love	*amatory, amative.*
ambul (L. *ambulare*)	walk	*somnambulist,* a sleep-walker; *funambulist,* a tight-rope walker.
ampl (L. *amplu*)	spacious, large	*amplify,* enlarge upon; *amplitude,* spaciousness.
ancien (F. *ancien*)	old, belonging to a former time	*ancient.*

Root or Stem	Meaning	Examples
angel (Gr. *angelos*)	messenger	*angel*, God's messenger; *evangelist*, a messenger of good tidings.
anism (L. *animus*)	mind, soul, spirit	*unanimous*, of one mind; *magnanimous*, great souled; *pusillanimous*, mean spirited.
anth (Gr. *anthos*)	flower	*anthology*, a collection of the flowers of poetry.
aper, apert (L. *aperire, apertus*)	open	*aperient*, a laxative; *aperture*, an opening; *April*, the month of opening buds.
apt (L. *aptus*)	fit	*adapt*, fit to.
aqu (L. *aqua*)	water	*aquatic, aqueous, aquaduct*.
ar (L. *arare*)	plow	*arable*, fit for plowing.
arbiter, arbitr (L. *arbiter*)	judge, umpire	*arbiter*, a judge; *arbitrary*, decisive judgment.
arc (L. *arcus*)	bow	*arc*, a bow-like section of a circumference.
arch (Gr. *archein*)	rule, govern	*anarchy*, the state of being without government.
archae, archai (Gr. *arche*)	ancient	*archaeology* (or *archeology*), the study of ancient life; *archaism*, an old form of expression.
argent (L. *argentum*)	silver	*argentiferous*, silver-yielding.
aster, astr (Gr. *aster*)	star	*asterisk*, a little star; *astrology*, fortune-telling by the stars; *aster*, the star flower.
aud (L. *audire*)	hear, listen	*audience*, a hearing—also a body of hearers; *audit*, to pass upon accounts.

Root or Stem	Meaning	Examples
aug, auct (L. *augere*, *auctus*)	increase, augment, bring forth	*august*, very grand; *auction*, a sale by means of increasing bids.
aur (L. *aureum*)	gold	*auriferous*, gold-producing; *aureate*, gilded.
av, au (L. *avis*)	bird	*aviary*, a place for birds; *auspice*, a token of good things, as indicated by the flight of birds (according to the old Roman superstition).
ball (Low L. *ballare*)	dance	*ball, ballet, ballad.*
band (It. *bando*)	ban, proclamation	*contraband*, subject to forfeiture for being against a proclamation.
bang (Skt. *banij*)	merchant	*banyan*, a wide-spreading tree of India, under whose shade merchants held their markets.
bar (Gr. *baros*)	weight	*barometer*, an instrument for indicating the weight of the atmosphere.
barrow (AS. *beorg, beorh*)	a hill	*barrow*, a burial mound.
bas, bass (Low L. *bassus*)	low	*base*, low; *bass*, the lowest part in music.
bat (L. *bature*, *batuere*)	beat, strike	*abate, battle, battalion, debate, rebate.*
bel, bell (L. *bellus*)	fair, fine, beautiful	*belladonna*, the drug nightshade, formerly used by ladies to dilate the pupils of their eyes, an effect thought very attractive; *belvedere*, beautiful to see.

Root or Stem	Meaning	Examples
bell (L. *bellum*)	war	*belligerent, bellicose, rebel.*
bene (L. *bene*)	well	*benefactor,* a helper or well-doer; *benevolent,* charitable well-wishing.
bi (Gr. *bios*)	life	*biography,* an account of a life; *biology,* the science of living things.
bibl (Gr. *biblos*)	book	*bibliomania,* a passion for books; *bibliography,* a list of the books on a given subject.
blanc (F. *blanc*)	white	*blanch,* to whiten; *blank,* white, empty; *Mont Blanc,* the white mountain.
bon (L. *bonus*)	good	*bonus, boon, bounty.*
bord (AS. *bord*)	edge, side	*starboard,* the steering or right-hand side; *larboard,* the lading side.
brev (L. *brevis*)	short	*brevet,* a short commission; *breviary,* a summary or short form of religious exercises.
burs (Low L. *bursa*)	purse	*bursar, disburse, reimburse.*
cachinn (L. *cachinnare*)	laugh	*cachinnation,* laughter.
cad; cas (L. *cadere, casus*)	fall	*cadence,* a falling off of the voice; *casual,* happening or befalling by chance.
caed, caes, cid, cis (L. *caedere, caesus*)	cut, kill	*caesura,* a pause in the middle of a verse, cutting the verse in two; *incisor,* a front cutting tooth; *homicide,* the killing of a human being.
calor (L. *calor*)	heat	*caloric, calorific.*

Root or Stem	Meaning	Examples
calypt (Gr. *calyptein*)	cover	*apocalypse,* a revelation, an uncovering.
camer (L. *camera*)	chamber	*camera,* the dark chambered instrument of photography.
camp, champ (L. *campus*)	field	*campestral,* growing in fields; *campaign,* a season of field service; *champion,* a combatant in the field.
candid (L. *candidus*)	white, clear, sincere	*candid,* frank, sincere; *candidate,* a seeker after office who in ancient Rome had to wear a white robe.
cap, capt (L. *capere, captus*)	take, seize, hold	*capable, capacious, captive, cable, captious.*
capit, cipit (L. *caput, capitis*)	head	*capitation,* so much per head; *captain,* the head man; *occiput,* the back of the head.
capr (L. *capra*)	goat	*caprice,* a sudden freak, like the frisk of a goat; *capricorn,* the horned goat; *caper,* to frisk about as a goat.
carn (L. *caro, carnis*)	flesh	*carnation,* flesh color; *carnival,* a period of levity before Lent, "a lightening to the flesh."
ced, cess (L. *cedere, cessus*)	go, yield	*cede,* yield up; *abscess,* a sore that discharges or yields pus; *access,* approach, go to; *antecedent,* going before.
celer (L. *celer*)	swift	*celerity, accelerate.*
cent (L. *centum*)	hundred	*century,* a hundred years; *centennial,* occurring once in a hundred years.

Root or Stem	Meaning	Examples
cern, cret (L. *cernere*, *cretus*)	separate, observe	*discern*, distinguish, separate one thing from another; *secret*, a matter kept private and separate.
charl (It. *ciarlari*)	prattle	*charlatan*, a pretentious prattler.
che (Gr. *cheo*)	pour out, mix	*chemist*, one who mixes and melts materials.
cheval (F. *cheval*)	horse	*chevalier*, a knight, a horseman; *chivalrous*, like a knight.
chlor (G. *chloros*)	pale green	*chlorophyl*, the green coloring matter in leaves of plants.
cnrom, chromat (Gr. *chrome*, *chromatos*)	color	*chromo*, a colored print; *chromatic*, relating to color; *achromatic*, without color.
chron (Gr. *chronos*)	time	*chronic*, having continued for a long time; *anachronism*, a blunder as to time.
cing, cinct (L. *cingere*, *cinctus*)	bind	*surcingle*, a girth bound over a saddle; *succinct*, compressed, bound tightly.
cit (L. *citare*)	arouse, summon	*cite*, summon; *excite*, arouse; *incite*, stir up or arouse to action.
civ (L. *civis*)	citizen	*civil*, *civilization*, *civic*.
claud, claus, clois, clud, clus (L. *claudere*, *clausis*)	shut, close	*clause*, a thought somewhat complete, or closed up, in itself; *cloister*, a monastery, an enclosure; *recluse*, a solitary, one shut back from the general public; *exclude*, shut out.
cognit (L. *cognoscere*, *cognitus*)	know	*cognition*, the act of knowing; *incognito*, unknown; *acquaint*, make known to.

Root or Stem	Meaning	Examples
commod (L. *commodus*)	fit, suitable, convenient	*commodity,* an article designed to suit the wants of people.
cor, cord (L. *cor, cordis*)	heart	*core,* the heart of a thing; *courage,* boldness of heart.
corn (L. *cornu*)	horn	*unicorn,* a fabulous beast with one straight horn in the forehead; *cornucopia,* horn of abundance.
corpus, **corpor** (L. *corpus, corporis*)	body	*corpuscle,* a little body; *corpse,* a dead body; *corporeal,* of a bodily or material nature.
cresc, **cret** (L. *crescere*)	grow, increase	*crescent,* the increasing moon; *concrete,* grown together; *excrescence,* a growing out.
culp (L. *culpa*)	fault, offense, blame	*culpable,* blamable; *culprit,* one charged with an offense.
cur (L. *cura*)	care, attention	*accurate,* exact through receiving care; *curate,* a priest having the care of souls.
curr, **curs** (L. *currere, cursus*)	run	*current,* the running; *cursory,* running along; *discursive,* running about; *precursor,* a forerunner.
cyn (Gr. *cyon, cynos*)	dog	*cynic,* a snappish, dog-like skeptic.
dat (L. *dare, datus*)	give	*date,* a given point in time; *perdition,* utter loss, a complete giving over.
decern, **decim** (L. *decem, decimus*)	ten, tenth	*December,* the tenth month in the Roman year; *decimate,* kill every tenth man.
dem (Gr. *demos*)	the people	*demagogue,* a leader (now, misleader) of the people.

ROOT OR STEM	MEANING	EXAMPLES
dent (L. *dens, dentis*)	tooth	*dentist, dentate, indent.*
dexter (L. *dexter*)	right hand	*dexterity,* righthandedness; *ambidextrous,* using either hand with the skill of the right.
dict (L. *dicere, dictus*)	speak, say	*contradict,* speaking against; *predict,* say beforehand; *valedictory,* a saying farewell.
dign (L. *dignur*)	worthy, merited	*dignify,* make worthy; *con dign,* fully merited; *disdain,* deem unworthy.
doc, doct (L. *docire, doctus*)	teach	*docile,* teachable; *doctrine,* the matter taught.
domin (L *dominus*)	lord, master	*dominate,* to master; *domain,* a dominion or territory of a lord.
drom (Gr. *dramein*)	a running	*hippodrome,* a race course for horses.
du (L. *duo*)	two	*dual,* consisting of two; *duel,* a fight between two.
duc, duct (L. *ducere, ductus*)	lead, bring	*adduce,* bring to; *conduce,* lead to; *conduit,* a leader, conductor; *ductile,* capable of being led or drawn out.
dur (L. *durus*)	hard	*indurate,* to harden · *obdurate,* hardened against; *duress,* hardship.
ego (L. *ego*)	I	*egotist,* a person admiring "I"; *egoism,* the philosophy of selfishness.
em, empt (L. *emere, emptus*)	take, buy	*exempt,* take out, free from liability; *redeem,* buy back.

Root or Stem	Meaning	Examples
equ (L. *equus*)	equal	*equanimity,* equalness or evenness of mind; *equation,* a statement of equality.
ero (Gr. *eros*)	love	*erotic, erogenous.*
etymo (Gr. *etymos*)	true	*etymology,* the science of the true sources of words.
ev (L. *aevum*)	life, age	*primeval, medieval, longevity.*
exo (Gr. *exo*)	outward	*exoteric,* of a popular nature. delivered to the outside public.
fa (L. *fari, fatus*)	speak	*affable,* of easy manners, easily spoken to; *fable,* a story spoken.
fac, fact (L. *facere, factus*)	make, form, act, do	*facsimile,* made alike; *factitious,* artificial, done for effect; *factotum,* a person of general usefulness; a do-all.
fall, fals (L. *fallire, falsus*)	err, beguile, deceive	*fallible, fallacy, default.*
fam (L. *fama*)	report	*fame, infamy, defame.*
fan (L. *fanum*)	temple	*fane,* temple; *fanatic,* an unreasoning enthusiast, like one religiously insane.
febru (L. *februare*)	expiate, cleanse	*February,* the month of expiation in Rome.
fecund (L. *fecundus*)	fruitful	*fecundity.*
feder (L. *foedus, foederis*)	treaty, league	*federation, confederate.*

Root or Stem	Meaning	Examples
fend, fens (L. *fendere, fensus*)	strike, ward off	*fend,* ward off; *fender,* a device for warding off injury; *fence,* to ward off.
fer (L. *ferire*)	strike	*ferule,* a striking rod of punishment.
ferr (L. *ferre*)	carry, bear, bring	*fertile,* bearing crops; *suffer,* undergo, bear under.
ferv (L. *fervere*)	boil	*fervent, effervesce, fervid.*
fil (L. *filum*)	thread, line	*filament,* a thread-like part; *file,* a line, as of soldiers.
fin (L. *finis*)	end, limit	*finite,* having an end; *fine,* a penalty that ends a case.
gain (AS. *gegen*)	against	*gainsay.*
gam (Gr. *gamos*)	marriage	*bigamy, polygamy, monogamy, amalgamate.*
garn (O.F. *garnir*)	warn, avert, protect, supply, adorn	*garnish,* to cover over, protect; *garniture,* adornment; *garment,* robe of protection.
gaster, gastr (Gr. *gaster*)	stomach	*gastric, gastronomy, gastro-intestinal.*
gaud (L. *gaudere*)	rejoice	*gaudy.*
ge (Gr. *ge*)	earth	*geography,* a description of the earth's surface; *georgic,* relating to husbandry, or working the earth.
gel (L. *geler*)	frost	*gelid,* frosty; *congeal,* to freeze; *gelatin,* an apparently frozen substance.
gen (L. *genu*)	knee	*genuflection,* a bend of the knee; *geniculate,* jointed.

Root or Stem	Meaning	Examples
gen, gener (L. *genus, generis*)	kin, kind, race, class	*genus,* a class; *general,* belonging to a whole class; *generate,* to produce, bring forth in kind; *gender,* kind.
gest (L. *gerere, gestus*)	carry, bring	*congestion,* a bringing together; *suggest,* bring under consideration.
gloss (Gr. *glossa*)	tongue, language, word	*gloss, glossary.*
gno (Gr. *gnonai*)	know	*prognostic,* a knowing beforehand; *agnostic,* one who does not know.
grad, gress (L. *gradi, gressus*)	step, go	*gradual,* step by step; *aggress,* go against; *transgress,* go beyond; *digress,* go aside.
gramm (Gr. *gramma*)	a letter, written character	*anagram,* change effected by rearranging letters of a word; *diagram,* a written figure or plan.
graph (Gr. *graphein*)	write	*autograph, biography, geography, stenography, graph.*
grat (L. *gratis*)	pleasing	*congratulate,* wish pleasure or joy; *gratify,* please.
greg (L. *gregarius, grex*)	herd, flock	*gregarious,* tending to flock together; *aggregate,* herd together.
gyn (Gr. *gyne*)	woman	*gynarchy, gynecology, gynandrous.*
habill (F. *habiller*)	dress, clothe	*habiliment, dishabille.*
hegemon (Gr. *hegemon*)	a guide, leader	*hegemony,* leadership.
helio (Gr. *helios*)	the sun	*heliocentric,* having the sun as center.

Root or Stem	Meaning	Examples
hepta (Gr. *hepta*)	seven	*heptarchy*, the rule of seven persons.
hier (Gr. *hieros*)	sacred, holy	*hierarchy, hierophant; hieroglyphic.*
homo (Gr. *homos*)	same	*homogeneous, homosexual, homopathy.*
hospit (L. *hospes, hospitis*)	host, guest	*hospitable, hospital, hospice.*
hum (L. *humus*)	ground	*exhume, inhume, humble, humus.*
hydr (Gr. *hydor*)	water	*hydra,* a watersnake; *hydraulics,* the science of water in motion; *hydrostatics,* the science of water at rest.
hypn (Gr. *hypnos*)	sleep	*hypnotic.*
ichthy (Gr. *ichthus*)	fish	*ichthyology,* the study or science of fish.
icon (Gr. *eicon*)	image	*iconoclast,* image breaker, assailant of established opinion.
imper (L. *imperare*)	command	*imperial, imperious, imperative.*
inan (L. *inanis*)	void, empty	*inane,* stupid, empty-minded; *inanition,* exhaustion, prostration, emptiness.
incend (L. *incendere*)	set on fire	*incendiary,* set on fire.
incip, incept (L. *incipere, inceptus*)	begin	*incipient, inception.*
insul (L. *insula*)	island	*insular,* belonging to an island; *insulate,* to cut off, separate as an island.

Root or Stem	Meaning	Examples
intim (L. *intimus*)	inmost	*intimate.*
ir (L. *ira*)	anger	*ire, irascible.*
iron (Gr. *eiron*)	a dissembler	*irony,* a disguised sarcasm or cutting criticism.
iso (Gr. *isos*)	equal	*isosceles.*
it (L. *ire, itus*)	go	*circuit, exit, ambition.*
jac (L. *jacere*)	lie	*adjacent,* lying against.
ject (L. *jacere, jectus*)	cast, hurl	*deject,* cast down; *inject,* cast into.
journ (L. *diurnus*)	daily	*journal,* daily record; *journey* (formerly), a day's travel.
judic (L. *judex*)	judge	*judiciary, judicial, adjudicate, prejudice, judicious.*
jug (L. *jugum*)	yoke	*subjugate,* bring under the yoke of a conqueror.
jur (L. *jurare*)	swear	*abjure,* swear away; *perjure,* swear falsely; *jury,* a sworn body of men.
la (L. *laos*)	the people	*laity,* the people as distinguished from the clergy.
labor (L. *labor*)	work	*collaborate,* work with; *elaborate,* work out; *laboratory,* a workshop.
lachrym (L. *lachryma*)	tears	*lachrymose, lachrymal.*
langu (L. *languere*)	be weak	*languid, languor, languish.*

Root or Stem	Meaning	Examples
lapid (L. *lapis, lapidis*)	stone	*lapidary,* a carver of precious stones; *dilapidated,* ruined, with stones torn apart.
lat (L. *latus*)	carry, lift, bring	*illative,* making an inference; *oblate,* with poles flattened or brought together.
leg (L. *legare*)	appoint, send, bring	*legate,* an ambassador, one sent abroad; *relegate,* to banish, send away.
leg, lect (Gr. *legein, lectos*)	gather, choose	*collect,* gather together; *eclectic,* selected, chosen; *eclege,* a selection.
leg (L. *lex, legis*)	law, legal	*legal, legitimate, legislate.*
leo, leon (L. *leo, leonis*)	lion	*leonine,* lion-like; *Leonard,* a veritable lion.
leps (Gr. *lambanein, lepsomai*)	seize, catch, take	*catalepsy, epilepsy.*
lev (L. *levari*)	lift, raise, rise	*lever,* an instrument for lifting; *levee,* a reception, formerly given in the morning on rising.
lib (L. *libare*)	taste, sip, pour out	*libation,* a pouring out of wine in honor of the gods.
liber (L. *liber*)	free	*liberty, liberate, liberal.*
libr (L. *libra*)	book	*library.*
lig (L. *ligare*)	tie, band	*ligament,* a band; *ligature,* a bandage; *league,* an alliance, or binding together.
line (L. *linum*)	line	*linear, lineal, delineate.*
lingu (L. *lingua*)	tongue	*lingual, linguist, language.*

Root or Stem	Meaning	Examples
lith (Gr. *lithos*)	stone	*lithography,* a process of drawing on stone; *monolith,* a single-stone shaft.
log (Gr. *logos*)	speech, word, reason, account	*eulogy, logic, dialog, syllogism, analogy, catalog.*
loqu, locut (L. *loqui, loqutus*)	speak, talk	*loquacious,* talkative; *obloquy,* calumny, a speaking against; *locution,* manner of speaking.
lud, lus (L. *ludere, lusus*)	sport, play, laugh, mock	*ludicrous,* laughable; *allude,* refer to lightly, as in sport; *illude,* deceive, mock.
lun (L. *luna*)	moon	*lunate,* shaped like a crescent moon.
lustr (L. *lustrum*)	purification	*lustrum, lustral, lustration.*
lut (L. *luere, lutus*)	wash	*ablution, dilute, pollute.*
macr (Gr. *macros*)	long, great	*macron,* the sign of the long sound.
magister, magistr (L. *magister*)	master	*magisterial, magistrate.*
magn (L. *magnus*)	great	*magnitude, magnificent, magnanimous.*
mal (L. *malus*)	bad, ill	*malice,* ill-will; *malady,* an illness; *malign,* ill-disposed.
mamm (L. *mamma*)	breast	*mammal,* an animal that suckles its young at the breast; *mammillary,* pertaining to the breasts.
man (L. *manus*)	hand	*manual, amanuensis, maintain, manage.*

Root or Stem	Meaning	Examples
mar (L. *mare*, *maris*)	sea	*marine*, belonging to the sea; *mariner*, a seaman; *cor- morant*, *rosemary*, *maritime*.
marti (L. *Mars*, *Martis*)	Mars	*martial*, warlike.
mater, matr (L. *mater*, *matris*)	mother	*maternal*, *matricide*, *matrimony*.
matin (L. *matutinus*)	morning	*matins*, morning service; *matinee*, an early perform- ance; *matutinal*, pertaining to the morning.
medi (L. *medius*)	middle, between	*medium*, *mediate*, *medieval*, *immediate*.
mel, mell (L. *mel*, *mellis*)	honey	*mellifluous*, flowing like honey.
memor (L. *memor*)	mindful	*memory*, *commemorate*, *memoir*.
mens (L. *mentini*, *mensus*)	measure	*mensuration*, *dimension*, *immense*.
merc (L. *merx*, *mercis*)	trade, reward, pay	*Mercury*, the god of trade; *amerce*, to fine, fix a sum to be paid; *mercantile*.
meter, metr (Gr. *metron*)	measure	*barometer*, *diameter*, *geometry*, *perimeter*.
migr (L. *migrare*)	wander	*migrate*, *emigrate*, *transmigrate*.
mill (L. *mille*)	thousand	*mill*, the thousandth part of a dollar; *millennium*, the thousand years of Christ's reign on earth.
mitt, miss (L. *mittere*, *missus*)	send, throw	*missile*, *missive*, *commit*, *demise*, *dismiss*, *emit*, *intermit*.

Root or Stem	Meaning	Examples
mon, monit (L. *monere, monitus*)	warn, advise, remind	*monument,* a memorial; *monition,* a warning; *admonish, premonition.*
mon, mono (Gr. *monos*)	single, alone	*monarch,* sole ruler; *monogram, monolog, monosyllable, monolith.*
mord, mors (L. *mordere, morsus*)	bite	*mordacity,* biting sarcasm; *morsel,* a little bite; *remorse,* a gnawing regret.
morph (Gr. *morphe*)	form, shape	*amorphous,* without form; *Morpheus,* the god of dreams—unreal shapes and forms.
mort (L. *mors, mortis*)	death	*mortal, mortify, mortgage.*
mot (L. *movere, motus*)	moved, move	*motion, motive, motor, promote, remote.*
mult (L. *multus*)	many	*multitude, multiply, multifarious.*
mur (L. *murus*)	wall	*mural, immure.*
mut (L. *mutare*)	change	*mutable, commute, mutual, permutation.*
myth (Gr. *mythos*)	fable	*mythology.*
nas (L. *nasus*)	nose	*nasal; nasturtium,* the flower whose odor twists the nose.
nat (L. *natus*)	born	*natal, innate, native, nature.*
necro (Gr. *necros*)	corpse	*necromancy,* divination by means of a corpse.
neur (Gr. *neuron*)	nerve	*neuralgia, neurosis, neural.*
noct (L. *nox, noctis*)	night	*nocturnal, nocturn, equinoctial.*

Root or Stem	Meaning	Examples
nom (Gr. *nomos*)	law	*astronomy*, laws of stars; *deuteronomy*, *economy*.
nom, nomen (L. *nomen*)	name, term	*binomial*, *misnomer*, *nomenclature*, *nominal*.
norm (L. *norma*)	rule	*normal*, *abnormal*, *enormous*.
not (L. *noscere*, *notus*)	known	*notice*, *notify*, *notion*, *notorious*.
nov (L. *novus*)	new	*novel*, *novice*, *innovate*, *renovate*.
numer (L. *numerus*)	number	*numerous*, *numerate*, *enumerate*, *innumerable*.
numism (L. *numisma*)	current coin	*numismatic*.
nounce, nunci (L. *nuntiare*)	bring tidings, tell	*announce*, *enunciate*, *nuncio*, *pronounce*.
nutr (L. *nutrire*)	nourish	*nutriment*, *nutrition*, *nurse*, *nurture*.
nymph (Gr. *nymphe*)	bride	*nymph*.
obel (Gr. *obelos*)	spit	*obelisk*, a pointed shaft, resembling a roasting spit.
octav (L. *octavus*)	eighth	*octave*, an interval in music embracing eight notes.
ocul (L. *oculus*)	eye	*ocular*, pertaining to the eye; *oculist*, one who treats the eye; *binocular*, two eyed.
od (Gr. *ode*)	song	*epode*, sung after; *monody*, a song with a single theme (grief); *prosody*, the study of song.
omal (Gr. *homalos*)	even	*anomoly*, something irregular, uneven.
omni (L. *omnis*)	all	*omnipresent*, *omnipotent*, *omniscient*, *omnibus*.

Root or Stem	Meaning	Examples
onym (Gr. *onyma*)	name	*anonymous*, without name; *homonyn*, having a name sounding like another.
ophi (Gr. *ophes*)	snake	*ophidian*, snake-like.
opt (L. *optare*)	wish, choose	*option*, *optative*, *adopt*.
or, orat (L. *orare*)	pray, address	*adore*, *oration*, *orison*, *peroration*, *inexorable*.
orama (Gr. *horao*)	a view	*diorama*, a view through a small opening; *panorama*, a view of all.
orbit (L. *orbita*)	a track	*orbit*, the path of a planet; *exorbitant*, excessive, going out of the beaten track.
ordin (L. *ordinare*)	order	*ordinal*, *ordinary*, *ordination*, *subordination*, *co-ordinate*, *inordinate*.
ortho (Gr. *orthos*)	straight, correct	*orthodox*, correct opinion; *orthoepy*, the correct pronunciation of words.
ov (L. *ovum*)	egg	*oval*, egg-shaped; *oviparous*, egg-producing; *ovule*, little egg.
oxy (Gr. *oxys*)	sharp, acid	*oxygen*, *paroxysm*, *oxymal*.
oz (Gr. *ozein*)	smell	*ozone*.
pachy (Gr. *pachys*)	thick	*pachyderm*, having a thick skin; *pachycephalous*, having a thick head.
paed, ped (Gr. *pais*, *paidos*)	child	*paedobaptism*, *pedagogue*, *pedophilia*.

Root or Stem	Meaning	Examples
palin (Gr. *palin*)	again	*palindrome*, a word or sentence reading the same backwards as forwards.
par (L. *par*)	equal	*disparity, disparage, parity, pair, par, peer.*
parl (L. *parler*)	speak	*parlance, parley, parliament, parlor, parole.*
pars, part (L. *pars, partis*)	part	*apart, apartment, parcel, partial, particle.*
past (L. *pascere, pastus*)	feed	*pasture*, a feeding place for animals; *pastor*, the feeder of a flock.
pater, patr (L. *pater*)	father	*paternal, patrician, patrimony, patron, patronymic.*
ped (L. *pes, pedis*)	foot	*pedal, biped, expedite, impede, pedestal.*
pen (L. *poena*)	pain, punishment	*penal, penitent, punish, impunity, subpena, pain.*
pend, pens (L. *pendere, pensus*)	hang, weigh	*pendant, pendulous, pensile, pension, pensive, append.*
phan (Gr. *phanein*)	show, bring to light, appear	*phantom*, a specter; *diaphanous*, transparent; *Epiphany*, the feast of the showing forth of Christ to the wise men of the East.
phil (Gr. *philos*)	fond, loving	*philanthropy*, love of fellow man; *philosophy*, love of wisdom; *philology*, love of words.
phor (Gr. *phoros*)	bringing	*phosphorous, metaphor.*
phthong (Gr. *phthongos*)	sound	*diphthong*, double sound; *aphthong*, without sound.

Root or Stem	Meaning	Examples
physi (Gr. *physis*)	nature	*physiognomy, physiology, physics.*
piano (It. *piano*)	even, smooth, soft	*pianoforte.*
pest, pist (L. *pinsere*)	pound	*pestle,* an instrument for pounding; *piston,* a pounding cylinder.
plaud, plaus (L. *plaudere*)	clap hands	*applaud, plaudit, plausible, explode.*
pleon (Gr. *pleos*)	more	*pleonasm,* a redundancy of speech.
plic (L. *plicare*)	fold, bend, embrace, twine	*complicated,* entwined; *explicate,* unfold, explain; *implicate,* involve.
plumb (L. *plumbum*)	lead	*plumb, plumbago, plumber plummet, plump.*
polis (Gr. *polis*)	city	*acropolis,* an upper city; *metropolis,* a great city.
pon (L. *ponere*)	to place, put	*component, deponent, exponent, opponent.*
pont (L. *pons, pontis*)	bridge	*pontoon,* a float used in the construction of a temporary bridge.
port (L. *portare*)	carry, bear, bring	*portable, porter, portage, portfolio, portmanteau, portly.*
pot (L. *potare*)	drink	*potion,* a draught; *potation,* a draft; *poison,* a destructive drink.
prehend, prehens (L. *prehendere, prehensus*)	take, seize, grasp	*apprehend, comprehend, reprehend, prehensile.*
psych (Gr. *psyche*)	soul, mind	*psychology, psychic, metapsychosis.*

Root or Stem	Meaning	Examples
pyr (Gr. *pyr*)	fire	*pyre, pyrotechnics, pyrean.*
quadr (L. *quadrus*)	square, fourfold	*quadrate, quadrangle, quadrennial, quadrilateral, quadruped, quadruple.*
quer, quisit (L. *quaerere*)	seek, ask	*query, inquire, inquiry, inquisition, perquisite, quest.*
quot (L. *quot*)	how many	*quota,* a share; *quotient,* the result of a division.
rap, rapt (L. *rapio*)	seize, grasp	*rapacious,* grasping; *rapine,* the seizing of plunder; *rapture,* a seizing.
rect (L. *regere, rectus*)	ruled, right, straight	*rectangle,* a figure having only right angles; *rectify,* make right.
reg (L. *regere*)	rule, govern	*regent,* one ruling in the stead of another; *regimen,* a course of life conforming to a rule.
rhe (Gr. *rhelin*)	flow	*diarrhea,* a flow through the bowels; *rheum,* a thin fluid secreted by the glands.
rhomb (Gr. *rhombos*)	a spindle	*rhombus,* a figure in the form of a spindle; *rhomboid,* resembling a rhombus.
rid, ris (L. *ridere, risus*)	laugh	*ridicule, ridiculous, deride, risible.*
rog, rogat (L. *rogare, rogatus*)	ask, demand	*abrogate, arrogate, derogate, interrogate, prorogue, surrogate, supererogation.*
rupt (L. *rumpere, ruptus*)	break	*rupture, corrupt, eruption, interruption, irruption, bankrupt.*

Root or Stem	Meaning	Examples
sacr (L. *sacer,* *sacri*)	holy	*sacrament,* a sacred vow or engagement; *sacrifice,* to make a holy offering.
sal (L. *sal*)	salt	*saline, salt, salary.*
salv (L. *salvus*)	save	*salvation, salvage, salver, salve.*
sanguin (O.F. *sanguin*)	blood	*sanguinary,* bloody; *consanguinity,* relationship by blood.
sat, satis (L. *sat, satis*)	enough, sufficient	*sate,* surfeit, give enough; *assets,* effects deemed sufficient to meet liabilities.
scan, scans (L. *scandere*)	climb	*scan, ascend, transcend.*
sci (L. *scire*)	know	*science,* classified knowledge; *conscious,* aware of.
scrib, script (L. *scribere,* *scriptus*)	write	*scribe, ascribe, describe, circumscribe, inscribe, proscribe, scribble, conscript.*
sec, sect (L. *secare,* *sectus*)	cut	*secant,* a radius that cuts the circumference of a circle; *sickle,* a cutting instrument.
sen (L. *senex*)	old	*senior,* older; *senate,* a council of elderly men; *seneschal,* an old servant.
sent, sens (L. *sentire,* *sensus*)	perceive, feel, think	*sentiment, presentiment, sentence, sensible, sensual.*
septem (L. *septem*)	seven	*September,* the seventh month of the Roman year, which began with March.
sequ, secut (L. *sequi,* *secutus*)	follow	*sequel, sequence, consequent, exequies, subsequent, execute, prosecute.*
sext (L. *sex*)	sixth	*sextuple,* six-fold; *sextant,* the sixth part of a circle.

Root or Stem	Meaning	Examples
sider (L. *sidus,* *sideris*)	star	*sidereal,* belonging to the stars.
sist (L. *stare*)	to place, stand	*assist,* step or stand to; *consist,* stand together.
sol (L. *sol*)	sun	*solar, solstice, parasol.*
solv, solut (L. *solvere,* *solutus*)	loosen	*dissolve, resolve, absolute, dissolute, solution.*
son (L. *sonare*)	sound	*consonant,* sounding with; *dissonant,* sounding apart, disharmonious.
soph (Gr. *sophos*)	wisdom	*sophistry, philosophy, sophisticate.*
spec, spect (L. *specere,* *spectus*)	look, see, appear	*species, specie, specimen, conspicuous, despicable, perspicacity, introspection.*
sper (Gr. *speirein*)	hope	*despair,* to be without hope; *prosper,* to have one's hopes advanced.
spir (L. *spirare*)	breathe	*spiracle,* a breathing hole; *spirit,* breath; *aspirate,* a breath sound.
st (L. *stare*)	stand	*contrast,* stand against; *obstacle,* something standing against.
string, strict (L. *stringere,* *strictus*)	draw tight, bind, compass, urge	*stringent, strict, constrain, district, distress, strait.*
stru, struct (L. *struere,* *structus*)	build	*construe, construct, instruct, structure, obstruct.*
syndic (Gr. *syndicos*)	censor, regulator, controller	*syndicate,* a combination to control a business.

Root or Stem	Meaning	Examples
tact (L. *tangere, tactus*)	touch	*contact,* touch together; *intact,* untouched; *tact,* delicacy of touch.
techn (Gr. *techne*)	art	*technical,* pertaining to an art; *pyrotechnics,* the art of fire works.
therm (Gr. *thermos*)	heat, warm	*thermal, thermometer, isotherm,* lines showing equal annual heat.
tom (Gr. *temnein*)	cut	*anatomy, atom, phlebotomy, tome, epitome.*
tort (L. *torquere, tortus*)	twist, wring	*contort,* twist together; *distort,* twist apart; *retort,* twist back; *torture,* a wringing pain; *tortuous,* crooked.
tract (L. *trahere, tractus*)	draw	*attract, contract, extract, protract, tract.*
tri (L. *tri*)	three	*triad, triangle, tribrach, trident, triennial, triglyph.*
trop (Gr. *trope*)	turn	*tropic, trophy, heliotrope.*
tum (L. *tumere*)	to swell, surge up	*tumiel, tumulus, tumult, tumefy, intumescence.*
typ (Gr. *typos*)	a blow, impression, model	*archetype,* original model; *antitype,* the copy formed against the model.
ultim (L. *ultimus*)	last	*ultimate, ultimo, penult, ultimatum.*
un (L. *unus*)	one	*unanimous,* of one mind; *unicorn,* the fabulous horse with one straight horn in the center of his forehead.
und (L. *unda*)	wave, flow	*undulate, inundate, redundant.*

Root or Stem	Meaning	Examples
uxor (L. *uxor*)	wife	*uxorious,* excessively fond of a wife; *uxoricide,* the killing of a wife.
vag (L. *vagari*)	wander	*vagabond, vagrant, vague, vagary, extravagant.*
val (L. *valere*)	be strong, be worth	*valid, valiant, valor, value, invalid, convalesce.*
val (Icel. *valr*)	the slain, slaughter	*Valhalla,* the hell of the slain, the paradise of the Northmen.
vale (L. *vale*)	farewell	*valedictory,* a farewell.
ven, vent (L. *venire, ventus*)	come	*convene, convenient, covenant, parvenu, souvenir, supervene.*
ver (L. *verus*)	true, truth	*veracious,* truthful; *verify,* determine the truth of.
verb (L. *verbum*)	word	*verbal, verbatim, verbose, proverb, verbiage.*
vert, vers (L. *vertere, versus*)	turn	*verse,* a line or turn of poetry; *version,* a translation or turning into another language.
vi (L. *via*)	road, way	*viaduct, obviate, obvious, pervious, envoy, invoice.*
vid, vis (L. *video*)	see, appear	*evident,* clearly visible; *provide,* foresee; *visor,* the face of a helmet; *vista,* a view.
vir (L. *vir*)	man	*virile, virago, virtue, triumvir.*
viv (L. *vivere*)	live	*vivacity, vivify, vivid.*
voc (L. *vox, vocis*)	voice	*vocal, vociferate, viva voce.*

Root or Stem	Meaning	Examples
volv, volu, volut (L. *volvere, volutus*)	roll, circumvolve	*convolve, devolve, revolve, revolt, vault, volute.*
vot (L. *vovere, votus*)	vow	*votive,* promised with a vow; *devout,* devoted; *devote,* vow away fully.
vuls, vult (L. *vellere, vulsus*)	pluck, tear	*convulsion, vulture, revulsion.*
xyl (Gr. *xyle*)	wood	*xylography, xylophone.*
zo (Gr. *zoon*)	animal	*zoology,* the science of animals; *zodiac,* the area of the twelve constellations, named almost entirely after animals.

BOOK THIRTEEN

Dictionary of Affixes:
PREFIXES AND SUFFIXES

Prefixes

Prefix	Meaning	Examples
a (AS.)	at; in; on	*ahead*, at the head; *asleep*, in sleep; *aground*, on ground
a (AS.)	Meaning and use are indefinite, but a generally has an intensive force (thus representing the AS. *ge*)	*aware, awake, awanting.*
a, ab, abs (L.)	from; away from	*avoid*, to part from; *avert*, to turn away from; *absolve*, to loose from; *abstract*, to draw from.
a, an (Gr.)	without; not	*abyss*, a place without a bottom; *atheist*, a man without God; *anarchy*, a society without a government; *anomalous*, not similar
ad; also a, ac, af, ag, al, an, ap, ar, as, at [for the sake of euphony, ad assumes the various forms listed, according to the letter with which	to; toward	*ascend*, to climb to; *accede*, to yield to; *accrue*, to grow to; *affix*, to fix to; *affiance*, to give faith to; *aggregate*, to collect into one mass; *aggravate*, to make heavy to; *allot*, to apportion to; *allocate*, to give a place to; *annex*, to tie to; *announce*, to tell to; *append*, to hang to; *applaud*, to clap the hands to; *arrive*,

Prefix	Meaning	Examples
the root begins] (L.)		to come to; *arrange,* to put in a row; *assign,* to allot to; *assist,* to stand to; *attract,* to draw to; *attest,* to bear witness to; *advance,* to go toward.
af *see* ad ag *see* ad al *see* ad		
am, amb, ambi, amphi (L. *ambi,* both: Gr. *amphi,* about, on both sides)	both; round; about	*amputate,* to cut off round about, as a leg: *ambidextrous,* using both hands as right: *ambition,* a going round: *amphibious,* able to live in both elements; *amphitheatre,* a theatre on all sides; *amphigens,* plants which increase by growth on all sides.
amb *see* am ambi *see* am amphi *see* am (Gr.) an *see* a, without an *see* ad		
ana (Gr.)	up; up through; back; again	*anatomy,* a cutting up through; *analogy,* a reasoning back; *analysis,* a loosening up through; *anachronism,* a dating up or back.
ant *see* anti		
ante [rarely, anti] (L.)	before, in time or place	*antechamber,* a chamber before the principal one; *antecedent,* going before; *anticipate,* to take before, to foresee.
anti (Gr. *anti,* against; Sans. *anti,* over against)	against; opposite	*antidote,* something given as good against; *antipathy,* a feeling against; *antarctic,* opposite the arctic or north.
anti *see* ante ap *see* ad		
apo (Gr. *apo;* Sans. *apa,* off, away)	away; from	*apostasy,* a standing away from; *apostle,* one sent from.

PREFIX	MEANING	EXAMPLES
ar *see* ad		
arch and archi (Gr.)	chief, principal, of the first order	*archangel*, an angel of the first order, *archenemy*, chief enemy; *architect*, principal builder.
as *see* ad		
at *see* ad		
be (AS.)	to make; to take from	*be* prefixed to a noun forms a verb, as in *becalm*, to make calm; *be* prefixed to a verb signifies *about*, *over*, *for*; as *begird*, to gird about; *bedaub*, to daub over; *bespeak*, to speak for; *be* as the first element in an adverb, a preposition, or a conjunction signifies *by* or *in*; *betimes*, in time; *because*, by cause of.
bi—also bis (L. *bis*, twice)	twice; two; double; in two	*bisect*, to cut into two equal parts; *bicipital*, having a double head.
bin *see* bi		
bis *see* bi		
cat *see* cata		
cata—also cat and cath (Gr.)	down; downwards; under; against; completeness	*catacombs*, hollow places under ground; *catechise*, to speak down to others; *catholic*, the whole, in completeness.
cath *see* cata		
circu *see* circum		
circum also circu (L.)	around; round about	*circumference*, that which goes round; *circumscribe*, to write around, to limit; *circuit*, a moving or passing round.
cis (L.)	on this side	*cisalpine*, on this side the Alps.
co *see* con		
cog *see* con		
col *see* con		
com *see* con		
con (L. *cum*; Gr. *syn*, with, together)	assumes the various forms co, cog, col, com, cor, according to the initial letter of the root, and signifies: together.	*concede*, to yield together; *coherent*, sticking together; *cognate*, born together; *collect*, to gather together; *commerce*, a trading together; *corrode*, to gnaw together.

PREFIX	MEANING	EXAMPLES
contra—also its forms counter and contro (L. contra, against) contro see contra cor see con counter see contra	against; in opposition to; the wrong way	*contradict,* to speak against; *counteract,* to act against; *controvert,* to contend against in words or writing.
de (L.)	down; from; separation	*degrade,* to put a step down; *demand,* to order from; *depose,* to put down; *de* is negative in *deform* and *destroy,* etc.; *de* is from *dis,* assunder, in *derange, depart,* etc.; *de* is intensive in *declare, desolate,* etc.
demi (F. *demi,* half— from L. *dimidius,* the half) di see dis	a half, or part of that of which it forms the prefix— generally separated by a hyphen	*demi-god,* a half or inferior god; *demi-semiquaver,* half a semiquaver (or a quarter of a quaver); *demi-wolf,* half-wolf and half dog.
dia (Gr. *dia,* through— from *duo,* two) dif see dis	two, through; asunder	*dialogue,* a conversation between two; *diaphanous,* letting light through; *diameter,* the measure through the center.
dis—also its forms di and dif (L. and Gr. *dis,* twice, in two parts)	not; the opposite of; asunder or apart; two	*disagree,* the opposite of agree; *dispell,* to drive asunder; *dissyllable,* a word of two syllables; *dis* becomes *di* before *s, v,* etc., as *disperse,* to spread asunder, *divert,* to turn aside or apart; *dif* before *f,* as *diffuse,* to pour apart; *differ,* to bear apart.
dys (Gr. *dys,* with difficulty, bad) e see ex ef see ex	an inseparable prefix denoting: badly; with difficulty, hard	*dyscrasia,* an ill habit of body; *dyspepsia,* bad digestion; *dysorexia,* bad appetite.
en—also em (AS.)	to make; to surround	*enable,* to make able, *ennoble,* to make noble; *embezzle,* to make as one's own what belongs to another; *employ,* to make use of; *embrace,* to surround with the arms.

Prefix	Meaning	Examples
en (F. *en;* L. *in;* Gr. *en;* AS., *em,* *in*)	in; on; into	*encage,* to put into a cage; *enclose,* to close in; *enkindle,* to set on fire; *embalm,* to put into balsam; *embosom,* to hold or enclose in the bosom; *empale,* to drive a stake into; *en* or *em* from the Greek, and used as a prefix in words derived from the Greek, as: *endemic,* on the people; *energy,* work or power in; *emphasis,* a speaking with the force of the voice on. (Some words are written indifferently with *en* or *in,* as *enclose* or *inclose.*)
ep and eph *see* epi		
epi—also its forms ep and eph (Gr.)	on; upon; during; on the outside or above; ep is used before a vowel; eph with an aspirate; and epi before a consonant	*epidermis,* a skin upon a skin; *epitaph,* a writing upon a tombstone; *epoch,* a point of time fixed on; *ephemeral,* existence only upon a day.
equi (L. equal)	equal: alike	*equilateral,* equal-sided; *equivalved,* having both valves alike.
ex with its forms e, ec, ef (L. and Gr. *ex;* Gr. *ek*)	from; out; out of; without	*exhaust,* to draw out; *exodus,* a going out; *expire,* to breathe out; *emerge,* to rise out of; *eccentric,* out of the center; *ecstasy,* a standing out of the body; *effect,* to work out; *effulgence,* a shining out: *ex* prefixed to the name of an office denotes that the person formerly held the office named, or does not now hold it, as *ex-mayor, ex-minister, ex-officio; ex parte,* from one side only, partial.
exo (Gr.)	without	*exotic,* that which is introduced from without.
extra (L.)	on the outside; beyond; in excess; additional	*extravagant,* wandering beyond limits; *extraneous,* that which is without or beyond a thing; *extra-judicial,* on the outside of ordinary court procedure.

Prefix	Meaning	Examples
Fitz Norman F. from Latin *filius*, son	son of	*Fitz-William,* the son of William
for (Ger. *ver;* Goth. *fra* or *fair;* F. *for,* away)	not; against, forth; away	*forbid,* to bid a thing away; *forget,* to lose from memory; *forgo,* to go without or against; *forfend,* to ward off.
fore (Ger. *vor,* before: AS. *for,* for)	before; in front of	*foreordain,* to ordain beforehand; *foretell,* to tell before; *foreground,* ground in front.
gain (AS.)	against	*gainsay,* to speak against
hemi (Gr. *hemi* —from *hemisu,* the half)	a half	*hemicrania,* pain on one side of the head only; *hemisphere,* a half sphere or globe; *hemistich,* a half line in poetry.
hepta (Gr. *hepta*)	a prefix signifying seven	*heptagon,* a figure with seven sides and angles; *heptarchy,* a government ruled by seven persons.
hetero (Gr. *heteros*)	another; one opposite or different; denoting dissimilarity; irregular; abnormal	*heterodox,* contrary to right doctrines or tenets; *heterarchy,* the government of an alien; *heterogeneous,* of a different kind or nature.
homo (Gr. *homos*)	same, similar, or alike	*homocarpous,* having all the fruits of a flowerhead alike.
hydr and **hydro** (Gr. *hydor*)	in scientific terms denoting the presence of water; also in certain chemical terms, the presence of hydrogen	*hydraulic,* relating to the conveyance of water through pipes; *hydrometer,* an instrument for measuring the density and strength of liquids; *hydropathy,* cure by water.
hyp and **hypo** (Gr. *hypo*)	under, beneath, indicating the deficiency or less than	*hypocrite,* one who keeps his real character under; *hypotenuse,* the line extended under the right angle; *hypalgia,* slight pain.
hyper (Gr. *hyper*)	above, over, beyond	*hyperborean,* beyond the north; *hypercritical,* judging overexactly.
ig *see* **in** **il** *see* **in** **im** *see* **in**		

Prefix	Meaning	Examples
in—also il, im, ir (L. *in*, in, within —akin to Sans. *an*; Gr. *en*; AS. *in*, into)	in as a prefix, with its forms il, im, ir, signifies in, into, on, in verbs and nouns	*include*, to shut in; *incur*, to run into; *incision*, a cutting into; *illuminate*, to throw light on; *immure*, to put within walls; *imbibe*, to drink in; *import*, to carry in; *irrigate*, to let water flow in.
in—also ig, il, im, ir (L. *in*, not— akin to Sans. and Gr. *an*; Goth. and Ger. *un*, not)	in, as a prefix, with its forms ig, il, im, ir, signifies *not* in adjectives	*incorrect*, not correct; *incapable*, not able to take; *ignoble*, not noble; *ignorant*, not knowing; *illicit*, not permitted; *immature*, not ripe; *imprudent*, not prudent; *irregular*, not according to rule.
in (AS.)	in (really, the preposition in)	*inborn, insight, inland*
infra (L. *infra*)	under or beneath	*infra-costal*, beneath the ribs: *infra-dig*, beneath dignity.
inter (L.)	between; among or amongst; in the midst	*intercede*, to go between; *interfere*, to strike amongst; *interpose*, to place amongst.
intra (L.)	within; on the outside; interior	*intramural*, within the walls.
intro (L.)	within; into; in	*introduce*, to lead within; *intromit*, to send in.
ir *see* in		
iso (Gr. equal)	equality or similarity	*isocheimal*, having the same or a similar winter temperature; *isochromatic*, having the same color.
juxta (L.)	close to; near to; nigh	*juxtaposition*, a position close to.
litho (Gr. *lithos*, a stone)	having reference to a stone, or a calculus	*litholysis*, the treatment for the solution of stone in the bladder; *lithoidal*, stony in appearance or structure.
Mac (Gael.)	son of, before proper name	*Mac Donald*, the son of Donald.
macro (Gr. *makros*, long)	denoting largeness or length	*macrocarpous*, having large fruit; *macrocosm*, the great world; *macrocephalous*, having a large head.
mal—also male (L. *male*, badly, ill; F. *mal*, evil, ill)	evil; ill; badly	*malformation*, an ill or wrong formation; *malefactor*, an evil or wrong doer; *malevolent*, ill-disposed towards others.

Prefix	Meaning	Examples
mega and **megalo** (Gr. great)	large; of great size	*megatherium,* a fossil creature of enormous size; *megalomania,* dementia marked by delusions of grandeur.
mes and **meso** (Gr. middle) **met** *see* **meta**	denoting the middle, intermediate	*mesophoeum,* the middle layer of the bark.
meta—also **met** (Gr. between, with, after)	beyond; after; over; a change or transference	*metaphor,* that which carries a word beyond its usual meaning; *metamorphosis,* a change of form.
micro (Gr. small)	denoting of small size	*micrometer,* an instrument for measuring minute objects under the microscope.
mis (Dan., Icel., and Goth.: implying error: Ger. *miss,* wrong: AS. *mis,* defect)	divergence; error; defect; wrong	*misapply,* to apply wrongly; *mislay,* to lay in a wrong place; *misbehavior,* ill behavior; *misconduct,* defect in conduct.
mis (OF. *mes,* less, ill—from L. *minus,* less)	degrading; ill; less	*misadventure,* ill adventure; *mischief,* that which turns out ill.
mon and **mono** (Gr. one, single) **mono** *see* **mon**	one; alone; solitary	*monandrous,* having one stamen; *monism,* philosophical doctrine of the oneness of mind and matter.
mult and **multi** (L. many, much)	many in number; much	*multangular,* having many corners or angles; *multiparous,* producing many at a birth.
ne or **n** (AS.)	no, not	*never,* not ever; *nescience,* no knowledge.
neo (Gr. new)	recent; new	*neoplasm,* a new formation or growth; *neophyte,* a new convert or proselyte; *neologism,* a new word
non (L.) **o** *see* **ob**	not—reversing the sense	*non-ability,* want of ability.
ob with its forms **oc, of, o, op** (L.) (Euphony determines which of the various forms is employed.)	in the way of; against; out	*object,* something cast in the way of; *obsolete,* grown out of use; *occasion,* a falling in the way of; *offend,* to strike against; *omit,* to leave out; *oppose,* to place against.

PREFIX	MEANING	EXAMPLES
oc *see* **ob**		
of *see* **ob**		
op *see* **ob**		
out (Icel. *ut*)	beyond; exceeding; above	*outbid,* to exceed in bidding; *outbreak,* a bursting above.
over (AS. *ofer* or *ober;* Ger. *ober,* upper, and *über,* over, above)	above, beyond, too much	*overawe,* to have influence to excess; *overcoat,* a coat above all others; *overwork,* work beyond the usual amount.
pan and **panto** (Gr. all)	all; everything	*pandemonium,* the place of all the demons; *pantomime,* a theatrical dumb show of all sorts of actions.
para (Gr. by, along)	side by side as if for comparison; like; alike; unlike; contrary to	*paradox,* that which is contrary to received opinion; *parody,* a poetical composition like in substance, but unlike in sense, to another.
penta and **pente** (Gr. five)	five	*pentaphyllous,* having five leaves; *pentagon,* a figure having five sides.
per and **pel** (L.)	through; thoroughly; by; for	*perennial,* lasting through the year; *per* becomes *pel* before *l,* only in *pellucid,* thoroughly clear; *per* standing alone signifies *by,* as *per annum,* by the year, yearly.
peri (Gr.)	round; about	*perimeter,* the measure round about; *period,* a round of time.
poly (Gr. *polys,* many)	many	*polyspermal,* containing many seeds; *polysyllable,* a word of many syllables; *polygamy,* having many wives.
por *see* **pro**		
post (L.)	behind; after; afterwards	*postfix,* that which is put after; *postscript,* that which is written afterwards.
prae or **pre** (Gr. *prae*)	before; priority of time, place, or rank	*precede,* to go before; *predict,* to say or tell before.
preter (L. *praeter*)	beyond; more than	*preternatural,* beyond the course of nature; *preterperfect,* more than perfect.
pro with its forms **por** and **pur** (L. *pro,* for; Gr. *pro,* before)	for; forward; forth	*proceed,* to go forward; *provoke,* to call forth; *portend,* to indicate events forward; *pursue,* to follow forward.

Prefix	Meaning	Examples
pros (Gr. *pros*)	to; towards	*proselyte*, one who comes to or towards.
prot and proto (Gr. *protos*, first)	first; lowest; in chem., a first degree of combination, as oxygen with metals	protoxide, that which combines with the first or smallest proportion of oxygen; *protoplast*, the thing first formed.
pseud and pseudo (Gr. false)	false or spurious	*pseudo-membrane*, a false membrane; *pseudonym*, a false name.
pyr and pyro (Gr. *pyr*, fire, *pyros*, of fire)	denoting relation to, or connection with, fire or heat	*pyrogenous*, produced or formed by fire.
re (L. *re* or *red*, back)	back or again; anew or a second time	*reaffirm*, to affirm again; *recommence*, to begin anew.
retro (L.)	back; backward;	*retrospect*, a looking back; *retrograde*, a going backward.
se (L.)	aside; a separating from	*secede*, to go aside, to separate from; *seduce*, to lead aside; *sedition*, a going aside.
semi (L.)	half; in part	*semicircle*, half a circle.
sex (L. *sex;* Gr. *hex*, six)	six	*sexennial*, happening once in six years, or lasting six years; *sextet*, a composition for six voices or six instruments.
sine (L.)	without	*sinecure*, an office which has an income but not employment.
sub, with its forms suc, suf, sug, sum, sup, sus (L.) (Euphony determines which of the variants of *sub* is employed.)	under; below, beneath	*subscribe*, to write under; *subside*, to settle under; *succeed*, to follow under or in order; *suffer*, to bear up under; *suggest*, to carry or lay under; *summon*, to warn beneath or secretly; *supplant*, to trip up beneath; *susceptible*, capable of being laid hold of beneath; *suspend*, to hang beneath.
subter (L.)	beneath; under	*subterfuge*, a flying under or beneath.
suc *see* sub		
suf *see* sub		
sug *see* sub		

Prefix	Meaning	Examples
sum *see* sub		
sup *see* sub		
super—also its form sur (L.)	above; over; in excess	*superhuman*, above human; *surcharge*, to charge in excess.
sur *see* super		
sus *see* sub		
sy *see* syn		
syl *see* syn		
sym *see* syn		
syn, with its forms sy, syl, sym (Gr.)	with; together	*syntax*, a putting together in order; *system*, that which is formed of parts placed together; *syllable*, several letters taken together to form a single sound; *sympathy*, feeling with another.
tra (L.) *see* trans		
trans—also its form tra (L.)	across; over; beyond; through	*transgress*, to go over or beyond; *traverse*, to turn or lie across.
tri (Gr. *treis*; L. *tres*)	three; in threes	*triangle*, a figure of three sides and angles; *trisect*, to cut into three parts.
ultra (L.)	beyond; on the other side; extreme	*ultramontane*, on the other side of the mountain; *ultraism*, advocating extreme measures.
un (AS. *un*, a privative or negative particle)	not· the opposite of	*unable*, not able; *un* before a verb signifies to deprive of, to undo; *uncrown*, to deprive of a crown; *un* is equivalent to the Latin prefix *in* when it signifies not.
under (AS.)	lower in rank or degree; beneath	*undercoat*, a coat beneath; *underclerk*, an inferior clerk.
uni (L. *unus*, one)	one	*uniparous*, having only one at a birth.
up (AS. *up*, exalted)	aloft; on high; upwards	*upcast*, to throw upward; *upbear*, to raise aloft.
vice (L. *vice*, instead)	acting in place of another, assisting	*vice-consul*, an assistant consul.
with (AS. *with*)	opposition; privation	*withdraw*, to draw from; *withstand*, to stand against.
y (AS., *ge*)	sign of past participle	*y-clad*, clad; *y-clept*, called.

Suffixes

Suffix	Meaning	Examples
able also ible and ile (L. termination bilis, able)	all form adjectives: able to be; fit to be; capacity or worthi- ness for being	*curable,* able to be cured; *visible,* able to be seen; *ductile,* capable of being drawn.
ac also al, ane, ar, ary, ic, ical, id, ile, ine, ory, ch, ese (L.) ish (AS.)	like, of, pertaining to	*cardiac,* pertaining to the heart; *vernal,* pertaining to spring; *human* and *humane,* like man; *Prussian,* pertaining to Prussia; *globular,* like a round body; *literary,* pertaining to learning; *gigantic,* like a giant; *as- tronomical,* pertaining to astronomy; *humid,* pertaining to moisture or wetness; *febrile,* pertaining to a fever; *marine,* pertaining to the sea; *consolatory,* tending to comfort; *French,* pertaining to France; *Chinese,* pertaining to China; *Eng- lish,* pertaining to England.
aceae (L. *aceus*)	in bot., a postfix which terminates the names of Orders	*Droseraceae,* the Sundew family of plants; *Oxalidaceae,* the Wood-sor- rel family of plants.
aceous and ous (L. *aceus*)	denotes resemblance to a substance	*carbonaceous,* partaking of the quali- ties or appearance of carbon; *ous* denotes the substance itself, as *mem- branous,* consisting of membranes.
acy (1) (L. *acia, asia, atia*); also age, ance, ancy, dom, ence, ency, hood, ism, or asm, ment, mony, ness, ry, ship, th, tude, ty or ity, ure, y	all form nouns, and signify: state, condition, or qual- ity of being	*celibacy,* state of being unmarried; *bondage,* state of being bound; *repentance,* state of repenting; *men- dicancy,* state of begging; *freedom,* state of being free; *diligence,* quality of being diligent; *falsehood,* state of being false; *barbarism,* condition of a savage; *enthusiasm,* state of being inspired, as by a god; *agreement,* state of being agreed; *acrimony,* quality of being sharp; *deafness,* state of being deaf; *bravery,* a qual- ity of being brave; *partnership,* state of being a partner; *mirth,* state of

SUFFIX	MEANING	EXAMPLES
		being merry; *gratitude,* quality of being thankful; *poverty,* state of being poor; *torture,* state of being tormented; *modesty,* quality of being modest.
acy (2) (Gr. *akos*) also **ate, dom,** **ric, ship**	all form nouns: rank; office, jurisdiction; dominion	*papacy,* the office of the Pope; *protectorate,* the jurisdiction of a protector; *kingdom,* the dominion of a king; *bishopric,* the office of a bishop; *clerkship,* the office of a clerk.
adae *see* **idae**		
ade (F. *ade*—from L. *atus*)	as a noun: concocted, made	*lemonade,* that which is concocted from lemons; *palisade,* that which is made of pales or posts.
age (1) *see* under **acy** (1)	state of being	
age (2) (F. *age*—fro L. *aticus*) also **.on,** **sion,** or **tion,** **ment, ure**	all form nouns: act of, thing done	*marriage,* the act of marrying; *union,* the act of uniting; *admission,* the act of admitting; *inspection,* the act of looking into; *concealment,* the act of hiding; *departure,* the act of leaving.
age (3) (F. *age*—from L. *aticus*) ; also **ry** **al** (L. *alis*) pert. to—*see* under **ac**	form nouns, and signifies persons or things collectively	*assemblage,* a collection of persons; *foliage,* the whole body of leaves; *gentry,* the whole body of gentlemen.
algia (Gr. *algos,* pain) **an** (1) or **ane** *see* under **ac**	denoting the presence of pain	*nephralgia,* pain in the kidney.
an (2) (L. *anus*) also **ant, ar, ard,** **ary, aster, ate,** **ee, eer, ent, er,** **ic, ist, ite** or **yte,** **ive** or **iff,** or **ster**	all form nouns and signify the person who acts or who is; one who	*equestrian,* one who rides on horseback; *vagrant,* one who wanders; *scholar,* one who attends school; *drunkard,* one who drinks intoxicants to excess; *lapidary,* one who cuts precious stones; *poetaster,* one who writes petty verses; *advocate,* one who pleads in behalf of others; *patentee,* one who holds a patent;

Suffix	Meaning	Examples
		mutineer, one who rebels against constituted authority; *student,* one who studies; *draper,* one who sells cloths; *rustic,* one who is a native of the country; *botanist,* one who is skilled in a knowledge of plants; *Israelite,* one who is descended from Israel; *neophyte,* one who is newly admitted, as into a religious order; *captive,* one who is taken prisoner; *plaintiff,* one who commences a suit in law against another; *benefactor,* one who confers benefits on another; *barrister,* one who pleads for others at the bar.
ana (L. *anus*)	signifying a collection of memorable sayings or random thoughts	*Johnsoniana,* a collection of the sayings, anecdotes, etc relating to Johnson.
ance and ancy *see* under acy (1)	state of being	
ant (1) *see* under an	one who	
ant (2) ; also ent (L. *ens,* being— gen. *entis*)	form adjectives and signify being or belonging to	*verdant,* being green; *belligerent,* being in a state that carries on war.
ar *see* under ac ar *see* under an ard *see* under an		
art *see* an	one who	*braggart,* one who is vain and boasting.
ary (1) (L. *arium*) also ery, ory, ry	form nouns and signify the place where or place which	*aviary,* a place where birds are kept; *drapery,* a place where linen goods are sold; *dormitory,* a place where persons sleep; *foundry,* a place where articles in metal are cast in molds.
ary (2) (L. *arius*); also ice, ment, mony, ory	form nouns and signify the thing which	*luminary,* that which gives light; *justice,* that which is just; *aliment,* that which nourishes; *patrimony,* that which is inherited from a father;

Suffix	Meaning	Examples
		territory, the district of country belonging to.
asm *see* under **acy** (1)		
aster *see* under **an**		
ate (1) *see* under **an** (2); **ate** (2) *see* under **acy** (2)		
ate (3) (L. *ate*) also **ful, lent, ose, ous, some, y**	form adjectives and signify full of; abundance	*desolate*, full of grief; *deceitful*, full of deceit; *violent*, full of the unnatural exercise of power; *verbose*, full of words; *beauteous*, full of beauty; *gladsome*, full of gladness; *flowery*, full of flowers.
ate (4) (L. *atus*) also **en, fy, ish, ise** or **ize**	form verbs and signify to make; to put; to take	*animate*, to put life into; *moisten*, to make moist; *qualify*, to make fit; *publish*, to make public; *fertilize*, to make fruitful.
ate (5) (L. *atus*)	in chem. substituted in the name of an acid ending in *ic*	*nitrate* of silver, that is, a combination of *nitric acid* with the salifiable base silver.
celli; also **cello** (It. *celli*—from L. *culus*)	little; a diminutive termination	*vermicelli, violoncello.*
ch *see* under **ac**		
cle (L. *culus*, a dim. termination) also **cule, ule, el**; or **le, en, kin, let, et** or **ot, ling, ock, y** or **ie**	form nouns and signify: little; diminution	*canticle*, a little song; *animalcule*, a very little creature; *globule*, a little globe; *satchel*, a little sack or bag; *sickle*, a little scythe; *kitten*, a little cat; *lambkin*, a little lamb; *bracelet*, a little brace or band for the arm; *coronet*, a little crown; *ballot*, a little ball used in voting; *gosling*, a little goose; *hillock*, a little hill; *Willy*, little William; *lassie*, a little lass.
cule *see* under **cle**	little	
dom *see* under **acy** (1 and 2)		

Suffix	Meaning	Examples
eae	in bot., a postfix terminating names of sub-Orders	*Phytolacceae,* a sub-Order of the Order Phytolaccaceae.
ed (AS.)	the sign of the past tense and past participle of regular verbs	*loved, learned:* often change into *t,* as *bent* (for *bended*); added to nouns, as in *talented.*
ee *see* under **an**		
eer *see* under **an**		
el; also **le** (AS.)	form nouns and signify: that which	*shovel,* an instrument for shoving earth; *settle,* that which forms a seat.
el; also **le** *see* under **cle**	little	
en (AS.)	forms adjectives and signifies: made of; belonging to	*earthen,* made of earth; *golden,* made of gold; *heathen,* belonging to those dwelling on the heath.
en *see* under **ate** (4)	to make	
en; also **n** and **ne** (AS.)	the sign of the past participle of many verbs	*woven, shorn, borne.*
en *see* under **cle**	little	
en (AS.)	a plural termination	*oxen, kine, children.*
ence; also **ency** *see* under **acy** (1)	state of being	
ene (L. *enus*)	belonging to	*terrene,* belonging to the earth.
ent *see* under **an**	one who	
ent *see* under **ant** (2)	being	
eous, same as **ous**		
er *see* **an**	one who; denoting: that which produces, that which receives, and also the thing contained	
er (AS.)	more—the sign of the comparative degree	*greater,* more great; *higher,* more high.

Suffix	Meaning	Examples
er (AS.)	a little; often	*glimmer*, to gleam a little.
erel (AS.: F. *erelle*)	little	*cockerel*, a little or young cock.
erly (AS.) also ward or wards	form adverbs and signify direction of	*southerly*, in the direction of the south; *homeward*, in the direction of home.
ern (AS.: L. *ernus*)	forms adjectives and signifies direction to or from	*southern*, in the direction of the south; *western*, in the direction of the west.
ery *see* under ary (2)	place where	
es and s (AS. and L.)	termination of the plural of nouns	*foxes, birds.*
escent forming adjectives, and escence forming nouns (L. *escens* or *escentem*)	growing; becoming; incipient state	*convalescence*, the state of growing in health; *putrescent*, becoming putrid; *putrescence*, the state of becoming putrid.
ese *see* under ac	like; as a noun, denoting a people	
esque (F. *esque*; It. *esco*; L. *iscus*)	forming adjectives and signifying belonging to; like	*picturesque*, vividly like a picture; *grotesque*, like the extravagant style of a grotto
ess (F. *esse*: L. and Gr. *issa*)	a termination indicating a noun of feminine gender	*tiger*, mas.; *tigress*, fem.
est (AS.)	(1) a termination indicating the superl. degree of adjectives (2) a termination of the second person singular present of a verb	(1) *smallest, largest, bravest;* (2) *eatest, walkest;* often contracted to *st*, as in *bidst, canst.*
et *see* under cle	diminutive termination	
eth (AS.)	a termination of the third pers. sing. of a verb	*cometh, goeth*—not now in general use.

SUFFIX	MEANING	EXAMPLES
ful (AS.)	denoting that the thing holds all it can contain	*pailful*, a water bucket which can contain no more; *pailfuls*, a water bucket whose contents, measured to its utmost capacity, is repeated again and again; *pails-full*, are two or more water buckets each completely filled.
ful *see* under ate (3)	abundance	
fy *see* under ate (4)	to make	
head hood is another spelling (AS. *had*, state, quality: Ger. *heit*, state)	forming nouns and signifying state; nature	*Godhead*, the nature of God; *maid-enhead*, the state of a maiden.
hood *see* acy	state of being	
ia; also ious (L. *ius*)	in botanical terms, a postfix which forms the titles of classes and orders	*monogynia, monogynious.*
ia (L. *ius*)	a postfix which forms the termination of medical terms, denoting a diseased condition	*leukemia*, a condition of the blood in which there is a deficiency of coloring matter; *dipsomania*, a condition in which there is an irresistible longing for alcoholic liquors.
ia (L. *ia*)	things belonging to	*regalia*, the ensigns or things belonging to royalty; *insignia*, badges or things belonging to an office.
ible *see* under able	able	
ic; also ical *see* under ac	pert. to— (NOTE: ical is really a compound postfix made up of ic and al)	
ic (1) (L. *icus*; Gr. *ikos*)	in certain chemical terms, a postfix denoting the acid containing the most oxygen	*nitric, sulphuric.*

Suffix	Meaning	Examples
ic (2) *see* under an (2)	one who	
ice *see* under ary (2)	things which	
ics (Gr. *ika*) ; also ism, ry, ure	form nouns and signify things relating to, as to an art or science; the practice, system, doctrines, or peculiarities	*optics,* things relating to the science of seeing; *Calvinism,* things relating to the doctrines of Calvin; *cookery,* things relating to the art of a cook; *agriculture,* things relating to the art of tilling the ground.
id *see* under ac		
ida *see* under idae		
idae; also adae and ides (Gr. *ides*)	descent: a postfix in many scientific terms, denoting a family or group exhibiting some points of likeness	*canidae,* the dog family, including dogs, foxes, and wolves (**ida** is only a corruption of **idae**).
ide, ides, plural (Gr. *eidos,* resemblance)	in chem. a postfix connected with such terms as *oxygen, chlorine, fluorine, iodine,* and the like; used to indicate combinations	*oxide,* of chlorine, *chloride,* of sodium, *iodide* of iron, etc.
idean (L. *ideus*—from Gr. *eidos,* resemblance)	relation to that which bears resemblance	*arytenoidean,* pert. to that which is *arytenoid* or funnel shaped.
ides; eides; and oides (Gr. *eidos,* resemblance or likeness)	in scientific terms, a postfix preceded by *o,* denoting resemblance or likeness to an object	*deltoides,* like the Greek letter delta; *cancroide,* like a crab; *typhoid,* like typhus.
ides *see* under idae		
ie *see* under cle	little	
iff *see* under an (2)	one who	

Suffix	Meaning	Examples
ile *see* under able	able	
im	a termination of Heb. nouns (plural)	*cherubim.*
ine *see* under ac		
ine	a feminine termination	*heroine.*
ine, or in (L. *inus*)	a common termination in chemical terms, but varying much in signification	*haematin,* the coloring matter resulting from the decomposition of *haemoglobin* by heat; *haematine,* the coloring matter of logwood; *stearin,* the solid fatty principal of animal fat; *e* is now pretty generally omitted in the terminations of such words.
ing (AS.)	the termination of the imp. of verbs	
ion *see* under age (2)	act of	
ior (L.)	more	*superior,* more above.
ique (F. *ique;* L. *iquus*)	belonging to	*antique,* belonging to what is ancient.
ise; also ize *see* under ate (3)	to make	
ish (1) (AS.) ; also like ly	form adjectives and signify like; becoming	*boyish,* like a boy; *foolish,* like a fool; *gentlemanlike,* like a gentleman; *warlike,* becoming a warrior; *brotherly,* becoming a brother; *friendly,* becoming a friend.
ish (2) (AS.)	little; somewhat	*brownish,* a little brown; *brackish,* somewhat salt; *feverish,* somewhat affected with fever.
ish (3) *see* under ac	pertaining to	
ish (4) *see* under ate (4)	to make	
isk (Gr. *iskos*)	little	*asterisk,* a little star.
ism; also asm *see* acy (1)	state of being	

Suffix	Meaning	Examples
ism *see* under ics	things relating to	
ist *see* under an (2)	one who	
ite (L. *itus*)	in chemistry, a postfix which is added to the name of an acid ending in *ous*	*sulphite* of potash, that is, a combination of *sulphurous* acid with the base potash.
ite *see* under an (2)	one who; that which	*appetite,* that which creates the desire for food.
ite (Gr. *lithos*)	in geology, a contraction of *lite,* meaning stone or resembling stone	*quartzite,* granular quartz; *ammonite,* a certain fossil shell.
itis (Gr. *itemi*)	in medicine, a postfix in Gr. names of organs, signifying inflammation of the organ indicated	*carditis,* inflammation of the heart; *laryngitis,* inflammation of the larynx.
ity *see* under acy (1)	state, condition, or quality of being	*comity,* the state or condition of being courteous.
ive (L. *ivus*)	able to do; or doing; capacity in an active sense	*cohesive,* able to stick together; *expansive,* able to spread out.
ive *see* under an	one who	
ix (L. *ix*)	a fem. termination	*testatrix,* a woman who leaves a will.
ize *see* under ate (4)	to make	
kin (AS. *cyn,* race: Ger. *kind,* a child)	little; a son of	*lambkin,* a little lamb, that is, the son of a lamb.
kind	kind or race	*mankind,* the race of man.
le *see* under el	that which	
le (AS.)	often, little	*sparkle, n.,* a little spark; *sparkle, v.,* to throw out sparks often.
lent *see* under ate (3)	full of	
less (AS. *laes;* Icel. *lauss*)	privation; without	*guiltless,* without guilt; *breathless,* without breath.
let *see* under cle	little	

Suffix	Meaning	Examples
like *see* ish (1)	like	
ling *see* under cle	little	
lite or lith *see* under ite (3)	in geology, signifies stone	*mellite,* honey-stone.
logy (Gr. *logia,* a word, a description)	science or study or systematized description of	*laryngology,* science or study of the larynx; *biology,* science of living things; *eulogy,* a very favorable description.
ly *see* under ish	like	
ly (AS. *lice*)	manner	*honestly,* in an honest manner; *candidly,* in a candid manner; *justly,* in a just manner.
ment *see* under acy	state of being	
ment *see* under ary (2)	the thing which	
mony *see* under acy (1) and under ary (2)	state of being	
most (AS.)	a termination indicating the superlative degree	*hindmost,* furthest behind; *inmost,* furthest within.
ness *see* under acy	state, condition, or quality of being	
ock *see* under cle	little	
oecium; also oecious (Gr. *oikos*)	in botany; denotes: the arrangement of stamens and pistils in flowers	*androecium,* the staminal organs, *monoecious,* possessing two kinds of unisexual flowers, that is, a plant having staminate and pistilate flowers.
oid (Gr. *eidos*)	likeness; resemblance	*spheroid,* resemblance to a sphere.
on; also one and oon (It. and F. *on*)	form nouns and signify large	*million,* a large thousand; *trombone,* a large deep-toned instr. of the trumpet kind; *balloon,* a large ball.
or *see* under an (2)	one who	
ory *see* under ac	pertaining to	
ory *see* under ary (2)	place where	
ory *see* under ary (1)	the thing which	

Suffix	Meaning	Examples
ose *see* under ate (3)	full of	
ot *see* under cle	little	
ous *see* under ate (3)	full of	
ous	in chem., a postfix denoting the compound which has a smaller quantity of oxygen than the one which ends in *ic*	*nitrous* acid, the acid which contains a smaller quantity of oxygen than *nitric* acid.
re (F.) another form of er		*theatre, centre.*
red (AS. *roeden*)	state or condition; those who	*kindred,* those who are kin, or related by blood.
ric *see* under acy (2.)	rank, jurisdiction, or office	
ry *see* under ics	things relating to	
ry *see* under ary (1) and age (3)	place where; persons or things collectively	
ry *see* under acy (1)	state of being	
s *see* under es		
se (AS.)	to make (contracted from ise)	*cleanse,* to make clean.
ship *see* under acy (1 and 2)	rank, jurisdiction, or office; state of being	
sion *see* tion and age (2)		
some *see* under ate (3)	full of	
son (AS.)	son	*Thomson,* the son of Thomas; *Johnson,* the son of John.
ster *see* under an (2)	one who	
stress (AS. *estre* or *istre,* and L. *ess*)	a fem. termination of nouns	*songstress.* a female singer.

Suffix	Meaning	Examples
teen (AS. *ten* or *tyn*)	ten to be added	*fourteen,* ten and four.
th *see* under **acy** (1)	state of being	
tion or **sion** *see* **age** (2)	act of; thing done	
tude *see* under **acy** (1)	state of being	
ty or **ity** *see* under **acy** (1)	state of being	
ty (AS. *tig;* Ger. *zig*)	ten, to be multiplied by	*seventy,* ten to be multiplied by seven.
ule *see* under **cle**	little	
ure *see* under **acy** (1) *see* under **age** (2) *see* under **ics**	state of being; the act of, or the thing done; things relating to	
ward also **wards** *see* under **erly**	direction of	
ways; also **wise** (Ger. *weise,* way, method; F. *guise,* manner, fashion; W. *gwis,* mode, custom)	manner; way of being or acting	*crosswise,* in a cross manner; *likewise,* in like manner; *lengthways,* in the direction of its length.
wise *see* **ways**		
y (1) *see* under **cle**	little	
y (2); also **ey** (AS. *ig*)	full of	*snowy,* full of snow; *frosty,* full of frost.
y (3) *see* under **acy** (1)	state, condition, or quality of being	
yte *see* under **an** (2.)	one who	

BOOK FOURTEEN

Rhetoric and Composition

Rhetoric has sloughed off its original connection with oratory. No longer may it be defined as "the art which teaches eloquence." Today *rhetoric* is generally used to signify "the art of effectively joining words together," or simply "composition."

There is an element of futility in the study of rhetoric. Three centuries ago Samuel Butler advised that

> . . . all a rhetorician's rules
> Teach nothing but to name his tools.

And in our day another skeptic, Burges Johnson, warned that

> Writing is an art and no art can be taught by recipe. A textbook that attempts to tell you just how you should organize your thoughts, and then how you should express them, would have just one good reason for existence. You might become a great writer by consciously violating every precept within its pages.

Perhaps Burges Johnson states the case against writings on writing a bit too strongly, but there is certainly a degree of truth in what he says. Accepted ways of arranging words, sentences, and paragraphs challenge the great writer to revolt: the history of literature is a record of successive revolutions in writing.

However, as Mr. Johnson goes on to say, the writer abandons a conventional mode "only when he is sure he has found something better." And there are certain modes which have never been improved upon. Several centuries before Christ, Aristotle insisted on the central importance of coherent organization: the principle is not noticeably less relevant today.

Rhetoric and Semantics

Rhetoric is concerned with *effective* language, which (since man is only in part a rational creature) implies *affective* or *emotive* language. Semantics is the study of meaning —or, as Ogden and Richards put it, of "the meaning of meaning."[1] Semantics studies more than the *denotation* of words, their impersonal or dictionary meaning: their personal or affective meaning, the *connotation* of words, comes under its scrutiny as well. Therefore, semantics has much to say about rhetoric.

The first purpose of rhetoric is to convince: that war is hell, perhaps; or that a rose is pretty. To accomplish its purpose, rhetoric employs a variety of tactics. Some of these tactics semanticists declare illegitimate. For example, a rhetorical trick often practiced is fixing a favorable epithet to a proposition one approves of, an unfavorable epithet to a proposition one disapproves of: "What an impartial man with no further purpose to serve would call 'public worship' or a 'system of religion,' is described by an adherent as 'piety' 'Godliness'; and by an opponent as 'bigotry,' 'superstition.' . . . What one seeks to prove is, first of all, inserted in the definition, whence it is then taken by mere analysis.[2]

What is the importance of semantics for the writer? First,

[1]Michel Breal originally used the word *semantics* to designate what is now generally called *semasiology,* the study that traces the successive changes in the meanings of words. In spite of the original signification, *semantics* "is now used more frequently to refer to the kind of inquiry initiated by Lady Viola Welby under the name 'significs.'" Professor Hayakawa offers the following definition for the term as currently employed: "The study of human responses to linguistic (and other) symbols; the study of human behavior with, and under the stimulus of, symbols." Perhaps a cautionary note should be added: any definition of *semantics* is open to semantic objection, since there are several distinct schools of semantics.

[2]Arthur Schopenhauer, *The Art of Controversy*—a delightfully ironic examination of rhetorical devices of the kind semanticists condemn.

it teaches him that his main duty is to be clear, and that clarity depends upon

> . . . the degree of agreement between the writer and his readers as to what the words of the writer represent. Simply by striving for a high degree of such agreement, the writer discovers, in some measure, his ingenuity in achieving it. He discovers the usefulness of conditional and quantifying terms, the confusion created by leaving out significantly differentiating details, the degree to which the meaning of a term varies from context to context, and the kinds of difference he must allow for among his readers' habits of interpreting words. He learns to rely less on the dictionary, and more on the linguistic habits of the people for whom he writes.[1]

Second, it frees him from the "verbal delusion," makes him realize that

> . . . there is no necessary connection between the "things" of the world and the words we use to describe them. You don't eat the printed restaurant menu. Any linguistic formulation is only a kind of map of something which, whatever it is, is *not* the words used to describe it.[2]

Finally, it enables him to be scrupulous in his use of words, prevents him from confusing levels of abstraction and from establishing false identities:

> Cow_1 is not cow_2; Jew_1 is not Jew_2; $politician_1$ is not $politician_2$, and so on.[3]

To summarize then, semantics teaches the honest writer how to be honest in writing. It teaches him how to write without unwitting rhetorical falsification. It teaches him how to write concretely and coherently through keeping the thing he is writing about—its similarities to other things and differences from them—continually in mind.

The Elements of Rhetoric

Clearness, unity, force, variety, euphony—these are the elements that critics agree are fundamental to effective ex-

[1] Wendell Johnson, "You Can't Write Writing," *ETC., A Review of General Semantics.*

[2] Francis P. Chisholm, "General Semantics in Reading Instruction," *Twentieth Century English.*

[3] S. I. Hayakawa, *Language in Action.*

pression.[1] The fusion of these elements—style—is not a mere mechanical matter. Style is organic; it bears the mark of the man—Buffon said style *is* the man. No set of prescriptions and proscriptions will make a master stylist of a writer who has not something compelling to say and an impelling interest in saying it. However, though each of us is a prisoner of his personality, though few of us have the ultimate talent for expression, any of us, by intelligent study and practice of the principles of rhetoric, can develop all the power of expression possible to him. This is a large consolation, for, as writers, most of us function far below our potentialities.

Clearness

The first and greatest demand that style imposes is clearness. "Clearness in thought and words," says Stopford Brooke, "ought to be a part of a writer's religion; it is certainly a necessary part of his morality." A basic analogy of semantics is of a map and a territory: a map is not a territory, nor is a word the thing it refers to. But there are accurate maps and inaccurate maps, those which represent well and those which represent poorly. So too there are accurate and inaccurate words. "The absolute accordance of expression to idea," declared Pater, whose concept of style was not narrow, is "the one indispensable beauty" of all literature. Flaubert thought that "Whatever be the thing one wishes to say, there is only one word to express it, only one verb to animate it, only one adjective to qualify it." Without subscribing to this literary mysticism, almost every critic has agreed that the unwearied search for the right word is the ultimate business of the man who wants to write effectively. Consider, therefore, before you write, whether you are describing a breeze, a gale, a blast, a gust, a storm, a tempest, a hurricane, or what. A dictionary of synonyms helps, of course, in choosing the accurate word. But even more valuable is the attitude that Landor commends: ". . . hate false words, and seek with care, difficulty, and moroseness those that fit the thing." Perhaps "years of literary gymnastic," as Stevenson warns,

[1]For statistical proof of this statement, see Helen F. Daringer's *Check List of Elements and Qualities of Style.*

will first be necessary before the quest for the right word is habitually successful; the prize is worth it.

Words must be not only accurate, but also specific and concrete. Herbert Spencer thought that the great law of style was: "economize the reader's or hearer's attention." To this "economy of the recipient's mental energy," he affirmed, was due the superiority of specific and concrete words over general words: the effort required to translate words into thoughts was reduced. He writes:

> That concrete terms produce more vivid impressions than abstract ones, and should, when possible, be used instead, is a current maxim of composition. As Dr. Campbell says, "The more general the terms are, the picture is fainter; the more special they are, 'tis the brighter." We should avoid such sentences as: "In proportion as the manners, customs, and amusements of a nation are cruel and barbarous, the regulations of their penal code will be severe." And in place of it we should write: "In proportion as men delight in battles, bull-fights, and combats of gladiators, will they punish by hanging, burning, and the rack."

Guy de Maupassant, similarly, sneers at "those who today write their descriptions without guarding against abstract terms, those who have the hail or the rain fall on the *cleanness* of the window-panes": they are the wielders of a "bizarre, complicated, crowded, and Chinese-like vocabulary"—and their art is basically false.

Unity

Unity demands the rejection of whatever is outside "the purpose or the feeling" of a phrase, paragraph, sentence, or an entire composition. The phrase, and every larger part, should be about one thing, or tend to produce one effect.[1] Length and unity are not necessarily incompatible. A short and simple sentence, for example, may lack unity:

Shelley liked poetry and died in 1822.

[1]Of course, in certain forms of composition, digression is not only allowable but even desirable. In almost any of Lamb's informal essays, for instance, disunity adds a peculiar charm to the style. "Delight condones offence." However, throughout this book we are commenting on descriptive, critical, reflective, expository, and editorial prose. For these kinds of prose, unity is almost invariably something devoutly to be wished—and worked for accordingly.

A long and complex sentence, on the other hand, may be perfectly unified:

> Is it possible, Gentlemen, that you can have read one, two, three, or more of the acknowledged masterpieces of literature without having it borne in on you that they are great because they are alive, and traffic not with cold celestial certainties, but with men's hopes, aspirations, doubts, loves, hates, breakings of the heart; the glory and vanity of human endeavour, the transience of beauty, the capricious uncertain lease on which you and I hold life, the dark coasts to which we inevitably steer; all that amuses or vexes, all that gladdens, saddens, maddens us men and women on this brief and mutable traject which yet must be home for a while, the anchorage of our hearts?[1]

Mass

Mass is synthetic—"the process of making the assertion act together as a whole, precipitating its force, as it were, upon the point desired and with the exact stress desired."[2] In speaking of mass, military metaphors come naturally: "As, in an army on the march, the fighting columns are placed front and rear, and the baggage in the center, so the emphatic parts of a sentence should be found either in the beginning or in the end, subordinate and matter-of-course expressions in the middle."[3] A less rhetorical statement of the same rhetorical principle would be: sentences (and larger units) must be planned so that their important elements will be featured. One way to accomplish the effect is by typographical means such as italicizing, bold-facing, underlining. However, that method has a limited value. Better resources are *parallelism, inversion, suspension,* and *repetition.*

Parallelism is achieved by balancing word against word, clause against clause, sentence against sentence. Its merit is that is allows no part to go lost; its danger, that it sometimes forces an alternation where none exists. Macaulay was a skillful maker of balanced sentences, and G. H. Lewes pays

[1]Arthur Quiller-Couch, *On the Art of Writing.*
[2]John F. Genung, *The Working Principles of Rhetoric.*
[3]Bain, *English Composition and Rhetoric.*

tribute to his style and cautions its imitators—doing both, while cleverly imitating the style:

> In our day there are many who imitate Macaulay's short sentences, iterations, antitheses, geographical and historical illustrations, and eighteenth century diction, but who accepts them as Macaulay's? They cannot seize the secret of his charm, because that charm lies in the felicity of his talent, not in the structure of his sentences; in the fulness of his knowledge, not in the character of his illustrations. Other men aim at ease and vigour by discarding Latinisms and admitting colloquialisms; but vigour and ease are not to be had on recipe.

Inversion is an obvious trick for focusing the attention of the reader. It consists simply of transposing the natural order of words. "Right you are," "The house beautiful," "Gone are the days," all invert the normal word-pattern, and thus succeed in being emphatic.

Suspension is a tactic closely related. Its purpose is to create distinction for the element suspended. A sentence based on the principle of suspension (or expectation) is called a **periodic sentence**. Minto describes the process by which meaning is held back till the end of a sentence. It is effected by

> . . . bringing on predicates before what they are predicated of, and, which is virtually a similar process, qualifications before they qualify; letting us know descriptive adjuncts, results, conditions, alternatives, oratorical contrasts, of subjects, states, and actions before we formally know the particular subjects, states, or actions contemplated by the writer.

The following sentence—a stock example—is periodic:

> At last, with no small difficulty, and after much fatigue, *we came,* through deep roads and bad weather, *to our journey's end.*

However, if the main assertion is placed first, if the suspension is not attempted, a **loose sentence** results:

> We came to our journey's end at last, with no small difficulty, after much fatigue, through deep roads and bad weather.[1]

[1]Genung, *op. cit.* Of course, a number of other revisions are possible.

Repetition for both effect and clarity is an important device. Matthew Arnold was excessively fond of it and used it as a sort of refrain:

> The practical genius of our people could not but urge irresistibly to the production of a real prose style, because for the purposes of modern life the Old English prose, the prose of Milton and Taylor, is cumbersome, unavailable, impossible. A style of regularity, uniformity, precision, balance, was wanted. These are the qualities of a serviceable prose style. Poetry has a different *logic,* as Coleridge said, from prose; poetical style follows another law of evolution than the style of prose. But there is no doubt that a style of regularity, uniformity, precision, balance, will acquire a yet stronger hold on the mind of a nation, if it is adopted in poetry as well as prose, and so comes to govern both. . . .

The phrase "regularity, uniformity, precision, and balance" is repeated several times more in the course of the essay. The reader can hardly fail to take away the idea that "regularity, uniformity, precision, and balance" are the marks of a "serviceable prose style."

Coherence

Coherence refers to the way the composition hangs together—the harmony and sequence of its parts. A simple outline is an excellent method of insuring coherence. Professor Johnson suggests another. He affirms that studying the cookbook has proved helpful to his students.

> By examining a cookbook they see at once that the organization of a description of procedure is determined simply by the order of the events that make up the procedure. First you do *a,* and then *b,* and then *c,* and you write it in that order because you do it in that order. This simple principle of order is fundamental in practically all descriptive, narrative, and expository writing, and it is obvious to anyone who is attempting to be considerate of the reader.

Perhaps the best statement of the principle of sequence is made by Herbert Spencer. In every sentence, he says,

> . . . there is some one order of words more effective than any other; and . . . this order is the one which presents the elements of the proposition in the succession in which they may

be most readily put together. As in a narrative, the events should be stated in such sequence that the mind may not have to go backwards and forwards in order to rightly connect them; as in a group of sentences, the arrangement should be such, that each of them may be understood when it comes, without waiting for subsequent ones; so in every sentence, the sequence of words should be that which suggests the constituents of the thought in the order most convenient for the building up of that thought.

A "topic sentence" and a smooth "transitional sentence" for each paragraph enhance the harmony of parts.[1] Francis Bacon's essay "Of Studies" presents a perfect instance of the topic sentence.

> Studies serve for delight, for ornament, and for ability.

Every sentence in the long paragraph that follows is intimately connected with the initial sentence. Nor was Bacon less expert in effecting his transitions. In his essay "Of Friendship" he analyzes the emotional value of friendship. This is the transitional (and topic) sentence to the next division of his essay:

> The second fruit of friendship is healthful to the understanding, as the first is to the affections.

Having said his full on the intellectual value of friendship, he proceeds:

> Add now, to make this second fruit of friendship complete, that other point, which lieth more open, and falleth within vulgar observation; which is faithful counsel from a friend.

Force

Some of the ways of achieving force or emphasis[2] are admittedly artificial; they are not to be disdained on that account. Contrivance is a necessary part of effective communication. However, no substitute for natural force—the force that inheres to "what oft was thought but ne'er so well

---

[1]Concerning the "proper length of sentence and paragraph," a favorite topic of writers on composition, only this much may validly be said: both ought to be no longer than the idea they contain requires them to be. An effective sentence may contain six or six hundred words; an effective paragraph one sentence or a hundred sentences.

[2]Analyzed above under the heading "Mass."

expresst"—is ever entirely satisfactory. The best writing is clean, hard, bare; it is *stripped conversation*. Thoreau, attuning sense to sentence, says:

> A sentence should read as if its author, had he held a plough instead of a pen, could have drawn a furrow deep and straight to the end.

Emerson in a sentence that "shall be proverb, [for] nobody shall be able to say it otherwise," suggests the best way to attain true force:

> Speak with the vulgar, think with the wise.

Economy of expression (Spencer's first "law" of style) helps to heighten speech. Brevity does not imply saying less than is needful, taking "a short sweep of view." A style consistently laconic, excessively terse, defeats itself: it becomes boring after a page or so. Moreover, as De Quincey points out, such a style "is fitted rather to aphorisms and maxims as upon a known subject, than to any process of investigation upon a subject yet to be fathomed." But all needless repetition must be shunned. Redundancy is the great stylistic sin. "It is," Schopenhauer says, "always better to omit something good than to add that which is not worth saying at all. . . . To use many words to communicate few thoughts is everywhere the unmistakable sign of mediocrity. To gather much thought into few words stamps the man of genius." The French have neatly summarized the matter: "The secret of boring is to say everything."

Variety

Variety is the writer's duty to the reader:

> The deadly snare of the jaded or perfunctory writer,—and, it may be added, of that much-vaunted being, the spontaneous writer—is, monotony of sentence structure, a wooden movement, with the same rise and fall, the same type of sentence, the same relative placement of stress, dominating the whole work.[1]

Not only monotony in the structure of sentences, but also monotony of climax—the mechanical employment of sus-

[1] Genung, *op. cit.*

pensions; monotony of cadence—the same rise and fall of the rhythm; in short, monotony anywhere "blunts the sensibilities . . . renders excellencies odious."[1]

Euphony

Euphony derives from the Greek words meaning "well sounding." Its antonym is *cacophony,* "harsh sounding." Why ought the former to be striven for and the latter avoided? Because the one attracts and the other distracts. The writer has failed if more attention is centered on how than on what he has written. Style is the groove of sense. Therefore, devices attractive in poetry—rime, assonance, alliteration—are condemned in straight prose *when they are employed to excess.* When they are sparingly employed, and for calculated purposes (as, for instance, to make a phrase more memorable) they can be thoroughly attractive. The same cautions apply to prose rhythms which approach the metrical regularity of verse. Those who use them mistake the nature both of prose and of poetry, Dryden warned; they do not realize that their harmonies are different. Perhaps a specimen of writing which employs with great ingenuity stylistic devices belonging to that "other harmony" of verse will best enforce the point. This is from John Lyly, whose *Euphues* gave the name to an elaborately artificial kind of writing.

> Therefore my good Euphues, for these doubts and dumps of mine, either remove the cause, or reveal it. Thou hast hitherto found me a cheerful companion in thy mirth, and now shalt thou find me as careful with thee in thy moan. If thou mayest not be cured, yet mayest thou be comforted. If there be anything either by my friends may be procured, or by my life attained, that may either heal thee in part, or help thee in all, I protest to thee by the name of a friend, that it shall rather be gotten with the loss of my body, than lost by getting a kingdom. Thou hast tried me, therefore trust me: thou hast trusted me in many things, therefore try me in this one thing. I have never failed, and now I will not faint. . . .

[1] The "Dictionary of Rhetoric" presents a full list of the stylistic devices, the "figures of speech," which help the writer to secure variety.

Peculiarly, this monomaniacal concern with euphony breeds its antibody: after any prolonged reading—and reading more than a page or two of *Euphues,* clever and dextrous as it is, seems a prolonged reading—one desires some good healthy cacophony, a succession of *k's* and *th's, v's* and *q's, s's,* and everything else the books on rhetoric inveigh against.

BOOK FIFTEEN

Dictionary of Rhetoric: The Figures of Speech

Alliteration.—The employment in close connection of two or more words that begin with the same letter.

I caught this morning morning's minion, kingdom of daylight's dauphin, dapple-dawn-drawn Falcon.—G. M. HOPKINS

The lisp of leaves, and the ripple of rain.—SWINBURNE

Apt alliteration's artful aid.—POPE

Allusion.—Reference to some person, fact, idea, or event which, it is assumed, is "embalmed in the deepest memory of all educated minds" (Macbeth).

Nature and Nature's laws lay hid in night:
God say "Let Newton be!" and all was light.—POPE

Religion is thus treated like Lear.—SCOTT

Anadiplosis.—*See* REPETITION (6).

Anaphora.—*See* REPETITION (3).

Anti-climax.—*See* CLIMAX.

Antithesis.—The balance of contrasted words, clauses, or ideas.

A man so various that he seemed to be,
Not one, but all mankind's epitome.
Stiff in opinion, always in the wrong;
Was everything by starts, and nothing long.—DRYDEN

Thus the successors of the old Cavaliers had turned demagogues; the successors of the old Roundheads had turned courtiers. Yet was it long before their mutual animosity began to abate; for it is the nature of parties to retain their original enmities far more firmly than their original principles. During many years, a generation of Whigs, whom Sidney would have spurned as slaves, continued to wage deadly war with a generation of Tories whom Jeffries would have hanged for Republicans.—MACAULAY

Antonomasia.—Using a proper as a common name, as when a traitor is called a *Quisling.*

> Some village Hampden, who, with dauntless breast,
> The little tyrant of his fields withstood;
> Some mute inglorious Milton here may rest;
> Some Cromwell guiltless of his country's blood.—GRAY

Aporia.—A form of dubitation (*q.v.*) in which the writer or speaker pretends that it is impossible for him to determine "either where to begin for the multitude of matters; or what to do or say in some strange or ambiguous thing" (J. Smith).

And what shall I more say? for the time would fail me to tell of Gideon, and of Barak, and of Samson, and of Jephthah; of David also, and Samuel, and of the prophets.—BIBLE

Aposiopesis.—"Sudden silence"; leaving a sentence unfinished because of emotion or some sudden consideration.

>   Heaven and earth:
> Must I remember? . . . And yet, within a month—
> Let me not think on't!—Frailty, thy name is woman!—SHAKSPERE

Apostrophe.—Turning aside from the regular course of the subject to address someone or something absent as if present.

Oh, Tiber! Father Tiber! You'd only be a suckling in that mighty land! And as for you, sweet Thames, flow gently till I end my song: flow gently, gentle Thames, speak softly and politely, little Thames, flow gently till I end my song.—THOMAS WOLFE

Asyndeton.—A special form of ellipsis, consisting of the omission of conjunctions.

The enemy said: I will pursue; I will overtake; I will divide the spoil; I will draw my sword; my hand shall destroy them. Thou didst blow with thy wind; the sea covered them; they sank like lead in the mighty waters.—BIBLE

I am your kin. You are Frenchmen; behold the enemy.—KING HENRY IV OF FRANCE (to his troops before battle)

See POLYSYNDETON.

Bathos.—*See* CLIMAX.

Bulk.—A representation of the size or clumsiness of an object by a commensurate use of words.

Leviathan, which God of all His works created hugest that swim the ocean stream.—MILTON

Bull.—A blunder consisting of "an apparent congruity and a real incongruity of ideas" (S. Smith).

I saw no corn standing on the ricks; a thing I never saw before, and would not believe had I not seen it.—COBBETT

Caesar never did wrong but with just cause.—SHAKSPERE

The bull is sometimes called Irish because of its allegedly greater frequency among the Irish. One Irishman is supposed to have accounted for the incidence of bulls among his countrymen by ascribing it to climate, and adding: "I fancy *if an Englishman was born in Ireland,* he would make as many."

Circumlocution.—Naming a thing in a round-about way.

Thus, Longfellow, in *Hiawatha,* gives the Indian name for September, *the moon of the falling leaves,* and Whitman in "When Lilacs Last in the Dooryard Bloom'd" calls September by its Quaker designation, *the ninth month.* Again, Johnson calls sunset *the gentle corruscations of declining day.*

Also called **Periphrasis.**

Climax.—A rising arrangement of parts so that the greatest strength or chief point of interest is at the end.

It is an outrage to bind a Roman citizen; to scourge him is a crime; to put him to death is almost parricide.—CICERO

The opposite of climax is **anti-climax** or **bathos**—a sort of "ladder to get down by." Pope calls it "the art of sinking."

I am told several pickpockets are here. Let them remember that the eye of God is on them, and also that there are a number of policemen in the house.—WESLEY

Conversion.—*See* REPETITION (4).

Correction.—Calling back an expression in order to put a stronger or more guarded one in its place.

It is a shame, Mr. President, that the noble bulldogs of the administration should be wasting precious time in worrying the rats of the opposition.—Rats, did I say?—mice! mice!—JOHN RANDOLPH

Also called **Epanorthosis.**

Dubitation.—A display, real or seeming, of doubt or hesitation.

> Thou speakst it falsely, as I love mine honor,
> And makst conjectural fears to come to me,
> Which I would fain shut out. If it should prove
> That thou art so inhuman;—'twill not prove so!
> And yet I know not.—Thou didst hate her deadly—
> And—she is dead.—SHAKSPERE

Echo.—*See* REPETITION (10).

Ecphonesis.—*See* EXCLAMATION.

Ellipsis.—The omission of one or more words necessary to complete the grammatical construction, but not necessary to make the meaning clear to the reader.

Women are the opposite of clocks: clocks serve to remind us of the hours; women [serve] to make us forget them.—FONTENELLE

So doth the moon with his pale light [shine] that the stars he obscureth in the heavens.—ALFRED

Emblem.—The expression of a moral idea such as might be pictured—in fact, often is pictured. Quarles, the most eminent English emblematist, calls it "Visible poetry . . . catching the eye and fancy at one draught." Emblem books, though now out of fashion, were popular till the close of the nineteenth century.

> Why dost thou shade thy lovely face? Oh why
> Does that eclipsing hand so long deny
> The sunshine of Thy soul-enlivening eye?—QUARLES

(The poem, which is based on the lines from Job "Why hidest thou thy face, and holdest me for thine enemy," is accompanied by a wood cut which depicts someone attempting to remove the face-eclipsing hand of a haloed being.)

Enallage.—The exchange of one part of speech, or of one modification of a part of speech, for another.

> This day will *gentle* his condition.—SHAKSPERE

> Your *most sweet* music's miracle.—E. B. BROWNING

Epanaphora.—*See* REPETITION (3).

Epanorthosis.—*See* CORRECTION.

Epidiplosis.—*See* REPETITION (7).

Epiphora.—*See* REPETITION (4).

Epithet.—An adjective, or a group of words employed adjectivally, that characterizes incisively. Epithets are very often called into use by epic poets, and particularly by Homer. Homer uses epithets as formulas, *e.g.*, the *wine-dark sea.* Keats, in a famous sonnet, imitates the Homeric epithet by calling its originator "broad-browed Homer."

Eroteme.—*See* RHETORICAL QUESTION.

Exclamation.—The "abrupt or elliptical expression that a strongly felt thought takes before it has calmed itself down to a logical affirmation" (Genung).

> What a piece of work is man! how noble in reason! how infinite in faculty! in form and moving, how express and admirable! in action, how like an angel! in apprehension, a god! the beauty of the world! the paragon of animals!—SHAKSPERE

Also called **Ecphonesis.**

Euphemism.—The conveying of a harsh or an unpleasant truth gently. "The smooth handle," Macbeth calls it.

> Thus: passed away═died
> obliquity of vision═squint
> unmentionables═women's underclothes

Gemination.—*See* REPETITION (2).

Hendiadys.—"Splitting in two" what is really a unity.

> They drank from goblets and from gold.—VIRGIL

> (That is to say, "They drank from golden goblets.")

Hypallage.—An interchange of construction; reversing the natural relations of two constructions.

> His coward lips did from their color fly.—SHAKSPERE

> (The *color* really flew from the *coward lips.*)

Hyperbaton.—*See* INVERSION.

Hyperbole.—Exaggeration.

He ran down the avenue, making a noise like ten horses at a gallop.—HARVEY KING

"Whoo-oop! bow your neck and spread, for the kingdom of sorrow's coming! Hold me down to the earth, for I don't feel my powers a-working! Whoo-oop! I'm a child of sin, *don't* let me get a start! Smoked glass, here, for all! Don't attempt to look at me with the naked eye, gentlemen! When I'm playful I use meridians of longitude and the parallels of latitude for a seine and drag the Atlantic ocean for whales! I scratch my head with lightning and purr myself to sleep with the thunder! When I'm cold, I bile the Gulf of Mexico and bathe in it; when I'm thirsty, I reach up and suck a cloud dry like a sponge; when I range the earth hungry, famine follows in my tracks!—MARK TWAIN

Hysteron-proteron.—An inversion of natural order; putting the first last and the last first (or, as Laurence Sterne defined it, "putting the cart before the horse").

Let us die, and rush into the heart of the fight.—VIRGIL

"He put on his shoes and stockings," Lubell points out, is an idiomatic instance of the figure—normally one puts on stockings and shoes.

Inversion.—Transposing the natural order of words.

Them, not the past, but the future, charmed.—BULWER

> Of man's first disobedience and the fruit
> Of that forbidden tree, whose mortal taste
> Brought death into the world and all our woe,
> Sing, heavenly Muse.—MILTON

Also called **Hyperbaton.**

Irony.—The "dry mock," in which the content and intent of the words employed are opposite; that is, the contrary of what is said is to be understood.

No doubt but ye are the people, and wisdom shall die with ye.—BIBLE

> What has the gray-hair'd prisoner done?
> Has murder stain'd his hands with gore?
> Not so. His crime's a fouler one—
> God made the old man poor.—WHITTIER

NOTE.—If the irony lies in a single word, it is termed antiphrasis: *e.g.*, to call someone with a low I.Q. a "brain-trust" is to indulge in the figure.

Kenning.—The substitution of the name of a characteristic of a thing for the name of the thing itself. It is a Norse word, and a form especially liked by the Northmen. In *Beowulf,* for example, the sea is variously called: *the whale's path, the water-street, the path of the swan, the foamy fields, the wave-battle.* A kenning is a metaphor (*q.v.*) that effects identification by periphrasis or circumlocution.

Litotes.—1. Understatement by the use of negatives.

> As lean was his horse as is a rake,
> And he was not right fat,
> I undertake.—CHAUCER

By "not right fat," Chaucer implies that his clerk was right lean.

2. Understatement, whether or not effected by negatives. This is probably the more widely accepted sense of the word, though precisionists prefer to consider understatement not effected by negatives as *meiosis* (*q.v.*).

Meiosis.—Understatement employed deliberately.

> I've studied human nature, and
> I know a thing or two;
> Though a girl may fondly love
> a living gent, as many do,
> A feeling of disgust upon her
> senses there will fall
> When she looks upon his body
> chopped particularly small.—W. S. GILBERT

If once a man indulges himself in murder, very soon he comes to think little of robbing; and from robbery he comes next to drinking and Sabbath-breaking, and from that to incivility and procrastination. Once begin upon this downward path, you never know where you are to stop. Many a man has dated his ruin from some murder or other that perhaps he thought little of at the time.—DE QUINCEY. *Cf.,* LITOTES

Metalepsis.—Compound metonymy (*q.v.*).

Thus, in an old song, a woman has sold her cow, Crummie, and her horse, Charlie. Her husband describes the aftermath:

> First she drank Crummie, and then she drank Charlie;
> O that my wife was drink hooly and fairly.

She did not drink Crummie or Charlie, of course: they stand for the money she got for them with which she bought whisky.

Metaphor.—An implied comparison between two (or more) unlike things; achieved by identifying one with the other.

> Military glory is a bubble blown from blood.—JERROLD

> Cathedrals,
> Luxury liners laden with souls,
> Holding to the east their hulls of stone.—AUDEN

A **mixed metaphor** is the junction of two inconsistent metaphors. The test for mixed metaphors, says Addison, is: "Try and paint them." Shakspere's line

> To take arms against a sea of troubles,

is—in spite of its failure to meet the test Addison poses— sometimes defended as a fused metaphor. *Cf.* SIMILE

Metonymy.—The substitution of the name of an adjunct or attribute of a thing for the name of the thing itself.

> In the sweat of thy face shalt thou eat bread.—BIBLE

(In the sentence quoted, *sweat* has been substituted for *work, eat bread* for *live.* Thus, the sentence means: "You shall have to work in order to live.")

In a famous metonymy, Milton called the bishops and pastors of his day "blind mouths," because (as Ruskin explains) they utterly reversed their functions: to see for the people and to feed them.

> Can gray hairs make folly venerable?

(*Gray hairs,* the effect of old age, stands for old age itself.)

Metastasis.—A change (or changes) of tense.

Widows are the very mischief! There's nothing like 'em. If they make up their minds to marry, it's done. I knew one that was terribly afraid of thunder and lightning, and every time a storm came on she runs into Mr. Smith's house (Mr. Smith was a widower), and clasps her little hands, and flies around like a hen with her head cut off, till the man was half distracted for fear she would be killed; and the consequence was, she was Mrs. John Smith before three thunder-storms had rattled over her head.—SAM SLICK

Onomatopeia.—The use of words whose sound is "an echo to the sense."

> How the pretty ladies talk—
> Tittle tattle, tittle tattle!
> Like their patters when they walk—
> Pittle pattle, pittle pattle.—E. DARWIN

> How does the water
> Come down at Lodore?
> Rising and leaping,
> Sinking and creeping;
> Dividing and gliding and sliding,
> And falling and brawling and sprawling,
> And bubbling and troubling and doubling,
> And rushing and flushing and brushing and gushing,
> And flapping and rapping and clapping and slapping,
> And thumping and pumping and bumping and jumping,
> And dashing and flashing and splashing and clashing,
> And at once and all o'er, with a mighty uproar—
> And this way the water comes down at Lodore.—SOUTHEY

Oxymoron.—The union of contradictory terms.

The term stems from the Greek words meaning "sharp" and "dull" or "wise" and "foolish," and so is in itself an instance of itself. The phrases "strenuous idleness" and "mildly magnificent" are oxymorons.

> How deep the silence, yet how loud the praise.—BARBAULD

> "And is he gone? And is he gone?"
> She cried, and wept outright;
> "Then I will to the water go,
> And see him out of sight."—HOOD

Paradiastole.—The abundant use of *neithers* and *nors*.

Shall neither the cries of innocence expiring in agony; nor the tears of pitying spectators; nor the majesty of the Roman commonwealth; nor the fears of the justice of his country, restrain the licentious cruelty of a monster who, in the confidence of his riches, strikes at the root of liberty, and sets mankind at defiance?—CICERO

Paralepsis.—A pretended suppression that really emphasizes what it pretends to pass by.

I will say nothing of his manners, though they have always been swinish; or of his morals, though they have always been hyenaish.—LIND

Also called **Preterition.**

Parallelism.—The pairing of similar ideas by casting them into similar forms.

If we do not hang together, we shall hang separately.—FRANKLIN

Paregmenon.—*See* REPETITION (9).

Paronomasia.—Pun; play on words which sound alike but which have different meanings.

One man's Mede is another man's Persian.—KAUFMAN

A bun is the lowest form of wheat.—ED WYNN

Period.—A sentence "consisting of several clauses, grammatically connected and rhetorically constructed. Hence, in *pl.*, rhetorical or grammatical language" (*NED*).

If you will not take this as an excuse, accept it at least as a well-turned period, which is always my principal concern.—GRAY

A **periodic sentence** is one in which the meaning is suspended till the close of the sentence.

What I like about Clive
Is that he is no longer alive.—BENTLEY

Periphrasis.—*See* CIRCUMLOCUTION.

Personification.—The ascription of life or personality to inanimate objects or to abstractions.

Then Ire came in, with sturt and strife,
His hand was aye upon his knife.—DUNBAR

Reason has moons, but moons not hers
    Lie mirrored on her sea,
Confounding her astronomers
    But O! delighting me:—RALPH HODGSON

Also called **Prosopopeia.**

Pleonasm.—Superfluity; using more words than necessary to convey the idea.

The spacious firmament on high,
With all the blue ethereal sky.—ADDISON

Come all ye brave Kentuckians,
    I'd have ye for to know,
That we against the enemy
    Are going for to go.

DICTIONARY OF RHETORIC 361

Polysyndeton.—The abundant use of conjunctions.

These things let us thoroughly know—that the man is our enemy, and has spoiled us of our dominions, and for a length of time has insulted us, and that all things whatever which at any time we hoped others would do for us are found against us; and that all the things which remain must be found in ourselves; and that if we will not to fight him there, here it is likely we may be forced to fight him.—DEMOSTHENES

Preterition.—*See* PARALEPSIS.

Prolepsis.—"The anticipative use of an adjective" (Loane).

> To scatter plenty o'er a *smiling* land.—GRAY

> The lazy nurse who snores the sick man *dead*.

Prosopopeia.—*See* PERSONIFICATION.

Rallying cry.—A short, rousing phrase, like a war-cry.

> Now's the day, and now's the hour;
> See the front of battle lour
> See approach proud Edward's power—
> > *Chains and slavery!*—BURNS

Regression.—*See* REPETITION (8).

Repetition.—Saying the same thing again—though perhaps with a difference.

There are dozens of forms of repetition. The more frequent are listed below:

1. **Ploce:** repetition of the same word in a different sense.

> There are *satins*—and there are *satins*.

Oliver Cromwell, who astonished mankind by his intelligence, did not derive it from spies in the *cabinet* of every prince in Europe; he drew it from the *cabinet* of his sagacious mind.—CHATHAM

2. **Gemination:** an immediate repetition of the same emphatic word; "a doubling."

> The bells! The bells!

3. **Anaphora** (or **Epanaphora**): repetition of a word at the beginning of successive clauses.

> Where is the wise? Where is the scribe? Where is the disputer of this world?—BIBLE

4. Conversion (or **Epiphora**): repetition of a word at the end of successive clauses.

> Government of the people, by the people, for the people.

5. Symploce: use of the same words at the beginning and at the end of successive clauses.

> *Spring* clothes the *trees; Spring* leads back the birds to the *trees.*

6. Anadiplosis: use of the same word at the end of one clause and at the beginning of another.

> Still he sought for *fame—fame,* that last infirmity of a noble mind.

7. Epidiplosis: use of the same word at the beginning and at the end of a sentence.

> *Justice* took no note of Joe; and he paid the same tribute to *justice.*

8. Regression (or **Epanodos**): the repetition of a word or words in an inverted order.

> Woe to them who call *evil good* and *good evil.*

9. Paregmenon: the use of several words of similar origin close together.

> He believes the best *defense* is to be *offensive.*—A. SALTER

10. Echo: repetition of sound, as if reflected from its source.

> Still the wood is dim and lonely;
> Still the flashing fountains play;
> But the past and all its beauty,
> Whither has it *fled away?*
> Hark! the mournful echoes say—
>
> > *Fled away!*—PROCTOR

Reverse.—Turning a familiar group of words around. Wilson, for example, said that Hazlitt was unable to appreciate a writer till he was dead—that Hazlitt thought *"a dead ass better than a living lion."* Again, the Yankee who said that *"if something does not turn up, I'll turn something up,"* was employing the reverse.

Rhetorical Question.—One asked for its probable effect on the audience, not because the speaker does not know the answer.

> And shall we allow these untruths to go unanswered, these misdeeds unreprimanded?—DAVIS

Also called **Eroteme.**

Simile.—A direct comparison between two (or more) unlike things; normally introduced by *like* or *as.*

> The evening is spread out against the sky
> Like a patient etherized upon a table.—T. S. ELIOT

> Fain would I kiss my Julia's dainty leg,
> Which is white and hairless as an egg.—ROBERT HERRICK

The man who has not any thing to boast of, but his illustrious ancestors, is like a potato—the only good belonging to him is under ground.—OVERBURY

The **Homeric** or **epic simile** is an extended comparison: the illustrative image is separately developed, sometimes at excessive length. The Homeric simile "generally is a comet, a small nucleus with a long tail" (Macbeth).

> As one who, dwelling in the distant fields,
> Without a neighbor near him, hides a brand
> In the dark ashes, keeping carefully
> The seeds of fire alive, lest he, perforce,
> To light his hearth must bring them from afar.—HOMER

Cf. METAPHOR

Syllepsis.—The adapting of a construction to the sense of a word, rather than to its gender or number.

> The *rock* on *whom* we trust,
> While Providence supports,
> Let saints securely dwell;
> That *hand* which bears all Nature up,
> Shall guide *his* children well.—DODDRIDGE

Also called **Synesis** or **Synthesis.**

Symploce.—*See* REPETITION (5).

Synecdoche.—A form of metonymy (*q.v.*) in which a part —usually an important part—is substituted for the whole; or the whole for a part.

> 1. Fifty *sails, hands, head of cattle.*
> 2. *Satan,* get thee behind me.

In the first illustration, *sails* stands for *ships, hands* for *workers, head of cattle* for *cattle*. In the second illustration, *Satan,* the alleged source of all temptation, stands for a particular temptation.

Synesis.—*See* SYLLEPSIS.

Trope.—A "word turned or diverted from its ordinary application, and pressed, as it were, into special service" (Minto).

Thus, only transferred epithets—such as "jovial wine," "merry bells," "the gentleman with the foolish teeth," "coward swords," "Heaven's forgiving rainbow"—are considered tropes by some writers. Other writers regard *tropes* as referring to implied comparisons (*e.g.*), metaphors, metonymys, personifications (*qq.v.*), and think the trope is opposed to the *simile* (*q.v.*), a direct comparison. The word *trope* has no settled signification, then. Most writers use it loosely, as a synonym for *figure of speech*.

Vision.—Speaking or writing of what is absent as if present.

> Ye sons of France, awake to glory!
> Hark! Hark! what myriads bid you rise
> Your children, wives, and grandsires hoary;
> Behold their tears, and hear their cries.—DE LISLE

Methinks I see it now—that one solitary, adventurous vessel, the Mayflower of a forlorn hope, freighted with the prospects of a future State, and bound across the unknown sea. I behold it pursuing . . . —EVERETT

Zeugma.—Yoking two words to a single word that does not apply equally to both, or does not apply in the same sense to both.

> Waging war and peace.
> He left in a huff and a taxi.

BOOK SIXTEEN

Prosody

Prosody

Poets have been attempting to define poetry ever since they began writing it. The definitions they have produced are, not astonishingly, excellent descriptions of their several kinds of poetry—but not of poetry. Pope thought poetry

> . . . nature to advantage dress'd,
> What oft was thought, but ne'er so well express'd.

Poe called it "the Rhythmical Creation of Beauty." Wordsworth said: "Poetry is the spontaneous overflow of powerful feelings: it takes its origin from emotion recollected in tranquillity." Thoreau affirmed that it was "nothing but healthy speech." Whitman held that poetry was that which gave "ultimate vivification to facts, to science, and to common lives, endowing them with the glows and glories and final illustriousness which belongs to every real thing and to real things only." In our day, T. S. Eliot has declared that poetry is "a *concentration,* and a new thing resulting from that concentration, of a great number of experiences—a concentration which does not happen consciously. . . . Poetry is not the assertion of something that is true, but the making of that truth more fully real to us."

And each one is right! What each poet includes and not

what he excludes is relevant to any definition of poetry. But how distinguish poetry from prose? Not on the basis of rime, for some prose is rimed and much poetry is not. Nor on the basis of regularity of rhythm, since certain kinds of prose are as rhythmical as certain kinds of poetry. Nor will Coleridge's distinction do ("prose,—words in their best order; poetry, —the best words in the best order"), since the aim of all writing that pretends to art is to place the best words in the best order. I. A. Richards, however, has suggested a distinction that has generally been accepted: prose, he says, is concerned with telling us about things; poetry is concerned with engendering attitudes. Both poetry and prose use words, of course. But prose uses words *symbolically,* "for the sake of the references they promote"; whereas poetry uses words *emotively,* "for the sake of the attitudes and emotions which ensue."

Verse, "the form of arranging words preferred by poetry," is the matter of prosody. That may require some amplification: prosody teaches not how to create poetry, nor even how to recognize it; it does teach how to construct and scan verse. "Prosody may be a means to an end," Thomas Hood once declared, "but it does not pretend to assure its attainment. Versification and logic are to poetry and reason what a parapet is to a bridge: they do not convey you across, but prevent you from falling in."

Some Preliminary Definitions

Rhythm means "a flowing," and implies recurrence. In verse a recurrent *accent* is the basis of rhythm. A rhythmic unit consists of an accented syllable accompanied by one or more stressed syllables. Such a unit is known as a *foot.* A definite pattern of feet in a measured and recurrent arrangement is known as *meter.* The metrical unit is normally the *line,* and each line is called a verse.[1] The arrangement of lines "into equal or obviously proportional masses" gives rise to the *stanza.*

[1] From the Latin *versus,* from *vertere,* to turn. In popular usage, a stanza is often called a verse.

Accent

Accent, the predominance of one syllable over another, is determined chiefly by *stress,* the force with which a syllable is spoken. Less important (but not unimportant) in determining accent is *quantity,* the length of time that it takes to say a syllable. Least important (but not negligible) is *pitch,* the height of sound that the syllable reaches. In other languages, the relative importance of stress, quantity, and pitch is different. In Latin verse, for instance, quantity was most important, and syllables were divided, according to the length of time it took to pronounce them, into long and short. In English, however, quantity is a far less considerable factor than stress. Therefore, Latin verse is called *quantitative,* English *qualitative* or *stressed.*

Foot

A specific combination of accented and unaccented syllables is called a foot. Accented syllables are generally indicated by an accent (´), unaccented syllables by a breve (˘). Coleridge's "Metrical Feet" makes an excellent introduction to this rhythmic unit.

> Trócheĕ tríps frŏm lóng tŏ shórt;[1]
> From long to long in solemn sort
> Slów Spóndeĕ stálks; stróng foót!
>   yet ill able
> Évĕr tŏ cóme ŭp wĭth dáctўl trĭsýllăblĕ.
> Ĭámbĭcs márch frŏm shórt tŏ lóng;—
> Wĭth ă leáp ănd ă boúnd thĕ swĭft Anăpaĕsts thróng;
> One syllable long, with a short at each side
> Ămphíbrăchўs hástes wĭth ă státelў stride;—
> Fírst ănd lást beĭng lóng, míddlĕ shórt, Ámphĭmácer
> Stríkes hĭs thúndérĭng hóofs lĭke ă proúd hígh-brĕd Rácer.

Prosodists, by looking hard, have discovered dozens of feet. They are, except for a very few, totally irrelevant to English prosody. Poe offered to scan "any true rhythm that human ingenuity can conceive" by employing "from among the numerous 'ancient' feet" only the spondee (˝), the

[1] Coleridge uses the macron (¯) and the breve (˘) to mark "long" and "short" syllables—an outmoded system of notation.

trochee (˘˘), the iambus (˘), the anapest (˘˘), the dactyl (˘˘), and the single accented syllable (´) to which no name has been given.[1] There is no doubt that Poe could have made good his boast.

Meter

Meter has been defined as "rhythm reduced to law." Prose, too, has rhythm, but the pattern of prose rhythm is not nearly so regular as the pattern of verse rhythm. Prof. Gordon points up the difference by contrasting a line—the unit of verse—with a sentence—the unit of prose:

VERSE: The *light* that *never was,* on *sea* or *land.*—WORDS-WORTH

PROSE: From the *very first,* the *at*mosphere, the *light,* the *in*fluence of *things,* seemed *dif*ferent from *what* they *knew.* —PATER

The line of verse flows far more regularly than the sentence of prose—and Pater's is a particularly rhythmic prose, at that.

Scansion

To scan a line is to divide it into its several feet, and say *how many* of feet and *what kind* there are. Depending on how many feet a line contains, a line is called:

monometer	(one foot)	hexameter	(six feet)
dimeter	(two feet)	heptameter	(seven feet)
trimeter	(three feet)	octameter	(eight feet)
tetrameter	(four feet)	nonameter	(nine feet)
pentameter	(five feet)		

Now, any of these line-lengths may be composed of any of the kinds of feet—iambic, trochaic, anapestic, dactylic, or another—indicated above. Very often, also, two kinds of rhythm combine in a stanza, or even in a single line. A few instances will make the matter plainer than will a lengthy explanation:

[1]Poe called the ´ a *caesura;* however, the caesura has long denoted a metrical pause. No one before or since Poe has, to our knowledge, called the ´ a caesura.

Iambic and Anapestic Dimeter—

> Thĕ wínd's | ŏn thĕ wóld
> Ānd thĕ níght | ĭs ă cóld
> Ánd Thámes | rŭns chíll
> Twĭxt meád | ănd híll . . .
> —MORRIS

Trochaic Dimeter—

> Rích thĕ | treásŭre
> Sweét thĕ | pleásŭre . . .
> —DRYDEN

Dactylic Dimeter—

> Toúch hĕr nŏt | scórnfŭllȳ
> Thínk ŏf hĕr | moúrnfŭllȳ
> Géntlȳ ănd | húmănlȳ;
> Nót ŏf thĕ | staíns ŏf hĕr
> Áll thăt rĕ | maíns ŏf hĕr
> Nów ĭs pŭre | wómănlȳ.
> —HOOD

Meters

The pentameter line is the most widely employed in English and American verse; with the tetrameter a close second. The rhythm English verse prefers above all others is unquestionably the iambic; however, it is a question whether American verse, particularly American verse since Whitman, does not employ the trochaic rhythm almost as frequently. Poets as various in technique as Archibald MacLeish and Karl Shapiro have both declared that trochaic is far closer to the speech rhythm of the American people. And it is basic speech rhythms that verse, being in essence "a heightened and measured speech," attempts to duplicate.

But other meters have their importance. To achieve particular effects—brevity or sonority—poets have employed meters as unusual as the monometer[1] and the nonameter. Below is a brief anthology of metrical combinations. Note that the designation given to each is approximate at best: each meter is subject to several kinds of variation. Poets measure by ear; they do not count with their fingers.

[1] Rarely is monometer employed other than as a refrain in lyrics.

Iambic Monometer

Thŭs Í
Păss bý
Ănd díe
Ăs óne
Ŭnknówn
Ănd góne.

—HERRICK

Iambic Dimeter (with some trimeter lines)

Thĕ Sphínx ĭs drówsў,
  Hĕr wíngs ăre fúrled:
Hĕr eár ĭs heávy,
  Shĕ broóds ŏn thĕ wórld.
"Whŏ'll téll mĕ mў sécrĕt
  Thĕ áges hăve képt?—
Ĭ awáited thĕ seér
  Whĭle theў slúmbĕred ănd slépt . . .

—EMERSON[1]

Anapestic Trimeter (with iambic variations)

Ŏ wéll fŏr thĕ físhĕrmăn's bóy,
  Thăt hĕ shoúts wĭth hĭs sístĕr ăt pláy!
Ŏ wéll fŏr thĕ saílŏr lád,
  Thăt hĕ síngs ĭn hĭs boát ŏn thĕ báy!

—TENNYSON

Iambic Tetrameter (with anapestic variations)

Rívĕrmŏuth Rócks ăre faír tŏ seé
Bў dáwn ŏr súnsĕt shóne ăcróss
Whĕn thĕ ébb ŏf thĕ seá hăs léft thĕm freé
Tŏ drý theĭr fríngĕs ŏf góld-greén móss . . .

—WHITTIER

Iambic Pentameter

Dráw fŏrth thў swórd, thoŭ míghtў mán-ăt-árms,
Ĭnténdĭng bút tŏ ráze mў chármĕd skín,
Ănd Jóve hĭmsélf wĭll strétch hĭs hánd frŏm heávĕn
Tŏ wárd thĕ blów ănd shiéld mĕ sáfe frŏm hárm.

—MARLOWE

[1]Scansion is very often a matter of personal preference. For example, Gay
Wilson Allen, in *American Prosody*, accents the *Who'll* in the fifth line. No two
persons read poetry alike and therefore no two will scan it alike. Professor
Allen's is a thoroughly valid reading—but not the only valid reading.

Dactylic Hexameter (with iambic variations)

Ónwărd o˘er súnkĕn sánds, thro˘ugh ă
wíldĕrnĕss sómbre wĭth fórĕsts,
Dáy ăftĕr dáy thĕy glídĕd ă dówn
thĕ túrbŭlĕnt rívĕr;
Níght ăftĕr níght, bў thĕir blázĭng
fíres ĕncámped o˘n ĭts bórdĕrs.

—LONGFELLOW

Iambic Heptameter (with anapestic variations)

Thĕre's nót ă jóy thĕ wórld căn gíve lĭke thát ĭt tákes ăwáy,
Whĕn thĕ glów o˘f eárlў thóught dĕclínes ĭn feélĭng's dúll dĕcáy;
'Tĭs no˘t o˘n yoúth's smoŏth cheék thĕ blúsh ălóne whĭch fádes so˘ fást,
Bút thĕ téndĕr blóom o˘f héart ĭs góne ĕre yóuth ĭtsélf bĕ pást.

—BYRON

Trochaic Octameter

Bút whĕn Í sĭt dówn to˘ reáso˘n, thínk to˘ táke mў stánd no˘r swérve,
Whíle Ĭ tríŭmph ó'er ă sécrĕt wrúng fro˘m nátŭre's clóse rĕsérve,
Ín yo˘u cóme wĭth yo˘ur cóld músĭc, tíll Í creép thro˘ugh évĕry nérve.

—BROWNING

Trochaic Nonameter

Rómăn Vírgĭl, thóu thăt síngĕst Ílĭo˘ns lóftў témplĕs róbed wĭth fíre,
Ílĭo˘n fállĭng, Róme ărísĭng, wárs, ănd fílĭăl faíth ănd Dído˘'s pýre . . .

—TENNYSON

Variation by Substitution

Iambic and anapestic are sometimes called *rising* or *ascending* meters, and trochaic and dactylic *falling* or *descending* meters. The reason for the designation is plain: the feet of rising meters begin with an unstressed and end on a stress; the opposite is true of the falling meters.

Another classification is into *double,* or *duple,* and *triple* meters: the iambic and the trochaic, which have two syllables, obviously belong to the former class; the anapest and the dactylic, which have three syllables, to the latter.

To substitute a trochee for an iamb, or an iamb for a trochee, is an effective and frequently employed method of varying meter. Such a substitution—termed *reversed accent* or *reversed feet*—is normally made at the beginning of a line or after a pause in the middle of a line. Here the reversal is initial:

> Dígg̈ing the grateful soil, where round him rise,
> Sóns ŏf the earth, the tall aspiring oaks.
>
> —FRENEAU

Here it takes place in the third foot, after a pause:

> First reached these coasts, híd frŏm the world beside . . .
> Mid woods and fields spént thĕ remains of life.
>
> —FRENEAU

A variation not so emphatic, but similarly preventing the rhythm from sinking, is the substitution of one of the rising meters for the other (anapest for iamb or *vice versa*) or one of the falling meters for the other (dactyl for iamb or *vice versa*). Instances are given above: in the anapestic trimeter lines from Tennyson and the iambic tetrameter lines from Whittier, of the substitution of one rising meter for another; in the dactylic hexameter lines from Longfellow and the trochaic nonameter lines from Tennyson, of the substitution of one falling meter for another.

Variation by Pause

Verse, though deriving from speech rhythm, is necessarily far more regular and ordered. From this fact stems one of the fundamental pleasures of verse—the clash of natural and metrical beat, an effect called *counterpoint*. The ground rhythm of Tennyson's "Break, Break, Break" is anapestic, but see how skillfully the poet manages counterpoint:

> ∧ Break, ∧ break, ∧ break,
> ʾOn thy cold gray stones, O Sea!

The omission of an unaccented syllable (or, occasionally, an accented syllable) compels a *metrical pause,* to give it the technical name, and enables the verse to escape the monotony inherent in an unbroken succession of anapests. Moreover, the pauses before each "break," in the lines quoted, give the words an accrued stress, thus fusing the sound and the sense into unity.

Another kind of pause is designated *caesural* or *rhythmic.*

A caesura is a break or "cut" in the line—usually near the middle of the line—that marks the end of a spoken unit. Its purpose, like that of the metrical pause, is the achievement of a variety in unity. In the following instance from one of Shakspere's sonnets, the caesura is marked by parallel lines:

> Not marble, ‖ nor the gilded monuments
> Of princes, ‖ shall outlive this powerful rime;
> But you shall shine more bright ‖ in these contents
> Than unswept stone, ‖ be smeared with slutish time.

The pause normally coincides with some mark of punctuation—marks of punctuation, it will be remembered, are also called *stops*. If the lines are consistently *end-stopped*—that is, if the mark of punctuation regularly comes at the end of the lines—monotony is fairly inescapable. Thus, poets vary the position of their stops, avoid having them consistently at the end of a line. When the sentence or sentence unit does not end with the line of verse, the line is said to be *run-on* or *enjambed*. The following quotation from Dwight's *The Conquest of Canaan,* one of the worst poems written in America, illustrates the dreadful results of unremittant end-stopping:

> On wasted plains unnumber'd corpses lay,
> And smokes far scatter'd climb'd upon the day,
> Still clouded flames o'er eastern mountains rise,
> And Ai's broad ruins sadden all the skies.

Now, for some of the advantages of judicious enjambment, consider these lines from Milton's *Paradise Lost,* one of the best poems written anywhere:

> Mammon, the least erected spirit that fell
> From heaven; for ev'n in heaven his looks and thoughts
> Were always downward bent, admiring more
> The riches of heaven's pavement, trodden gold,
> Than aught divine or holy else enjoy'd
> In vision beatific. . . .

Variation by Adding or Dropping Syllables

The metrical pattern may be effectively varied either by adding or dropping syllables. Almost invariably the added syllables are unaccented. Preceding a trochaic or dactylic line, such an *extra-metrical* addition is termed *anacrusis.* Following an iambic or dactylic line, such an extra-metrical addition is termed a *hypercatalectic* or *feminine* ending. Sometimes the extra syllables are of little weight and do not significantly halt the reader; then we have *elision,* a slurring of syllables (as in the following line) :

> Impressed | the efful | gence of | his glo | ry abides.

Sometimes the extra syllables are to be not slurred but eliminated; then we have *apocope,* a cutting of syllables (as in *fev'r, o'er, fi'ry*).

Syllables may also be lacking. Thus, very often a trochaic or dactylic line has not its full complement of unaccented syllables; then we have a form of truncation known as *catalexis* (as in this line from Tennyson, technically called *trochaic octameter catalectic*) :

> Cómrădes, | leáve mě | hére ă | líttlĕ whíle ăs | yét 'tĭs | eárlў | mórn˘.
>   ^

Or, in an iambic or anapestic line, the lacking syllable may be, not at the end (as in catalexis), but at the beginning; then we have a form of truncation known as *clipping,* and the clipped line is called *headless* (as in this iambic tetrameter line from Freneau) :

> ˘Seés   this earth   a dis   tant star.
> ^

Variation by Stress

The shifting of accent to relieve us from the "continual tyranny of the same sound" as well as to make us "more sensible of the harmony of the pure [*i.e.,* basic] measure" is an allowable poetic license. So said Dr. Johnson, who hated irregularity in poetry, prose, or politics alike. Poets have availed themselves of the license—as they had before he granted it.

Variation of the metrical pattern through the substitution of accented for unaccented syllables and of unaccented for accented syllables has already been described. However, thus far accent has been treated as if it were a constant, as if all accented syllables were of equal weight. That they are not, a little analysis will sufficiently prove. Consider this famous line:

Tŏ bé ŏr nót tŏ bé.

The three stressed syllables are of differing force, though all are indicated by the same accent mark. The *not* is less heavily stressed than the first *be* and more heavily than the second *be*. Yet all three stressed syllables are clearly of greater weight than the unstressed. An accurate system of notation, one which indicated the relative weights of the stressed and unstressed syllables, would be unreasonably cumbersome.

Thus, scansion has its limitations. If the real meter of a poem has "to be butchered and carved into anapest and iamb and spondee," the reader will discover little about it but its regularities and irregularities. Scansion helps the reader discern the basic pattern, but is no substitute for the perceptive and sympathetic reading of a poem.

Rime

Rime serves a two-fold purpose: first, as a combining agency for the stanza; second as a musical device giving pleasure in itself. The "laws of rime" were once strictly set: in riming words, the sounds of the accented vowels and all sounds coming after them had to be identical; the sounds of the consonants preceding the accented vowels had to be different. Thus *sober* and *October, begins* and *wins, beaver* and *weaver, though* and *low,* conform to the laws and are rimes. On the other hand *sober* and *robber, visible* and *invisible, head* and *hood, whether* and *rather* do not conform and are not rimes. However, poets consistently refused to obey the laws, claiming the while that they were making rimes. Finally their claims received attention. The meaning of *rime* has been extended to include some interesting modifications of **perfect rime** (or **full rime**), as rimes conforming to the laws outlined above are called.

In **imperfect rime** (or **half rime**), as in perfect rime, unlike consonant sounds are followed by like accented vowel sounds; but—and this constitutes the difference—the sounds following the accented vowels are unlike. Thus, imperfect rime is characterized by echoing vowel and contrasted consonant sounds. Accordingly, *bird* and *fern, chase* and *faze, like* and *right* are imperfect rimes. One value of this modification of rime is that it consorts better with certain states of mind. It is not metaphysical to say that uncertainty is better connoted by a vague rather than a definite echo. Emily Dickinson uses imperfect rimes to achieve the effect of indecision and allied moods. Another value of imperfect rime is that it permits a colloquial casualness. Louis Untermeyer cites this stanza from "our own brief epic of the Negro steel-driver":

> John Henry started at the right side,
> The steam-drill started at the *left.*
> "Before I'd let that steam drill beat me down,
> Lord, I'd hammer my fool self to *death.*"

Suspended rime differs from perfect rime only in that the accented vowel sounds are unlike: *moves* and *loves, blot* and *naught, blood* and *stood.* (Sometimes—for obvious reasons—such rimes are designated **eye rimes.**) They have, as C. M. Lewis observes, "partly been foisted into our system of verse by changes in pronunciation; for though words that were formerly sounded alike may have become differentiated in speech, their familiar use by old poets sometimes induces us still to accept them as making rhymes." But that is not the whole story. Poets employ suspended rime deliberately, to achieve calculated effects. For instance, the soft tenderness of Tennyson's lovely lyric, "Come Into the Garden, Maud," is enhanced by his alternation of faint and sharp rimes:

> All night have the roses *heard*
> The flute, violin, *bassoon;*
> All night has the casement jessamine *stirred*
> To the dancers dancing in *tune;*
> Till a silence fell with the waking *bird,*
> And a hush with the setting *moon.*

Alliteration, assonance, and **consonance**—or beginning, middle, and final rime[1] are three rime-devices closely related. *Alliteration* is the repetition of the same sound, vowel or consonant, at the beginning of a series of words, or at the beginning of stressed syllables within words:

For all *th*is, *n*ature is *n*ever spent;
*Th*ere lives *th*e *d*earest freshness *d*eep *d*own *th*ings.—G. M. HOPKINS

Assonance is the repetition of similar (not necessarily identical) vowels situated within words. It is easier exemplified than defined: *begin* and *him* and *wing* and *ripe* and *eye* all exhibit assonance. In Tennyson's lines,

The moan of doves in immemorial elms
The murmur of innumerable bees,

both assonance and alliteration are beautifully deployed. Assonance and alliteration, however, rarely function as end rime. Rather they are, in modern poetry, occasional embellishments. However, *consonance,* which refers to the repetition of final consonant, does function as end rime. Consonantal end rime is a relatively new development in English, having been introduced by Hopkins (who transplanted it from Icelandic verse). Dylan Thomas employs it ingeniously, to tighten the stanza pattern while concealing the tightening process. That stanzas like this rime, Leslie Fiedler points out, has eluded critics generally:

Light breaks where no sun shi*nes;*
Where no sea runs, the waters of the hear*t*
Push in their ti*des.*
And broken ghosts with glowworms in their hea*ds,*
The things of ligh*t*
File through the flesh where no flesh decks the bo*nes.*

The rime is *abccba.*

Another departure from traditional rime is what Day Lewis calls **alliterative assonance,** Edmund Blunden **pararhyme,** and Louis Untermeyer (most validly) **dissonance-**

---

[1]This nomenclature may be misleading. *Final* rime is to be distinguished from *end* rime. The former comes at the end of a word; the latter at the end of a line. Final rime has *alliteration* (or initial) rime as its antithesis; end rime has *internal* (or interior) rime as its antithesis. (Interior rime: At length did *cross* an *albatross* . . .)

consonance. It consists of identical consonant sounds, initial and final, and differing vowel sounds: *groined* and *groaned. leaves* and *lives, birds* and *bards, escaped* and *scooped.* Wilfrid Owen, incomparably the greatest poet of World War I, is responsible for this technical innovation. Its chief merit will best be demonstrated by quoting from his most completely successful poem, "Strange meeting." The final couplet reads:

> And by his smile, I knew that sudden *hall;*
> By his dead smile I knew we stood in *Hell.*

Hell could not easily have been used as a perfect rime: the preceding rime-word would have deprived it of its necessary shock. Poets since Owen have imitated this technical resource widely.

Split rime is chiefly associated with humorous poetry, but occasionally serious poetry employs the device:

> In Texas a great gusher, a grain–
> Elevator in the Ukraine plain.

A slightly different classification is into **masculine** or **single** rime, in which only single syllables correspond (*could* and *understood, abound* and *sound*); and feminine or double rime, in which two syllables correspond (*potion* and *lotion, bleeding* and *seeding*).[1] The normal rime of iambic lines is, obviously, masculine; of trochaic, feminine.

Sometimes accent is displaced—"wrenched" from the syllable on which it normally would fall—and thrown on a syllable normally unaccented, or only slightly accented. When, as frequently in the popular ballad, such displacement forces a rime between an accented and unaccented syllable, **wrenched rime** is the outcome. (*Countreé* and *me, gum* and *quarrelsóme*).

Lines and Stanzas

Lines may be composed of various numbers of the different kinds of feet, and stanzas of various numbers of the dif-

---

[1] Triple rime, based on the correspondence of three syllables, "is usually a humorous device: but Hood, in a serious poem, employs such rimes as *tenderly* and *slenderly.*

ferent kinds of lines. Consequently, to attempt an exhaustive listing of stanza-forms, as Hood comments, "would be to enter upon an arithmetical progression alarming to think of." Nevertheless, a few instances of the stanzas most commonly employed in English and American verse will be suggestive.

First, though, let us look briefly at some non-stanzaic forms. **Blank verse**—unrimed iambic pentameter—has proved compellingly attractive to poets, especially dramatic poets. Marlowe's "mighty line" and Auden's exceedingly fluid one demonstrate the diverse values of blank verse: its power and its plasticity.[1]

Blank verse offers the poet who knows his craft a unique combination of freedom and discipline. The discipline is more apparent than the freedom in the **couplet**—a pair of riming lines—yet the great practitioners of the form, Dryden and Pope, moved freely in it. And they were addicted to its most rigid variation, the **heroic couplet**.[2] These iambic pentameter couplets were "closed"—that is, each pair expressed a complete thought. Almost every line was end-stopped and divided into neat halves by the *caesura*. Balance, alliteration, antithesis were the hinges on which the lines turned. But because of the restrictions imposed on it, the heroic couplet was beautifully suited for hard, compact, epigrammatic expression. The masters of the form could achieve any effect they wanted to—except perhaps the ultimate poetic effect, that which Shakspere achieved, and Wordsworth at his best, and Walt Whitman at his. However, poetry is a house of many mansions. Auden's couplet,

> The pious fable and the dirty story
> Share the total literary glory,

is the only possible credo for the critic who does not needlessly narrow his horizons. The following heroic couplets from Pope are poetry of a different but not necessarily of an inferior order than Wordsworth's. It may be that beginning poets have more to learn from Pope than from Wordsworth

[1] Specimens of blank verse from Marlowe and Milton have been quoted previously.

[2] So called because it was used in Restoration heroic tragedy, in place of the blank verse of Elizabethan tragedy.

concerning their craft: These lines are perfect of their kind
—clear, crisp, beautifully managed:

> But most by Numbers judge a Poet's song;
> And smooth or rough, with them is right or wrong:
> In the bright Muse though thousand charms conspire,
> Her voice is all these tuneful fools admire;
> Who haunt Parnassus but to please their ear, ⎫
> Not mend their minds; as some to Church repair, ⎬
> Not for the doctrine, but the music there. ⎭
> These equal syllables alone require,
> Though oft the ear the open vowels tire;
> While expletives their feeble aid do join;
> And ten low words oft creep in one dull line:
> While they ring round the same unvaried chimes,
> With sure returns of still expected rhymes;
> Where'er you find 'the cooling western breeze,'
> In the next line, it 'whispers through the trees';
> If crystal streams 'with pleasing murmurs creep,'
> The reader's threatened (not in vain) with 'sleep';
> Then, at the last and only couplet fraught
> With some unmeaning thing they call a thought,
> A needless Alexandrine ends the song
> That, like a wounded snake, drags its slow length along.

Note the three lines braced: they form a **triplet** (*ear, repair,*
and *there* were perfect rimes in the eighteenth century),
one of the few licenses permitted. The **Alexandrine,** the
iambic hexameter line which ends the quotation, had a more
dubious status, but even the purists indulged themselves in
an occasional Alexandrine.

Only one other of the many couplet forms needs specific
attention here—the **Hudibrastic couplet,** named from Samuel Butler's *Hudibras.* This seventeenth-century satire was
constructed of crude, rugged, and often cacophonous four-
stressed iambic lines:

> He was in logic a great critic,
> Profoundly skilled in analytic;
> He could distinguish and divide
> A hair 'twixt south and south-west side . . .

The nineteenth-century Romantics occasionally used the
couplet; but it was a different kind of couplet: run-on, open,

with rime (and with the epigrammatic point which rime sharpened) suppressed. Mostly, though, they sought more congenial forms. The **tercet,** or three-line stanza, was a favorite. The **triplet,** riming *aaa, bbb, ccc,* and so on, was employed not only as a variation, but also as a set stanza-form. A more complex tercet, the **terza rima,** was adopted from the Italian where Dante had used it "with astonishing diversity of effect." The first and third lines of the *terza rima* rime; the second supplies the rime for the first and third lines of the following stanza; and so on to the end. (Thus: *aba, bcb, cdc,* etc.) In English verse, either a separate couplet or a separate quatrain riming *abab* brings the *terza rima* to a close. The opening lines of Shelley's "Ode to the West Wind" illustrate the form:

> O Wild West Wind, thou breath of Autumn's being,
> Thou, from whose unseen presence the leaves dead
> Are driven, like ghosts from an enchanter fleeing,
>
> Yellow, and black, and pale, and hectic red,
> Pestilence-stricken multitudes: O thou,
> Who chariotest to their dark wintry bed
>
> The wingèd seeds, where they lie cold and low,
> Each like a corpse within its grave, until
> Thine azure sister of the Spring shall blow
>
> Her clarion o'er the dreaming earth, and fill
> (Driving sweet buds like flocks to feed in air)
> With living hues and odours plain and hill:
>
> Wild Spirit, which art moving everywhere;
> Destroyer and preserver; hear, oh, hear!

No other English stanza-form has been so widely and continuously popular as the four-line stanza, or **quatrain.** The **ballad,** riming *abcb,* and usually alternating tetrameter and trimeter lines as well as rimes, was the "poetry of the people" long before any of the more sophisticated forms came into being:

> The wind doth blow today, my love,
>   And a few small drops of rain;
> I never had but one true love,
>   In cold grave she was lain.

> "I'll do as much for my true-love
> As any young man may;
> I'll sit and mourn her at her grave
> For a twelvemonth and a day."

Other quatrains consist:

1. Of "a couplet divided by a couplet" (*e.g.,* Tennyson's "In Memoriam"—sometimes called the *"In Memoriam" stanza*).

2. Of iambic pentameter lines riming alternately (*e.g.,* Gray's "Elegy"—sometimes called the *heroic quatrain* or the *elegiac stanza*).

3. Of a triplet divided by an unrimed line, as *aaba* (*e.g.,* Fitzgerald's *The Rubáiyát of Omar Khayyám*—sometimes called the *rubáiyát stanza*).

The five-line stanza, or **quintain,** some think, is "one of the most musical forms of stanza we possess. It is capable of almost endless variety, and the proportions of rhymes, three and two, seem to be especially conducive to harmony." Browning was extremely fond of the quintain, and he rung all its changes. Only a single illustration will be quoted:

> Is it your moral of life?
> Such a web, simple and subtle,
> Weave we on earth here, in impotent strife
> Backward and forward each throwing his shuttle—
> Death ending all with a knife?

The six-line stanza, or **sestet,** may be composed of three couplets, a quatrain and a couplet, a tercet enclosing another, and any variety of other combinations. This is Burns's characteristic stanza:

> Wee modest, crimson-tipped flower—
> Thou'st met me in an evil hour,
> For I maun crush among the stour
> Thy slender stem;
> To spare thee now is past my power,
> Thou bonny gem.

Of the seven-line stanza, or **septet,** but one variation is sufficiently distinctive to require analysis. The **rime-royal** or

Chaucerian stanza[1] is seven-line iambic pentameter, riming *ababbcc*. Here Chaucer is complaining to Adam, his copyist, of the latter's carelessness in transcription:

> Adam scriveyn, if ever it thee bifalle
> Boece or Troilus to wryten newe,
> Under thy lokkes thou most have the scalle
> But after my making thou wryte trewe.
> So ofte a daye I mot thy werk renewe,
> Hit to correcte and eek to rubbe and scrape;
> And al is through thy negligence and rape.

The eight-line stanza, or **octet,** has one form that has appealed to poets for its humorous and satiric possibilities. From Byron to Mac Neice, the *ottava rima,* an Italian importation, has been popular in spite of its apparent difficulties. It consists of two triplets enclosing each other and a final couplet; thus *abababcc*. In the following, Byron employs the *ottava rima* for serious purposes—which indicates its (and his) versatility.

> Thus lived—thus died she; nevermore on her
>   Shall sorrow light or shame. She was not made
> Through years or moons the inner weight to bear,
>   Which colder hearts endure till they are laid
> By age in earth; her days and pleasures were
>   Brief but delightful; such as had not staid
> Long with her destiny. But she sleeps well
> By the sea-shore whereon she loved to dwell.

The stanza composed of nine lines, the **nonet,** similarly has one notable form—the **Spenserian stanza.** Shelley, who adopted "the stanza of Spenser (a measure inexpressibly beautiful)," did so, he declares, because he was enticed "by the brilliancy and magnificence of the sound which a mind that has been nourished upon musical thoughts can produce by a just and harmonious arrangement of the pauses of this measure." Spenser had, in a like manner, been enticed by the stanza of Chaucer; and the Chaucerian is obviously the ancestor of the Spenserian stanza. The latter consists of eight five-stressed iambic lines plus a closing Alexandrine, and rimes *ababbcbcc*. The Romantics at times introduced some

[1] Both James I of Scotland and Chaucer used this form—whence its names.

slight variations (preferring two rimes to three), but the stanza as Spenser conceived it is the most popular:

> So fashioned a porch with rare device,
> Archt over head with an embracing vine,
> Whose bounches, hanging downe, seemd to entice
> All passers by to taste their lushious wine,
> And did them selves into their hands incline,
> As freely offering to be gathered:
> Some deepe empurpled as the hyacine,
> Some as the rubine laughing sweetely red,
> Some like faire emeraudes, not yet well ripened.

The Fixed Verse-Forms

The Sonnet

From the early sixteenth century, when Wyatt imported the form to England, to the present, the sonnet has appealed to more, and more diverse, talents than any other form. Shakspere, Milton, Wordsworth, Keats, Poe, Longfellow, Cummings, Masefield, Millay—all have occasionally found it

> . . . pastime to be bound
> Within the sonnet's scanty plot of ground.

There have been conflicting suggestions as to the classification of the distinct types of sonnet. Two types, though, are clearly distinguishable: the **Petrarchian**[1] or **Italian sonnet,** and the **Shaksperian**[2] or **English sonnet.**

The Petrarchian sonnet is a strict form. A fourteen-line poem in iambic pentameter, it is divided into *octet* and *sestet.* Professor Gayley describes their functions: "The octave bears the burden; a doubt, a problem, a reflection, an historical statement, a cry of indignation, or desire, a vision of the ideal. The sestet eases the load, resolves the problem or the doubt, answers the query, solaces the yearning, realizes the vision. It gilds the thought with the tracery of instance, crowns it with the sufficient and inevitable actuality that

---

[1]Petrarch, a fourteenth-century Italian poet, devised the sonnet.

[2]Shakspere did not invent the sonnet form associated with his name, but he was its greatest exponent. Henry Howard, Earl of Surrey, was the inventor of the "Shaksperian" sonnet.

lies within the wisdom of art." The octave has an unvarying
rime scheme: *abbaabba*. The sestet may have one of several: *cdecde* or *cdcdcd* or *cdeedc*. Here Theodore Watts-
Dunton defines and illustrates at the same time.

> Yon silvery billows breaking on the beach
> Fall back in foam beneath the star-shine clear,
> The while my rhymes are murmuring in your ear
> A restless lore like that the billows teach;
> For on those sonnet-waves my soul would reach
> From its own depths and rest within you, dear,
> As, through the billowy voices yearning here,
> Great Nature strives to find a human speech.
>
> A sonnet is a wave of melody:
> From heaving waters of the impassioned soul
> A billow of tidal music one and whole
> Flows in the "octave"; then, returning free,
> Its ebbing surges in the "sestet" roll
> Back to the deeps of Life's tumultuous sea.

The Shaksperian sonnet is a more flexible form. It mini-
mizes the division into octet and sestet, substituting a sum-
marizing couplet at the end. The rime scheme is normally
abab cdcd efef gg. Other possibilities are *abab abab cdcd
ee* and *abab bcbc cdcd ee*.[1] Watts-Dunton makes this perceptive comment on the Shaksperian form: ". . . the sweet-
est of all possible arrangements in English versification is a
succession of decasyllabic quatrains in alternate rhymes knit
together and clinched by a couplet—a couplet coming not
so far from the initial verse as to lose its binding power, and
yet not so near the initial verse that the ring of epigram dis-
turbs the 'linked sweetness long drawn out' of this movement, but sufficiently near to shed its influence on the poem
back to the initial verse." This is Shakspere's magnificent
proof of Watts-Dunton's contention:

> When to the sessions of sweet silent thought
> I summon up remembrance of things past,
> I sigh the lack of many a thing I sought,
> And with old woes new wail my dear time's waste.

[1] The linking of the three quatrains in an *abab bcbc cdcd ee* rime scheme was
Spenser's effective variation of the form: occasionally it is referred to as the
Spenserian sonnet.

Then can I drown an eye, unused to flow,
For precious friends hid in death's dateless night,
And weep afresh love's long since cancelled woe,
And moan the expense of many a vanish'd sight.
Then can I grieve at grievances foregone,
And heavily from woe to woe tell o'er
The sad account of fore-bemoanèd moan,
Which I new pay as if not paid before.
But if the while I think on thee, dear friend,
All losses are restored and sorrows end.

Perhaps the **Miltonic sonnet** ought to be classified as a distinct form. Though it is in its rime scheme modeled on the Petrarchian, it discards the octet-sestet structure. Its integral, swelling theme needs fourteen uninterrupted lines to contain it. Neither the epigrammatic comment of the Shaksperian sonnet, nor the break marking a new phase of thought of the Petrarchian, is relevant to this form. Milton and Wordsworth are its two great exponents.

The **irregular sonnet** is a hybrid form. It uses what combination of structure and rime scheme it considers appropriate to its subject. And often the combination is very unlike any traditional sonnet form. Some purists insist that *irregular sonnet* is a misnomer, that *fourteener* would be a better name for this composite variety. However, the many modern poets—and they have the last say—who practice the form declare that they are writing sonnets. Cummings, Spender, Day Lewis, Stevens, Crane, among the moderns, have all written irregular sonnets of a high degree of excellence.

The Ode

The **ode** (Edmund Gosse defines) "is any strain of enthusiastic and exalted lyric verse directed to a fixed purpose and dealing progressively with one dignified theme." The **regular** or **Pindaric ode** imitates, as best it can, the scheme of the Greek ode as practiced by Pindar. The latter consisted of three movements: the *strophe,* an iambic stanza chanted by the chorus as it "turned"; the *antistrophe,* a stanza arranged to correspond, that is, symmetrical to the strophe, chanted as the chorus "reversed"; and the *epode,* a trochaic stanza chanted as the chorus came to a "stand." The true Pindaric ode is rare in English; Gray's "Progress of Poesy" and "The Bard" are the two closest approximations to the form.

Of the **false Pindaric** or **Cowleyan ode,**[1] however, instances are numerous: Dryden's "Alexander's Feast," Wordsworth's "Ode: Intimations of Immortality," Moody's "An Ode in Time of Hesitation," Allen Tate's "Ode to the Confederate Dead" are a few of the many that might be cited. In the English form, no two stanzas are alike—not because (as sometimes has been supposed) Cowley and his contemporaries did not quite understand the structure of the Pindaric ode, but rather because they thought it not adapted for English verse.

The **stanzaic** or **Horatian ode** is an English imitation of Horace's ode. The Horatian ode is of uniform stanza-structure—though the stanzas may be short, simple, and unrimed, as in Collins's "Ode to Evening"; or long, complex and rimed as in Keats's "Ode on a Grecian Urn."

French Forms

The French forms are the most rigid of all in regard to structural requirements. They were cultivated in the pre-classic period of French literature, and while occasionally attempted during Chaucer's day, when the English court was dominated by French modes, they did not take root in English verse until the 1870's. Credit for their transplantation is chiefly due to Edmund Gosse, who conceded that the majority of them "are not suited for nor are they intended to rival the more approved national rhythms in the treatment of grave and elevated themes. What is modestly advanced for them . . . is that they may add a new charm of buoyancy—a lyric freshness—to amatory and familiar verse, already too much condemned to faded measures and outworn cadences." That the French forms are delightfully

[1]Also, and perhaps more properly, called the **English ode,** since Cowley was neither the first to write in the form, nor its best exponent.

suited for *vers de société,* the success of Lang, Dobson, Chesterton, Henley, Bunner, Matthews, Robinson, and Untermeyer in employing them abundantly attests. The following are those most often met with:

1. **Rondeau:** composed of thirteen lines, having but two rimes, and those in a prescribed order, throughout; the refrain is unrimed. If *R* stands for the refrain, the rime scheme may be represented thus: *aabba, aabR, aabbaR.* This is Austin Dobson's version of a rondeau by Voiture:

> You bid me try, blue eyes, to write
> A rondeau. What!—forthwith?—to-night?
> Reflect. Some skill I have, 'tis true;
> But thirteen lines—and rhymed on two—
> "Refrain," as well. Ah, hapless plight!
>
> Still, there are five lines—ranged aright.
> These Gallic bonds, I feared, would fright
> My easy Muse. They did till you—
> *You* bid me try!
>
> This makes them nine. The port's in sight;
> 'Tis all because your eyes are bright!
> Now, just a pair to end with 'oo'—
> When maids command, what can't we do?
> Behold! the rondeau—tasteful, light—
> You bid me try!

2. **Rondel:** a variation of the rondeau, composed of fourteen lines and having only two rimes; the first and second lines are repeated in their entirety as the seventh and eighth lines, again as the thirteenth and fourteenth.

3. **Roundel:** Swinburne's distinctive variation of the rondel; it is not really a French form at all. Here is Swinburne's exemplification—"The Roundel":

A roundel is wrought as a ring or a star-bright sphere,
With craft of delight and with cunning of sound unsought,
That the heart of the hearer may smile if to pleasure his ear
A roundel is wrought.

Its jewel of music is carven of all or of aught—
Love, laughter or mourning—remembrance of rapture or fear—
That fancy may fashion to hang in the ear of thought.

As a bird's quick song runs round, and the hearts in us hear
Pause answer to pause, and again the same strain caught,
So moves the device whence, round as a pearl or a tear,
              A roundel is wrought.

4. **Triolet:** a single stanza composed of eight lines, having
only two rimes; the first is repeated as the fourth, and the
first and second as the seventh and eighth. This is H. C.
Bunner's "A Pitcher of Mignonette":

> A pitcher of mignonette,
>   In a tenement's highest casement:
> Queer sort of a flower-pot—yet
> That pitcher of mignonette
> Is a garden in heaven set,
>   To the little sick child in the basement—
> The pitcher of mignonette,
>   In the tenement's highest casement.

5. **Villanelle:** composed of five triplets and a quatrain,
having but two rimes throughout.[1] The most rigid villanelles
follow this form: The opening line is repeated as the third
of the second and fourth triplets and as either the last or
the next to the last line of the concluding quatrain; the third
line is repeated at the end of the third and fifth triplets and
as either the last or next to the last line of the concluding
quatrain; the first and third lines of each triplet all rime
together, as do the second lines of each triplet. Illustration
will be more enlightening than any schematic representation. In this villanelle by L. S. Bevington, the poet has introduced one slight modification: he has varied the last line of
the quatrain, and in theory it ought to be identical with the
last line of the first, third, and fifth triplets:

> There are roses white, there are roses red,
>   Shyly rosy, tenderly white;
> Which shall I choose to wreathe my head?
>
> Which shall I cull from the garden-bed
>   To greet my love on this very night?
> There are roses white, there are roses red.

---

[1] Less strict villanelles are of indefinite length; the sticklers, though, say that
these are not properly villanelles.

The red should say what I would have said;
Ah! how they blush in the evening light!
Which shall I choose to wreathe my head?

The white are pale as the snow new spread,
Pure as young eyes and half as bright;
There are roses white, there are roses red.

Roses white, from the heaven dew-fed,
Roses red for a passion's plight,
Which shall I choose to wreathe my head?

Summer twilight is almost fled,
Say, dear love! have I chosen right?
There are roses white, there are roses red,
All twined together to wreathe my head.

6. **Ballade:** most popular of all the French forms; composed of three stanzas of eight lines each and a half-stanza, called the *envoy*, a "message." Like the rondeau, it is based on the triple use of a refrain. The rimes and arrangement of the first stanza are repeated in the others. The refrain ends the three stanzas and the envoy. Some variation in the length of stanza and the number of rimes is often seen, but the typical form is that used in the following "Ballade of Things Known and Unknown" by François Villon, translated by John Payne:

Flies in the milk I know full well:
    I know men by the clothes they wear:
I know the walnut by the shell:
    I know the foul sky from the fair:
    I know the pear-tree by the pear:
When things go well, to me is shown:
    I know who work and who forbear:
I know all save myself alone.

I know the pourpoint by the fell:
    And by his gown I know the frère:
Master from varlet can I tell:
    And nuns that cover up their hair:
    I know a swindler by his air,
And fools that fat on cates have grown:
    Wines by the cask I can compare:
I know all save myself alone.

I know how horse from mule to tell:
  I know the load each one can bear:
I know both Beatrice and Bell:
  I know the hazards, odd and pair:
  I know of visions in the air:
I know the power of Peter's throne
  And how misled Bohemians were:
I know all save myself alone.

ENVOY

Prince, I know all things: fat and spare,
  Ruddy and pale, to me are known;
And Death that endeth all our care:
  I know all save myself alone.

7. **Ballade variations:** (a) the **double ballade** has six stanzas with the same rime scheme and the same last line; (b) the **triple ballade** has nine stanzas with the same rime scheme and the same last line; (c) the **chant royal** has five stanzas of eleven lines with the same rime scheme and the same last line. The double and triple ballades may, and often do, discard the envoy; the *chant royal* usually retains the envoy (of five lines).

8. **Sestina:** the most complex of the French forms; composed of six six-lined stanzas, each of which ends with the same six words, plus an envoy of three lines, containing all the six words—three at the end of the lines, three near the middle. The rime throughout is therefore identical—it consists of repeating words. Modern variations, however, include perfect rimes. In either case, whether identical or perfect rime has been employed, the rime scheme is: *abcdef, faebdc, cfdabe, ecbfad, deacfb, bdfeca, b/e d/c f/a.* Kipling, Swinburne, Auden, and Gosse have all attempted this exceedingly difficult form. It is from the last-named that the following "Sestina" is quoted:

In fair Provence, the land of lute and rose,
Arnaut, great master of the lore of love,
First wrought sestines to win his lady's heart,
For she was deaf when simpler staves he sang,
And for her sake he broke the bonds of rhyme,
And in this subtler measure hid his woe.

"Harsh be my lines," cried Arnaut, "harsh the woe.
My lady, that enthorn'd and cruel rose,
Inflicts on him that made her live in rhyme!"
But through the meter spake the voice of Love,
And like a wild-wood nightingale he sang
Who thought in crabbed lays to ease his heart.

It is not told if her untoward heart
Was melted by the poet's lyric woe,
Or if in vain so amorously he sang;
Perchance through cloud of dark conceits he rose
To nobler heights of philosophic love,
And crowned his later years with sterner rhyme.

This thing alone we know: the triple rhyme
Of him who bared his vast and passionate heart
To all the crossing flames of hate and love,
Wears in the midst of all its storm of woe—
As some loud morn of March may bear a rose—
The impress of a song that Arnaut sang.

"Smith of his mother-tongue," the Frenchman sang
Of Launcelot and of Galahad, the rhyme
That beat so blood-like at its core of rose,
It stirred the sweet Francesca's gentle heart
To take that kiss that brought her so much woe,
And sealed in fire her martyrdom of love.

And Dante, full of her immortal love,
Stayed his dear song, and softly, fondly sang
As though his voice broke with that weight of woe;
And to this day we think of Arnaut's rhyme
Whenever pity at the laboring heart
On fair Francesca's memory drops the rose.

Ah! sovereign Love, forgive this weaker rhyme!
The men of old who sang were great at heart,
Yet have we too known woe, and worn thy rose.

Modern Techniques

Free Verse

Free verse or *vers libre* is simply verse that has no fixed metrical pattern. Terms like "iambic pentameter" or "trochaic tetrameter," always inexact, are thoroughly out of place when applied to free verse. In free verse, rhythm is a reflex of meaning, advancing or retreating with it. Not the image of footsteps hitting the ground, says D. H. Lawrence, but "of a bird with broad wings flying and lapsing through the air" is appropriate to the cadences of free verse. Its rhythm can expand or contract to embrace any of the million rhythms of the world about us. The unit is no longer the line, but the emotion—or rather the passage that contains it. In fact, one possible definition of free verse is *emotional rhythm.*

It is customary to trace the development of free verse from the 1920's, when Amy Lowell and the Imagists propagandized so effectively for it. In a famous couplet, Keith Preston weeps over

> The graves of little magazines
> That died to make verse free.

However, only the term is new; the thing has been in English poetry at least since the King James version of the BIBLE. Milton, Blake, Whitman—all wrote great free verse. For the line from Ecclesiastes, "There is no new thing under the sun," this passage from The Songs of Songs serves as evidence:

> The voice of my beloved! behold he cometh,
> Leaping upon the mountains, skipping upon the hills.
> My beloved is like a roe or a young hart:
> Behold, he standeth behind our wall,
> He looketh in at the windows,
> He showeth himself through the lattice.
> My beloved spoke, and said unto me,
> "Rise up my love, my fair one, and come away.
> For, lo, the winter is past,
> The rain is over and gone;
> The flowers appear on the earth;
> The time of the singing of birds is come,
> And the voice of the turtle heard on our land;
> The fig tree ripeneth her green figs,
> And the vines are in blossom,
> They give forth their fragrance.
> Arise my love, my fair one, and come away.

> O my dove, thou art in the clefts of the rock, in the covert
>   of the steep place,
> Let me see thy countenance, let me hear thy voice;
> For sweet is thy voice, and thy countenance is comely."[1]

In the foregoing quotation, note how the verse is linked together by repetition, by balance, by inversion, by alliteration, by assonance. Note, too, how the thought and emotion encompassed determine the length and the force of the breath-sweep. This, surely, is what Amy Lowell meant by "organic rhythm," "the poem built on cadence."

That free verse is a form capable of all the greatness of any of the regular metrical patterns is beyond doubt. H. D., Eliot, Sandburg, Fletcher, Jeffers, have proved false Edward Anthony's comment:

> *Vers libre*
> Is anything
> At all,
> Arranged
> Like this—

except, of course, when practiced by *vers librettists* who have not learned their craft. But one effect free verse, even at its best, cannot achieve: the counterpoint between meter and speech rhythm, the "delightful discord" between a pattern and the variation that can be played upon it. For this reason, to gain once more the clash of the natural and metrical beat which Day Lewis calls "that most desirable of rhythmical effects," free verse has in the last decade partly indentured itself to meter. T. S. Eliot has declared that "the ghost of some simple metre should lurk behind the arras in even the 'freest' verse, to advance menacingly as we doze and withdraw as we rouse." By accepting a more regular rhythmic base, yet not at all relinquishing its right to be irregular when sense and feeling demand it, free verse gains a new solidity while it loses none of its versatility.

Sprung Rhythm

Gerard Manley Hopkins, a late nineteenth-century poet, was perhaps the greatest technical innovator in the history

---

[1] The arrangement is that of E. S. Bates, *The Bible Designed to Be Read as Living Literature.*

of modern English verse. More than any other modern, he refurbished and revitalized its technique. His distinctive contribution is "Sprung Rhythm," and no other prosodic innovation has had so pervasive an effect on so many contemporary poets. Auden, Spender, Day Lewis, Mac Neice, Thomas, Lowell, Shapiro—almost every poet now writing who has something new to say and wants a new way of saying it—have been fundamentally influenced by Hopkins's metrics.

For prosodic purposes, Hopkins divided English verse into that written in "Running Rhythm, the common rhythm in English use," and that written in "Sprung Rhythm." The latter is the prosodic result of a continuous counterpointing of running rhythm; for, he says, "if you counterpoint throughout, since only one of the counter rhythms is actually heard, the other is really destroyed or cannot come to exist, and what is written is one rhythm only and probably Sprung Rhythm." Essentially, sprung rhythm is a wholly qualitative or stressed verse. In theory, stress would always fall on the first syllable of a line; but that would give rise only to falling rhythms. Actually, therefore, two licenses are necessary (and natural, Hopkins affirms) to sprung rhythm, namely *rests,* or *pauses;* and *hangars* or *outriders,* which consist of usually not more than three unstressed or "slack" syllables. These are "added to a foot and not counted in the nominal scanning." Thus, Day Lewis points out, lines such as Hopkins's

High there how he hung upon the rein of a wimpling wing.
No wonder of it: sheer plod makes plough down sillion

are metrically equivalent to

When you shall these unlucky deeds relate,

since each has five stresses.

Hopkins says that "Sprung Rhythm is the most natural of things." It is found in nursery rimes and weather saws; in highly counterpointed verse, such as Milton's *Samson Agonistes;* in music and verse closely corresponding to music, such as choral verse; in common speech. It is from

Samson Agonistes that Hopkins specifically traces his method; since Milton's poem is counterpointed throughout, the ground rhythm is obliterated and sprung rhythm results. However, as Hopkins points out, "the old English verse seen in Pierce Ploughmen" is sprung. So, too, is Coleridge's "Christabel."[1]

The great advantage of sprung rhythm, the reason that so many contemporary poets accorded it an eager welcome, is that it enables the poet to catch "the hover and swoop a kestrel" and to effect "the heavy determination of *sheer* plod" (in the line quoted above)—the cumulative result of the preceding unstressed syllables. Even more important, sprung rhythm enables a poet to use scientific and technical words without dislocating the pattern, or "inscape," to use one of Hopkins's neologisms, of his verse.

Note in the following lines how internal, suspended, split, cross rimes, vowel modulations and vowel harmonies, assonance, and—above all—alliteration, simultaneously fuse the verse and direct the stress:

I caught this morning morning's minion, kingdom of daylight's
   dauphin, dapple-dawn-drawn Falcon in his riding
Of the rolling level underneath him steady air . . .

Sometimes, Hopkins forces his stress; at other times he slights it. Sometimes he is cryptic because of the ellipses and dislocations his verse breeds. Sometimes he employs alliteration and other devices too exuberantly. Sometimes he "explores the limbo which divides the ridiculous from the sublime."[2] But in spite of all of these tendencies, the necessary product of daring experimentation, no other poet of the last hundred years has offered so much real "hope for poetry."

[1] Coleridge's introduction to "Christabel" anticipates Hopkins's theory in many ways; and the poem itself anticipates Hopkins's poetry.
[2] Untermeyer, *Modern British Poetry*.

ab or **abb**: bab, blab, cab, crab, dab, drab, gab, Mab, nab, scab, St. Abb, slab, stab.

abe: astrolabe, babe.

ac: almanac, ammoniac, aphrodisiac, arrack, attack, back, black, brach, bric-a-brac, clack, crack, demoniac, hack, hypochrondriac, jack, knack, lac, lack, maniac, pack, quack, rack, sack, slack, snack, stack, symposiac, tack, thwack, track, wrack, Zodiac.

ace: abase, ace, apace, base, brace, carapace, case, chase, dace, debase, deface, disgrace, displace, efface, embrace, face, grace, grimace, interlace, lace, mace, misplace, pace, place, populace, race, retrace, space, thrace, trace.

act: abstract, act, attract, cataract, co-act, compact, contact, contract, counteract, detract, distract, enact, exact, extract, fact, fract, infract, intact, pact, protract, re-act, retract, subact, subtract, tact, tract, transact, the preterits and participles of verbs in **ack**.

ad or **add**: as in *bad*. Add, bad, brad, cad, chad, clad, dad, fad, gad, glad, had, lad, mad, pad, plaid, sad, shad, etc.
As in *wad*. *See* **od**.

ade: afraid, aid, ambuscade, arcade, bade, blade, blockade, braid, brigade, brocade, cade, cannonade, cascade, cavalcade, cockade, crusade, degrade, dissuade, esplanade, evade, fade, gambade, glade, invade, jade, lade, lemonade, made, maid, masquerade, palisade, persuade, raid, renegade, retrograde, rhodomontade, serenade, shade, spade, staid, trade, upbraid, wade.

afe: chafe, safe, vouchsafe.

aff: behalf, calf, cenotaph, chaff, distaff, draff, epitaph, gaff, graph, half, laugh, paragraph, photograph, quaff, staff, telegraph.

aft: abaft, craft, daft, draft, draught, graft, haft, handicraft, ingraft, raft, shaft, and the preterits and participles of verbs in **aff** and **augh,** etc.

ag: bag, brag, Brobdingnag, cag, crag, drag, fag, flag, gag, hag, jag, knag, lag, nag, quag, rag, sag, scrag, shag, snag, stag, swag, tag, wag.

age: age, assuage, cage, concubinage, disengage, engage, enrage, equipage, gage, gauge, heritage, hermitage, mage, page, parentage, parsonage, pasturage, patronage, personage, pilgrimage, presage, rage, sage, stage, swage, villanage, wage.

ah: ah, bah, pah, shah.

ai: ai, almai, ay, papai, serai.

ail: Abigail, assail, ale, avail, aventail, bail, bale, brail, countervail, curtail, dale, detail, entail, exhale, fail, flail, frail, gale, grail, hail, hale, impale, jail, mail, male, nail, nightingale, pail, pale, prevail, quail, rail, regale, retail, sail, sale, scale, shale, stale, swale, tail, tale, trail, vale, veil, wail, wale, wassail, whale.

ain: abstain, amain, appertain, arraign, attain, bane, blain, brain, cain, campaign, cane, chain, champagne, complain, constrain, contain, crane, Dane, deign, detain, disdain, distrain, drain, enchain, entertain, explain, fain, fane, feign, gain, grain, hurricane, Jane, lain, lane, main, maintain, mane, obtain, ordain, pain, pertain, plain, plane, profane, rain, refrain, regain, reign, rein, remain, restrain, retain, skein, slain, Spain, sprain, stain, strain, sustain, swain, thane, train, twain, vain, vane, vein, wain, wane.

aint: acquaint, ain't, attaint, complaint, constraint, distraint, faint, feint, mayn't, plaint, quaint, restraint, saint, taint.

air and **aire:** *see* **are.**

aith: baith, faith, rath, wraith.

ake: ache, alcaic, awake, bake, bespake, betake, brake, break, cake, caique, drake, flake, forsake, hake, lake, make, mandrake, mistake, opaque, overtake, partake, quake, rake, sake, shake, snake, spake, stake, steak, strake, take, undertake, wake.

al: admiral, animal, arsenal, cabal, canal, cannibal, capital, cardinal, carnival, comical, conjugal, corporal, criminal, critical, fal-lal, festival, fineal, funeral, gal, general, hospital, interval, liberal, literal, madrigal, magical, mall, mineral, musical, mystical, natural, original, pal, pastoral, pedestal, personal, physical, poetical, political, principal, prodigal, prophetical, rational, reciprocal, rhetorical, sal, satirical, several, schismatical, shall, temporal, tragical, tyrannical.

alk: auk, balk, baulk, calk, catafalque, caulk, chalk, hawk, stalk, talk, walk.

all: all, appal, awl, ball, bawl, brawl, call, caul, crawl, enthral, fall, forestall, gall, Gaul, hall, haul, install, mawl, pall, scrawl, sprawl, shawl, squall, stall, tall, thrall, wall.

alm, alms: balm, becalm, calm, embalm, palm, psalm; plurals and third persons singular rime with **alms**, as becalms, calms, etc.

alt: as in *halt*. Assault, default, exalt, fault, halt, malt, salt, vault. As in *shalt*. Asphalt, alt, shalt.

alve: as in *calve*. Calve, halve, salve. As in *valve*. Alve, valve.

am and amb: am, anagram, clam, cram, dam, damn, dram, epigram, flam, ham, jam, jamb, kam, lam, lamb, ma'am, oriflamme, pam, ram, Sam, sham, swam, telegram.

ame: acclaim, aim, became, blame, came, claim, dame, defame, exclaim, fame, flame, frame, game, inflame, lame, maim, misbecame, misname, name, overcame, proclaim, reclaim, same, shame, tame.

amp: as in *camp*. Camp, champ, clamp, cramp, damp, decamp, encamp, lamp, stamp, vamp. As in *swamp*. Pomp, romp, swamp.

an: as in *ban*. Artisan, ban, barracan, began, bran can, caravan, clan, courtesan, Dan, fan, foreran, man, Nan, pan, partisan, pelican, plan, ran, scan, shandydan, span, tan, than, trepan, unman, van. As in *wan*. Swan, wan. *See* **on.**

ance: advance, arrogance, chance, circumstance, complaisance, concordance, consonance, countenance, dance, deliverance, dissonance, enhance, exorbitance, expanse, extravagance, France, glance, ignorance, inheritance, intemperance, intrance, lance, maintenance, mischance, ordinance, prance, romance, sufferance, sustenance, temperance, trance, utterance, vigilance.

anch: blanch, branch, ganch, stanch.

and: as in *band*. And, band, bland, brand, command, contraband, countermand, demand, disband, expand, gland, grand, hand, land, rand, reprimand, sand, stand, strand, understand, withstand, and preterits and participles of verbs in **an.** As in *wand*. Wand. *See* **ond.**

ang: bang, chang, clang, fang, gang, hang, harangue, lang, pang, rang, sang, slang, stang, swang, tang, twang.

ange: arrange, change, estrange, exchange, grange, range, strange.

ank: bank, blank, brank, clank, dank, disrank, drank, frank, hank, lank, mountebank, plank, prank, rank, shank, slank, spank, stank, thank, Yank.

ant: as in *ant*. Absonant, adamant, ant, arrogant, aslant, aunt, can't, cant, chant, combatant, complaisant, consonant, conversant, cormorant, covenant, displant, disputant, dissonant, elegant, elephant, enchant, exorbitant, extravagant, gallant, grant, ignorant, implant, inhabitant, insignificant, militant, pant, petulant, piant, predominant, protestant, rant, recant, shan't, significant, slant, supplant, sycophant, transplant, vigilant, visitant.
As in *want*. Font, upon't, want.

ap: as in *cap*. Affrap, cap, chap, clap, dap, entrap, enwrap, fap, flap, gap, hap, knap, lap, map, mayhap, mishap, nap, pap, rap, sap, scrap, slap, snap, strap, tap, trap, wrap.
As in *swap*. Swap. See **op**.

ape: ape, cape, chape, crape, escape, grape, jape, nape, rape, scape, scrape, shape, tape, trape.

apse: apse, elapse, lapse, perhaps, relapse, and the plurals of nouns and third persons singular present tense of verbs in **ap**.

apt: adapt, apt. Rimes the preterits and participles of verbs in **ap**.

ar: afar, angular, are, avatar, bar, calendar, car, char, catarrh, caviar, cinnabar, debar, far, jar, mar, par, particular, perpendicular, petar, popular, regular, scar, scimitar, secular, singular, spar, star, tar, titular, unbar, vinegar.
As in *war*. See **or**.

arb: barb, garb, rhubarb.

arce: farce, parse, sarse, sparse.

arch: as in *march*. Arch, countermarch, larch, march, parch, starch.
As in *hierarch*. Heresiarch, hierarch. See **ark**.

ard: as in *bard*. Bard, basilard, bombard, card, discard, disregard, guard, hard, interlard, lard, nard, regard, retard, shard.
As in *ward*. Afford, restored, sward, ward, etc.

are: as in *bare:* Affair, air, aware, bear, beware, care, chair, compare, coheir, dare, debonnair, declare, despair, e'er, elsewhere, ensnare, ere, fair, fare, flare, forbear, forswear, gare, glaire, glare, hair, hare,

howe'er, heir, howsoe'er, impair, lair, mare, ne'er, pair, pare, pear, prepare, repair, scare, share, snare, spare, square, stair, stare, sware, swear, tare, tear, their, there, vair, ware, wear, were, whate'er, whene'er, where, where'er, yare.
As in *are*. Rimes **ar**.

arf: dwarf, wharf.

arge: barge, charge, discharge, enlarge, large, marge, o'ercharge, surcharge, targe.

ark: ark, bark, cark, chark, clark, dark, embark, heresiarch, hierarch, lark, mark, park, remark, shark, spark, stark.

arl: carl, gnarl, harl, marl, parle, snarl.

arm: as in *arm*. Alarm, arm, barm, charm, disarm, farm, harm.
As in *warm*. Swarm, warm. *See* **orm**.

arn: as in *barn*. Barn, darn, tarn, yarn.
As in *warn*. Forewarn, warn. *See* **orn**.

arp: as in *carp*. Carp, counterscarp, harp, sharp.
As in *warp*. Warp. *See* **orp**.

arsh: harsh, marsh.

art: as in *art*. Apart, art, cart, counterpart, dart, depart, hart, heart, mart, part, smart, start, tart.
As in *wart*. *See* **ort**.

arth: forth, north, swarth.

arve: carve, starve.

as: as in *was*. 'Coz, poz, was.
As in *gas*. Gas. *See* **ass**.
As in *has*. As, has.

ash: as in *ash*. Abash, ash, bash, brash, cash, clash, crash, dash, flash, gash, gnash, hash, lash, plash, pash, rash, sash, slash, splash, thrash.

ask: ask, bask, cask, casque, flask, hask, mask, task.

asm: cataplasm, chasm, enthusiasm, miasm, phantasm, plasm, spasm.

asp: asp, clasp, gasp, grasp, hasp, rasp.

ass: alas, alias, amass, ass, brass, class, cuirass, gas, grass, lass, mass, morass, pass, surpass.

ast: aghast, avast, blast, cast, fast, forecast, hast, mast, outcast, overcast, past, repast, vast, the preterits and participles of verbs in **ass**.

aste: baste, chaste, distaste, haste, paste, taste, waist, waste, and the preterits and participles of verbs under **ace.**

at: as in *at.* At, bat, brat, cat, fat, flat, gnat, hat, lat, mat, pat, rat, sat, tat, that, vat.
As in *what. See* **ot.**

atch: as in *catch.* Attach, catch, detach, dispatch, hatch, latch, patch, ratch, scratch, slatch, smatch, snatch, swatch, thatch.
As in *watch. See* **otch.**

ate: abate, abdicate, abominate, abrogate, accelerate, accommodate, accumulate, accurate, adequate, adulterate, advocate, affectionate, aggravate, agitate, alleviate, animate, annihilate, antedate, anticipate, antiquate, arbitrate, arrogate, articulate, assassinate, await, bait, bate, belate, calculate, candidate, capacitate, capitulate, captivate, celebrate, celibate, circulate, coagulate, collate, commemorate, commiserate, communicate, compassionate, confederate, congratulate, congregate, consecrate, considerate, consulate, contaminate, cooperate, corroborate, create, cultivate, date, debate, debilitate, dedicate, degenerate, delegate, deliberate, delicate, denominate, depopulate, deprecate, derogate, desolate, desperate, dilate, disconsolate, discriminate, dislocate, dissipate, educate, effeminate, eight, elaborate, elate, elevate, emulate, equivocate, eradicate, estate, estimate, evaporate, exaggerate, exasperate, expostulate, exterminate, extricate, facilitate, fate, fortunate, gate, generate, grate, gratulate, great, hate, hesitate, illiterate, illuminate, imitate, immoderate, importunate, imprecate, inanimate, ingrate, innate, inovate, instigate, intemperate, intimate, intimidate, intoxicate, intricate, invalidate, inveterate, inviolate, legitimate, magistrate, mate, meditate, mitigate, moderate, necessitate, obstinate, participate, passionate, pate, penetrate, perpetrate, personate, plate, potentate, prate, precipitate, predestinate, predominate, premeditate, prevaricate, procrastinate, profligate, prognosticate, propagate, rate, rebate, recriminate, regenerate, regulate, reiterate, relate, reprobate, reverberate, ruminate, sate, sedate, separate, skate, slate, sophisticate, state, stipulate, straight, strait, subjugate, subordinate, suffocate, terminate, tête-à-tête, titivate, tolerate, translate, unfortunate, vindicate, violate, wait, weight.

ath: as in *bath.* Aftermath, bath, hath, path, swath, wrath.
As in *rath. See* **aith.**

athe: bathe, rathe, scathe, swathe.

aud: abroad, applaud, broad, defraud, fraud, laud, and the preterits and participles of verbs under **aw.**

aught: as in *draught*. Draught, quaffed, etc.
As in *caught*. *See* **aut.**

aunt: aunt, avaunt, daunt, gaunt, haunt, jaunt, taunt, vaunt.

ause: applause, because, cause, clause, gauze, pause, the plurals of nouns and third persons singular of verbs in **aw.**

aut: caught, distraught, fraught, nought, ought, sought, taught, taut.

ave: architrave, behave, brave, cave, crave, deprave, engrave, forgave, gave, grave, lave, misgave, nave, outbrave, pave, rave, save, shave, slave, stave, wave.

aw: chaw, claw, craw, daw, draw, flaw, foresaw, gnaw, jaw, law, maw, paw, raw, saw, scraw, shaw, straw, thaw, usquebaugh, withdraw.

awn: aun, awn, brawn, dawn, drawn, fawn, lawn, pawn, prawn, shaun, spawn, withdrawn, yawn.

ax: ax, flax, knickknacks, lax, pax, relax, tax, wax, the plurals of nouns and third persons singular of verbs in **ack.**

ay: affray, allay, array, astray, away, aye, belay, betray, bewray, bray, clay, convey, day, decay, defray, delay, disarray, dismay, disobey, display, essay, fay, flay, forelay, fray, gainsay, gay, gray, inlay, inveigh, jay, lay, may, nay, neigh, obey, pay, play, pray, prey, purvey, ray, relay, repay, roundelay, say, shay, slay, spray, stay, stray, survey, sway, they, tray, tway, virelay, way, weigh, yea.

aze: amaze, blaze, craze, draze, gaze, glaze, graze, maze, paraphrase, phrase, raise, and the nouns plural and third persons singular of the present tense of verbs in **ay, eigh,** and **ey.**

each: beach, beech, beseech, bleach, breach, each, impeach, leech, peach, preach, speech, teach.

eague: fatigue, intrigue, league, Teague.

eak: as in *beak*. Antique, beak, bespeak, bezique, bleak, cheek, creak, creek, clique, critique, eke, freak, leak, leek, meek, oblique, peak, pique, reek, seek, shriek, sleek, sneak, speak, squeak, streak, tweak, weak, week, wreak.
As in *break*. *See* **ake.**

eal: anneal, appeal, conceal, congeal, deal, eel, feel, heal, heel, keel, kneel, leal, meal, peal, peel, real, reel, repeal, reveal, seal, squeal, steal, teal, veal, weal, wheal, wheel, zeal.

ealth: commonwealth, health, stealth, wealth.

eam: beam, beseem, beteem, blaspheme, bream, cream, deem, disesteem, dream, enseam, esteem, extreme, gleam, misdeem, redeem, scheme, scream, seam, seem, team, teem, theme.

eamt: attempt, dreamt, empt, exempt.

ean: bean, between, careen, clean, convene, dean, demean, demesne, foreseen, glean, green, intervene, keen, lean, machine, mean, mien, obscene, queen, screen, seen, serene, spleen, teen, wean.

eans: means, rimes plural of nouns, and third persons singular present of verbs, in **ean, een, ene.**

earl: churl, curl, earl, furl, girl, pearl, purl, thirl, twirl, whirl.

earth: berth, birth, dearth, earth, mirth, Perth, worth.

ease: as in *cease*. Apiece, cease, decease, decrease, fleece, frontispiece, geese, grease, increase, lease, niece, peace, piece, release.
As in *disease. See* **eeze.**

east: beast, east, feast, least, priest, the preterits and participles of verbs in **ease,** as in *cease*.

eat: as in *bleat*. Beat, bleat, cheat, complete, concrete, defeat, discreet, eat, effete, entreat, escheat, estreat, feat, feet, fleet, greet, heat, meat, meet, neat, obsolete, replete, retreat, seat, sheet, sleet, street, sweet, treat, wheat.
As in *great. See* **ate.**
As in *threat. See* **et.**

eath: as in *breath*. Breath, death, Elizabeth, saith, etc., and antiquated third person singular present, accented on the antepenult (*e.g.,* encount*er*eth).
As in *heath*. Beneath, heath, sheath, teeth, wreath.

eathe: bequeathe, breathe, inwreathe, seethe, sheathe, wreathe.

eave: achieve, aggrieve, believe, bereave, cleave, conceive, deceive, disbelieve, eve, grieve, heave, interweave, inweave, leave, perceive, receive, relieve, reprieve, retrieve.

eb and **ebb:** bleb, ebb, neb, web.

eck and **ec:** beck, check, deck, fleck, geck, hypothec, neck, peck, spec, speck, wreck.

ect: affect, architect, circumspect, collect, correct, deject, detect, direct, disaffect, disrespect, effect, elect, eject, erect, expect, incorrect, indirect, infect, inspect, intellect, neglect, object, project, protect, recollect, reflect, reject, respect, sect, select, subject, suspect.

ed: abed, bed, behead, bled, bread, bred, dead, dread, fed, fled, head, inbred, lead, led, misled, o'erspread, read, red, said, shed, shred, sped, spread, Ted, thread, tread, wed.

edge: allege, edge, fledge, hedge, kedge, ledge, pledge, privilege, sacrilege, sedge, sortilege.

ee: agree, be, bee, calipee, cap-a-pie, decree, degree, disagree, flea, flee, foresee, free, glee, gree, he, jubilee, key, knee, lee, me, o'ersee, pedigree, plea, sea, see, she, tea, thee, three, tree, we.

eed: bead, bleed, breed, concede, creed, deed, exceed, feed, glede, heed, impede, indeed, intercede, knead, lead, mead, meed, need, plead, precede, proceed, read, recede, rede, reed, seed, speed, steed, succeed, supersede, weed.

eep: asleep, cheap, creep, deep, heap, keep, neap, peep, sheep, sleep, steep, sweep, weep.

eer: as in *beer*. Adhere, appear, auctioneer, austere, bandolier, beer, besmear, bier, cannoneer, cohere, chanticleer, charioteer, cheer, clear, compeer, dear, deer, disappear, domineer, ear, endear, engineer, fear, fere, fleer, gear, hear, here, hemisphere, interfere, jeer, leer, mere, mountaineer, mutineer, near, peer, persevere, pickeer, pier, pioneer, privateer, rear, revere, severe, sheer, smear, sneer, spear, sphere, steer, tear, tier, veer, year.
As in *e'er*. See **are**.

eeze: appease, breeze, cheese, disease, displease, ease, seize, sneeze, squeeze, tease, these, wheeze, and the plurals of nouns in **ea, ee,** etc.

ef: clef, deaf, kef, nef.

eft: bereft, cleft, left, theft, weft.

eg and **egg:** beg, egg, keg, leg, Meg, peg, Winnipeg.

el and **ell:** asphodel, befell, bell, calomel, cell, citadel, compel, dispel, dwell, ell, excel, expel, fell, foretell, hell, impel, infidel, knell, mell, muscatel, parallel, petronel, quell, refel, repel, sell, sentinel, shell, smell, spell, swell, tell, well, yell.

eld: beheld, eld, geld, held, upheld, withheld, etc., the preterits and participles of verbs in **el, ell.**

elf: delf, elf, himself, Guelf, Guelph, pelf, self, shelf.

elk: elk, kelk, whelk.

elm: elm, helm, realm, overwhelm, whelm.

elp: help, kelp, whelp, yelp.

elt: belt, dealt, dwelt, felt, gelt, melt, pelt, smelt.

elve: delve, helve, shelve, twelve.

em: anadem, apothegm, condemn, contemn, diadem, gem, hem, kemb, parapegm, stem, stratagem, phlegm.

empt: attempt, contempt, dreamt, exempt, tempt.

en: den, denizen, fen, hen, ken, men, pen, ten, then, when, wren.

ence: abstinence, benevolence, cense, circumference, commence, concupiscence, condense, conference, confidence, consequence, continence, defence, dense, difference, diffidence, diligence, dispense, eloquence, eminence, evidence, excellence, expense, fence, frankincense, hence, immense, impenitence, impertinence, impotence, improvidence, impudence, incense, incontinence, indifference, indigence, indolence, inference, innocence, intelligence, intense, magnificence, munificence, negligence, offence, omnipotence, pence, penitence, preference, prepense, pretence, propense, providence, recompense, reference, residence, reverence, sense, suspense, thence, vehemence, violence, whence.

ench: bench, blench, clench, drench, intrench, quench, retrench, stench, trench, wench, wrench.

end: amend, apprehend, ascend, attend, befriend, bend, blend, commend, comprehend, condescend, contend, defend, depend, descend, discommend, distend, dividend, end, expend, extend, fend, forefend, friend, impend, lend, mend, misspend, offend, portend, pretend, recommend, rend, reprehend, reverend, send, spend, suspend, tend, transcend, unbend, vend.

enge: avenge, revenge.

ength: length, strength.

ens: lens, plural of nouns and third person singular present of verbs in **en.**

ent: absent, abstinent, accident, accomplishment, acknowledgment, admonishment, aliment, arbitrament, argument, ascent, assent, astonishment, attent, augment, banishment, battlement, bellipotent, benevolent, bent, blent, brent, cement, chastisement, circumvent, competent, complement, compliment, confident, consent, content, continent, corpulent, descent, detriment, different, diligent, discontent, disparagement, dissent, document, element, eloquent, embellishment, eminent, equivalent, establishment, event, evident, excellent, excrement, exigent, experiment, ferment, firmament, foment, fraudulent, government, hent, imminent, impenitent, impertinent, implement, impotent, imprisonment, improvident, impudent, incident, incompetent, incontinent, indent, indifferent, indigent, innocent, insolent, instrument, intelligent, intent, invent, irreverent, lament, languishment, lent, ligament, lineament, magnificent, malcontent, management, meant, medicament, misspent, monument, negligent, nourishment, nutriment, occident, o'erspent, omnipotent, opulent, ornament, ostent, outsent, penitent, pent, permanent, pertinent, precedent, present, president, prevalent, prevent, provident, punishment, ravishment, redolent, regiment, relent, rent, repent, represent, resent, resident, reverent, rudiment, sacrament, scent, sent, sediment, sentiment, settlement, shent, spent, subsequent, supplement, temperament, tenement, tent, testament, tournament, turbulent, unbent, underwent, vehement, vent, violent, virulent, went.

ep: demirep, nep, rep, skep, step.

ept: accept, adept, crept, except, intercept, kept, sept, slept, wept.

er and err: administer, ampitheater, arbiter, astrologer, astronomer, aver, bur, burr, canister, character, chorister, concur, confer, cottager, cur, defer, demur, deter, dowager, err, fir, flatterer, forager, foreigner, fur, gardener, grasshopper, harbinger, her, idolater, incur, infer, inter, interpreter, islander, lavender, lawgiver, loiterer, mariner, massacre, messenger, minister, murderer, myrrh, officer, passenger, philosopher, pillager, prefer, presbyter, prisoner, provender, purr, refer, register, sepulchre, sir, skirr, slanderer, slur, sophister, sorcerer, spur, stir, theater, thunderer, transfer, traveler, usurer, villager, voyager, wagoner, whir.

erm: affirm, chirm, confirm, firm, germ, infirm, term, turm, worm.

ern: burn, concern, dern, discern, earn, eterne, fern, hern, learn, quern, stern, turn, yearn.

erne: eterne. *See* **ern.**

erp: discerp. *See* **urp.**

erse: absterse, accurse, adverse, amerce, asperse, averse, coerce, converse, curse, disburse, disperse, hearse, imburse, immerse, intersperse, nurse, perverse, purse, reimburse, terse, universe, verse, worse.

ert: advert, assert, avert, blurt, concert, controvert, convert, desert, dirt, divert, exert, expert, flirt, hurt, insert, invert, pervert, shirt, spurt, squirt, subvert, wert.

erth: berth, birth, dearth, earth, girth, mirth, perth.

erve: conserve, curve, deserve, disserve, nerve, observe, preserve, reserve, serve, subserve, swerve.

es, ess, or **esse:** access, acquiesce, address, adultress, ambassadress, assess, bashfulness, bitterness, bless, caress, cess, cesse, cheerfulness, chess, childishness, comeliness, comfortless, compress, confess, depress, digress, diocess, dispossess, distress, dizziness, dress, drowsiness, drunkenness, duress, eagerness, easiness, emptiness, evenness, excess, express, fatherless, filthiness, foolishness, forgetfulness, forwardness, fruitfulness, fulsomeness, gentleness, giddiness, governess, greediness, guess, happiness, haughtiness, heaviness, heinousness, hoariness, holiness, hollowness, idleness, impress, lasciviousness, lawfulness, laziness, less, lioness, littleness, liveliness, loftiness, lowliness, manliness, masterless, mess, mightiness, motherless, motionless, nakedness, neediness, noisomeness, numberless, oppress, patroness, poetess, possess, press, profess, prophetess, ransomeless, readiness, recess, redress, repress, righteousness, shepherdess, sorceress, sordidness, spiritless, sprightliness, steadiness, stress, stubbornness, sturdiness, success, surliness, tenderness, thoughtfulness, transgress, ugliness, uneasiness, unhappiness, usefulness, votaress, wakefulness, wantonness, wariness, weaponless, weariness, wickedness, wilderness, willfulness, willingness, wretchedness, yes.

esh: afresh, flesh, fresh, mesh, refresh, thresh.

esk and **esque:** arabesque, burlesque, desk, grotesque, moresque, picturesque.

est: abreast, arrest, attest, bequest, best, breast, chest, contest, crest, detest, digest, divest, guest, infest, interest, invest, jest, lest, manifest, molest, nest, obtest, palimpsest, pest, protest, quest, request, rest, suggest, test, unrest, vest, west.

et and **ette:** abet, alphabet, amulet, anchoret, bassinet, beget, beset, bet, cabinet, cadet, coronet, debt, epaulette, epithet, forget, fret, get, jet, let, met, net, parapet, parroquet, piquette, regret, rivulet, rosette, set, silhouette, sweat, threat, violet, wagonette, wet, whet, yet.

etch: fetch, sketch, stretch, wretch.

eur: amateur, bon-viveur, connoisseur.

ew: accrue, adieu, anew, askew, avenue, bedew, blew, blue, brew, chew, clue, coo, crew, cue, dew, do, drew, due, endue, ensue, eschew, few, flew, glue, grew, hew, hue, imbrue, imbue, interview, Jew, knew, mew, new, ormolu, perdue, pooh, purlieu, pursue, renew, residue, retinue, revenue, review, screw, shoe, slew, stew, subdue, sue, threw, too, true, view, who, withdrew, woo, yew, you.

ex: annex, circumflex, complex, convex, perplex, sex, vex, and the plurals of nouns and third persons singular of verbs in **ec, eck.**

ib: bib, crib, drib, glib, nib, rib, squib.

ibe: ascribe, bribe, describe, diatribe, imbibe, inscribe, kibe, prescribe, proscribe, scribe, subscribe, superscribe, transcribe, tribe.

ice: advice, concise, device, dice, entice, ice, mice, nice, paradise, precise, price, rice, sacrifice, slice, spice, splice, thrice, trice, vice.

ick: arithmetic, brick, Catholic, chick, choleric, kick, lick, lunatic, nick, pick, politic, quick, rhetoric, sick, splenetic, stick, thick, trick.

ict: addict, afflict, contradict, convict, inflict, Pict, strict, the preterits and participles of verbs in **ick.**

id: bestrid, bid, chid, forbid, hid, katydid, kid, lid, pyramid, quid, rid, slid, squid.

ide: abide, aside, astride, beside, bestride, betide, bide, chide, confide, decide, deride, divide, glide, gride, guide, hide, misguide, nide, preside, pride, provide, ride, side, slide, stride, subside, tide, wide.

idge: abridge, bridge, fidge, midge, ridge.

ie or y: alibi, alkali, ally, amplify, apply, awry, beautify, bely, buy, by, certify, comply, crucify, cry, decry, defy, deify, deny, descry, die, dignify, dry, edify, espy, eye, falsify, fie, fly, fortify, fry, glorify, gratify, hie, high, imply, indemnify, justify, lie, magnify, modify, mollify, mortify, nigh, outfly, outvie, pacify, petrify, pie, ply, prophesy, pry, purify, putrify, qualify, ratify, rectify, rely, reply, rye, sanctify, satisfy, scarify, shy, sigh, signify, sky, sly, specify, spy, stupefy, sty, supply, terrify, testify, thigh, tie, try, untie, verify, vie, villify, vitrify, vivify, why.

ief: beef, belief, brief, chief, grief, leaf, reef, relief, sheaf.

iege: assiege, besiege, liege, siege.

ield: afield, field, shield, wield, yield, and the preterits and participles of verbs in **eal.**

iend: As in *fiend.* Rimes preterits and participles of verbs in **ean, een.** As in *friend.* Rimes **end.**

ierce: fierce, pierce, tierce.

ieve: as in *sieve. See* **ive.** As in *grieve. See* **eave.**

if, iff: cliff, hieroglyph, if, skiff, sniff, stiff, tiff, whiff.

ife: fife, knife, life, rife, strife, wife.

ift: adrift, drift, gift, lift, rift, shift, sift, thrift, and the preterits and participles of verbs in **iff.**

ig: big, dig, fig, gig, grig, jig, pig, prig, rig, sprig, swig, twig, Whig.

ike: alike, dike, dislike, glike, like, pike, shrike, spike, strike.

il, ill: bill, chill, codicil, daffodil, distill, drill, fill, fulfill, gill, hill, ill, instill, kill, mill, pill, quill, rill, shrill, skill, spill, still, swill, thrill, till, trill, will.

ilch: filch, milch.

ild: as in *child*. Rimes mild, wild, etc., the preterits and participles of verbs of one syllable in **ile,** or of more syllables, provided the accent be on the last.
As in *gild*. Rimes build, rebuild, etc., and the preterits and participles of verbs in **ill.**

ile: aisle, awhile, beguile, bile, chyle, compile, defile, exile, erewhile, file, guile, isle, mile, pile, reconcile, revile, smile, style, tile, vile, while.

ilk: bilk, milk, silk, whilk.

ilt: built, gilt, guilt, hilt, jilt, milt, quilt, spilt, stilt, tilt.

ilth: filth, spilth, tilth.

im: brim, dim, grim, him, hymn, limb, limn, prim, rim, skim, slim, trim, whim.

ime: chime, climb, clime, crime, grime, lime, mime, paradigm, prime, rime, slime, sublime, time.

imp: gimp, imp, jimp, limp, pimp.

in, inn: baldachin, begin, bin, cannikin, chin, din, discipline, fin, grin, in, inn, javelin, kin, limn, pin, shin, sin, skin, spin, thin, tin, twin, whin, win, within.

ince: convince, evince, mince, prince, quince, rinse, since, wince.

inch: clinch, finch, inch, pinch, winch.

inct: distinct, extinct, instinct, precinct, succinct, tinct, etc., and the preterits and participles of certain verbs in **ink,** as linked, pinked.

ind: as in *bind*. Behind, blind, find, grind, kind, mind, remind, rind, unkind, wind, etc., and the preterits and participles of verbs in **ine, ign,** etc.
As in *rescind*. Preterits and participles of verbs in **in.**

ine. as in *dine*. Assign, brine, chine, combine, concubine, condign, consign, countermine, decline, define, design, divine, enshrine, entwine, eyne, fine, incline, indign, interline, kine, line, mine, nine,

opine, pine, porcupine, recline, refine, repine, Rhine, shine, shrine, sign, superfine, supine, thine, trine, twine, undermine, vine, whine, wine.
As in *discipline*. *See* in.

ing: bring, cling, fling, ging, king, ring, sing, sling, spring, sting, string, swing, thing, wing, wring, etc., and the participles of the present tense in **ing**, with the accent on the antepenultimate, as *recovering*.

inge: cringe, fringe, hinge, singe, springe, swinge, tinge, twinge.

ink and inque: appropinque, bethink, blink, brink, chink, cinque, clink, drink, forethink, ink, link, pink, shrink, sink, skink, slink, stink, swink, think, wink, zinc.

int: asquint, dint, flint, hint, lint, mint, print, quint, sprint, squint.

inth: hyacinth, labyrinth, plinth.

inx: jinx, methinks, minx, sphinx, plural of nouns and third person singular present of verb in **ink**.

ip: chip, clip, dip, drip, eldership, equip, fellowship, hip, lip, nip, rip, rivalship, scrip, ship, sip, skip, slip, snip, strip, tip, trip, whip.

ipe: archetype, gripe, pipe, prototype, ripe, snipe, stripe, type, wipe.

ire: acquire, admire, aspire, attire, conspire, desire, dire, entire, expire, fire, gipsire, gire, hire, inquire, inspire, irc, lyre, mire, pyre, quire, require, retire, sire, spire, squire, tire, transpire, wire.

irk: burke, dirk, firk, kirk, murk, quirk, shirk, stirk, work.

is: pronounced like *iz*. His, is, whiz.

isc: disc, risk, whisk. *See* isk.

ise and ize: advise, agonize, authorize, canonize, chastise, civilize, comprise, criticize, despise, devise, disguise, enterprise, excise, exercise, guise, idolize, immortalize, premise, prize, revise, rise, sacrifice, signalize, size, solemnize, suffice, surmise, surprise, sympathize, tyrannize, wise.

ish: cuish, dish, fish, pish, squish, wish.

isk: basilisk, brisk, disc, frisk, risk, tamarisk, whisk.

ism: abysm, anachronism, cataclysm, chrism, criticism, egotism, heroism, organism, prism, schism, solecism, syllogism, witticism.

isp: crisp, lisp, wisp.

iss: abyss, amiss, bliss, Dis, dismiss, hiss, kiss, miss, remiss.

ist: alchemist, amethyst, anatomist, annalist, antagonist, assist, consist, desist, Eucharist, evangelist, exist, exorcist, fist, herbalist, humorist, insist, list, mist, oculist, organist, persist, resist, satirist, subsist, twist, wrist.

it: acquit, admit, benefit, bit, commit, emit, fit, flit, grit, hit, knit, omit, outwit, permit, perquisite, pit, quit, refit, remit, sit, split, submit, transmit, twit, wit, writ.

itch: bewich, ditch, enrich, fitch, flitch, itch, niche, pitch, rich, stitch, switch, twitch, which, witch.

ite and **ight:** accite, aconite, affright, alight, appetite, bedight, benight, bite, blight, blite, bright, cite, contrite, delight, despite, disunite, excite, expedite, fight, flight, foresight, fright, height, incite, indite, invite, kite, knight, light, might, mite, night, oversight, parasite, pight, plight, polite, proselyte, quite, recite, requite, reunite, right, rite, sight, slight, smite, spite, spright, tight, trite, unite, upright, unsight, white, wight, write.

ith: frith, pith, sith, smith.

ithe: blithe, hithe, lithe, scythe, tithe, writhe.

ive: as in *five*. Rimes alive, arrive, connive, contrive, deprive, derive, dive, drive, gyve, hive, revive, rive, shrive, survive, thrive.
As in *give*. Rimes, fugitive, live, positive, sensitive, sieve.

ix: affix, crucifix, fix, infix, intermix, mix, nix, prefix, transfix, etc., and the plurals of nouns and third persons singular of verbs in **ick**.

ixt: betwixt. Rimes the preterits and participles of verbs in **ix**.

o: adagio, ago, beau, below, bestow, bo, bow, calico, Co., crow, doe, dough, flow, foe, forego, foreknow, foreshow, fro', glow, go, grow, ho, hoe, know, lo, low, mistletoe, mo', mow, no, oh, outgrow, overflow, overthrow, owe, portico, roe, seraglio, sew, show, sloe, slow, snow, so, strow, tho', though, toe, undergo, woe.

oach: abroach, approach, broach, coach, encroach, loach, poach.

oaves: cloves, groves, loaves, roves, etc.

oax: coax, hoax, rime plurals of nouns and third persons singular present of verbs in **oke**.

ob: bob, cabob, cob, hob, knob, lob, mob, nob, rob, sob, squab, swab, throb.

obe: conglobe, globe, lobe, probe, robe.

ock: block, brock, clock, cock, crock, dock, epoch, flock, frock, hock, knock, loch, lock, mock, rock, shock, sock, stock.

od: clod, cod, God, hod, nod, odd, plod, pod, quod, rod, shod, sod, tod, trod.

ode: abode, a-la-mode, bode, code, commode, corrode, episode, explode, forebode, goad, incommode, load, mode, ode, road, rode, toad, and the preterits and participles of verbs in **ow, owe**.

odge: bodge, dodge, lodge, hodgepodge.

off: cough, doff, off, scoff.

oft: aloft, croft, oft, soft, and the preterits and participles of verbs in **off**.

og: agog, bog, catalog(ue), clog, cog, dialog(ue), dog, epilog(ue), fog, frog, Gog, hog, jog, log, pedagog(ue), pollywog, prog, quog, Quogue, shog, synagogue, tog.

oge: gamboge, rouge.

oice: choice, rejoice, voice.

oid: alkaloid, asteroid, avoid, devoid, varioloid, void, and the preterits and participles of verbs in **oy**.

oil: boil, coil, despoil, disembroil, embroil, moil, oil, recoil, soil, spoil, toil, turmoil.

oin: adjoin, coign, coin, conjoin, disjoin, enjoin, foin, groin, join, loin, proin, purloin, rejoin.

oint: anoint, appoint, aroint, counterpoint, disappoint, disjoint, joint, oint, point.

oir: as in *choir. See* **ire,** but the foreign sound, as in *devoir, reservoir,* is nearer **ar.**

oise: counterpoise, equipoise, noise, poise, etc., and the plurals of nouns and third persons singular present tense of verbs in **oy**.

oist: foist, hoist, moist, the preterits and participles of verbs in **oice**.

oit: adroit, doit, exploit, quoit, etc.

oke: bespoke, broke, choke, cloak, coke, equivoque, invoke, joke, moke, revoke, smoke, soak, spoke, stroke.

ol: alcohol, capitol, doll, extol, loll, Moll, Poll.

old: behold, bold, cold, enfold, foretold, gold, hold, manifold, marigold, mold, old, scold, sold, told, unfold, uphold, withhold, preterits and participles of verbs in **oll, owl, ole,** and **oal**.

ole: aureole, bole, bowl, cajole, coal, condole, console, control, dole, droll, entol, foal, girandole, goal, hole, jole, mole, parole, patrol, pistole, pole, poll, roll, scroll, shoal, sole, soul, stole, toll, troll, whole.

olt: bolt, colt, dolt, holt, jolt, molt, revolt, thunderbolt.

olve: absolve, convolve, devolve, dissolve, involve, resolve, solve.

ome: dome, foam, home, loam, mome, roam.

omp: pomp, romp, swamp.

on: as in *don*. Rimes anon, con, upon.
As in *won. See* **un.**

ond: abscond, beyond, blonde, bond, correspond, despond, diamond, pond, vagabond, and the preterits and participles of verbs in **on.**

one: as in *bone*. Alone, atone, blown, cone, dethrone, disown, drone, enthrone, flown, groan, grown, known, loan, lone, moan, overthrown, own, postpone, prone, shone, shown, sown, stone, throne, thrown, tone, zone.
As in *done. See* **un.**
As in *gone. See* **awn, on.**

ong: as in *long*. Along, belong, prolong, prong, song, strong, thong, throng, wrong.
As in *among. See* **ung.**

onse: sconce, ensconce, response.

ont: as in *font*. Rimes want. As in *front. See* **unt.** (The abbreviated negatives, *don't, won't,* rime together.)

ood: as in *brood. See* **ude.**
As in *wood*. Rimes brotherhood, could, good, hood, likelihood, livelihood, neighborhood, stood, understood, widowhood, withstood, would.
As in *blood. See* **ud.**

oof: aloof, behoof, disproof, hoof, proof, reproof, roof, woof.

ook: betook, book, brook, caoutchouc, cook, crook, forsook, hook, look, mistook, rook, shook, stook, took, undertook.

ool: befool, buhl, cool fool, pool, rule, school, spool, stool, tool.

oom: assume, bloom, boom, consume, doom, entomb, fume, gloom, groom, loom, perfume, plume, presume, resume, rheum, room, spoom, spume, tomb, whom, womb.

oop: coop, droop, dupe, group, hoop, loop, poop, scoop, soup, stoop troop, whoop.

oor: as in *boor*. Rimes amour, contour, paramour, pure, sure, tour. As in *door*. *See* **ore.**

oose: *see* **use.**

ooth: truth, uncouth, youth.

ooze: abuse, choose, lose, ooze, use, whose, the plurals of nouns and third persons singular present tense of verbs in **ew, ue.**

op: chop, crop, drop, fop, flop, hop, pop, prop, shop, slop, sop, stop, swop, top, underprop.

ope: antelope, aslope, cope, elope, grope, heliotrope, hope, horoscope, interlope, mope, ope, pope, rope, scope, slope, telescope, trope.

oque: *see* **oke.**

or: abhor, ambassador, ancestor, bachelor, competitor, conqueror, conspirator, counselor, creditor, emperor, for, governor, metaphor, or, progenitor, senator, etc.

orb: corb, orb, sorb.

orch: porch, scorch; torch.

ord and **orde:** as in *cord*. Rimes abhorr'd, aboard, accord, afford, board, ford, hoard, horde, lord, record, sword, and the preterits and participles of verbs in **oar, ore.**

ore: abhor, adore, afore, albicore, ashore, boar, bore, Bucentaur, core, corps, deplore, door, encore, explore, floor, forbore, forswore, four, gore, hellebore, heretofore, implore, lore, more, oar, o'er, ore, pore, restore, roar, score, senator, shore, snore, soar, sore, store, swore, sycamore, tore, wore.

orge: disgorge, forge, George, gorge, regorge.

ork: cork, fork, ork, pork, stork, York.

orm: as in *form*. Rimes chloroform, conform, deform, inform, misinform, multiform, perform, reform, storm, swarm, transform, uniform. As in *worm*. *See* **erm.**

orn: adorn, born, capricorn, corn, foreborne, forsworn, forewarn, forlorn, horn, lorn, lovelorn, morn, mourn, overborne, scorn, shorn, sworn, suborn, thorn, torn, unicorn, warn, worn.

orp: thorp, warp.

orse: coarse, corse, course, endorse, force, horse, morse, remorse, torse.

ort: consort, court, distort, exhort, extort, fort, mort, morte, port, quart, report, resort, retort, short, snort, sort, swart, thwart, wart.

ose: as in *jocose*. Rimes close, dose, engross, gross, morose, verbose.
As in *pose*. Arose, chose, close, compose, depose, disclose, discompose, dispose, dose, enclose, expose, foreclose, froze, glose, gloze, hose, impose, interpose, nose, oppose, propose, prose, recompose, repose, rose, suppose, those, transpose, etc., and the plurals of nouns and apostrophized preterits and participles of verbs in **ow, oe, o**.
As in *lose*. *See* **use**.

osh: bosh, swash, wash.

osque, osk: kiosk, mosque.

oss: albatross, across, boss, cross, doss, dross, emboss, loss, moss.

ost: as in *cost*. Rimes accost, frost, holocaust, lost, etc., and the preterits and participles of words in **oss**.
As in *ghost*. Rimes boast, coast, most, post, toast, and the old second person singular present of verbs in **ow**, as ow'st.

ot: allot, apricot, begot, blot, clot, complot, cot, counterplot, forgot, got, grot, hot, jot, knot, lot, melilot, not, plot, polyglot, pot, quat, rot, scot, shot, sot, spot, trot, what, yacht.

otch: blotch, botch, crotch, notch, Scotch, watch.

ote: afloat, anecdote, antidote, bloat, boat, coat, denote, devote, dote, float, gloat, goat, moat, mote, note, oat, overfloat, promote, quote, remote, rote, smote, throat, tote, vote, wrote.

oth: as in *broth*. Rimes cloth, froth, troth, wroth.
As in *both*. Rimes both, growth, loath, loth, oath, sloth.
As in *moth*. Rimes cloth.

ouc: *see* **ook**.

ouch: as in *couch*. Avouch, crouch, pouch, slouch, vouch.
As in *touch*. *See* **utch**.

ouche: buche, cartouche.

oud: aloud, cloud, crowd, loud, proud, etc., and the preterits and participles of verbs in **ow**.

ought: aught, besought, bethought, bought, brought, caught, forethought, fought, methought, naught, nought, ought, sought, taught, thought, wrought.

ould: cold, fold, mould, old, and the preterits and participles of verbs in **owl, oll**, and **ole**.

ounce: bounce, denounce, flounce, ounce, pounce, pronounce.

ound: as in *bound*. Abound, aground, around, compound, confound, expound, found, ground, hound, mound, pound, profound, propound, rebound, resound, round, sound, surround, wound, and the preterits and participles of verbs in **own**.

As in *wound*—the noun. Rimes preterits and participles of verbs in **oon, une**.

ount: account, amount, count, discount, fount, mount, remount.

our: as in *hour*. Rimes bow'r, deflow'r, devour, lour, our, scour, sour, tow'r, etc.

As in *pour*. See **ore**.

As in *tour*. See **ure**.

ourne: bourne, rimes **orn**.

ous: bowse, douse, house, mouse, rouse.

oust: Faust, joust.

out: about, bout, clout, devout, doubt, drought, gout, grout, misdoubt, out, pout, redoubt, rout, scout, shout, snout, spout, sprout, stout, throughout, tout, trout, without.

outh: mouth, south, drouth.

ove: as in *wove*. Alcove, behove, clove, drove, grove, hove, interwove, inwove, rove, stove, strove, throve.

As in *dove*. Above, glove, love, shove.

As in *move*. Approve, disapprove, disprove, groove, improve, prove, reprove.

ow: as in *now*. Allow, avow, bough, bow, brow, cow, disallow, endow, how, mow, plough, prow, slough, sow, trow, vow.

As in *blow*. See **o**.

owl: cowl, fowl, growl, howl, owl, prowl, scowl, etc.

own: as in *drown*. Adown, clown, crown, down, drown, embrown, frown, gown, noun, renown, town.

As in *thrown*. See **one**.

owze: blowze, browse, carouse, espouse, rouse, spouse, touse, the verbs to house, mouse, etc., and the plurals of nouns and third persons singular present tense of verbs in **ow**.

ox: box, equinox, fox, heterodox, orthodox, ox, the plurals of nouns and third persons singular present tense of verbs in **ock**.

oy: alloy, annoy, boy, buoy, cloy, convoy, coy, decoy, destroy, enjoy, employ, joy, toy.

ub: chub, club, cub, drub, dub, grub, hub, rub, shrub, snub.

ube: cube, tube.

uce: abstruse, abuse, conduce, deduce, deuce, disuse, excuse, induce, introduce, juice, misuse, obtuse, produce, profuse, puce, recluse, reduce, seduce, sluice, spruce, traduce, truce, use.

uck: buck, duck, luck, pluck, struck, suck, truck, tuck.

uct: aqueduct, conduct, deduct, instruct, obstruct; the preterits and participles of verbs in **uck**.

ud: blood, bud, cud, flood, mud, scud, stud.

ude: allude, altitude, aptitude, brood, conclude, crude, delude, elude, exclude, exude, feud, food, fortitude, gratitude, habitude, illude, inaptitude, include, ingratitude, interlude, intrude, lassitude, latitude, lewd, longitude, magnitude, mood, multitude, obtrude, plenitude, promptitude, prude, rood, rude, seclude, servitude, similitude, snood, solitude, vicissitude.

udge: adjudge, budge, drudge, fudge, grudge, ludge, nudge, prejudge, sludge, smudge, trudge.

uff: bluff, buff, chough, chuff, counterbuff, cuff, enough, gruff, huff, luff, puff, rebuff, rough, ruff, slough (cast skin), snuff, stuff.

uft: tuft, rimes the preterits and participles of verbs in **uff**.

ug: bug, drug, dug, hug, jug, lug, mug, pug, rug, shrug, slug, smug, snug.

uke: chibouque, duke, fluke, puke, rebuke.

ul and **ull**: as in *cull*. Rimes annul, dull, gull, hull, lull, mull, null, skull, trull.
As in *full*. Rimes bountiful, bull, dutiful, fanciful, merciful, pull, sorrowful, wonderful, wool, worshipful.

ulch: gulch, mulch.

ule: buhl, fool, misrule, mule, pule, overrule, ridicule, rule. tool.

ulge: bulge, divulge, indulge, etc.

ulk: bulk, hulk, skulk, sulk.

ulp: ensculp, gulp, pulp, sculp.

ulse: convulse, expulse, impulse, pulse, repulse.

ult: adult, catapult, consult, difficult, exult, insult, occult, result. etc.

um: become, burdensome, chum, come, crum, crumb, cumbersome, drum, dumb, encomium, frolicsome, glum, gum, hum, humorsome, mum, opium, overcome, plum, quarrelsome, scum, succumb, sum, swum, thrum, thumb, troublesome.

ump: bump, clump, jump, lump, plump, pump, rump, stump, thump, trump.

un: begun, bun, done, dun, gun, none, nun, one, pun, run, shun, son, spun, stun, sun, ton, tun, undone, won.

unce: dunce, once.

unch: bunch, crunch, hunch, lunch, munch, punch, scrunch.

unct: defunct, disjunct, rimes preterits and participles of verbs in **unk.**

une: boon, buffoon, cocoon, coon, croon, dragoon, dune, hewn, jejune, June, lampoon, moon, noon, poltroon, prune, raccoon, shalloon, soon, spoon, swoon, triune, tune, untune.

ung: among, bung, clung, dung, flung, hung, rung, slung, sprung, strung, stung, sung, swung, tongue, unsung, wrung, young.

unge: expunge, plunge, sponge.

unk: bunk, chunk, drunk, funk, hunk, monk, punk, shrunk, slunk, stunk, sunk, trunk.

unt: blunt, brunt, front, grunt, hunt, runt, etc.

up: cup, dup, pup, sup, up.

upt: abrupt, corrupt, interrupt, the participles and preterits of verbs in **up,** etc.

urb: curb, disturb, herb, verb.

urch: birch, church, lurch, perch, search, smirch.

urd: absurd, bird, curd, gird, heard, herd, sherd, word, and the preterits and participles of verbs in **er, ur,** and **ir.**

ure: abjure, adjure, allure, amour, assure, calenture, conjure, contour, coverture, cure, demure, dure, endure, epicure, forfeiture, furniture, immature, immure, insure, inure, investiture, lure, manure, mature, miniature, moor, nouriture, obscure, overture, poor, portraiture, primogeniture, pure, secure, sure, temperature, your.

urf: scurf, serf, surf, turf.

urge: diverge, gurge, purge, scourge, surge, thaumaturge, urge, verge.

urk: irk, jerk, lurk, murk, perk, quirk, Turk, work.

url: churl, curl, earl, furl, girl, hurl, pearl, purl, twirl, uncurl, unfurl, whirl.

urn: adjourn, burn, churn, discern, earn, overturn, rejourn, return, sojourn, spurn, tern, turn, urn.

urp: chirp, discerp, extirp, usurp.

urst: accurst, burst, curst, durst, first, thirst, versed, worst.

us or **uss:** adulterous, adventurous, ambiguous, amorous, arquebus, blasphemous, boisterous, buss, calamitous, clamorous, credulous, cuss, dangerous, discuss, dolorous, emulous, fabulous, fortuitous, frivolous, generous, gluttonous, gratuitous, hazardous, incredulous, incubus, idolatrous, infamous, lecherous, libidinous, magnanimous, miraculous, mischievous, mountainous, mutinous, necessitous, numerous, obstreperous, odoriferous, ominous, overplus, perilous, poisonous, ponderous, populous, prosperous, pus, ravenous, ridiculous, rigorous, riotous, ruinous, scandalous, scrupulous, sedulous, slanderous, solicitus, thus, timorous, traitorous, treacherous, truss, tyrannous, unanimous, ungenerous, us, valorous, venomous, vigorous, villainous.

use: as in the noun *use*. Rimes abuse, deuce, disuse, goose, juice, loose, moose, noose, sluice, truce.
As in *muse*. Rimes the verbs abuse, accuse, amuse, bruise, choose, diffuse, excuse, infuse, lose, misuse, peruse, refuse, shoes, suffuse, transfuse, use, and the plurals of nouns and third persons singular of verbs in **ew** and **ue**, etc.

ush: as in *blush*. Rimes brush, crush, flush, gush, hush, lush, rush, tush. As in *bush*. Rimes push.

usk: busk, dusk, husk, musk, tusk.

ust: adjust, bust, crust, disgust, distrust, dust, intrust, just, lust, mistrust, must, rust, thrust, trust, unjust, the preterits and participles of verbs in **us, uss,** etc.

ut or **utt:** abut, but, butt, cut, englut, glut, gut, hut, jut, nut, rut, scut, shut, slut, smut, strut.

utch: crutch, Dutch, hutch, much, touch.

ute: absolute, acute, attribute, boot, bruit, brute, compute, confute, constitute, contribute, coot, depute, destitute, dilute, dispute, dissolute, execute, fruit, glute, hoot, impute, institute, lute, minute, mute, persecute, pollute, prosecute, recruit, refute, resolute, salute, shoot, substitute, toot.

ux: crux, dux, flux, lux, reflux. The plurals of nouns and third persons singular of verbs in **uck.**

BOOK EIGHTEEN

The History of the English Language—From Anglo-Saxon to Anglo-American

English, Then and Now

Faether ure, thu the eart on heofenum
Father our, thou that art in heavens

Si thin nama gehalgod
Be thy name hallowed

To becume thin rice
Arrive   thy kingdom

Geweorthe thin willa on eorthan swa swa on heofenum
Be-done   thy will on earth   so-as   in heavens

Ure daeghwamlican hlaf syle us to daeg
Our daily   loaf give us to day

And forgyf us ure gyltas, swa swa we forgifath urum gyltendum
And forgive us our debts, so   as we forgive   our   debtors

And ne gelaede thu us on   costnunge, ac alys us of yfle
And not lead   thou us into temptation, but lose us of evil

Sothlice
Soothly (Amen).[1]

Were it not for the literal translation in italics, you might not have been able immediately to identify the prayer above

---

[1] Old English had a separate letter, called *thorn,* used for either of the two sounds of Modern English *th* (*th*in, *th*en). Throughout, we have employed modern characters in place of the old.

as being the Lord's Prayer; but certainly you would have realized that it was in a language which, if not English, was strangely like English. The language *is* English—Old English. How our Modern English developed from it makes a story not less interesting than instructive.

The Invasion

The story begins in the middle of the fifth century A.D. Hengist and Horsa, two Jutish chiefs, and their followers came over to Britain in 449 A.D. from their homes in northern Germany. They had been invited by the Romans who, having kept the native Celtic inhabitants of Britain in subjugation for about four centuries, were in serious trouble. Rome had been invaded by the "barbarians from the north," and to defend herself had to recall legion after legion from Britain. The Celts had never accepted Roman rule, and now saw their opportunity. They swarmed from the mountains to which they had been driven and attacked the Romans of the cities (who, having always had the imperial legions to do their fighting, were inexpert in the business of war).

Hengist and Horsa at first fought the Celts with a will. But when they saw how helpless the Romans were, how desirable the land was, they shifted their objectives. They called upon their Germanic kinsmen of the mainland, and proceeded to fight both Roman and Celt. Before long, they were masters of the country.

The Celtic Influence

The three tribes which conquered Britain were the Angles, Saxons, and Jutes. The Jutes apparently settled in Kent and the Isle of Wight, but they have been almost entirely lost to history. The Angles occupied the north and east of the country, the Saxons the south and west. The country came to be called *England* ("land of the Angles") and the language *English* ("tongue of the Angles").

English spread through the land. The Highlands of Scotland, however, retained their Celtic speech, Gaelic. Wales, too, held fast to its native tongue, Welsh, which is akin to Gaelic.

Their conquerors did not learn many words from the Celts. Only a meager handful could be added to this list of Celtic loan-words:[1] *bannock, brock* (badger), *clout, cradle, crock, down* (hill), *dun, slough, cumb* (valley), *torr* (hill). (Most of these words are descriptive of terrain to which the Germanic tribesmen were strangers.) Place-names formed a larger group. *Thames, Wye,* and *Avon* are Celtic river-names, and the Celtic word for river or water appears, slightly altered, in *Usk, Ux, Axe, Exe,* and *Esk.* The first syllable of *Winchester, Manchester, Gloucester, Exeter,* and *Salisbury* are Celtic loans; and so are some city-names: *York, London, Kent.* Most of these words are of popular origin: they came into English as the result of daily contact between Celt and Anglo-Saxon. A few others were introduced by the Irish missionaries. (The Anglo-Saxons had not adopted Christianity and the Celts had.) Among the words missionaries taught the Anglo-Saxons were *ancor* (hermit), *cross, clugge* (bill), *mind* (diadem), *dry* (magician).

The Latin Influence

The Celts, then, did not directly affect the language the Anglo-Saxons had brought with them to any significant degree. However, the Britons had been under Roman domination for about four centuries, and Celtic was intimately tinctured with Latin. How extensive were the Anglo-Saxon borrowings from Latin through Celtic? The answer is partly clouded by doubt, since several million Germans lived within the Roman empire and undoubtedly had picked up a good many Latin words on the Continent before they came over to Britain. The following, though, is probably an authentic list of their borrowings from Latin through Celtic:—

Caester, Chester: AS. *caester,* Latin *caestrum* (camp or fortified place); seen in such place-names as *Chester,* Glou*cester,* Ex*eter* (for Ex*cester*), Don*caster.*

[1]Loan-words, as the name would indicate, are **words** English has borrowed from foreign languages.

Coln: Lat. *colonia* (military settlement); seen in such place-names as Lin*coln*, *Colne*, *Col*chester.

Port: AS. *port*, Lat. *portus* (harbor); seen in such place-names as *Por*chester, *Ports*mouth, Daven*port*.

Wick, wich: AS. *wic*, Latin *vicus* (a town or village); seen in such place-names as *Wick*ham, *Wig*ton.

Pool: AS. *pol*, Welsh *pwll*, Lat. *padulis* (a marsh): Hartle*pool*, Liver*pool*.

Perhaps, as Baugh says, words like *street* (Lat. *strata via*), wall (Lat. *vallum*), wine (Lat. *vinum*), etc., which had been acquired by the Germanic tribes in their homeland, survived in English because of the reinforcing presence of the same words in Celtic.

The two principal occupations of the Teutons—war and trade—account for many of the words of Latin origin that they brought with them. *Camp* (battle), *sen* (banner), *mil* (mile), *milestre* (courtesan) belong to the first class; *mangian* (to trade), *mynltere* (money-changer), *pund* (pound), *ceap* (bargain), *mynet* (coin) belong to the second.

From A.D. 597, when St. Augustine and forty monks landed in Kent to convert the heathen to Christianity, to 1066 A.D., the time of the Norman conquest, a variety of additional Latin words were introduced. Most of the following terms, it is probable, came into English between the seventh and eleventh centuries.

(1) Church terms of Latin origin: *altar, candle, chalice, cowl, creed, cup, disciple, font, mass, nun, shrine, shrive*, etc.

(2) Church terms of Greek or Hebrew origin borrowed through Latin: *alms, angel, anthem, amen, apostle, bishop, canon, Christ, church, clerk, deacon, devil, martyr, minister, monk, pope, priest, psalm, school, stole*, etc.

(3) Trade words and words for articles of commerce and agriculture: *beet, box, cheese, fan, fork, kettle, linen, mat, mulberry, pease, pear, penny, poppy, pound, sock, spend, ton*, etc.

(4) Miscellaneous: *ass, belt, castle, chalk, coulter, fever, fiddle, fennel, hemp, kitchen, lake, mill, noon, pillow, shambles, sickle, sole, tile, tunic, verse, dish*, etc.

The Northumbrian Kingdom

Though Kent received the Gospel first, Northumbria became chief of the Christian nations in England. "It is evident," one historian comments, "that there was great and substantial progress in religion, civilization, and learning; of which fact the permanent memorial is the name and words of Baeda, who died in 735." Northumbria was an Anglian nation, and the admiration she excited in her neighbors caused them to emulate her example, to read her books, to form their language after hers, and to call it *Englisc*. The peoples of the southern and western and south-eastern parts of the kingdom continually called themselves *Saxons* (witness such local names as *Wessex, Essex, Sussex, Middlesex*), yet almost invariably they called their language *Englisc*.

The Invasion of the Northmen

The Northumbrian culture was soon nearly obliterated by successive invasions from the North. The invasions of the Northmen fall into three periods. At first, their goal was immediate—they wanted simply to plunder; later, they developed larger ambitions—they wanted to set up local dynasties; finally, their purpose was comprehensive—they wanted to place a Danish king on the throne of England. For a long while, through the heroism of Alfred and his successors, they were thwarted in the last purpose. In the end, however, they were successful in that too: in the year 1017, the Danish king Cnut became King of England.

The effect on English of the Danish conquest was not so great as might be supposed. Of course, hundreds of Danish words came into English, but the structure of English was not fundamentally disturbed. "The Danes," Prof. Krapp comments, "accepted the Anglo-Saxon language, which indeed closely resembled their own. It is for this reason that the language of the country did not become Danish . . ." The following is a partial list of English words that have come in through Danish agency:

ale, anger, call, cast, cow, dwell, egg (*verb*), fellow, flat, gain, gust, hansel, hap, hit, husband, hustings, ill, irk, kid, law, meek, odd, plough, quandary, ransack, score, scrap, scrape, shallow, skill[1], skin, sky, slouch, swain, take, thrall, thrift, tiding, ugly, want, windlass, window[2].

Alfred and Anglo-Saxon

Because the Danish invaders gave Northumbrian culture such a definitive set-back, the cultural leadership passed on to Wessex and its great king, Alfred. It is the language of Wessex to which we really refer when we say "the Anglo-Saxon language." Actually Anglo-Saxon is only one of three Old English dialects. But of the other two, Northumbrian (the Anglian or northern dialect—that spoken "north of the Humber") and Mercian (the dialect spoken between the Humber and the Thames) little literary record remains: both Northumbria and Mercia fell into the barbaric hands of the Danes. Wessex, the dialect imported by Saxon tribes and spoken south of the Thames, owed its importance to three causes:

1. The unification of England under the Saxon kings, whose capital, Winchester, was in the kingdom of Wessex.
2. The preservation of a large part of Wessex literature.
3. The influence and example of Alfred, who wrote in the Wessex dialect and who supervised the translation of many works into the vernacular.

The Characteristics of Anglo-Saxon

If we look at a page of Modern English, we see not only nouns, verbs, adjectives, and adverbs, but also particles—little words that interpret the relations existing among the greater words. These are the pronouns, articles, prepositions, and conjunctions. In Old English the particles were generally absent. The relations were indicated not so much by means of small secondary and auxiliary words as by changes made in the main words themselves. For Anglo-Saxon was, to a far greater extent than Modern English, an inflected language: Anglo-Saxon expressed by modifications of form what Modern English expresses mostly by arrangement of

[1] *Sk* at the beginning of a word is indicative of Scandanavian origin.

[2] The list does not include the Danish suffix for forming patronymics: *son,* as in *Anderson, Ericson, Robertson.* (The Anglo-Saxon suffix is *ing* as in Harding, Manning.) Nor does it include any of the more than 1400 Scandinavian place-names that have been counted.

words. In the following passage of Anglo-Saxon, the inflectional endings are italicized.

Upahafen*um* eag*um* on the heahnys*se* and athend*um* earm*um* ongan gebidd*an* mid thaera weler*a* styrung*um* on stilnes*se*

The translation below italicizes those words which are contained in the inflectional endings:

With uplifted eyes to the heights and *with* outstretched arms *she* began *to* pray with stirrings *of* the lips in stillness.

Note that prepositions exist side by side with inflectional endings in the Anglo-Saxon (*on the heahnysse,* to the heights). The inflections are no longer completely self-sufficient in Anglo-Saxon; and as time goes on, as more particles are added, there will be a general shedding of inflections. Some will remain, but they will be grammatical vestiges.

The Norman Conquest and the Beginning of Middle English

The Danish rule endured from 1016 A.D. to 1042 A.D. Then the Saxon Dynasty was restored: Edward the Confessor came to the English throne and reigned over a united England until 1066. At his death in 1066, Harold, who was not in the direct line of succession, was chosen and crowned. His right to the throne was opposed by William, the sixth Duke of Normandy, first cousin of Edward the Confessor. William had the force to implement his claim to the throne. At the battle of Hastings (1066), the power of Harold was broken and William became master of England.

Who were the Normans? The word Norman—a modified form of *Northmen*—itself supplies part of the answer. They were kinsfolk of those Scandinavian raiders and conquerors who had overrun Northumbria several centuries back. Their depredations had extended to the French coast. But having conquered, they had not (as had the Danes) blotted out a superior culture. Instead they had adopted the ways of the native Franks, had intermarried with them, and had accepted their language and religion. "The name of Norman," one historian writes, "still clings to the new home; but all else that was Norse disappeared . . ."

The Norman conquest of England produced two great results. First, it brought to an insular nation a new and larger, a continental culture. Second, it forced on England "the national idea," a concept against which the Saxons had long struggled. However, the influx to English of French words is not to be dated from this time. Not till after 1300 A.D. did any considerable number of French words come into English—and then they came from Central or Parisian French rather than from the Norman dialect.

The reasons for this surprising lack of influence are to be sought in the social set-up following the Conquest. The Normans who came over were, quite definitely, upper-crust: royalty, nobility, clergy, and army:

There was [Shaw says] no mass of common people whose station would compel them to mingle with the despised Saxons. The Royal family used the Norman speech, and continued to exert every influence in its behavior until the close of the fourteenth century. There was no attempt on the part of the king to understand the language of the subjects; the nobles, under the system of feudalism, needed not to talk with those whom they oppressed; the churchmen were satisfied with their ecclesiastical benefices without understanding the confessions of humble worshippers; and the military forces, trained to consider themselves as men placed on guard against these discontented and dangerous Englishmen, did not seek companionship with them. The circumstances were unfavorable to grand changes in the form and structure of the English language. The mutual repulsion of the two races continued for a century; then followed a century of seeming indifference; but in the third century after the Conquest the people were united in their common interest in the foreign wars of England.

The subjugated English were not killed off, nor were they driven from their country. But they were relegated to the status of an "inferior people"—good swineherds and servants—if occasionally surly in either capacity—but obviously unfit associates for gentlemen. Norman French became the only polite speech. The native tongue, despised not only because it was unknown, but also because it was the language of a subject people, was left to the use of boors and serfs. In *Ivanhoe,* Walter Scott graphically points up the class relations of Norman French and Anglo-Saxon. The dialog that follows is carried on by Gurth, a Saxon swineherd, and Wamba, a jester.

"Why, how call you those grunting brutes running about on their four legs?" demanded Wamba.

"Swine, fool, swine," said the herd; "every fool knows that."

"And swine is good Saxon," said the jester; "but how call you the sow when she is flayed and drawn and quartered, and hung up by the heels like a traitor?"

"Pork," answered the swineherd.

"I am very glad every fool knows that, too," said Wamba, "and pork, I think, is good Norman-French; and so when the brute lives, and is in charge of a Saxon slave, she goes by her Saxon name; but becomes a Norman, and is called pork, when she is carried to the castle hall to feast among the nobles; what doest thou think of this, friend Gurth, ha?"

"It is but too true doctrine, friend Wamba, however it got into a fool's pate!"

"Now I can tell you more," said Wamba, in the same tone; "there is old Alderman Ox continues to hold his Saxon epithet while he is under the charge of serfs and bondsmen, such as thou, but becomes Beef, a fiery French gallant, when he arrives before the worshipful jaws that are destined to consume him. Mynheer Calf, too, becomes Monsieur de Veau in the like manner; he is Saxon when he requires tendance, and takes a Norman name when he becomes matter of enjoyment."

The Triumph of Midland

Norman French was a class language, never the speech of England. "The low man," as a contemporary put it, "holden to English and their own speech still." However, the language of the "low men" decayed as a literary language. The three main dialects of England were still Northumbrian, Wessex, and Mercian; but for the period under discussion they are better termed **Northern, Southern,** and **Midland.** All were "standard": each writer (there were not many) chose the dialect of his section.

The three dialects exhibited a number of differences. Northern held most firmly to the old sounds: for example, it stuck to the old guttural *k* and *g* (as in *kirk* and *brig*), which in Southern became *ch* and *j* (as in *church* and *bridge*). Southern was characterized by its refusal to part with the old inflections. The Midland followed the South in discarding some of the earlier consonantal sounds, and the North in discarding the earlier inflections.

Midland is the chief ancestor of Modern English—not Southern (the Wessex of Alfred the Great) or Northern (the Northumbrian of Bede). Why did Midland triumph? There are a variety of cogent reasons. For one, the Midland area included London—marked by nature to be England's capital.[1] Again, two great writers, Wyclif and Chaucer,[2] arose who both employed the Midland dialect. Third, Midland was an intermediate dialect, as its name implies, and intelligible to Northerners and Southerners alike, whereas these could often not understand each other. "The Mercians," writes Trevisa in 1387, "who are men of the middle of England, being as it were partners with the extremities, better understand the side-languages, Northern and Southern, than Northern and Southern understand each other." Finally, when Caxton in 1477 introduced the printing press to England, the triumph of Midland was underwritten; for the printers patronized the Mercian or Midland dialect, and any Englishman who wanted to be published wrote in that dialect.

The Periods of English

The history of English has been divided into periods. Of course the periods overlap, and any one is only approximate. Still, if the fact is kept in mind that changes in language are never periodic and abrupt, but always continuous and gradual, the divisions will be found convenient for reference:

1. Old English: from A.D. 450 to about 1200
2. Middle English: from A.D. 1200 to about 1500
3. Modern English: from A.D. 1500 to the present.

Prof. Sweet has called Old English the period of *full endings;* Middle English, the period of *leveled endings;*

---

[1]"It is a curious reflection," Prof. Skeat says, "that if London had been built on the south side of the river, the speech of the British Empire and of the greater part of North America would probably have been very different from what it is."

[2]Chaucer, as Prof. Kittredge cautions, did not create Modern English. "None the less, he was a powerful agent in setting the language."

and Modern English, the period of *lost endings. Leveled endings* means that the final vowels, *a, o, u,* are changed or leveled to *e. Lost endings* means that only a few have remained, and these few have for most part become nonsyllabic.

OLD	MIDDLE	MODERN
leorn-*ian*	lern-*en*	learn
mon-*a*	mone-*e*	moon
stan-*as*	ston-*es*	stones
sun-*ne*	sun-*ne*	sun
sun-*u*	sun-*e*	son

Middle English

The periods of Middle English have been further subdivided:

Early: 1200 A.D. to 1300 A.D.
Late : 1300 A.D. to 1400 A.D.
Transitional (to Modern English) : 1400 A.D. to 1500 A.D.

Perhaps three brief selections—one from each of the centuries indicated above—will best show how English altered during the middle period and became more and more like the English we use today. In the selections that follow, note especially the progressive decay of inflectional endings:

1. From "Genesis and Exodus" (Early)

The chapmen skinden here fare,

in to Egipte ledden that ware;
with Putifar the kinges stiward,
he maden swithe bigetel forward;
so michel fe thor is hem told;

he hauen him bogt, he hauen sold.

The chapmen hastened their departure,
into Egypt led that chattel;
with Potiphar the king's steward,
they made very profitable bargain;
so much money there is them told;

these have him bought, and those have sold.

2. From Chaucer, *Troilus and Criseyde* (Late)

And for there is so gret diversite
In Englissh, and in writyng of oure tonge,
So prey I god that non myswrite the,
Ne the mys-metre for defaute of tonge

3. From Caxton, "Prologue" to his translation of Virgil's *Encydos* (Transitional)

I doubted that it sholde not please some gentylmen whiche late blamed me sayeing, y in my translacyons I had ouer cyryous termes, whiche coud not be understande of comyn peple, and desired me to vse olde and homele termes in my translacyons. And fayn wolde I satysfy, every man; and so to doo, toke an olde boke and redde therim; and certaynly the englysshe was so rude and brood that I coude not wele vnderstande it. And certaynly it was wreton in suche wyse that it was more lyke to dutche than englysshe; I coulde not reduce ne brynge it to be vnderstonde.

It is apparent that the quotation from Chaucer needs no translation. And with Caxton's complaint, we are on the threshold of Modern English.

French Influence on English Vocabulary

When, a few generations after the Conquest, English began to be again employed for general literature in place of French, most of the terms to express ideas other than those in connection with daily living had to be borrowed from French. Professor Jesperson has chartered these borrowings. The first hundred years after the Conquest saw little increase in the adoption of French words. After that the borrowing process was accelerated, and from 1250 A.D. to 1700 A.D. it was in full force. From 1400 A.D. on, borrowings decreased in number and extent, until today they are hardly more than casual.

The following is a severely abridged list of the words that came into English during the middle period. Note that most —though by no means all—are learned rather than popular words.

Government and Law: *people, parliament, crown, reign, tax, allegiance, noble, peer, prince, state, governor, warden, homage, manor, servant, bar, judgment, verdict, blame, arrest.*

Religion: *religion, sermon, baptism, hermit, friar, lesson, penance, prayer, clerk, crucifix, Bible, convent, creator, virgin, mercy, pity.*

War: *aid, banner, captain, arms, trumpet, army, navy, peace, war, battle, combat, brandish, besiege, defend.*

Society: *fashion, dress, lace, button, adorn, recreation, dance, carve, music, chess, melody, leisure.*

Cookery: *beef, veal, pork, mutton, pullet, repast, feast, pottage, salad, spice, stew, fry, grate, mince.*

Learning: *art, sculpture, music, beauty, literature, prose, rime, romance, story, tragedy, physician, surgeon, malady, gout.*

Modern English

As nearly as limits may be placed, Modern English dates from Caxton and the establishment of printing in England. Though the language has certainly changed, the changes have been neither so profound nor so wide since Caxton as before.

Modern English is usually subdivided into three periods:

1. Tudor, from about 1500 to 1625 (when James I died). The Authorized Version of the Bible, which appeared in 1611, acted as a tremendous stabilizing influence.

2. From 1625 to 1700. The Renaissance brought a new influx of classical and, later, French words, many of them never assimilated. *Its* as the possessive of *it* was established during this period.

3. From 1700 to the present. The first two periods, as Prof. Sweet declares, are "periods of experimentation and comparative license, both in the importation of new words and in the formation of idioms and grammatical constructions." The period from 1700, on the other hand, "is marked by selection and organization." Perhaps the most marked characteristic of the period is the ascendancy of the Midland dialect and the decay of all others. Samuel Johnson's *Dictionary of the English Language* (1775) was a powerful force in fixing the language.

Borrowings of Modern English

1. Greek:

Greek borrowings have been continuous from the fifth century to the present, but up to the Revival of Greek learning (about A.D. 1540) they entered the language at second or third hand. Since, Greek words have been freely borrowed to supply deficiencies in English: when new words are required for new facts, Greek has frequently supplied them.

(a) **Greek borrowings through French, having first passed through Latin:**—*blame, frenzy, ink, place, slander, surgeon, palsy, dropsy.*

(b) **Greek borrowings direct:**—*analysis, monopolist, telephone, telegraph, anthology, zoology, epidemic, epilepsy, epicure, utopia, anesthetic, cosmetic, psychology.*

2. Italian:

The Renaissance, or Revival of Learning, which originated in Italy, led to a study of Italian literature. Dante, Tasso, Ariosto, and Petrarch were all translated into English. The poems of Surrey, Wyatt, Spenser, and Milton all show an intimate acquaintance with Italian. In the reigns of the Tudors Italian was as necessary to every courtier as French was in the time of Charles II. The tide receded with the establishment of the Commonwealth, and was entirely thrown back by the overwhelming taste for French that set in with the accession of Charles II. But the borrowings were rather numerous, while the fashion lasted.

(a) **Direct from Italian:**—*balcony* (It. *balcone,* a stage); *bandit* (It. *bandito,* outlawed); *canto; comply* (It. *complire,* Lat. *complere); contraband* (Lat. *contra,* against, *bannum,* a decree); *ditto* (a thing already said, from Lat. *dictum,* said); *duel; duet; monkey* (It. *monicchio); gusto* (Lat. *gustus,* taste); *fresco* (of the same root as *fresh); milliner* (a dealer in *Milan* goods); *isolate* (It. *isolato,* detached); *imbroglio; grotto; portico; quota; rebuff,* etc.

NOTE.—We are indebted to Italian for many of our terms in music, poetry, and painting:—

MUSIC:—*concert, sonata, spinet, fugue, breve, duet, contralto, opera, piano, prima donna, quartet, quintet, solo, soprano, trio, canzonet, tremolo, falsetto,* etc.

POETRY:—*canto, sonnet, stanza, improvise, ottava rima.*

PAINTING:—*miniature, profile, vista, model, palette, pastel, mezzotint, amber,* etc.

(b) **Through French:**—*alert* (It. *all'erta,* on the watch); *arcade, artisan; bankrupt* (It. *banco, rotto,* afterwards changed to Lat. *rupta); brusque* (It. *brusco); bust* (It. *busto); caprice* (It. *capriccio,* a whim); *canteen* (It. *cantina,* a cellar); *cartoon* (It. *cartone,* Lat. *charta); cavalcade* (It. *cavalcata,* a troop of horsemen); *cascade* (It. *cascata,* a waterfall); etc.

3. Spanish:

Our borrowings from Spain were not due to a study of Spanish literature, but to our commercial and political relations with Spain, and to the descriptions of the country and her colonies furnished by English travelers. Spanish borrowings are almost as numerous as Italian. The *al* prefixed to some Spanish nouns is the Arabic article, *al.*

(a) **Direct from Spanish:**—*alligator* (*al ligarto,* a lizard); *armada* (armed fleet); *booby* (*bobo,* a blockhead); *buffalo; canoe* (West Indian); *cargo; cigar; armadillo* ("the little armed one," an animal); *cork* (*corcho,* Lat. *corticem,* bark); *domino; don; filibuster* (Sp. *filibuster;* corruption of Dutch *vrijbuiter,* Eng. *freebooter*); *peccadillo* (dim. of *pecado,* a sin); etc.

(b) **Through French:**—*bizarre; calenture; cask* (Fr. *casque,* It. *casco*); *castanets* (of the same root as *chestnut*); *escalade, garble, parade* (*prada,* a show); *risk* (*risco,* a steep rock), etc.

4. Portuguese:

Albatross, albino, apricot, caste, corvette (small frigate), *firm* (mercantile, association), *lingo* (language), *marmalade, molasses, parasol, tank* (*cf.* Lat. *stagnum,* a pool of standing water), *fetish* (Lat. *factitius,* artificial).

5. German (High German):

Landau (a kind of carriage), *meerschaum, mesmerize, plunder, poodle, swindler, waltz, zinc, carouse* (through Fr. *carous,* Ger. *gar-aus,* lit. "quite out," "a bumper drunk right off"), *kindergarten, noodle, pretzel, sauerkraut.*

6. Dutch:

Deck, freebooter, hoist, hold, hull, yacht, boom, cope, dollar, guilder, hogshead, boor, burgomaster, frolic, fumble, loiter, landscape, ruffle, sniff, slope, easel, landscape, kraal, trek.

7. Russian or Slavonic:

Knout, mammoth, argosy, mazurka (Polish dance), *sable* (an animal), *rouble, polka, slave, steppe, vampire, czar.*

8. Persian:

Bazaar, bezique (a game), *caravan, divan, orange* (P. *naring*), *check* (or *cheque*), *chess, dervish, exchequer, hazard, jackal, jasmine, jujube, lemon, lilac, checkmate* (*shah mat,* "the king is dead").

9. Sanskrit:

Banyan (a kind of tree), *camphor, chintz, crimson, ginger, hemp,* *indigo, jungle, loot* (to plunder), etc.

10. Hindustani (Northern India):

Bangle (a ring bracelet), *chutney* (a kind of pickle), *dacoit* (highway robber), *topee* (a sunshade for the head), *khaki.*

11. Hebrew:

Balsam (*cf.* older form *balm,* through French), *alphabet* (through Greek), *amen, bedlam* ("mad-house," corruption of *Bethlehem*), *cinnamon, cherub, cider* (through French), *maudlin* (corruption of *Magdalene*), *jubilee, jockey* (corruption of *jackey,* dim. of *Jack,* Hebrew *Jac-ob*), *hallelujah* (*halelu jah,* praise ye God), *seraph* (coined from the plural *seraphim*), *shekel,* etc.

12. Syriac:

Abbess, abbot, abbey (all from *abba,* father), *damask* (from *Damascus*), *damson* (a *Damascene* plum), *muslin* (from the town *Mosul*), *mammon* (riches), *Messiah* (anointed), etc.

13. Arabic:

Rather numerous; some have come from the Levantine trade through Greek or Italian; others by way of Spain, in which country the Arab-speaking Moors were dominant for about 700 years; others more indirectly, by way of France:

Admiral (spelt by Milton as *ammiral;* Arab, *amir,* prince), *alcove* (a recess), *algebra, Arabesque, arsenal, artichoke, assassin, caliph, caraway* (seed), *cipher, coffee, cotton, garbage, nadir, zenith,* etc.

14. Turkish:

Bey (provincial governor), *horde, bosh* (nonsense), *ottoman* (from *Ottoman,* founder of the Turkish empire), *vataghan* (a dagger-like sword), *janizary, horde,* etc.

15. Dravidian (Southern India):

Teak (a kind of timber), *bandicoot, mongoose, curry, cheroot, coolie* (laborer), *mango* (kind of fruit), *tope* (mango-orchard), *pariah* (outcast), etc.

16. Malay:

Bamboo, caddy (small tea-chest), *cockatoo, gong, mangrove, orangutan, paddy* (rice), *rattan* (cane), *sago, upas* (a fabled poisonous tree), *amuck* (as in the phrase "to run amuck").

17. Chinese:

China (in the sense of porcelain), *iea*, (Ch. *tsa, cha;* the last, though not used in England, is universally used in India, where it became current through the Portuguese), *nankeen* (a kind of cloth, from Nankin).

18. Thibetan:

Lama (Buddhist high priest at Llassa), *yak* (Thib. ox).

19. Australian:

Boomerang, kangaroo, paramatta (so called from the place).

20. Polynesian:

Taboo (a prohibition), *tattoo.*

21. Egyptian:

Behemoth, sack (hence, dim. *satchel,* and *sack-cloth*), *gum, gypsy, ibis, oasis, paper* (papyrus).

22. North African:

Barb (a horse), *morocco* (from the country), *fez* (Moorish cap).

23. West African:

Canary, chimpanzee, guinea, gorilla, yam (sweet potato).

24. North American:

Caucus (previously, one who pushes on; now, a preliminary meeting for a political purpose), *moose, skunk, squaw, tobacco, tomahawk, totem* (ancestral symbol), *wigwam* (Indian hut), *opossum, raccoon.*

25. Mexican:

Cocoa (orig. *cacao*), *chocolate, copal, jalop, tomato, chili, coyote.*

The English Language in America

Anglo-American or American English is English subjected to a new set of environmental circumstances. The new life in America, the new habits of thought it engendered, the new influences operative—all these combined to make the language spoken in America unlike that spoken in England.

The differences of vocabulary are the most striking. Indian place-names are like none in England. *Potomac, Niagara, Tallahassee, Susquehanna, Mississippi, Allegheny, Chicago, Kalamazoo* give, as H. L. Mencken remarks, "a barbaric brilliancy to the American map." Other words of Indian origin—*skunk, hickory, squash, caribou, raccoon, possum, moose, woodchuck, hominy, pone, toboggan, squaw*—are distinctively and unmistakably American.

American English and British English exhibit other dissimilarities in vocabulary, arising from variant usages rather than variant sources:

American English	British English
sidewalk	foot-path or pavement
subway	tube
gasoline	petrol
cracker	biscuit
pie	tart
elevator	lift
checkers	draughts

American spelling and British are similarly divergent. The advantage is on the American side. *Armor, behavior, color, harbor, honor* are better (because simpler) than the British versions: *armour, behaviour, colour, harbour, honour.* Again, *theatre, calibre, fibre* are less logical than *theater, caliber, fiber.* The Americans, quite reasonably, do not retain the diphthong in *anaemia, anaesthetic, encyclopaedia,* or the compound consonants in *barque, cheque, plough.*

The differences between American and British pronunciation are perhaps the most pervasive of all. The British tend to use broad *a* instead of the American short *a* in words like *bath, class, half.* They prefer the long to the short *i* in *civilization, organization, agile.* They stress heavily the accented syllables and consequently level the unstressed vowels, either obscuring or eliding them.

American		British
*med*isin	(medicine)	*med*s'n
adver*tize*ment	(advertisement)	ad*ver*'tizmnt
*san*itary	(sanitary)	*san*uhtree
sekruh*teh*ree	(secretary)	*sec*ruhtree
clerk	(clerk)	clark
*sked*ule	(schedule)	*shed*ule
loo*ten*ant	(lieutenant)	lef*ten*ant
*auto*mobeel	(automobile)	auto*mo*'bil

BOOK NINETEEN

Dictionary of World Literature

Acrostic.—Verses in which the initial or other letters taken in order form a word or words. Now regarded as a species of literary tomfoolery, acrostics were once in high repute. Sir John Davies, an Elizabethan poet of some excellence, had twenty-six poems called "Hymns to Astrea," each being an acrostic on *Elisabetha Regina*.

Allegory.—A work that attempts to enforce some moral, or some system of morality, by clothing abstract ideas in story. Essentially, an allegory is an extended metaphor.

Allegory has been defined as "a sort of translation into the concrete of the abstract." There must be, in properly managed allegory, some congruence between the abstraction and its embodiment. The great English allegories are Langland's *Vision of Piers Plowman*, Spenser's *Faerie Queene*, and Bunyan's *Pilgrim's Progress*.

Anagram.—A transposition of the letters of a word that results in a new word. Jeremy Taylor speaks of anagrammatizing his "art into a vermin," by which he means effecting the transposition: *art* into *rat*.

Anecdote.—A pointed and usually humorous story, interesting in its own right even when detached from a larger whole.

Aphorism.—A short, pithy statement of a precept or a principle.

Better a living ass than a dead lion.

Belles Lettres.—No attempt to translate this French phrase has met with unqualified success: *beautiful letters* is unsatisfactory but perhaps sufficiently definitive.
See LITERATURE.

Bestiary.—Poem, story, or treatise, setting forth "the nature of various beasts and birds—lion, panther, eagle, and the like—with an explanation of the meaning of each as a symbol of points in religion" (Osgood). Very popular during the Middle Ages, the type "still survives in the secular use of animal alphabets or skits in humorous periodicals."

Biography.—The history of an individual (*e.g.*, Boswell's *Life of Johnson*). Closely allied to the type are the **autobiography,** the story of a man's life told by himself (*The Education of Henry Adams*); the **confession** (De Quincey's *Confessions of an English Opium-Eater*), the **memoir** (Anne Grant's *Memoirs of an American Lady*), and the **biographical novel** (Stone's *Lust for Life*).

Burlesque.—Comic writing that is derisively imitative of a literary convention, style, attitude, or the like. Chaucer's "Sir Thopas" and Cervantes' *Don Quixote* both were burlesques of the conventions of medieval romance.

Chronogram.—"A phrase, sentence, or inscription, in which certain letters (usually distinguished by size or otherwise from the rest) express by their numerical values a date or epoch" (*NED*). In 1666, a fast-day was decreed in the expectation of a naval engagement between the English and Dutch. A pamphlet issued in reference to the fast-day had this sentence, constituting one of the few perfect chronograms, imprinted on the bottom of the page where normally the date was placed:

LorD haVe MerCIe Vpon Vs.

Classicism.—The adherence to or the advocacy of the principles of classic literature. G. N. Clark says:

The classical tendency meant harmony, dignity, and purity, not only in words, but in sentiments.

Employed in that sense, classicism is merely a term of praise; and a case can be made for calling Wordsworth a classicist and Ovid a non-classicist. More useful and more objective is the view that considers classicism as the tendency to look to the culture of Greece and Rome for literary inspiration. *See* NEOCLASSICISM.

Colloquy.—A dialog: *e.g.*, Erasmus's *Colloquies.*

Comedy.—Drama that treats amusing subjects amusingly. However, even this generalized definition is open to exception, since Shaw's comedies sometimes treat *unamusing* subjects amusingly. Shaw's comedies conform to another definition (which, however, is of even more limited application than the one given above) : comedy is "thoughtful laughter" (Meredith).

The kinds usually distinguished are **romantic comedy** (Rostand's *Cyrano de Bergerac*), **comedy of manners** (Congreve's *Way of the World*), **serio-comedy** (Barrie's *Dear Brutus*), **sentimental comedy** (Chase's *Harvey*), **intrigue comedy** (Shakspere's *Merry Wives of Windsor*), **farce comedy** (Thomas's *Charley's Aunt*), **satiric comedy** (Aristophanes' *The Birds*), **intellectual comedy** (Shaw's *Major Barbara*). The adjective element characterizes each type as well as it can be characterized.

Conceit.—A "far-fetched" and ingenious comparison, the mode of the Metaphysical (*q.v.*) poets:

> Our two souls therefore, which are one,
>> Though I must go, endure not yet
> A breach, but an expansion,
>> Like gold to airy thinness beat.

Cubism.—A term taken from painting and applied to literature, where it refers to the technique of dislocation of rhythm, logic, words, and syntax; and "the substitution of the discontinuous for the continuous" (Michaud). Deriving from Guillaume Apollinaire (who wrote the manifesto of the movement) and affecting many French writers and artists in the second decade of this century, cubism has had a limited influence abroad. However, the poetry of E. E. Cummings indicates that its influence has not been totally negligible.

Cycle.—A group of poems, romances, novels that centers about an event or epoch of history (real or mythological), or about a person or place, and forms a continuous narrative: *e.g.,* The Arthurian Cycle.

Originally, the word referred to the *Epic Cycle,* the poems of the Cyclic poets of Greece who, by filling in the time gaps of Homer's *Iliad* and *Odyssey,* presented a continuous narrative of the Trojan Wars. In modern usage, Galsworthy's *Forsyte Saga* and Proust's *Remembrance of Things Past* are, by extension, called *cycles.*

Dadaism.—A form of purposeful irrationality, characterized by such stunts as André Breton's construction of a poem from telephone-directory extracts. All restrictions on the free play of impulse were attacked with savage humor. Tristan Tzara was the founder of the school, which endured from about 1916–1922; its main importance is its subsequent development into surrealism (*q.v.*). The name was chosen at random from a dictionary.

Dialog.—A literary work in the form of a conversation between two or more persons: *e.g.,* Landor's *Imaginary Conversations,* Hope's *Dolly Dialogues,* Plato's *Republic.*

Drama.—A composition, either prose or verse, having some degree of unity and intended for stage presentation. No more specific definition is possible of a type that includes *Antigone* and the Japanese *No* plays; moralities, miracles, and masques; *The Doll's House* and *No Exit; Strange Interlude* and *Waiting for Lefty; Hamlet* and *The Dog Beneath the Skin.* Even the phrase "intended for stage presentation" is not invariable, since closet dramas (*e.g.,* Hardy's *Dynasts*) are intended only to be read.
See COMEDY, TRAGEDY.

Distich.—A couplet, especially one that achieves complete expression by itself:

> A little learning is a dangerous thing;
> Drink deep, or taste not the Pierian Spring.
> —POPE

Eclogue.—A short poem in dialog, especially pastoral dialog, as Virgil's *Bucolics,* Spenser's *Eclogues.*

Elegy.—A "poem of meditative calm written in a measure to conduce thoughtfulness" (Shepard) ; usually, though not necessarily, elegies are songs of lamentation. Gray's "Elegy," Wordsworth's "Elegiac Stanzas," Whitman's "When Lilacs Last in the Dooryard Bloomed" are diverse examples of the type.

Epic.—A narrative poem, written in "the grand style," that represents the signal actions and achievements of some real or mythical hero. The *Iliad* and *Odyssey* are traditionally exampled as types of the true epic. There are variations however:

The National or Folk Epic: a poem in the elevated style depicting a nation's past history, or (as Fowler emends) a nation's conception of its past history. De Camoën's *Lusiads* is the national epic of Portugal. *Beowulf* is sometimes considered England's national epic (even though it recounts the exploits of a Geatish hero).

Literary or Art Epic: a conscious and artistic imitation of an epic, as Spenser's *The Faerie Queene,* Milton's *Paradise Lost,* Virgil's *Aeneid.*

Mock Epic: a burlesque of the epic style and machinery, as Pope's *The Rape of the Lock,* Cowper's *The Task,* Barlow's *The Hasty Pudding.*

Epigram.—A terse, pointed, witty saying, either prose or verse (usually achieving its effect by antithesis).

> What is an Epigram? A dwarfish whole;
> Its body brevity, and wit its soul.
> —COLERIDGE

Epilogue.—"(1) The concluding part of a speech; (2) the concluding part of a literary work; an appendix; (3) a speech or short poem addressed to the spectators by one of the actors after the conclusion of a play" (*NED*).

Epistle.—A literary work in the form of a letter. St. Paul, Horace, Pope, Auden, and Mac Neice all practiced the form.

Epistolary Novels, in which the story is told by means of letters that the characters send one another, were extremely popular in the eighteenth century. All of Richardson's novels were epistolary. The form is still practiced—*e.g.,* K. Taylor's *Address Unknown*—though hardly fashionable.

Epitaph.—An inscription on a tombstone, or intended for one. Some are the product of no small literary art; others have become literature for different reasons (as this one, often erroneously credited to George MacDonald):

> Here lie I, Martin Eldinbrodde,
> Ha' mercy on my soul, Lord God,
> As I would do, were I Lord God,
> And thou wert Martin Eldinbrodde.

Epithalamium.—A nuptial song, praising bride and bridegroom and praying for their prosperity, as Spenser's "Epithalamion," written for his own marriage.

Essay.—A "short piece of prose [or, occasionally, verse], not attempting to treat its subject completely or logically, but rather giving the author's opinions of it" (Heydrick). The opinions may vary from the serious to the humorous, the style from heavy to light, the length from a few hundred words to several thousand. Montaigne's two volumes of *Essays* (1580) are the first modern instances of the type, but the history of the essay goes back further than Greece or Rome. Lamb, Hazlitt, Stevenson, Ruskin, Pater, Wilde, Eliot, More, all were (or are) devoted to the essay. The kinds of essays usually distinguished are **personal, descriptive, critical, reflective, appreciative, editorial**—all of which are self-explanatory. The approach may be **informal** or **formal**.

Euphuism.—A high-flown, extremely affected style, taking its name from the chief character in John Lyly's *Euphues, The Anatomy of Wit* (1578). The characteristics of the style are: relentless counterpoise and balance; an artificial rhythm, close to verse; an excessive amount of alliteration, direct and crossed (as in "The *h*ot *l*iver of a *h*eedless *l*over," or "Let my *r*ude *b*irth excuse my *b*old *r*equest"); an oversubtle refinement of expression, and an overabundant use

of rhetorical figures ("often drawn from the fabulous qualities ascribed to plants, minerals, and animals"). Very popular in its day, it fell into disrepute early in the seventeenth
century. Today it is employed as a loose synonym for affected,
periphrastic language.

Existentialism.—The current French philosophic-literary
movement which has for its "first principle . . . [that] man
is neither more nor less than what he makes himself"
(Sartre), or, phrased differently, that *"existence* precedes
essence"; second, that the will of man is free to choose or
deny; next, that existence is absurd and meaningless, since
there is no God, and consequently there is no objective
system of values; finally, that since man is free and defined by
his acts, he can become what he desires.

The source of this atheistic doctrine, paradoxically, is
ultimately the great Danish theologian Soren Kierkegaard.
Kierkegaard declared that existence was absurd without God
and that the idea of God was absurd; but only by flinging
himself across the abyss of reason and embracing the absurd,
by subjecting his will to God's, can man be saved. Kierkegaard's immediate followers were Jaspers and Heidegger,
and from them, particularly from the latter, modern existentialism stems. The philosopher of the school is Jean Paul
Sartre, its best novelist Albert Camus. No others of the school
have yet been published in America.

Expressionism.—That development of Impressionism (*q.v.*)
which seeks to project suitable symbols for the writer's moods,
feelings, attitudes. Its mode is "the externalization of the
inner." Most influential in the drama, expressionism numbers among its full- or part-time adherents Ernst Toller, T.
S. Eliot, W. H. Auden, Elmer Rice, Clifford Odets, Archibald MacLeish.

Exemplum.—A moral story or illustration, popular with
medieval preachers and their audiences. Chaucer's "Par-
doner's Tale" is a surviving instance of the type.

Fable.—A short moral tale, usually having animals as its
characters. The fable is an ancient form, dating back to the

Indian *Panchatantra.* Phaedrus, Aesop, La Fontaine, Ambrose Bierce, and George Ade were all fabulists. (Ade's *Fables in Slang,* incidentally, has people rather than animals as its actors.)

Fabliau.—A short tale in verse, normally in octosyllabic couplets, dealing with the incidents of daily life in humorous, realistic, and often vulgar fashion: *e.g.,* Chaucer's "Miller's Tale" and almost any of Boccaccio's tales. Very popular in medieval times, the fabliau is sometimes considered the precursor of the short-story.

"Frame-story."—A story (or stories) within a story: *e.g., The Canterbury Tales, The Arabian Nights, The Decameron.*

Futurism.—A short-lived but influential literary movement which had "speed, force, and dynamism" for its principles. Founded by F. T. Marinetti, with the blessings of Guillaume Apollinaire, futurism "threw a bomb in art and letters . . . He [Marinetti] demanded an entirely new technique based on free invention of words, simultaneous and onomatopoetic descriptions (like his own battle of Tripoli) and the substitution of noise for music" (Michaud). The machine, the electric sign, the moving pictures were hailed as potent sources of inspiration.

Gnomic.—Aphoristic, dealing in maxims. The Gnomic poets of Greece flourished in the sixth century B.C. They were given their designation simply because they embodied "sententious maxims on life and morals in their verse" (Symonds). By extension, writers in an aphoristic vein— Francis Bacon, for example—are called *gnomic.* Gnomic verse is found very early in English literature: in *Beowulf,* for example, sayings like "Fate goes ever as she is bound" and "Far countries are seemliest sought by a man sure of himself" abound.

Humanism.—"The New Learning," devoted to the "more human writings" (*literae humaniores*)—the classics rather than theology. An off-shoot rather than the cause of the Renaissance (generally given the dates 1453 to 1603, or from the Fall of Constantinople to the death of Elizabeth), humanism was a revolt against the other-worldliness of medievalism, against the veiled presentation of the supernatural; it joyously received the here and the now and the natural, for all of which it found its inspiration in the study of Greek and Roman culture. Its "fundamental precept was the law of measure . . . ('There is a measure in things') of Horace . . . Pagan in its revulsion from medieval mysticism and symbolism, in its revolt against the bondage of intellectual and ecclesiastical authority, it aimed at liberating the free human personality" (Otis and Needleman).

The great humanists were Colet, Lily, Erasmus, Petrarch, Boccaccio, More, Ascham, Bacon.

See NEO-HUMANISM.

Idyl(l).—A descriptive poem, presenting in idealized form a picture of country life, as the *Idylls* of Theocritus. Whittier's "Snow-Bound" is in the idyllic tradition, but Tennyson's *Idylls of the King* marks a significant departure in that it depicts almost nothing of country life.

Imagism.—The body of poetic doctrine, urging the following aims: to use "the language of common speech" and to employ the exact rather than "the merely decorative word"; to liberalize poetic rhythms and to create new ones; to choose subjects freely; to present *"images";* to write "poetry that is hard and clear, never blurred or indefinite"; to produce a concentrated rather than diffuse poetry.

The imagist school was founded by Ezra Pound and T. E. Hulme. Its chief adherents were D. H. Lawrence, Richard Aldington, F. S. Flint (British); and Hilda Doolittle, John Gould Fletcher, and Amy Lowell (Americans).

Impressionism.—The reproduction of the impressions and feelings a scene, event, object, or the like has stimulated in the artist or writer.

If impressionism is viewed as a creative literary technique, Dorothy Richardson, Virginia Woolfe, and Sherwood Anderson may be numbered among its adherents. More usually it is considered to be a critical technique—"the adventures of a soul among masterpieces": Walter Pater, Anatole France, James Huneker have all labeled themselves *impressionists* in criticism.

Interlude.—Short plays, usually farcical, with plot minimized and dialog central. They were most often "performed in the intervals of banquets and entertainments" (Chambers), but probably were independently presented on occasion. They form a link between the old miracle and morality (*qq.v.*) plays and the modern drama. John Heywood (about 1497 to about 1580) was the most notable writer of interludes.

Invocation.—A poetic convention, in which the poet calls upon the Muses (or some deity) for aid in carrying out the plan of his poem, as in the initial lines of Milton's *Paradise Lost*.

Lay.—A short poem, usually telling a story, meant to be sung. The original lays (or *lais*) were the short stories of the middle ages (Nitze). Adventure, romance, history, and legend form their dominant themes. Marie de France was the pre-eminent practitioner of the form. In English literature, *Sir Orfeo* is perhaps the best surviving lay. Modern extensions of the form include Macaulay's *Lays of Ancient Rome*, Scott's *Lay of the Last Minstrel*, and Aytoun's *Lays of the Scottish Cavaliers*.

Literature.—The expression of what has been done, thought, felt; particularly expression characterized by beauty of form, emotional impact, and permanence. De Quincey's distinction is famous:

There is first the literature of *knowledge,* secondly the literature of *power*. The function of the first is—to teach; the function of the second is—to move; the first is a rudder, the second an oar or a sail. The first speaks to the *mere* discursive understanding; the second speaks ultimately, it may happen, to the higher understanding or reason, but always *through* affections of pleasure and sympathy.

Cf. BELLES LETTRES.

Local-Color Story.—One concerned largely with the physical background of a particular locality; carefully indicating dialect differences, sketching character types, noting interests peculiar to it. Bret Harte was greatly influential in the development of the local-color story in America. Edward Eggleston, Joaquin Miller, Lafcadio Hearn, George Washington Cable, E. W. Howe arc other important local-colorists.

Masque (or **Mask**).—A form of dramatic entertainment, involving music, dance, and spectacle, "in which the spectacular and musical elements predominated over plot and character" (Harvey). The masque was extremely popular in seventeenth-century England, which had borrowed the idea of the masque from Italy. Beaumont, Fletcher, Chapman, Middleton, and many other contemporaries wrote masques or pseudo-masques.

Metaphysical Wit.—The name given by Drummond of Hawthornden and popularized by Dr. Johnson to the style of writing practiced by Daniel, Donne, Cowley, Herbert, Waller, Denham, Crashaw, Vaughan, Davenant, Marvell —often thought of as comprising the "metaphysical school of poetry." Their wit, Dr. Johnson says, may be considered a kind of concord in discord: "a combination of dissimilar images or discovery of occult resemblances in things apparently unlike . . . If they frequently threw away their wit upon false conceits, they likewise sometimes struck out unexpected truth; if their conceits were far-fetched, they were often worth the carriage."

Modern followers of the metaphysical school include G. M. Hopkins, T. S. Eliot, Hart Crane, Horace Gregory, E. E. Cummings, Wallace Stevens, John Crowe Ransom. *See* CONCEIT.

Miracle.—A dramatization of some portion of the Bible. Miracle Plays were of religious origin, and at first were acted by the clergy. Later, as the plays became more popular, secular action supplanted the clergy. They were in vogue during the fourteenth and fifteenth centuries. The distinction between miracle and morality—the one dealing with

Biblical themes, the other with incidents in the lives of the saints—is valid in French but not in English literature.
Cf. MORALITY

Morality.—A dramatized moral allegory. *Everyman* is the best serving instance of the Morality Play.
Cf. MIRACLE

Naturalism.—A thoroughgoing form of realism (*q.v.*) that has for its aim complete objectivity. Zola, one of the great writers in this tradition, declared that his purpose was to give fiction "the absolute truth of science with regard to human life." As his literary ancestors he claimed Balzac, Stendhal, and Flaubert. To Zola and his school, naturalism implied science, and they employed texts like Claude Bernard's *Study of Experimental Medicine* to learn the method of science. Zola believed with Taine that "vice and virtue are products like vitriol and sugar," and that it was the business of the writer to examine causes and note effects with scientific dispassion.

Modern naturalists—Norris, Dreiser, Farrell—adopt the method, but most of them discard the philosophical base.

Neo-classicism.—The tendency towards imitation of the great writers of Greece and Rome, and the attempt to duplicate their characteristics: simplicity, unity, restraint, universality, uniformity, correctness. Neo-classic writers held that the business of the writer was

. . . to examine, not the individual, but the species. He does not number the streaks of the tulip, or describe the different shades in the verdure of the forest: he is to exhibit in his portraits of nature such prominent and striking features, as recall the original to every mind . . .

—JOHNSON

They believed that the rules of writing could be derived from the classics: to imitate them was to imitate nature, because the rules were "nature methodized." They frowned on irregularities and had only contempt for "enthusiasm" (that is, lack of restraint). The "unities" (*q.v.*) in drama, and the heroic couplet in poetry were their literary ideals. Man, they affirmed, was the proper study of mankind. But the study had for its purpose not only knowledge but correction also: "For 'tis but half a judge's task, to know." Correction was the aim of art, but the correction has to be administered cleverly:

> Men must be taught as if you taught them not,
> And things unknown proposed as things forgot.

Neo-classicism was dominant in English literature for more than a century—from about the middle of the seventeenth to about the end of the eighteenth century. From then to the first decade of this century it has had scarcely a defender. Today, however, there seems to be an upsurge of neo-classicism. T. S. Eliot has proclaimed himself a "classicist"; Allen Tate, Mark Van Doren, the Sitwells, Robert Graves, and Humbert Wolfe have strong affinities with neo-classicists. However, applied to modern poets, the term is perhaps too general to be useful.

See CLASSICISM.

Neo-Humanism (or **New Humanism**).—A philosophical and critical (as opposed to creative) movement that stressed the continuity of "the traditional Christian and classical controls," the necessity for "the ethical or generalizing imagination, the permanence of objective esthetic values" (Babbit). The term implies "doctrine and discipline, and is applicable not to men in general but only to a select few—it is, in short, aristocratic and not democratic in its implications" (More).

The movement flourished in the third decade of this century, but since has died down if not died. However, the neo-humanist school has been influential out of all proportion to the number of its followers: Foerster, Shafer, Clark, and others sharing the neo-humanist point of view have edited a large number of widely adopted college texts that foster their doctrine.

Nonsense Verse.—Verse which has no meaning, and does not pretend to have. Its subject, where a subject can be discerned, is intentionally absurd. Edward Lear and Lewis Carroll are the great English masters of the type.

> The sun was shining on the sea,
> 　Shining with all her might:
> He did his very best to make
> 　The billows smooth and bright—
> And this was odd, because it was
> 　The middle of the night.—
>
> 　　　　　—CARROLL

Novel.—A narrative, usually in prose but sometimes in verse, containing at least fifty thousand words. This is the only definition possible if narratives as different as *Don Quixote, Finnegans Wake, Remembrance of Things Past, Clarissa Harlowe, War and Peace,* and *Bambi* are to be included by it. The narrative may be continuous or it may continually break off. It may be impressionistic, symbolic, or naturalistic in form. Almost always its actors are human, but they may be animals. It may emphasize the story element, or it may emphasize mood and character. It may take place in a day —or less—or over several generations—or longer. It may contain incidental essays, asides, letters, or it may be "pure" narrative.

Occasional Verse.—Verse written for special occasions: *e.g.,* Emerson's "Concord Hymn."

Parody.—A derisive imitation of a poem or other writing, by exaggerating or burlesquing its characteristic features. In the following brief quotation, Swinburne parodies his own occasionally over-done alliterativeness:

> Blank is the book of his bounty beholden
> 　of old, and its binding is blacker
> 　　　than bluer,
> Out of blue into black is the scheme of
> 　the skies, and their dews are the
> 　　　wine of the bloodshed of things.

Pastoral Poetry.—Poetry that portrays some phase of country life. Originally as the etymology would imply, pastorals (from Latin *pastor,* shepherd), as those of Theocritus who developed the form, exhibited shepherds in characteristic moments. The meaning of the term has increasingly widened, until now pastoral denotes a poem having a rustic background. Milton, Wordsworth, Shelley wrote some of the great pastorals in English.

Poetry: Types.—The following is a list of the types of poetry most often distinguished. It must be noted, however, that types overlap:

1. **Epic:**—*See* EPIC.

2. **Narrative:**—telling a story.
    a. **metrical romance** (*see* ROMANCE).
    b. **verse tale** (Noyes's "The Highwayman").
    c. **verse novel** (Benet's *John Brown's Body*).
    d. **ballad** ("Sir Patrick Spens," "Frankie and Johnny," Rossetti's "Sister Helen").

3. **Dramatic:**—employing dialog as its medium.
    a. **poetic drama** (Shakspere's *King Lear,* Auden's *Dog Beneath the Skin*).
    b. **dramatic monologue** (Browning's "My Last Duchess").

4. **Lyric:**—dominated by strong personal feeling and musical in style.
    a. **meditative** (Wordsworth's "Lines Composed a Few Miles above Tintern Abbey," E. A. Robinson's "The Man Against the Sky").
    b. **religious** (Emerson's "Brahma").
    c. **love** (Emily Dickinson's "Of All the Souls That Stand Create," Poe's "To Helen").
    d. **nature** (Bryant's "Inscription for the Entrance to a Wood").
    e. **dramatic** (E. A. Robinson's "Richard Cory").
    f. **elegy** (*see* ELEGY).
    g. **lament** (Tennyson's "Break, Break, Break").
    h. **sonnet** (Hardy's "Hap").
    i. **ode** (Keats's "Ode to a Nightingale").
    j. **pastoral** (*see* PASTORAL).

5. **Didactic:**—teaching or enforcing a lesson (Longfellow's "A Psalm of Life").

6. **Satiric:**—*See* SATIRE.

7. **Light** (or **familiar** or **vers de société**):—having amusement as its prime purpose.
   a. **burlesque** (Butler's *Hudibras*).
   b. **nonsense** (Lear's "Pobble Who Has No Toes").
   c. **parody** (Swinburne's *Nephelidia*).
   d. **humorous** (Carryl's *Grimm Tales Made Gay*).
   e. **serious** (Lowell's *Biglow Papers*).

Polyphonic Prose.—A "many voiced prose," developed by a French poet, Paul Fort, and adapted to English by Amy Lowell. The form has as its basis "the long flowing cadence of oratorical prose" and makes use of all the "voices" of poetry—"meter, *vers libre,* assonance, alliteration, rhyme, and return" (Lowell). ("Return" denotes the recurrence of a dominant thought or image.) The following is a brief specimen of polyphonic prose:

Due East, far West. Distant as the nests of the opposite winds. Removed as fire and water are, as the clouds and the roots of the hills, as the wells of youth and age.   —AMY LOWELL

Primitivism.—The advocacy or imitation of the way of life "natural to man unspoiled by cities and their culture." Rousseau is the central source of primitivism in modern literature, though others had advocated it before him and others have since. Primitivist ideas have been especially influential on modern poetry, from Wordsworth to Robinson Jeffers. Gertrude Stein, J. M. Synge, William Faulkner, and Ernest Hemingway, have, with more or less justification, also been labeled *primitivists.*

Purple Patch.—An eloquent or over-ornate (depending on whether the phrase is used as a compliment or as a criticism) passage of description in a work. Ruskin's and Macaulay's essays are tissues of purple patches (in both senses, favorable and unfavorable, of the phrase).

Realism.—Works of literature that describe real life and the real world. Naturalism and veritism (*qq.v.*) are more emphatic forms of realism. Why naturalists and veritists chose to dissociate themselves from realists by adopting another name may become clear after this passage, in which realism is defined by one of its chief American exponents, has been read. Realism, Howells says,

derives from Hawthorne and George Eliot . . . ; but it studies human nature more in its wonted aspects, and finds its ethical and dramatic examples in the operation of lighter but not less vital motives; the moving accident is certainly not its trade; and it prefers to avoid all manner of dire catastrophes. It is largely influenced by French fiction in form, but it is the realism of Daudet rather than the realism of Zola that prevails with it, and it has a soul of its own which is above recording the brutish pursuit of a woman by a man, which seems to be the chief end of the French novelist.

Regionalism.—The movement based on the doctrine that the chief concern of literature should be to get the essence of particular sections—history, background, setting, and "the radically different patterns of feeling and thinking" which make up the environment. In fiction, the regionalist's aim is "to show the character in terms of the region in which he lives" (Walcutt). Robert Frost, Thomas Wolfe, and Richard Wright are regionalists though their "prime concerns are not consciously regional" (Walcutt).

Romance.—(1) A fiction that attempts "to create an illusion which is the antithesis of common human experience" (Walley and Wilson), as *Treasure Island* in prose or *The Lady of the Lake* in verse; (2) a form of narrative verse, widely popular in the middle ages (and often called **metrical romance**), that embodied "the adventures of some hero of chivalry," as *The Song of Roland,* Chaucer's "The Knight's Tale," and *Sir Gawaine and the Green Knight.*

Romanticism.—The movement which extolled the free, untrammeled expression of personality; the strange and even the Satanic; medievalism, revolution, transcendentalism; the wild and unordered in nature; the particular rather than the universal; inspiration rather than reason. Such a diversity could of course never be comprehended by any one romantic: the love of the strange, for example, was not always found in combination with revolutionary politics. Professor Lovejoy has analyzed romanticism penetratingly. He affirms that "Romanticism is a sign that has lost its significance." There may be some identical element in all attempts at definition, but if so it has not been demonstrated. Not only do definitions differ, but also the source has been differently located by different men: Gosse says that Joseph Warton was the first romantic and Whibley says the devil was. Lovejoy suggests, therefore, that we speak not of "romanticism" but of "romanticisms." There is no unit concept to which we can give the name "romanticism," but there are "smaller, simpler, diversely combinable intellectual and emotional complexes" to which we can give the name "romanticisms."

Among the "great romantics" of the nineteenth century, the period during which romanticism(s) dominated, were Wordsworth, Coleridge, Byron, Keats, and Shelley. Today, writers like Edna St. Vincent Millay, E. E. Cummings, Stephen Spender, Day Lewis, Robert Lowell are often termed romantics because of real or imagined affinities with the attitudes and styles of the nineteenth-century writers mentioned above.

Saga.—The Icelandic and Norwegian prose narratives, for the most part embodying historical and mythological traditions; compiled between the twelfth and fifteenth centuries (A.D.). The *Volsunga* and the *Sturlinga* sagas are probably the best known.

Satire.—Poem or other writing ridiculing or denouncing vice or folly. Three types are traditionally distinguished:

1. **Horatian:** urbane, amused comment, after the manner of Horace, on the person or object satirized (*e.g.,* Pope's *The Rape of the Lock*).

2. **Juvenalian:** vehement, unamused denunciation, after the manner of Juvenal, of the person or object satirized (*e.g.,* Samuel Johnson's *London*).

3. **English:** vigorous, uninhibited attack on the person or object satirized (*e.g.,* Samuel Butler's *Hudibras*).

Short Story.—A short prose narrative that aims at a single effect. Such was Poe's definition—a definition that writers have largely ignored. Frequently, the short story is indistinguishable from the tale, and sometimes even from the character sketch. In the modern short story the narrative element tends to be suppressed, the mood or background dominant.

Surrealism (or **Super Realism**).—That revolt against reason in literature which attempts to derive from the creative unconscious "a perpetual flow of irrational thought in the form of images" (Gascoyne). It is a lineal descendant of dadaism (*q.v.*) and numbers among its adherents several former dadaists. Its chief sources have been French mysticism and symbolism on the one hand and psychoanalysis on the other. Its method is "free-association"—that is, pouring forth ideas and images as they occur, without any attempt to edit them. It is "Pure psychic automatism, by means of which one proposes to express, either verbally or by means of writing, the real functioning of thought. Dictated by thought, in the absence of any control exercised by reason, and without regard to any aesthetic or moral preoccupations" (Breton).

Symbolism.—A literary movement, "based on a new mysticism," the adherents of which believed that every mood, thought, and feeling had a specific image appropriate to it, and that it was the business of the writer to apprehend and express that image. "To symbolize," said Jules Tellier, "consists plainly, after one has found an image expressive of a state of the soul, in expressing not this state of the soul, but only the image that materializes it." "In place of *description*," Professor Cargill points out, "the symbolists substituted and defended *suggestion*."

Symbolism has, of course, a very long history: in medieval literature the symbolic technique was pervasive. But the peculiar form described above was a late nineteenth-century development. It originated in France, and had Baudelaire, Rimbaud, and Verlaine as ancestors and Mallarmé as its conscious high-priest. Symbolism has been widely influential on contemporary English and American literature. Few writers have been untouched, but the influence is most apparent in Eliot, Yeats, Synge, O'Neill, Joyce and their innumerable imitators.

Tragedy.—Drama which treats serious subjects seriously. According to Aristotle, tragedy "is an artistic imitation of an action that is complete in itself, serious, and of adequate magnitude [in language]." It depicts the great fall of a noble personage. Applicable to the classic drama he knew, Aristotle's definition does not cover such significant tragedies as T. S. Eliot's *Murder in the Cathedral,* Clifford Odets's *Awake and Sing!,* Eugene O'Neill's *The Iceman Cometh.*

The **fate tragedy** in which the catastrophe is the result of a malignant force external to the protagonist, and the **flaw tragedy,** in which the catastrophe is the result of an inner weakness of the protagonist, are often distinguished. Greek tragedy is of the former kind, Elizabethan of the latter.

Transcendentalism.—The philosophy which affirms the freedom of the will, the existence of God, and the reality of immortality. Deriving from Kant, it went through a broadening and widening process before it arrived in New England. There it came to be applied "to whatever in man's mental and spiritual nature is conceived of as above experience and independent of it. Whatever transcends the experience of the senses is transcendental" (Goddard). Transcendentalism meant for its disciples that the innate, original, and intuitive were to be exalted. Emerson, Alcott, Thoreau, Ripley, Margaret Fuller, Parker—all were admittedly of the school.

Unities.—Three unities—time, place, and action—were declared essential to properly negotiated drama by Aristotle. Every part of the action should be such that its elimination would destroy the integrity of the play; the time should be confined to about one day; the episodes should be "confined to a narrow compass." Neo-classical critics made the requirements for dramatic unity even more stringent—some even declaring that the time of the action should be no greater than the time it took to present the drama.

BOOK TWENTY

History of English and American Literature—

from BEOWULF TO THOMAS WOLFE

English Literature

OLD ENGLISH PERIOD (600–1066)

OF OLD ENGLISH LITERATURE, only a small (but not insignificant) portion survives: the earliest poetry does not bulk much larger than Milton's *Paradise Lost,* the earliest prose than Gibbon's *Decline and Fall of the Roman Empire.*

Poetry always develops before literary prose, and narrative poetry before the other kinds. English literature is no exception. *Beowulf,* a "folk epic" recounting the deeds and death of its (Scandinavian) hero, dates from the late seventh century. (That is, it was written down at that time; long before, however, it had been shaped by the *scops,* or poets, from the stuff of Teutonic legend and sung by the *gleemen,* or minstrels.) *Andreas,* a later poem, dealing with the life of St. Andrew; the fragment *Judith,* a version of the Apocryphal story; "The Song of Brunanburh" (937), describing the victory of Aethelstan, the King of Wessex, over Constantine, King of Scotland—all illustrate divergent types of narrative. But the epic tone, the manner of *Beowulf,* is common to them all.

Other themes received treatment. "The Wanderer" (which has been translated or imitated by poets as various as Tennyson, Pound, and Auden) is a poignant mourning "over the desolation of the whole world of man." "The Seafarer," a dialog between an old and a young sailor, extraordinarily modern, conveys the perennial fascination of the sea. (Both "The Wanderer" and "The Seafarer," the high-water marks of Anglo-Saxon poetry, fuse pagan and Christian elements—the latter probably being tacked on by a monkish coypist.) Two poems, "The Wife's Lament" and "The Husband's Message," are the only love-poems in Old English literature. Riddles, charms, and incantations, and gnomic verses constitute another series of themes.

Caedmon (*ca.* 670) and Cynwulf (*ca.* 800) are the only Anglo-Saxon poets we know by name. It was formerly the amiable custom of scholars to assign to either of these two most poems of doubtful date or superior merit. Better counsel has prevailed; and now only one poem, "Hymn of the Creation," is definitely credited to Caedmon; four to Cynwulf, generally conceded the best Anglo-Saxon poet.

Deep seriousness, the English climate of thought from the beginnings, manifests itself in the pervasive melancholy of Anglo-Saxon poetry. Christianity added a hopeful note, but did not alter the dominant mood. Nor did it alter the virtues the verse extolled: loyalty of thane to lord, generosity of lord to thane. It buttressed the fundamental morality of Anglo-Saxon poetry, and added to its themes.

The structure of Anglo-Saxon verse requires some comment. Each verse (or line) contains four accented and a varying number of unaccented syllables. Each verse is divided into two half-verses (*hemistichs* or *staves*). The half-verses are linked by alliteration of accented syllables. Syllables alliterate when they begin with the same consonant sound, or with a vowel sound (not necessarily the same vowel sound). The third accented syllable (called the *rime-giver*) alliterates with either the first or the second, or with both. The fourth accented syllable may alliterate with whichever accented syllable in the first half-verse does not alliterate with the third accented syllable. This metrical translation of the opening lines of *Beowulf* will make the conventions of form clearer (corresponding sounds are italicized):

Lo, *P*raise of the *p*rowess   of *p*eople-kings
of *s*pear-armed *D*anes   in *d*ays long *s*ped
we *h*ave *h*eard   and what *h*onor the athelings won!

Note that the fourth accented syllable does not alliterate with the third. This is a "rule" of Anglo-Saxon verse—but one not always adhered to.

Anglo-Saxon prose comes into its own with Alfred (848–901). He supervised and probably engaged in the translation of Latin works (Gregory, Orosius, Bede, Boethius); and he revised and enlarged the Anglo-Saxon *Chronicle,* the first continuous historical record in England. The *Blickling Homilies* (sermons written in the tenth century) deserve mention, as do the translations from the Old Testament by Aelfric "the Grammarian" (*ca.* 955—*ca.* 1023), the best stylist of his time. The Latin writings of Bede do not properly belong to English literature, but his *Ecclesiastical History of the English Race* contains invaluable source material.

MIDDLE ENGLISH PERIOD (1066–1476)

The Middle English period spans the more than four centuries between the Norman Conquest (1066) and Caxton's establishment of a printing press at Westminster (1476). Toward the beginning of the period, French threatened to displace English as the literary language; but English slowly regained the ascendancy, and with Chaucer and Caxton all doubt as to which was to be the medium for literature was resolved. Old English alliterative poetry (through contact with French poetry) was gradually transformed, until, with Chaucer, English poetry became essentially modern in form and structure. Rime, an accidental feature of Anglo-Saxon verse, supplanted alliteration.

The period under consideration is too extensive and encompasses too many tendencies to be treated conveniently as a unit. Accordingly, these arbitrary subdivisions will be employed: Anglo-Norman Age (1066–1340); Age of Chaucer (1340–1400); Fifteenth Century (1400–1476).

Anglo-Norman Age (1066–1340)

English literature from the Conquest to the birth of Chaucer is remarkable for its variety rather than its merit. The *Ormulum* ("Orm's little book"), a poem of some ten thousand lines consisting of paraphrases of the gospels, supplemented by homilies on each; the mystical poetry of Richard Rolle of Hampole; the anonymous *Poema Morale* ("Moral Ode"); the prose *Ancren Riwle* ("The Rule of Anchoresses") are more important for the light they cast on the language and interests of the age than for purely literary reasons. The same is true of the chronicles and histories. Geoffrey of Monmouth's *History of the Kings of Britain* (a Latin work) and Layamon's *Brut* (English verse), however, are valuable for the stimulus they gave to the Arthurian legend, a staple of the metrical romances.

The English metrical romances, stemming from French counterparts, employed four "matters" (or kinds of material): the matter of France—the tales centering about Charlemagne and his peers; the matter of Rome—the stories of Thebes, Troy, Alexander, and Aeneas; the matter of England—the (originally Germanic) stories of *King Horn, Havelock, Bevis of Hampton, Guy of Warwick,* and *Robin Hood;* and the matter of Britain—the tales centering about Arthur and his knights.

Perhaps what is usually referred to as "miscellaneous literature" is the best of the period. The ballads, though not yet written down, were current. Other popular forms—the *fabliaux,* the *exempla,* and the casual lyrics (of which "The Cuckoo-Song" is unquestionably the finest)—succeed in being interesting to our day, whereas more pretentious works remain deservedly unread.

The Age of Chaucer (1340–1400)

Chaucer dominates his time. *The Canterbury Tales* and *Troilus and Creseyde* are permanent literature. "Long before Balzac, Chaucer conceived and exhibited the Human Comedy," Lowes comments. "He is next to Shakspere in his vividness and appropriateness of character dramatization and in his infinite variety," declares another critic.

But Chaucer is not the whole of English literature during the sixty years under consideration. William Langland, the putative author of *The Vision of William concerning Piers the Plowman,* pictures the life of the poor, indicates something of the spirit of social unrest of the age—thus supplementing Chaucer, who does not at all look at this side of the Human Comedy.

Wyclif's translation of the Bible (the first complete translation in English) exerted a tremendous influence, both on English prose-style and on religious thought.

John Gower's *Confessio Amantis* deals poetically with each of the seven sins, while committing an eighth far greater: being unabatingly dull. The poem "has a certain charm for congenial minds," Prof. Shaw declares—a severe criticism of the minds.

To an unknown author of this age are attributed four fine poems: *Gawain and the Green Knight, The Pearl, Patience,* and *Cleanness.* Only Chaucer and Langland of his contemporaries are superior to him.

The Fifteenth Century

Lydgate's *Troy Book* and *Falls of Princes,* and James I of Scotland's *King's Quair* (or book) are "the monuments of the early fifteenth century," and the usual connection between what is dead and the monument holds. However, there are lines in the *King's Quair*—such as those describing the glimpse James catches of his queen as she walks under his prison-window—that indicate real poetic feeling. Except for the folk ballads, which took their approximately final shape in this century, no other poetry is worth mentioning.

The Miracle and Morality Plays, which grew out of the short dialogs in Latin delivered as part of the liturgy, were written down in this century. One still retains interest, the allegory of *Everyman.* The verse is rough, but the drama has a force and immediacy even for a more skeptical age.

Malory's *Morte d'Arthur* is the great work of fifteenth-century English prose. Its strong masculine style more than compensates for its narrative looseness.

THE PERIOD OF THE RENAISSANCE (1476–1660)

The Renaissance (or "rebirth") covers the two centuries of seed-time and harvest between Caxton's establishment of the printing press and the restoration of the Stuart line. It was a period of unbounded horizons. Man threw off the yoke of otherworldliness and found joy in "a liberated animality." He discovered again the great classics of Greece and Rome and they supplied a new impetus to his freedom. He pushed back the limits of the known further and further. The growth of capitalism and nationalism gave rise to a wave of exploration and invention. All things combined to free the creative spirit of Renaissance man—in thought, religion, and literature.

For more convenient organization, these arbitrary subdivisions of the period will be employed: Age of Experiment (1476–1579); Age of Shakspere (1579–1616); Puritan Age (1616–1660).

The Age of Experiment (1476–1579)

The Age of Experiment begins with the dominance of the "Scottish Chaucerians"—Henryson, Dunbar, Douglas, and Lindsay. It ends with the publication of Spenser's *The Shepheardes Calender*. The superiority of Spenser to the Scottish Chaucerians is a measure of the distance literature traveled in the century.

The English humanists, of whom More was the chief, revived English interest in the classics, "the humane letters." More's *Utopia,* a description of an ideal commonwealth, written by a "scholar who had fallen asleep over his Plato," is a thoroughly modern work in spite of its date (1516). Surrey's translation of the *Aeneid,* Colet's *Latin Grammar,* Roger Ascham's *Toxophilus* and *The Schoolmaster,* Erasmus's *Praise of Folly* are the fruits of humanistic study. But so, in a different way, are Skelton's magnificent doggerel attacks on Cardinal Wolsey, the clergy, and the court; and William Tyndale's translation of the New Testament and parts of the Old.

The influence of the Italian scholars and poets on English was scarcely less effective. Wyatt and Surrey were inspired by Italian models; and Tottel's *Miscellany,* in which Wyatt and Surrey (among other writers of songs and sonnets) were first printed, testifies to the widespread (and on the whole beneficial) influence of Petrarch and his countrymen.

The first English comedies, Udall's *Ralph Roister Doister* and Stevenson's *Gammer Gurton's Needle,* though dealing with English types and in an English way, were stimulated by Plautus and Terence, the great Latin writers of comedy. Similarly, Sackville and Norton's *Gorboduc,* the first English tragedy, manifests the influence of Seneca, the Roman writer of tragedies. In the earlier interludes, however, particularly those of John Heywood, the foreign influence is negligible; and the historical plays, such as Bale's *King John,* seem to be peculiarly English genres.

The Age of Shakspere (1579–1616)

Shakspere bestrides his age like a colossus, while being (as his contemporary Jonson saw) "not of an age but for all time." The thirty-seven plays—history, comedy, tragedy —reach the highest point of world literature. The sonnets, the *Venus and Adonis,* and *The Rape of Lucrece* are second in enduring worth only to the plays.

But admiration for Shakspere's supreme genius ought not to obscure the achievements of his contemporaries. England assumed for the first time a leading position among the nations: the achievements of the statesmen and soldiers were matched by the achievements of her writers. The exploits of Drake, the defeat of the Spanish Armada, the triumph of Protestantism, result from the same expanding nationalism and are of a piece with the unfolding creativity of the poets, dramatists, and prose writers.

Translation, "an Elizabethan art," is represented by three superb efforts: North's *Plutarch's Lives,* Chapman's *Iliad,* and Florio's *Montaigne.* Near the end of the age, the "King James Bible" (the "Authorized Version" of the Old and New Testaments), the result of the collaboration of forty-seven scholars and divines, was published (1611). No other book in the history of English literature has exerted so powerful an effect as this. Huxley's praise is famous: ". . . this book has been woven into all that is noblest and best in English history . . . it is written in the noblest and purest of English, and . . . abounds in exquisite beauties of literary form . . ."

The poetic outbreak during the Age of Shakspere was unprecedented—both as to kind and extent. Much of the poetry was artificial, imitative, and "too honey-sweet." But sometimes the Elizabethan poets reached the peaks of song. The sonnet and the sonnet sequence were extremely popular. Sidney's *Astrophel and Stella,* Daniel's *Delia,* Spenser's *Amoretti,* Drayton's *Idea,* and Shakspere's *Sonnets* are poetry of the highest order. Gascoigne, Constable, Barnes, and (chiefly in their dramas and romances) Lyly, Peele, Greene, Lodge, Nash, Jonson, and Marlowe added to the flood tide. Next to Shakspere, Spenser is the poet most widely admired—"the poet's poet," Keats called him. His sonnets, his *Shepheardes Calender* (a dozen youthful pastorals), and, above all, his *Faerie Queene* (a glorification of Elizabeth and of England in the guise of romance) fairly entitle him to his rank, even if modern taste finds him somewhat cloying.

Prose was finding itself during the age. Frequently it adopts the techniques of verse and drama. However, the *Voyages* of Hakluyt, the picaresque novels of Nash (*The Unfortunate Traveller*), even the intricately artificial cadenced prose of Lyly (*Euphues, Euphues and his England*) are enjoyable today—though not in large doses. Sidney's *Arcadia,* a romance in which prose and verse commingle not unattractively, takes second place to his stirring *A Defense of Poesie,* an eloquent reply to Gosson's *School of Abuse.* Raleigh's strong and vigorous prose is yet capable of a grandeur which has no counterpart in any previous English prose. In spite of its loose and rambling style, its "unerudite erudition and easy scholarship," Raleigh's *The History of the World,* many critics hold, contains the best prose of the age— with one exception. That exception, of course, is the *Essays* of Francis Bacon. Shrewd, worldly, disillusioned; crisply, brilliantly phrased—they are like nothing in English before or (for that matter) since.

Pre-eminently, however, Shakspere's was the age of drama. Lyly's *Sapho and Phao* and *Endymion* introduced the "Euphuistic drama." Kyd's *The Spanish Tragedy* set the "tragedy of blood" fashion. Greene's *The Scottish History of James the Fourth* gave new life to the Chronicle Play, and from his *Friar Bacon and Friar Bungay,* Shakspere (that "upstart crow," as Greene called him in *A Groatsworth of Wit*) chose several feathers with which to beautify himself. All three are important to the development of English drama and interesting in their own right. But the English drama first attains greatness with Marlowe. *Tamburlaine, Doctor Faustus, The Jew of Malta,* and *Edward II* are occasionally clumsy, both in thought and structure, but their total power is not the less impressive. His dominant theme—"the aspiring mind"—is clothed in verse which fits it perfectly. His "mighty line" matches the primordial energy of his thought.

Some of the dramatic contemporaries of Shakspere fall outside of the time limits assigned to his age, but belong to it so inevitably that they must be mentioned here. Ben Jonson's "comedy of humour" is exemplified by *Every Man in His Humour*—a play whose humor depends so largely on an understanding of the "humours" that it has lost much of its effectiveness for today. Still occasionally presented are *Volpone* and *The Alchemist,* both excellent comedies that play far better than they read. His tragedies, imitated from classical models, are now wholly without interest. Chapman's best comedy, *Eastward Ho!* (written with Jonson and Marston), and his best tragedy, *Bussy D'Ambois,* are still not to be consigned to the "lumber room of literature" (especially not the comedy). Ford's *The Broken Heart* and *'Tis a Pity She's a Whore;* Beaumont and Fletcher's *Philaster;* Massinger's *A New Way to Pay Old Debts*—all are read by potential Ph.D's and by lovers of Elizabethan literature. There is real passion in the tragedies, real exuberance in the comedies. Latterly, T. S. Eliot's essays on the Elizabethan dramatists have caused a revival of interest in them; and it is with shock that moderns first see the manifold excellencies underlying the patent absurdities. John Webster, particularly, has been singled out for praise by Eliot, MacLeish, and others. There is a forgetive intensity in his plays, most notably in *The Duchess of Malfi* and *The White Devil,* a poignancy and power of expression, that are unmatched by any other English dramatist with the (understood) exception of Shakspere. Thomas Dekker's *The Shoemaker's Holiday* is one of the few realistic dramas of the age. A presentation of this earthy, not to say rowdy, play three hundred and forty years after its premier was hailed with delight.

The Puritan Age (1616–1660)

The Puritan Age saw "the greatest moral and political reform which ever swept over a nation in the short space of half a century." A corrupt nobility, the theory of "the divine right" of kings, and the head of Charles I fell together. National Presbyterianism carried, along with its reforms, a large variety of restraints, and counter-revolution was inevitable. But for the brief while it lasted (1649–1660), the Puritan movement ushered in a "second renaissance," a new flowering hardly less remarkable than the first.

The theater, of course, suffered: the Puritans regarded stage presentations as immoral. Poetry, though, both Puritan and Cavalier, flourished—less luxuriantly but hardly less beautifully. Milton is the great name of the age. Derivative, certainly, and completely humorless, he nevertheless presents an instance of self-integration about an ideal unique in English literature. *Paradise Lost, Paradise Regain'd, Samson Agonistes* are his three master-works, and represent a cumulative hardening and baring of style. Many critics prefer the last-named to the first. His "minor works," *L'Allegro* and the symmetrical *Il Penseroso,* "On the Morning of Christ's Nativity," *Comus,* and the *Sonnets* would be important for their consummate metrical dexterity, even if they were not the revelations of a great and noble personality.

John Donne and the "metaphysical school" of which he is

the center have had a new access of popularity in our day. Their tight-knit thought, their passionate vision, the wit which fuses their poetry have made them the ancestors of much modern poetry. Herbert, Crashaw, and Vaughan are the best of the other metaphysicals.

The Cavalier poets, Carew, Suckling, Lovelace, and Herrick, are slighter: but their lyrics sometimes achieve perfect grace, perfect melody. A dozen of Herrick's poems, and perhaps as many of the others' combined, are "ultimate expression—beyond praise."

Cowley and Marvell are transitional poets: one foot in the renaissance poetic tradition, one in the neo-classic. Cowley's *Pindarique Odes* are historically important because they initiated a form; but it is now difficult to discern the reasons for their former popularity. The cycle of his love poems called *The Mistress* consists of far cleverer pieces. Cowley is more a neo-classic than a renaissance poet. The reverse is true of Marvell. In the great burst of Elizabethan song some of Marvell's lyrics would have been completely in place, and in a high place: *e.g.,* "To His Coy Mistress," "A Horatian Ode upon Cromwell's Return," "The Garden," "Burmudas."

The prose of the Puritan Age is of the first order. Jeremy Taylor's *Holy Living* and *Holy Dying,* much admired by Lamb, still can hold the interest, if read in small amounts. Fuller's *Worthies of England* is of some historical importance. The organ-voiced prose of Thomas Browne (*Religio Medici* and *Urn Burial*) and of Robert Burton (*Anatomy of Melancholy*) have, with sufficient reason, had devoted readers from Dr. Johnson to the present. Nor has Izaak Walton's *The Compleat Angler* ever lacked its enthusiasts.

But time has placed its laurels chiefly on John Bunyan, whose plain, homely style has appealed to generations of readers—some of whom were violently anti-Puritan. Though written after the Restoration, *The Holy War, Grace Abounding,* and "that peerless allegory" *Pilgrim's Progress* obviously belong in spirit and substance to the Puritan Age.

PERIOD OF NEO-CLASSICISM (1660–1798)

The Period of Neo-Classicism—of proportion, measure, correctness, common sense—lasted from the Restoration of Charles II and the Stuart line to the publication of the *Lyrical Ballads* (1798). Usually this period is further sub-divided: The Age of Restoration (1660–1700); The Age of Pope (1700–1740); The Age of Johnson (1740–1798). However, because of the rules it imposed on itself, this is a much narrower period, and it may be considered as a whole without too much impropriety. Dryden dominates the first part of the period, Pope the second, Johnson the third.

Dryden's crisp, epigrammatic wit, his power of incisive satire, were largely unappreciated during the nineteenth and early twentieth centuries. Van Doren and Eliot have done much to rehabilitate his literary reputation. *Absalom and Achitophel, Mac Flecknoe,* and *The Medal* are brilliant satire. The verse, flexible and vigorous, is perfect of its kind. His political and religious poetry has been long suspect because of a different sort of flexibility. The date of his "Heroic Stanzas consecrated to the Memory of his Highness Oliver Cromwell" (1658) and of his celebration of the return of Charles II, *Astrea Redux* (1660), are indicative. When the court was Anglican, so was Dryden's poetry (*Religio Laici*); when Roman Catholic, so was Dryden's poetry (*The Hind and the Panther*). Dr. Johnson said that Dryden merely changed with the nation, but later critics have taken a darker view. Nevertheless, whatever the faults of the man and however they hurt his poetry, his satires and incidental poems (such as "Alexander's Feast" and "Ode for St. Cecelia's Day") are brilliantly successful.

Pope has an infinity of wit, incomparable dexterity in versification, and the "power to sum up, in a couplet, a moral or ethical sentiment or an observation on life, which is thus delivered in a neat package, ready to be addressed." He is a classic not of our prose (as Arnold asseverated) but of our poetry. It is an inferior definition of poetry which cannot encompass *The Rape of the Lock, An Essay on Criti-*

cism, An Essay on Man, Epistle to Dr. Arbuthnot, and—above all—*The Dunciad.*

Samuel Johnson, it is something of a surprise to remember, was a poet. But *London* and *The Vanity of Human Wishes,* both imitations of Juvenal, though strong, direct verse, are read voluntarily only by those whom Boswell's *Life* has rendered Johnsonophiles. His *Irene* was deemed a failure at its premier and has steadily gone down in critical estimation since. *Rasselas,* which Johnson wrote in a week, is worthless as a story, but of some interest as a classic exposition of neo-classic principles. But, for criticism that (in spite of all its prejudices, freaks, and preconceptions) is utterly free from cant and pretense, always shrewd and illuminating, Johnson is pre-eminent. *The Lives of the Poets* is, most modern critics agree, by far his best work. The *Rambler* and *Idler* essays rank second. (Of course, in another sense, Boswell's *Life* is Johnson's masterpiece.)

Butler's *Hudibras,* a Restoration verse satire on the Puritans, is pungent, clever, and vigorous doggerel. Waller's smooth, neat, masterful couplets were immensely influential in the development of neo-classicism. At least two of his lyrics, "Go, Lovely Rose" and "On a Girdle," are equal to any of the Elizabethan.

Dryden, Butler, and Waller are the only three Restoration poets who deserve mention in this brief history. The Age of Pope adds a few more names that cannot be slighted: Gay, whose amiable wit and lively verse are best perceived in his *Fables* and *Trivia;* Prior, "The English Horace," whose delightful, glittering society verse (undeservedly forgotten now) is best seen in brief poems like "Jinny the Just," "To a Child of Quality," "A Better Answer," *Down Hall,* and "For My Own Monument"; and Goldsmith, whose genial and sentimental (if somewhat factitious) *The Traveller* and *The Deserted Village* are among the most popular poems in the language.

Goldsmith's poetry straddles the neo-classic and romantic schools; he is the first of the important precursors of the eventually triumphant romanticism. From Goldsmith's *Deserted Village* to the publication of the *Lyrical Ballads* of Wordsworth and Coleridge in 1798, the romantic tendency overshadows the neo-classic. Some of the poems cited in the following paragraph are not of a high order of literary merit. But all were instruments of the romantic triumph: some because of their humanitarianism, others because of their medievalism, still others because of their "irregularity" in theme or style.

James Thomson's *The Seasons* is an early landmark (1726–1730) of the ascendant romanticism, through its (blank verse) description of rural scenery. The "graveyard school" of poetry is representative of that mood of ruminative melancholy to which the later, greater romantics were addicted. The chief poems the school produced were Edward Young's *Night Thoughts on Life, Death, and Immortality* (1742–1745); Robert Blair's *The Grave* (1743); and Thomas Gray's "Elegy Written in a Country Churchyard" (1751). Other poems and collections of poetry that swelled the romantic tide which in the next century was to engulf English poetry include: Shenstone's "The Schoolmistress" (1742); William Collins's *Odes* (1746); Thomas Gray's "The Bard" (1757); Percy's collection of old Scots and English ballads and songs, *Reliques of Ancient English Poetry* (1765); Macpherson's superb but fraudulent "Ossianic" epics (1765); Chatterton's inspired forgeries, *The Rowley Poems* (1777).

But all the poetry thus far mentioned is "pre-romantic" rather than romantic. It illustrates a tendency, but does not constitute a movement. From 1780 on, however, romanticism is in the saddle. Cowper's *The Task* manifests a real, not posed, love of nature. Crabbe's *The Village* is an unsentimental, an anti-sentimental, series of realistic pictures. With Blake's *Songs of Innocence* (1789) and *Songs of Experience* (1794), romanticism comes into its own. Blake's passionate, apocalyptic vision is on a wholly different plane from Goldsmith's *Deserted Village* and the other sentimental outpourings of the pre-romantics. And Burns's lyrics bring into English poetry a beauty and tenderness absent since the Elizabethans. The keen and caustic wit of his epistles and satires have an emotional humanitarianism (rather than an intellectual) foreign to the great body of English verse until his time.

The diary of John Evelyn is a valuable and occasionally interesting chronicle of the years it covers (1640–1706). Less informative of public affairs but more intimately revelatory of the man who kept it, the diary of Samuel Pepys (1660–1669) is still a favorite browsing-book.

Not, however, till the Age of Pope does modern prose develop from hint to fact. Daniel Defoe, a versatile journalist, will be occasionally remembered for *Moll Flanders, Essay on Projects,* and *Journal of the Plague Year;* always, for his masterpiece of imaginative projection, *Robinson Crusoe.* Jonathan Swift, whose sentences are whips, is, like Defoe, generally considered a one-book author—*Gulliver's Travels* being the book, of course; however, his *A Modest Proposal* and *A Tale of a Tub* are scarcely less trenchant satires. Addison and Steele collaborated on the *Tatler* and the *Spectator,* two journals which criticized with not less point than humor the morals and manners of the age.

In the Age of Johnson appeared the greatest English biography, Boswell's full-size portrait of Dr. Johnson, and the greatest English history, Gibbon's *The Decline and Fall of the Roman Empire.* Even more important, there arose that most protean of forms, the novel. From the sentimental epistolary novels of Samuel Richardson (*Pamela, Clarissa Harlowe*) to the rich, vital production of perhaps the greatest novelist in the history of English fiction, Henry Fielding (*The Adventures of Joseph Andrews, Jonathan Wild the Great,* and—above all—*Tom Jones*), the novel traveled the complete distance from infancy to maturity. Laurence Sterne's *The Life and Opinions of Tristram Shandy* is halfway between the novel and the discursive essay, but it is not the less delightful for that; and to this day a fierce band of Shandyists hold that their author is supreme in English fiction. Fewer are the devotees of Tobias Smollett, but they urge as vigorously the claims of *The Adventures of Roderick Random, The Adventures of Peregrine Pickle,* and (chiefly)

The Expedition of Humphrey Clinker—three superb picaresque novels. The "Gothic" novel (featuring gloomy castles, trapdoors, and all the paraphernalia of horror) had a large vogue during the age: *The Castle of Otranto* is the best exemplar of the type. The sentimental novel, too, was exceedingly popular (and excessively, it seems to moderns): Goldsmith's *The Vicar of Wakefield* is the least reprehensible instance of the form, Henry Mackenzie's *The Man of Feeling* the most.

Of the Restoration drama, only one tragedy deserves mention here: Thomas Otway's powerful, somber *Venice Preserv'd,* perhaps the best tragedy since the golden age of the Elizabethans. Comedy, however, flourished mightily, for this was the age of William Wycherley and William Congreve. Wycherley's *The Country Wife,* a sardonic, bawdy farce, is still successfully revived. Concerning Congreve's *The Way of the World,* only superlatives are possible: it is, simply, the most consummately witty comedy of manners ever written.

The comedy of the Age of Pope is saved from desolation by John Gay, whose *Beggar's Opera* is the most brilliant example of a genre little practiced in England—the burlesque-opera.

Oliver Goldsmith and Richard Brinsley Sheridan are the most considerable writers of comedy in the following age. Goldsmith's *She Stoops to Conquer* is a comedy of intrigue, which differs from most others in that its complications are truly laughable and its dialog truly funny. Two of Sheridan's comedies, *The Rivals* and *The School for Scandal,* are in the same style and even more successful: dialog is more sparkling, the complications more ingenious.

THE ROMANTIC PERIOD (1798–1837)

The Romantic Period is customarily dated from the publication of the *Lyrical Ballads* by Coleridge and Wordsworth in 1798 to the accession of Victoria in 1837. Since dates are convenient, these will do: but the tissue of tendencies called romanticism had its genesis more than half a century before the publication of *Lyrical Ballads* and has endured up to the present day—in fact, one or another "romanticism" has never been totally absent from English literature, or from any other literature.

In *Lyrical Ballads,* the real and the supernatural were the dual themes—both treated in language which renounced the conventions of poetic diction, in the simple language of the common man. Wordsworth took the real for his province, and kept within it for the whole of his long poetic career. Some of his poems are "fair as a star when only one is shining in the sky"; others are unadulterated moonshine. To the former class belong the ineffably beautiful "Intimations of Immortality," "Tintern Abbey," "I Wandered Lonely as a Cloud," "The Solitary Reaper," most of the early sonnets, parts of *The Prelude,* and a dozen or so assorted poems. Coleridge took the supernatural for his province. He was not nearly so prolific a writer, but his achievement is small only in quantity. "Kubla Khan" is sheer magic; "Christabel" is a distillation of the spirit of romance; "The Ancient Mariner" is a perfect handling of a supernatural theme. In prose, his *Biographia Literaria* contains (along with much dross) some of the most profound insights into the nature of the poetic process of any English critical work.

Contemporary with Coleridge and Wordsworth were Walter Scott, whose facile genius embraced both poetry (*The Lady of the Lake, Marmion, The Lay of the Last Minstrel*) and the novel (*Ivanhoe, Kenilworth, Quentin Durward, Rob Roy*) with equal success; Robert Southey, whose lyrics and epics collect deserved dust; Thomas Moore, whose songs are hauntingly lovely things; Landor, whose amber epigrams and chiseled prose are the joy of connoisseurs of the chaste English style; Jane Austen, whose novels (*Sense and Sensibility, Pride and Prejudice, Emma, Northanger Abbey*), rendering the ordinary exquisite, are the perennial delight of "Janeites" from Scott to Auden.

The essay during the first part of the Romantic Period achieved a new sensitivity and range. Charles Lamb's *Essays of Elia* blend whimsy and wit, charm and shrewdness, drollery and realism in a style at once individual and quaint. William Hazlitt's *Essays* are models of modern prose: perceptive, firm, individual, vivid, masculine. The "impassioned prose" of Thomas De Quincey's *Confessions of an English Opium Eater* has a cadenced eloquence and "picture-making power" that (rightly) compel admiration and often (wrongly) imitation.

The second generation of romantics bred three great poets: Lord Byron, Percy Bysshe Shelley, and John Keats. They are frequently lumped together, a triunity; but they are separate and individual talents. Byron was a satirist in a romantic age. How well he fitted his talent to his time, is manifest in the genuine lyric quality of "She Walks in Beauty" and "Maid of Athens"; the sweep and grandeur of set passages from the longer narrative poems; the parade of self as hero and rebel and martyr in *Manfred* and *Childe Harold*. But nimble humor, biting criticism of cant and corruption, are aspects of Byronism at least as fundamental: *The Vision of Judgment, Beppo,* and his epic-satire, *Don Juan,* are characteristic Byron. Shelley has been misrepresented as an impractical visionary. In fact, he was a profoundly philosophical poet, aware of his purpose and his direction. His *Adonais,* "Hymn to Intellectual Beauty," and *Prometheus Unbound* were not the products of a "pale, ineffectual angel" but of a heaven-aspiring idealist. His pure lyric gift, however, is more attractive to most readers than his philosophy, and his odes "To a Sky-Lark," "The Cloud," "To the West Wind" are perfect marriages of sense and music. Keats, one of the "inheritors of an unfulfilled renown," wrote some poems that are as close to "beauty bare" as anyone has ever come. A few of the sonnets (particularly, "Bright Star, Would I Were Steadfast as Thou Art" and "When I Have Fears that I May Cease to Be"), two of the odes ("On a Grecian Urn" and "To a Nightingale"), one ballad ("La Belle Dame sans Merci"), one narrative poem ("The Eve of St. Agnes"), and parts of the longer poems (particularly *Endymion* and *Hyperion*)—these are quintessential poetry.

THE VICTORIAN PERIOD (1837–1901)

The sixty-four years of Victoria's reign is a period of flux in science, politics, morals, industry, literature. The old certainties were going down; and writers were looking to the life boats.

The prose-writers of the period took on the garb of prophets. Thomas Carlyle forged from German idealism both a program and a style. Repugnant to most moderns, his teachings were undeniably eloquent. His cragged, picturesque, impassioned comments on man, history, and society were listened to everywhere—and nowhere more attentively than in America. *Sartor Resartus, The French Revolution, Heroes and Hero-Worship,* and *Past and Present* are characteristic productions. Macaulay was more superficial, but perhaps also more solidly founded. *The History of England from James II* is his masterpiece, though now only browsed through. The essays are informative and entertaining: though fact-laden, they bear their burden lightly. John Ruskin's essays and his art criticism are based on the concept of the unity of art and morality; but even those most fundamentally in disagreement with his thesis can thoroughly savor the grace of his pictorial style. Matthew Arnold, the apostle of a new humanism, and Thomas Huxley, "Darwin's bulldog," present clearly and vividly in their essays two divergent trends of thought.

The novel had another renaissance. Charles Dickens, in spite of an overweening sentimentality, gives us the most perceptive and fullest portrait of an age in such novels as *Oliver Twist, Nicholas Nickleby, David Copperfield, Great Expectations.* William Makepeace Thackeray, adopting an ironic and anti-heroic method, paints a narrower but not shallower canvas in *Vanity Fair, The Newcomes, Henry Esmond.* George Eliot, employing simple realism without abandoning her high critical intelligence, wrote *Adam Bede, The Mill on the Floss, Romola, Silas Marner.* Thomas Hardy fused naturalism and regionalism in his uncompromising novels of character and environment—*Far from the*

Madding Crowd, The Mayor of Casterbridge, Tess of the D'Urbervilles, Jude the Obscure. George Meredith, with subtlety, wit, and intelligence rarely met with in the English novel, scrutinized the ways of man and society in *The Ordeal of Richard Feverel, Beauchamp's Career, The Egoist.* Robert Louis Stevenson treated the matter of romance in *Treasure Island, Kidnapped, The Black Arrow, David Balfour, The Strange Case of Dr. Jekyll and Mr. Hyde*—in a style so captivating that hardened realists cannot help applauding. Samuel Butler is (declares Bernard Shaw, and many agree) "in his own department the greatest English writer of the late XIX century" by virtue of his satiric Utopian romance *Erewhon* and his profoundly honest autobiographical novel *The Way of All Flesh.*

The unduly sentimental romanticism of Victorian poetry made it anathema to the poets and critics of the generation preceding ours. Today, the many excellencies of the poetry (as well as its several defects) are acknowledged. Alfred Lord Tennyson wrote a deal of poor stuff: but also he wrote some great poetry. "Break, Break, Break," "Ulysses," "The Lotus-Eaters," some of the lyrics from *The Princess,* some parts of the *Idylls of the King* are magnificent achievements. Even the intellectual poetry—"Locksley Hall," for example —is admirable for its attempt to assimilate modern ideas into poetry. Robert Browning's profoundly dramatic genius is now again recognized. *The Ring and the Book,* "Cavalier Tunes," "My Last Duchess," "Porphyria's Lover," "Fra Lippo Lippi," "Saul"—any of the dramatic monologs, in fact—exhibit a unique penetrative power matched by a rugged power of expression. Matthew Arnold, thoroughly imbued with the classic spirit, wrote at least one great poem, "Dover Beach," and "a half-dozen nearly faultless ones"— "The Scholar-Gypsy," *Sohrab and Rustum,* "Thyrsis," "Requiescat." William Morris's superb narrative gift (especially as exhibited in *The Earthly Paradise*); Charles Algernon Swinburne's metrical dexterity and miraculous diction (*Songs Before Sunrise, Poems and Ballads, Atlanta in Calydon*); Elizabeth Barrett Browning's bitter-sweet lyricism

(*Sonnets from the Portuguese*); George Meredith's tight-knit, "psychological wit" (*Modern Love, Poems and Ballads of the Tragic Life*); Dante Gabriel Rossetti's passionate medievalism ("The Blessed Damozel," "The White Ship," "The King's Tragedy"); Christina Rossetti's poignant, wistful music ("When I Am Dead, My Dearest," "My Heart Is Like a Singing Bird," "Uphill," "Dream Love," "Monna Innominata"); Thomas Hardy's transmutation of determinism into poetry (*Wessex Poems, Satires of Circumstance, Late Lyrics and Earlier, The Dynasts*); Gerard Manley Hopkins's burning vision, and technical virtuosity—all these make the Victorian a period of dynamic importance, not less for its achievements than for its influence.

THE TWENTIETH CENTURY

The drama of the twentieth century is notably superior to that of the Victorian age. Of Victorian dramas, only Oscar Wilde's brittle epigrammatic comedies (*Lady Windemere's Fan, The Importance of Being Earnest,* and a few others written in the last decade of the nineteenth century); and William Schwenk Gilbert's delightful librettos for the comic operas written in collaboration with Arthur Sullivan (*H.M.S. Pinafore, The Mikado, Iolanthe*) still hold the stage. In the twentieth century, the intellectual comedies of George Bernard Shaw (*The Doctor's Dilemma, Candida, Caesar and Cleopatra*) are worthy of comparison with Congreve's. James Matthew Barrie's charming humor (*Peter Pan, The Admirable Crichton, The Ten Pound Look*) is scorned only by determined intellectuals. John Galsworthy's problem dramas (*The Silver Box, Justice, Strife*) still rank high. The plays of the Irish dramatists John Millington Synge (*Riders to the Sea, The Playboy of the Western World*), Lady Gregory (*Spreading the News*), Lennox Robinson (*Whiteheaded Boy*), and Sean O'Casey (*Juno and the Paycock, The Plough and the Stars, Within the Gates*) are effective drama and effective poetry at once.

Modern prose has forged new and diverse paths. G. K.

Chesterton's paradoxical wit (*Heretics*); H. G. Wells's intellectual force (*Outline of History*); Max Beerbohm's urbane brilliance (*A Christmas Garland*); Lytton Strachey's lucid irony (*Queen Victoria*) are qualities that have been instrumental in the remaking of modern prose.

The twentieth-century novel is even more emphatically experimental than is non-fictional prose. No simple summary of tendencies can be made. Joseph Conrad (*Lord Jim*), Somerset Maugham (*Of Human Bondage*), Galsworthy (*The Forsyte Saga*), and Wells (*Tono-Bungay*) are in the great tradition of the novel. But D. H. Lawrence (*Sons and Lovers*), Aldous Huxley (*Point Counter Point*), Virginia Woolf (*To the Lighthouse*), James Joyce (*A Portrait of the Artist as a Young Man, Ulysses, Finnegans Wake*), E. M. Forster (*A Passage to India, Howard's End*), Christopher Isherwood (*The Last of Mr. Norris*) have revolted from the tradition: no generalization as to style or content can be at all discriminating if it is to be broad enough to cover the writers enumerated above.

The "well-made" story convention has been undermined, too. Joyce, Katherine Mansfield, Lawrence, Christopher Isherwood, Stephen Spender frequently write stories without beginning, middle, or end. Maugham, "Saki," Galsworthy, Rudyard Kipling are more nearly in the tradition.

In poetry, intransigency is the rule. Only a handful of twentieth-century poets who can be read with enjoyment adhere to the conventions. A. E. Housman (*A Shropshire Lad, Last Poems, More Poems*) is the only great poet of our century squarely in the tradition. Kipling (*Departmental Ditties, Barrack-Room Ballads*) and John Masefield (*Salt-Water Ballads*) both have unconventional vocabularies and themes. William Butler Yeats, beyond doubt the chief poet of this century, has come the whole way from lush pre-Raphaelitism to clean, bare modernism. W. H. Auden, Stephen Spender, Cecil Day Lewis, Louis Mac Neice, Dylan Thomas—the most considerable contemporary poets—have continued the experiments of Hopkins, Yeats, and Eliot in rhythms, syntax, and "associative reference."

American Literature

THE COLONIAL PERIOD (1606–1765)

THE BELLETRISTIC MOTIVE was insignificant in the Colonial Period. Colonial literature had one controlling purpose: the glorification of God. The graces of literature were suspect unless they contributed to the carrying out of the purpose.

Consequently, the great work of the period is Cotton Mather's *Magnalia Christi Americana,* a fascinating anthology of history and pseudo-history, biography and demonology, sermon and theology, which has this unifying aim: to praise God and the men who served Him according to Mather's Puritan light. William Bradford's *History of Plymouth Plantation* is a record of special providences, and so is John Winthrop's *Journal.* Somehow, though, plain speech and unadorned sincerity lift both works to the plane of literature. To Samuel Sewall's *Diary,* an intimate record of an era and a faith, the same sort of interest attaches as to Pepys's *Diary.* Colonial poetry is rarely as interesting. Michael Wigglesworth's *The Day of Doom* is "a Poetical description of the Great and Last Judgment" written in a rocking-horse rhythm that consorts ludicrously with the theme. Anne Bradstreet in an occasional verse attains to poetry, but the "quaternion" nonsense ("Four Monarchies," "Four Seasons," etc.) of her major efforts is relevant to the history of literature—not to literature. The pamphlets that record the theological feuds of Roger Williams and John Cotton, the *Indian Grammar* of John Eliot, the verse of *The Bay Psalm Book* are important documents of American history but are negligible as American literature. Jonathan Edwards who, in the *Freedom of the Will,* left us the most reasoned statement of the Puritan faith, is sometimes read because he sums up the thought of an era in lucid, perspicuous prose.

A handful of men and women outside the Puritan frame of

reference—who did not accept the dogmas of the inherent wickedness of man, of predestination, of salvation through the free (and apparently erratic) grace of God—produced what most moderns regard as the best writing of the period. John Woolman's *Journal,* the record of a Quaker life, does not exhibit more esthetic sensibility than the Puritan writings, but it does exhibit a far less sectarian concern with the welfare of society: with gentle but irrefragible logic, it denounces war, slavery, cruelty in all forms. *The Journal of Madam Knight* gives a lively picture of Colonial frontier life, and gives it in vivid, racy language. William Byrd's cavalier *The History of the Dividing Line* performs the same service (and in much the same way as Madam Knight's Journal) for North Carolina life during the period.

REVOLUTIONARY AND FORMATIVE PERIOD (1765–1815)

From the Stamp Act Congress of 1765 to the close of the War of 1812 was a tumultuous, event-packed period. Other interests than literary were uppermost in men's minds. Still, some good, forceful writing was produced during the half-century.

Benjamin Franklin straddles the Colonial and Revolutionary Periods. One of the most versatile men who ever lived, Franklin regarded the creation of literature as an incidental concern: he wrote, Prof. Hubbel comments, "to promote practical ends." Nevertheless, "his prose style is one that almost any eighteenth-century writer might have envied; it has charm as well as clearness, force, and flexibility." The *Autobiography* is, of course, his chief work; but parts of *Poor Richard's Almanac,* some of the essays, and most of the letters are scarcely less excellent.

Thomas Jefferson's *Notes on Virginia,* the *Declaration of Independence, A Summary View of the Rights of British America* are written with rhetorical vigor, precise command of the language, and literary polish. Hamilton's *The Federalist* papers are forceful, but without the merits of his great rival's writings. Thomas Paine's *Common Sense, The Rights of Man, The Age of Reason* need no critical allowances: they are the productions of a master of style. Gamaliel Bradford was moved to say of them: ". . . what speed, what ease, what inimitable, careless natural mastery of words!" *The Letters from an American Farmer* by Crèvecoeur are full of keen observations, though slightly romanticized. They are worth reading if only because they are among the few pictures of early eighteenth-century America by a contemporary who was not of English stock.

The Hartford Wits—John Trumbull, Timothy Dwight, Joel Barlow—have caused one critic to inquire: "If these were the wits of Hartford, what was the rest of the population like?" Trumbull's *The Progress of Dulness,* Dwight's *The Conquest of Canaan,* Barlow's *The Columbiad* are deadly dull. Barlow's *The Hasty Pudding* is somewhat more amusing, but less than engrossing. Philip Freneau is the best poet of the period. Poems like "The House of Night," "The Beauties of Santa Cruz," "To a Wild Honeysuckle," "The Indian Burying Ground," "Eutaw Springs" are lovely in their own right and important for their influence on the later romantics. His political poems ("A Political Litany," "To the Memory of the Brave Americans," "Arnold's Departure") make him "in every respect worthy to bear the title of 'the father of American Poetry.' "

Charles Brockden Brown, the author of *Wieland, Ormond, Edgar Huntley, Arthur Mervyn,* is the first American novelist who today is even remotely readable. The profusion (and confusion) of events in his novels, their conventionally macabre settings, their lack of continuity are the defects, intensified, of the Gothic school; but the brooding intensity, the realistic use of detail, the realistic employment of native backgrounds are Brown's peculiar virtues.

THE ROMANTIC PERIOD (1815–1870)

In the Romantic Period the flickering promise of the earlier periods is fulfilled. America loosed the cultural chains which still bound her to Britain.

The divorce was not abrupt. Washington Irving, usually called "The Father of American Literature," was entranced his whole life long by European forms and attitudes. But, as Edward J. O'Brien points out, in *Rip Van Winkle,* for example, he transmuted the substance of an old German legend into significant American reality, so that now it is "an integral part of our racial memory." The *Knickerbocker's History of New York, The Sketch Book, The Alhambra,* though, are not altogether American stuff—as Irving himself realized and admitted. However, they were written by an American, and Longfellow (for one) testifies to the stimulus the pleasant humor, melancholy tenderness, atmosphere of reverie in Irving's tales gave to young American writers. James Fenimore Cooper deliberately set out to write "a work that should be purely American." In his recollections of the Indians, traders, and trappers that he had observed in his boyhood, he found materials for an American saga. Sentimentalized (after the manner of Scott), stilted, artificial, the Leather-Stocking Tales (especially *The Last of the Mohicans*) nevertheless have an energy that has made them live on to our day.

William Cullen Bryant, Lowell remarked, had unqualified merits, but lacked "the one merit of kindling enthusiasm." That is a fair estimate. Yet "Thanatopsis," "Inscription for the Entrance of a Wood," "To a Waterfowl," "A Forest Hymn," "To a Fringed Gentian" are, in spite of their tacked-on morals, chastely beautiful lyrics.

Most historians are inclined to date a distinctively American literature from Ralph Waldo Emerson. Holmes called *The American Scholar* America's intellectual Declaration of Independence. Emerson's essential message was: throw off the bonds of the past. In *Nature,* his *Essays* (First and Second Series), *Representative Men,* he stated it over and over again in pithy, gnomic sentences that were in the nature of proverb. His poetry, generally unappreciated in his own time, in ours has come to rank above his essays.

Henry David Thoreau called himself "a mystic, a transcendentalist, and a natural philosopher." Perhaps most readers would be willing to forgive all three and remember that he was also "a prose-stylist of singular and signal excellence" who left behind him one great book—*Walden*.

Nathaniel Hawthorne, "a New England Balzac," was at once "a product of his Puritan cnvironment and a living protest against it," Prof. Boynton declares. He recoiled from Puritan theology, but could not evade a Puritan awareness of sin. *The Scarlet Letter, The House of Seven Gables, The Marble Faun* all exhibit this strange ambivalence. For artistic creation of effects, his short stories arc supcrior cvcn to his novels. Among the best are "The Great Stone Face," "The Gray Champion," "Dr. Heidegger's Experiment," "The Birthmark," "Rappaccini's Daughter."

Herman Melville is currently being rediscovered and put with "Rabelais, Swift, Shakespeare and other minor and disputable worthies." More and more, he is being called America's greatest novelist. *Moby Dick* will remain "America's unarguable contribution to world-literature," Clifton Fadiman believes. *Typee, Omoo, Redburn, White-Jacket, Pierre, The Piazza Tales, Billy Budd* are variously indicative of Melville's great and distinctive achievement.

Henry Wadsworth Longfellow, James Russell Lowell, and Oliver Wendell Holmes—the "Boston Brahmins"—are suffering a decline in reputation almost as great as the rise Melville is enjoying. Yet, in the case of all three, if their original valuation was too high, their present one is too low. Time will right matters. Longfellow's *Evangeline, The Song of Hiawatha, The Courtship of Miles Standish,* the *Divine Comedy* sonnets, and a dozen minor lyrics are first-rate poetry. Lowell is uniformly amusing and interesting—in prose or verse; his *The Biglow Papers* and *A Fable for Critics* are shrewd, delightful satires, certain of permanence. Holmes's poetry is never great, but always engaging; his prose works—particularly the novels (*Elsie Venner, The Guardian Angel, A Mortal Antipathy*)—are now having a minor renaissance because they are alleged to have anticipated psychoanalysis.

John Greenleaf Whittier's idyls and pastorals—"Snow-

Bound," "Maud Muller," "Barbara Frietchie," "The Barefoot Boy" are never mistaken for great poetry. But they have risen beyond literary judgment, become part of the American heritage.

Edgar Allan Poe, "an ordered chaos," was a highly conscious artist. To American literature he taught something it needed to learn: the necessity of form. Among the short stories best representing his strange, febrile genius are: "The Cask of Amontillado," "The Pit and the Pendulum," "The Black Cat," "The Fall of the House of Usher," "The Gold Bug"; among the poems: "To Helen," "Israfel," "The City in the Sea," "The Raven," "The Bells," "Annabel Lee."

Emerson wrote to Walt Whitman shortly after the publication of the latter's *Leaves of Grass* (1855): "I find it the most extraordinary piece of wit and wisdom America has yet contributed." It is nearly one hundred years since Emerson's letter, but few contemporary critics would seriously modify his statement. *Leaves of Grass,* Mumford said, is more than a book: it is a literature.

TRANSITIONAL PERIOD (1870–1918)

The years from 1870 to 1918 saw the slow, inevitable triumph of realism and allied movements. The local-colorists—Bret Harte (*The Luck of Roaring Camp*), Edward Eggleston (*The Hoosier Schoolmaster*), George Washington Cable (*Old Creole Days*), Joel Chandler Harris (*The Songs and Sayings of Uncle Remus*), Sarah Orne Jewett (*Tales of New England*)—are transitional even within the Transitional Period: they approached realistic materials romantically.

Mark Twain began as a local-colorist; but he transcends any label. "Sole, incomparable," he is in Howell's memorable phrase, "the Lincoln of our Literature." In *The Adventures of Huckleberry Finn, The Adventures of Tom Sawyer, Life on the Mississippi,* Mark Twain gave three epics to America. *A Connecticut Yankee in King Arthur's Court, The Man That Corrupted Hadleyburg, The Mysterious*

Stranger represent three other facets of Twain's versatile genius.

William Dean Howells was America's first avowed realist, but his was a "reticent realism": writers, he affirmed, ought to concentrate on the more smiling aspects of life, because those are the more American. His three best novels—*The Rise of Silas Lapham, A Hazard of New Fortunes,* and *A Modern Instance*—(fortunately) do not completely adhere to his strictures.

Hamlin Garland's *Main Travelled Roads,* Stephen Crane's *The Red Badge of Courage,* and Frank Norris's *The Octopus, The Pit,* and *McTeague* carried the doctrine of realism much further than Howells; their novels, though never as happily phrased as Howells's, dig deeper into life. Jack London (*The Call of the Wild, The Sea-Wolf, The Iron Heel, Martin Eden*) might have surpassed them all, were it not for his inability to divorce himself from a sentimental approach to his materials.

Henry James abjured the stark, but told the truth—which is the essential requirement of realism. He aspired "to write in such a way that it would be impossible to an outsider to say whether I am at a given moment an American writing about England or an Englishman writing about America (dealing as I do with both countries)." He chose to deal with both countries because it presented the path of greatest difficulty; and the difficult came to intrigue James above all else. *The American, Daisy Miller, Portrait of a Lady* are the early fruits of his cosmopolitan interest. In his later tales and particularly in three of his later novels, *The Wings of the Dove, The Golden Bowl,* and *The Ambassadors* (which last he considered his best book), "he reached," Prof. Shafer says, "a purity of form and a height of imaginative creation which has not been equaled or even approached by any other American writer, and which is not soon likely to be."

Edith Wharton, who, to some extent, was a follower of James, wrote two novels that compare favorably with James's: *Ethan Frome* and *The Age of Innocence.*

Henry Adams's two remarkable books, *Mont-Saint-Michel and Chartres* and *The Education of Henry Adams,* are complementary works: one is a study of medieval unity, the other, of modern multiplicity. *The Education* is a magnificent exercise in an almost unique form: the ironic autobiography.

Poetry during the half-century from 1870–1918 (if Whitman, who published new editions of the *Leaves* till his death in 1892, be excepted) has but one great practitioner: Emily Dickinson. The pertness and patness of her verse, its exquisite perceptions, its unobtrusive metaphysicality constitute her the peer of any of her English contemporaries. Sidney Lanier's verse occasionally strikes a pure lyric note which, had it been sustained, would have made him the equal of Poe. "May the Maiden," "The Marshes of Glynn," "Evening Song," "The Revenge of Hamish," "The Symphony" are superb poems. Edwin Markham's "The Man with the Hoe" and "Lincoln, the Man of the People"; William Vaughn Moody's *Gloucester Moors and Other Poems*— these are the cream of the other poetry of the period.

THE CONTEMPORARY PERIOD

The drama of the Contemporary Period is far superior to that of the foregoing periods. Eugene O'Neill's *Anna Christie, Strange Interlude, The Hairy Ape, Emperor Jones, Mourning Becomes Electra* have an imaginative intensity, a poetic power, an inevitable progression that makes American drama before him appear shallow and tawdry. Maxwell Anderson's *Winterset,* Sidney Howard's *Yellow Jack,* Paul Green's *In Abraham's Bosom,* Elmer Rice's *Street Scene,* Susan Glaspell's *Allison's House;* Marc Connelly's *The Green Pastures,* S. N. Behrman's *Biography,* Philip Barry's *The Animal Kingdom,* Morrie Ryskind and George S. Kaufman's *Of Thee I Sing!* illustrate the remarkable excellence no less than the remarkable diversity of the modern theater.

The novel still retains its lead as a literary form. The overwhelming honesty, the complete fearlessness of Theodore Dreiser (*An American Tragedy, Jenny Gerhardt, The Finan-*

cier) establish him as the outstanding naturalist of our day. James T. Farrell (*Studs Lonigan*) is in the Dreiser tradition and hardly less effective a writer. Upton Sinclair (*The Jungle, Boston*) is a sociological novelist, an impassioned and eloquent fictional crusader. Sinclair Lewis (*Arrowsmith, Babbitt, Dodsworth*) is America's outstanding prose satirist. Ernest Hemingway (*For Whom the Bell Tolls, Farewell to Arms, Winner Take Nothing*) is allied with no school, susceptible of no facile description; perhaps our chief novelist, he has "made Midwestern speech into a prose living and alert, capable of saying at all times what he wanted it to say." Sherwood Anderson (*Dark Laughter, Winesburg, Ohio, Tar*) is a "fluid impressionist" who floats naturalism down the stream of consciousness. Willa Cather (*O Pioneers!, Death Comes for the Archbishop, My Antonia*) is America's foremost poetic realist. Thomas Wolfe (*Look Homeward, Angel; Of Time and the River; The Web and the Rock; You Can't Go Home Again*) powerfully fuses epic vision and Whitmanesque prose. John Steinbeck (*The Grapes of Wrath, Of Mice and Men, The Wayward Bus*) is a sentimental naturalist—excellent when he renounces sentimentality and concentrates on naturalism. John Dos Passos (*The 42nd Parallel, 1919, The Big Money*) chooses the social background of the nation for his protagonist and achieves not only a range but also a depth perhaps beyond any of his contemporaries. William Faulkner (*Sanctuary, Light in August, The Hamlet*) analyzes degeneracy with acute force and bitter comedy.

Contemporary poetry does not lag. Edgar Lee Masters (*Spoon River Anthology*) is an authentic American equivalent of *The Greek Anthology*. Edwin Arlington Robinson's "bare Yankee Speech" is the sufficient instrument of a criticism of life at once "independent, pertinent, and valuable." Amy Lowell (*Men, Women, and Ghosts, Can Grande's Castle, Selected Poems*) has written brilliant pictorial if not profoundly moving poetry. Robert Frost is easily the chief pastoral poet in American literature: his verse mingles "traditional New England individualism and stoic renunciation," austerity and nobility, simplicity of diction and depth of insight. Carl Sandburg (*Good Morning, America, Chicago Poems, Smoke and Steel*) is vigorous and sensitive—"the synthesis of hyacinths and biscuits." Vachel Lindsay is evangelist and lyricist; the noise and the exuberance of his verse envelop a real beauty. T. S. Eliot—"an Anglo-Catholic in religion, a classicist in literature, a royalist in politics"—is, in spite of being a reactionary in politics, a revolutionary in verse: the most vitalizing influence on American poetry since Hopkins. Hart Crane offers "a fresh vision of the world, so intensely personalized in a new creative language that only the strictest and most unprepossessed effort of attention can take it in." Robinson Jeffers is America's pre-eminent tragic poet: beauty is the brief interlude of his doom-haunted universe. Archibald MacLeish is a balanced Eliot—without his metrical skill or poetic intensity, but with more eloquence and infinitely more humanity. Stephen Vincent Benét (*John Brown's Body*) is the most successful practitioner of a difficult form—the verse novel. Elinor Wylie (*Nets to Catch the Wind, Black Armor, Trivial Breath*) possesses a fragile, brilliant talent, precise and polished. Edna St. Vincent Millay, at her best, has the singing quality of the great Elizabethans, a quality unimpaired by a passionate social-conscience. Muriel Rukeyser (*Theory of Flight, U.S. 1*) tempers a "hurtling" emotionalism by an acute critical intelligence.

APPENDIX I

CHRONOLOGY: English Literature

449	Hengist and Horsa land in Britain	1563	Foxe's *Book of Martyrs*
670	Caedmon's *Paraphrase of Scriptures*	1570	Ascham's *Schoolmaster*
700	*Beowulf*	1575	Stevenson's *Gammer Gurton's Needle*
731	Bede's *Ecclesiastical History* (Latin)	1577	Holinshed's *Chronicle*
793	Cynwulf's poems	1579	Spenser's *Shepheardes Calendar*
871	Accession of Alfred		North's *Plutarch's Lives*
886	Alfred begins his literary work. *Anglo-Saxon Chronicle* carefully edited	1580	Lyly's *Euphues*
		1581	Sidney's *Arcadia*
1066	Defeat of English by Normans at Hastings. Accession of William I	1584	Dramas of Peele and Green
		1587	Marlowe's *Tamburlaine*
1154	Anglo-Saxon *Chronicle* ends	1588	Marlowe's *Faustus*
1205	Layamon's *Brut*	1589	Shakspere's career as dramatist begins with *Henry the Sixth*
1215	Orm's *Ormulum*. The Great Charter		Hakluyt's *Voyages*
1250	*King Horn; Genesis* and *Exodus*	1590	Spenser's *Faerie Queene*
1262	Miracle plays acted by Guilds	1591	Harrington's translation of Ariosto
1268	The Love Lyric begins in such verse as the "Throstle and the Nightingale" and the "Cuckoo Song"		Shakspere's *Love's Labours Lost*
		1593	Donne's *Satires*
1300	*Havelok the Dane*		Shakspere's *Venus and Adonis*
1321	Dante's *Divine Comedy*	1596	Ben Jonson's dramas
1353	*Decameron* of Boccaccio	1597	Bacon's *Essays*
1363	Langland's *Vision of Piers the Plowman* (A. Text)	1598	Chapman's *Homer* (first part)
		1599	Shakspere's *Hamlet*
1370	*Gawain and the Green Knight, Pearl, Cleanness,* and *Patience*	1600	Fairfax's translation of Tasso
		1603	Florio's translation of Montaigne
1375	Barbour's *Bruce*	1605	Bacon's *Advancement of Learning*
1380	Wycliff's translation of the BIBLE	1606	Cervantes' *Don Quixote*
1383	Chaucer's *Troilus and Creseyde*		Drayton's *Poems*
1388	Chaucer's *Canterbury Tales*	1609	Shakspere's *Sonnets*
1393	Gower's *Confessio Amantis*	1610	Dramas of Beaumont and Fletcher
1421	Lydgate's *Troy Book*	1611	"Authorized Version" of the BIBLE
1422	James I of Scotland: *King's Quair*	1614	Raleigh's *History of the World*
1425	Lydgate's *Falles of Princes*	1621	Burton's *Anatomy of Melancholy*
1460	Poems of Robert Henryson	1623	Webster's *Duchess of Malfi*
1470	Malory's *Morte d'Arthur*		Waller's first poems
1476	Caxton sets up printing press	1632	Milton's "Allegro," "Penseroso"
1503	Dunbar's *Thistle and Rose*	1635	Sir Thos. Browne's *Religio Medici*
1513	Douglas's translation of the *Aeneid*	1640	Thomas Carew's poems
1516	Sir Thos. More's *Utopia* (Latin)	1641	Evelyn's *Diary* begins (ends 1697)
1518	Skelton's *Colin Clout*	1644	Milton's *Areopagitica*
1520	Heywood's Interludes	1647	Cowley's *Mistress*
1527	Tyndale's *New Testament*		Herrick's *Noble Numbers; Hesperides*
1532	Rabelais's *Gargantua*	1648	Poems of Suckling and Lovelace
1535	Lyndsay's *Satire of the Three Estates*	1649	Commonwealth
1541	Udall's *Ralph Roister Doister*	1650	Marvell's poems
1545	Ascham's *Toxophilus*		Vaughan's poems
1552	English *Prayer Book*	1653	Izaak Walton's *Compleat Angler*
1557	Tottel's *Miscellany*	1659	Pepys's *Diary* begins (ends 1669)
1558	Accession of Elizabeth	1663	Butler's *Hudibras* (Part I)
1561	Sackville and Norton's *Gorboduc*		

1667 Dryden's "Essay on Dramatic Poesy"
Milton's *Paradise Lost*
1671 *Paradise Regained. Samson Agonistes*
Dramas of Wycherley
1678 Bunyan's *Pilgrim's Progress* (Part I)
1681 Dryden's *Absalom and Achitophel*
1687 Newton's *Principia*
1688 The Revolution. Accession of William III
1693 Congreve's dramas
1697 Vanbrugh's dramas
1698 Farquhar's dramas
1709 Prior's poems
1711 Addison & Steele's *The Spectator*
1712 Pope's *Rape of the Lock*
1719 Defoe's *Robinson Crusoe*
1726 Swift's *Gulliver's Travels*
1727 Gay's *Fables.* 1728, *Beggar's Opera*
1728 Pope's *Dunciad* (First form)
1730 Thomson's *Seasons*
1732 Pope's *Essay on Man*
1740 Richardson's *Pamela*
1742 Gray's *Poems*
1746 Collins's *Odes*
1748 Smollett's *Roderick Random*
Thomson's *Castle of Indolence*
1749 Fielding's *Tom Jones*
1755 Johnson's *Dictionary*
1759 Johnson's *Rasselas*
1760 Sterne's *Tristram Shandy*
Macpherson's *Ossian*
1764 Chatterton's *Poems*
1765 H. Walpole's *Castle of Otranto*
1766 Goldsmith's *Vicar of Wakefield*
1768 Plays of Goldsmith and Sheridan
1776 Adam Smith's *Wealth of Nations*
Gibbon's *Decline and Fall of the Roman Empire*
1779 Johnson's *English Poets*
1783 Crabbe's *Village*
1785 Cowper's *Task*
1786 Burns's first poems
1789 Blake's *Songs of Innocence*
1791 Boswell's *Life of Johnson*
1794 Blake's *Songs of Experience*
1798 Coleridge and Wordsworth's *Lyrical Ballads*
Landor's *Gebir* and other poems
1805 Scott's *Lay of the Last Minstrel*
1807 Wordsworth's *Poems*
T. Moore's *Irish Melodies*
1811 Jane Austen's *Sense and Sensibility*
1812 Byron's *Childe Harold*
1814 Scott's *Waverley*
1816 Coleridge's "Christabel," "Kubla Khan"
1817 Coleridge's *Biographia Literaria*
1819 Byron's *Don Juan*
1820 Keats's *Hyperion* and other poems
Shelley's *Prometheus Unbound*

1821 De Quincey's *Confessions*
Lamb's *Essays of Elia*
Hazlitt's *Table Talk*
1828 Landor's *Imaginary Conversations*
1834 Carlyle's *Sartor Resartus*
1836 Dickens's *Pickwick Papers*
1842 Tennyson's *Poems*
Macaulay's *Essays*
1844 E. B. Browning's *Poems*
1848 Thackeray's *Vanity Fair*
1849 Dickens's *David Copperfield*
1850 Tennyson's *In Memoriam*
Wordsworth's *Prelude*
1854 Arnold's *Poems*
1857 Trollope's *Barchester Towers*
Baudelaire's *Fleurs de mal*
1859 George Eliot's *Adam Bede*
Darwin's *Origin of Species*
Fitzgerald's *Omar Khayyám*
Ruskin's *Modern Painters*
1860 Tolstoy's *War and Peace*
1862 Meredith's *Poems*
Hugo's *Les Misérables*
1866 Swinburne's *Poems and Ballads*
1868 Browning's *Ring and the Book*
1870 Morris's *Jason, The Earthly Paradise*
D. G. Rossetti's *Poems*
1873 Arnold's *Literature and Dogma*
1876 Spencer's *Principles of Sociology*
1878 Hardy's *Return of the Native*
1879 Meredith's *The Egoist*
Ibsen's *A Doll's House*
1880 Zola's *Nana*
1883 Stevenson's *Treasure Island*
Marx's *Capital*
1887 Kipling's *Plain Tales from the Hills*
1892 Wilde's *Lady Windermere's Fan*
1893 Shaw's *Widower's Houses*
F. Thompson's *Hound of Heaven*
1894 Yeats's *The Land of Heart's Desire*
Moore's *Esther Waters*
1896 Housman's *A Shropshire Lad*
1900 Conrad's *Lord Jim*
1903 Butler's *The Way of All Flesh*
1904 Barrie's *Peter Pan*
1905 Synge's *Riders to the Sea*
Chesterton's *Heretics*
1908 Bennett's *Old Wives' Tale*
1909 Wells's *Tono-Bungay*
1911 Beerbohm's *Zuleika Dobson*
Lawrence's *Sons and Lovers*
1914 World War I
1915 Maugham's *Of Human Bondage*
1921 Strachey's *Queen Victoria*
1922 Galsworthy's *The Forsyte Saga*
Joyce's *Ulysses*
1928 Woolf's *Orlando*
1932 Huxley's *Brave New World*
1934 Auden, Day Lewis, Spender, MacNeice all publish volumes of poetry

CHRONOLOGY: American Literature

Jamestown settled
Smith's *A True Relation*
Plymouth Colony founded
Bay Psalm Book
Bradford's *Plymouth Plantation*
Anne Bradstreet's *The Tenth Muse*
Sewall's *Diary* (1652–1730)
Wigglesworth's *Day of Doom*
Mather's *Magnalia Christi Americana*
Byrd's *History of the Dividing Line*
Poor Richard's Almanac (1733–1757)
Edward's *Freedom of the Will*
Woolman's *Journal* (begun)
Franklin's *Autobiography* (begun)
Paine's *Common Sense*
Declaration of Independence
Treaty of Paris
Crèvecoeur's *Letters from an American Farmer*
Dwight's *Conquest of Canaan*
Freneau's *Poems*
Barlow's *Vision of Columbus*
Hamilton's *The Federalist* papers
Brown's *Weiland*
Webster's *Compendious Dictionary*
War with England (1812–1814)
Key's "Star-Spangled Banner"
Irving's *Sketch Book*
Bryant's "Thanatopsis"
Poe's *Poems*
Holmes's *Poems*
Emerson's *The American Scholar*
Dana's *Two Years before the Mast*
Poe's *Tales*
Cooper's *Deerslayer*
Emerson's *Essays* (First Series)
Lowell's *Poems*
Emerson's *Poems*
Longfellow's *Evangeline*
Lowell's *Biglow Papers*
Hawthorne's *Scarlet Letter*
Whittier's *Songs of Labor*
Melville's *Moby Dick*
Stowe's *Uncle Tom's Cabin*
Thoreau's *Walden*
Whitman's *Leaves of Grass*
Civil War (1861–1865)
Whitman's *Drum Taps*
Harte's *Luck of Roaring Camp*
Eggleston's *Hoosier Schoolmaster*
Twain's *Tom Sawyer*
Lanier's *Poems*
James's *Portrait of a Lady*
Howe's *Story of a Country Town*
Twain's *Life on the Mississippi*
Twain's *Huckleberry Finn*
Howells's *Rise of Silas Lapham*
Bellamy's *Looking Backward*
Garland's *Main Travelled Roads*
Emily Dickinson's *Poems*

1892	Bierce's *In the Midst of Life*
1894	Crane's *The Red Badge of Courage*
1898	Spanish-American War
1899	Markham's "The Man with the Hoe"
	Veblen's *Theory of the Leisure Class*
1901	Moody's *Poems*
	Norris's *The Octopus*
1903	London's *Call of the Wild*
	H. James's *The Ambassadors*
1904	Porter's *Cabbages and Kings*
1906	U. Sinclair's *The Jungle*
	Adams's *Education*
1907	W. James's *Pragmatism*
1909	Stein's *Three Lives*
1913	Cather's *O Pioneers!*
	Lindsay's *General William Booth*
1914	World War I
	Frost's *North of Boston*
1915	Masters' *Spoon River Anthology*
	Teasdale's *Rivers to the Sea*
1916	A. Lowell's *Men, Women and Ghosts*
	Sandburg's *Chicago Poems*
1917	World War I (U.S. entry)
1919	Peace Treaty at Versailles
	Cabell's *Jurgen*
	Anderson's *Winesburg, Ohio*
	Mencken's *The American Language*
1920	Wharton's *Age of Innocence*
	Lewis's *Main Street*
1921	Robinson's *Collected Poems*
1922	Lewis's *Babbitt*
	O'Neill's *The Hairy Ape*
	Eliot's *The Waste Land*
1925	Dreiser's *An American Tragedy*
1926	Wilder's *Bridge of San Luis Rey*
1927	Parrington's *Main Currents in American Thought* (Vols. I and II)
1928	Benét's *John Brown's Body*
	O'Neill's *Strange Interlude*
	MacLeish's *Hamlet of A. MacLeish*
1929	Hemingway's *A Farewell to Arms*
	Wolfe's *Look Homeward, Angel*
1931	O'Neill's *Mourning Becomes Electra*
	Wilson's *Axel's Castle*
	Faulkner's *Sanctuary*
1932	Caldwell's *Tobacco Road*
	Dos Passos' *1919*
1934	Saroyan's *Daring Young Man on the Flying Trapeze*
	Sherwood's *Petrified Forest*
1935	Wolfe's *Of Time and the River*
	Odets's *Awake and Sing*
1936	Dos Passos' *The Big Money*
	Santayana's *The Last Puritan*
	Mitchell's *Gone with the Wind*
1939	Steinbeck's *The Grapes of Wrath*
	Wolfe's *The Web and the Rock*
1940	Hemingway's *For Whom the Bell Tolls*
	Wolfe's *You Can't Go Home Again*

APPENDIX II

SHORT LIST OF BOOKS RECOMMENDED FOR FURTHER STUDY

REFERENCE

Benet, William R., *Reader's Encyclopedia*, 1955.

Fowler, H. W., *A Dictionary of Modern English Usage*, 1940.

Gerwig, Henrietta, *Handbook for Readers and Writers*, 1925.

Hart, James D., *The Oxford Companion to American Literature*, 1941.

Harvey, Paul, *The Oxford Companion to English Literature*, 1937.

Hornstein, Lillian H., *The Reader's Companion to World Literature*, 1956.

Shipley, Joseph T. (editor), *Dictionary of World Literature*, 1943.

Thrall, W. F., and Hibbard, C. A., *A Handbook to Literature*, 1936.

Walsh, William S., *Handy-Book of Literary Curiosities*, 1925.

Weseen, M. H., *Dictionary of English Grammar and Handbook of American Usage*, 1928.

GRAMMAR

Curme, George Oliver, *Parts of Speech and Accidence*, 1935. *Syntax*, 1931.

Jesperson, Otto, *Philosophy of Grammar*, 1924.

Kennedy, Arthur G., *Current English*, 1935.

Kittredge, G. L., and Farley, F. E., *An Advanced English Grammar*, 1913.

SPELLING

Mawson, C. O. S., *The Dictionary Companion*, 1932.

PUNCTUATION

Summly, George, Jr., *American Punctuation*, 1949.

United States Government Printing Office, *Style Manual*, 1953.

University of Chicago Press, *A Manual of Style*, 1949.

PRONUNCIATION

Kenyon, J. S., *American Pronunciation*, 1952.

Kenyon and Knott, *A Pronouncing Dictionary of American English*, 1944.

McLean, M., *Good American Speech*, 1941.

USAGE

Evens, Berger and Evans, Cornelia, *A Dictionary of Contemporary American Usage*, 1957.

Krapp, George P., *A Comprehensive Guide to Good English*, 1927.

Leonard, S. A., *Current English Usage*, 1932.

Perrin, Porter G., *Writer's Guide and Index to English*, 1950.

RHETORIC

Brown, Rollo W., *The Writer's Art*, 1921.

Foerster and Steadman, *Sentences and Thinking*, 1919.

Genung, John F., *The Working Principles of Rhetoric*, 1900.

Macbeth, J. W. V., *The Might and Mirth of Literature*, 1876.

Watt, Willier W., *American Rhetoric*, 1957.

VOCABULARY

Brown, Ivor J. C., *Ivor Brown's Book of Words*, 1944.

Greenough and Kittredge, *Words and Their Ways in English Speech*, 1901.

Greever and Bachelor, *The Century Vocabulary Builder*, 1923.

O'Connor, Johnson, *English Vocabulary Builder*, 1939.

Waldhorn, Arthur and Zeiger, Arthur, *Word Mastery Made Simple*, 1956.

PROSODY

Allen, Gay W., *American Prosody*, 1935.

Gordon, Ralph, *Verse and Prose Technique*, 1931.

Hood, Tom, *The Rhymster*, 1882.

Saintsbury, George, *History of English Prosody*, 1906-1910.

Untermeyer and Davidson, *Poetry: Its Appreciation and Enjoyment*, 1934.

LITERATURE

Ford, Boris (editor), *The Pelican Guide to English Literature*, 5 vols., 1950 and after.

Legouis and Czamian, *A History of English Literature*, 1929.

Parrington, Vernon L., *Main Currents of American Thought*, 1939.

Spiller, Thorpe, Canby, and Johnson (editors), *Literary History of the United States*, 1948.

Trent, Erskine, Sherman, and Van Doren (editors), *The Cambridge History of American Literature*, 1917-1921.

Ward and Waller (editors), *The Cambridge History of English Literature*, 1916-1931.

Wilson, F. P., and Dobie, B., *The Oxford History of English Literature*, several vols., 1945 and after.

Index